Encyclopedia
of the
Clinton Presidency

Encyclopedia
of the
Clinton
Presidency

Peter B. Levy

Greenwood Press
Westport, Connecticut • London

Library of Congress Cataloging-in-Publication Data

Levy, Peter B.
    Encyclopedia of the Clinton presidency / Peter B. Levy.
      p. cm.
    Includes bibliographical references and index.
    ISBN 0–313–31294–X (alk. paper)
    1. United States—Politics and government—1993–2001—Encyclopedias. 2. United
States—Foreign relations—1993–2001—Encyclopedias. 3. Clinton, Bill,
1946—Encyclopedias. I. Title.
E885.L48 2002
973.929—dc21   2001033683

British Library Cataloguing in Publication Data is available.

Library of Congress Catalog Card Number: 2001033683
ISBN: 0–313–31294–X

First published in 2002

Greenwood Press, 88 Post Road West, Westport, CT 06881
An imprint of Greenwood Publishing Group, Inc.
www.greenwood.com

Printed in the United States of America

The paper used in this book complies with the
Permanent Paper Standard issued by the National
Information Standards Organization (Z39.48–1984).

10 9 8 7 6 5 4 3 2 1

CONTENTS

INTRODUCTION

As the year 2000 came to a close, newspapers, magazines, television and radio shows, public pollsters, and others weighed in on President Bill Clinton's legacy. Nearly all agreed that Clinton oversaw one of the most robust economies in American history. Not only did he fulfill his pledge to create millions of new jobs, he left office with a large federal **budget** surplus, something virtually no one had predicted was even possible when he was elected in 1992. The deficit was $290 billion in 1993. The budget surplus ran close to $200 billion when he left office. Serious **crimes**, the welfare rolls, unemployment, **inflation**, and **poverty** were all down. Home ownership, economic productivity, and the number of people attending college were all up. In the realm of foreign affairs, the mass media noted, Clinton left office still hoping to bring peace to the **Middle East**, **Northern Ireland**, and the Balkans. Yet even if these diplomatic efforts fell short of their goals, they observed, President Clinton could claim that the United States was secure from any major threats and that the nation had essentially enjoyed eight years of peace during his presidency. Nonetheless, as nearly all commentators concluded, the opening line in Clinton's political epitaph most likely would read: Second president in American history to be impeached.

A quantitative analysis of the 200 plus entries in this *Encyclopedia of the Clinton Presidency* supports this view. A high proportion of them deal with either his **impeachment** or one of the many scandals that surrounded his presidency. Even before he was elected, Clinton had to overcome stories that he had had an affair with **Gennifer Flowers**, had dodged the draft so as to avoid fighting in **Vietnam**, and had lied about whether he had used illegal **drugs** as a youth. Before he ever encountered **Monica Lewinsky**, Clinton and his aides had been accused of several misdeeds: **Whitewater**, **filegate**, and **travelgate**. Although he had pledged to run the most ethical administration in history, several of his **cabinet** members stood accused of various crimes. Worse yet, some claimed that Clinton, Vice President **Al Gore**, and their top aides had violated campaign finance laws and had allowed **China** to gain access to technology that jeopardized America's national security. A hard core of his critics even claimed that President Clinton bore responsibility for the deaths of **Ron Brown** and **Vincent Foster**, his commerce secretary and deputy White House counsel, respectively.

A qualitative analysis of many of these entries, however, might show that the accusations against Clinton, though many, had little merit. Not only did four separate investigations clear the president of the worst of these charges, killing Vincent Foster, the independent counsel's office ultimately reported that there was not enough evidence to charge Bill or **Hillary Clinton**, who also stood accused of various misdeeds, with any **crime** related to **Whitewater**, **travelgate**, or **filegate**. Nor did the president, vice president, or their top aides face any charges related to alleged campaign finance violations or espionage. Indeed, one can disagree with Hillary Clinton's claim that a "vast conspiracy" to topple Bill Clinton was responsible for the charges against the president, yet recognize that President Clinton was impeached along party lines and that he was acquitted of all charges by the **U.S. Senate**.

The tragedy of the Clinton presidency, hence, is that he allowed himself to fall prey to such attacks. If he had not had an affair with Monica Lewinsky, then he could have truthfully informed the public that he had not lied to **Paula Jones**'s attorney in his deposition in what would be ruled essentially a frivolous lawsuit by Judge **Susan Webber Wright**. Or if he had admitted to his affair with Lewinsky in his deposition and/or to the American public when the story first emerged, then he might not have been charged with an impeachable offense. In other words, if Clinton had reacted differently to his admittedly improper relations with Lewinsky, then at worst his political epitaph might have read: The first president to publicly admit to an affair while in office. But most likely, historians would have taken little note of his tryst since it was hardly the first by an American president.

Indeed, the Lewinsky scandal and Clinton's impeachment tended to obscure several of Clinton's other notable accomplishments. Most obviously, he was the first Democrat to be elected president in two consecutive elections in over half a century. In 1992, he reversed years of setbacks for the Democratic Party, which had lost five of the previous six presidential elections. At the same time, some of his early political missteps, most prominently his attempt to enact **health care reform**, contributed to the Democrats' losses in the off-year **election of 1994**. Still, as his reelection in 1996 showed, politics was not one of Clinton's weaknesses; rather, it was one of his greatest strengths. Termed irrelevant by some in 1995, he staged a comeback in 1996 that left his Republican opponent, Senator **Robert Dole**, essentially out of the race even before it began. Somewhat similarly, even as the **House of Representatives** voted to impeach him, his standings in the public opinion polls remained high. **George W. Bush**'s election as president in 2000 suggested that Clinton's moral lapses could prove a liability to the Democratic Party. Yet the facts that Clinton's vice president Al Gore won the popular vote, but not the presidency, and that the Democrats gained a tie in the U.S. Senate and that Hillary Clinton became one of its members suggested to many that Bill Clinton remained a political asset, not a liability.

A careful reading of the entries in this encyclopedia will reveal several other themes. Like his political hero, John F. Kennedy, Bill Clinton brought with him advisers, aides, and cabinet members who were achievers and could be described, as Kennedy's team was, as the "best and the brightest." A review of these biographees reveals that nearly all were highly educated—a number were Rhodes scholars—and had excelled in school, politics, and the business world. **Robert Rubin**, who served as Clinton's top economic adviser and secretary of the Treasury, attended Harvard University as an undergraduate, earned his law degree from Yale Law School, and rose to the post of co–senior partner at Goldman Sachs and Company, one of the most prominent investment banking firms in the nation, before he reached middle age. Likewise, **Robert Reich** and **Janet Reno** had distinguished careers. Like Clinton, Reich was a Rhodes scholar who earned his law degree from Yale Law School and went on to become a prominent professor at Harvard University. Although Reno was rarely described as an intellectual heavyweight, she was one of only 16 women out of more than five hundred students in Harvard University's law class of 1963. Blocked from law clerkships because she was a woman, Reno earned a reputation as one of the top attorneys through her years of service as state's attorney in Dade County, Florida.

In addition to achievement, youth was another theme that much of the administration shared. Bill Clinton was the first person of his generation to occupy the White House—he was the third-youngest man to become president—and he brought many baby boomers with him to Washington, D.C. Arguably the youth of many of these aides produced some of the administration's early political missteps. Yet at the same time, the relative youth of the president and of many of his top aides virtually assures that Clinton's ultimate legacy will not be fully determined for years to come. Bill Clinton will have an unprecedented ability to shape his legacy and/ or the perception of it. Many members of his administration probably will remain politically active long after Clinton has left office, influencing the public's views of the Clinton years in the process.

Last, and perhaps appropriately, Bill Clinton played a key role in shaping his legacy even as he readied to leave office. In his final two days as president, Clinton did two things that epitomized his presidency. First, in a brief farewell address, President Clinton succinctly and forcefully summarized his accomplishments. "Our economy is breaking records with more than 22 million new jobs, the lowest unemployment in 30 years, the highest home ownership ever, the longest economic expansion." Turning to foreign affairs, Clinton declared that under his lead, "America had been a force for peace and prosperity in every corner in the globe." In a jibe at the incoming Bush administration, the president also warned against enacting large tax cuts that would jeopardize the chance the nation had to pay off its federal debt for the first time since 1835. Furthermore, Clinton counseled against isolationism. "In his first inaugural address," Clinton remarked, "Thomas Jefferson warned of entangling alliances. But in our times, America cannot and must not disentangle itself from the world. If we want the world to embody our shared values, then we must assume shared responsibility."

It was a masterful speech delivered by a man long acknowledged as a great communicator. Yet it left out one key aspect of his legacy. The following day, less than twenty-four hours before George W. Bush was sworn in as the forty-third president, Clinton reminded the nation of this other part of his presidency. On January 19, 2001, Clinton lawyers and independent counsel **Robert Ray** finalized a deal whereby Clinton admitted that he had testified falsely in his deposition in the Paula Jones case and Ray agreed not to prosecute Clinton for any of his statements or actions stemming from his affair with Monica Lewinsky. Clinton also agreed to pay $25,000 in legal fees and to the suspension of his law license in the state of Arkansas for five years. This last-minute deal allowed Bill Clinton to return to private life without any legal troubles. Since Ray had already ruled that there was not enough evidence to charge either Clinton or his wife with any crimes stemming from the Whitewater or other investigations of the 1990s, all legal cases against him were formally closed. Yet the deal cemented in the mind of the public the one act of his presidency he most wished they would forget. To make matters worse, Clinton's first weeks in private life were dogged by accusations that he had illegally and/or unethically pardoned a slew of F.O.B.s (friends of Bill). Perhaps the only thing missing in the strange ending was greater attention to the fact that the deal confirmed what many Democrats and Clinton had argued all along, that Clinton had never committed an impeachable offense. Rather, he had had a sexual affair, had lied about this affair in a civil suit that was ultimately thrown out of court, had lied to his wife, aides, and the public about his affair, and had been fined $25,000 in legal fees for doing so, nothing more, nothing less.

Several criteria were used to determine entries. The author sought to provide a degree of continuity between this encyclopedia and *The Encyclopedia of the Reagan–Bush Years* (1996). As much as possible, an effort was therefore made to include parallel entries. For example, both works contain entries on the economy, foreign policy, and the Supreme Court. Both works include entries on prominent cabinet members and political advisers. And both works contain entries on key legislative initiatives, both those that were enacted and those that were defeated. Both works also contain foreign policy entries on many of the same countries and regions, such as China, Latin America, and the Middle East. However, regions and nations that figured more prominently during the Clinton administration than they did during the Reagan and Bush presidencies, such as Rwanda and Kosovo, have received special attention in this book. Conversely, some nations that figured prominently during the Reagan-Bush years but not during the Clinton presidency and were covered in separate entries in *The Encyclopedia of the Reagan–Bush Years* are not covered separately in this book.

Each item is accompanied by suggested readings. References to related entries are made either below the entry or in the text of the entry itself (in boldface print). In addition, cross-references to entries are provided throughout the text. Readers are also encouraged to use the subject index to find specific items of interest.

Every effort was made to provide the date, month, year, and place of birth for all entries on individual figures. However, in many cases, it was not possible to provide all of this information for all individuals listed. Every effort was also made to double-check the accuracy of web sites listed in the suggested readings. The ever-changing nature of the World Wide Web, however, means that some of the sites listed will undoubtedly disappear or have their URLs (web addresses) changed. On the positive side, readers will discover a vast amount of material on the web that will help them understand the Clinton presidency. A good place to start is the Clinton Presidential Materials Project, accessible at http://search2. nara.gov. The Washingtonpost.com and CNN.com also have a great deal of archived material, especially on Whitewater and the 2000 election. Researchers may need to be patient when trying to access this material because specific material often disappears from its original address.

I would like to thank the various editors of Greenwood who enhanced this work immeasurably, especially Barbara Rader, Betty C. Pessagno, and Charles Eberline. I would also like to thank York College, especially the Faculty Enhancement Committee and the Research and Publications Committee, for grants that allowed me to complete this work in a timely manner. I would also like to thank my chairperson, Phil Avillo, and Dean Jean Wyld for their support, and last but not least, my wife, Diane, and children, Brian and Jessica. It is hard to believe that Brian and Jessica were only three and six years old, respectively, when Bill Clinton was elected. I still remember boosting Jessica on my shoulders at a Clinton-Gore campaign rally in Cleveland, Ohio, in 1992 and trying to explain to my son the Lewinsky affair. I did a much better job with the former than I did with the latter, and I hope that this book will allow them to better understand the not-so-distant past.

A

ABORTION, PARTIAL BIRTH. One of the more contentious issues of the 1990s was the battle over "partial birth abortion," the name given to describe late-term abortions—abortions performed in the last trimester. Several times Congress passed laws banning partial birth abortion. In each instance, President Clinton vetoed the bill. Republicans sought to overturn his veto but fell short of the two-thirds majority necessary to do so. In 1998, the vote was very close in the Senate, 64–36. In vetoing the bill, Clinton proclaimed that the ban did not provide for exceptions to allow for the protection of a woman's health. A number of the president's supporters argued that Republicans knew that they did not have the votes to override his veto but enacted the ban anyway to score political points. In reference to the proposed federal ban and to numerous statewide laws against partial birth abortion, prochoice advocates contended that enactment of the partial birth abortion law would erode the right to choose and would lead to a slew of other restrictions if it were allowed to stand. The American Civil Liberties Union, for instance, observed that a Nebraska law prohibited an "array of safe and common abortion procedures used throughout pregnancy" (Sealey, "Considering Partial Birth Bans").

Until the spring of 2000, the **Supreme Court** stayed out of the fray. Some state partial birth abortion laws were overturned, while others were upheld. In April 2000, the Supreme Court heard arguments in the case of *Steinberg v. Carhart* on the constitutionality of the aforementioned Nebraska law. A lower federal court had struck down the law, agreeing with the plaintiffs that it was so broadly worded that it could prohibit nearly all second-trimester abortions as well as third-trimester abortions. State officials countered that they sought to ban a procedure known as dilation and extraction that involved removing a fetus through the birth canal. The Alan Guttmacher Institute, a family planning organization, stated that only 650 out of 1.4 million abortions in 1996 used this procedure and that late-term abortion is performed largely to protect the life of the mother. In a 5–4 ruling, the Supreme Court upheld the lower courts and found that the Nebraska law violated the Constitution.

Often the debate over partial birth abortion turned gruesome, with advocates of the laws using graphic language and images to describe the procedure. Comparing the procedure to the Holocaust, Henry Hyde, a Republican congressman from Illinois long identified with the prolife cause, declared, "Our beloved America is becoming the killing fields" (*CQ Almanac*, 1998, pp. 5–7). These prolife campaigns proved somewhat effective, as public polls showed that a broad majority of the public favored legislation that banned partial birth abortions. Nonetheless, President Clinton continued to oppose the bans, maintaining that he felt that it was wrong to take the decision over whether or not to have an abortion away from health care providers and patients, where it belonged, and place it with the state instead.

Suggested Readings: American Public Health Association, "Partial-Birth Abortion Ban: Fact Sheet," December 1998, http://www.apha.org/legislative/factsheets.htm; "Clinton Again Vetoes Abortion Ban," *Congressional Quarterly Almanac*, 1997, pp. 6–12; Geraldine Sealey, "Considering Partial Birth Ban," www.abcnews.com, April 25, 2000; "Senate Sustains Veto of 'Partial Birth' Abortion for a Second Time," *Congressional Quarterly Almanac*, 1998, pp. 3–7.

Related Entry: Women.

AFFIRMATIVE ACTION. At a time when affirmative action, a policy aimed at overcoming past and ongoing racial and sexual discrimination, especially in education and the workforce, faced increasing legal scrutiny and restrictions, the Clinton administration remained committed to it. As Bill Clinton declared in July 1995, while affirmative action had "not always been perfect," the administration's policy was to "mend it" rather than to "end it." In the face of **Supreme Court** rulings that increasingly restricted or narrowed affirmative action, the president ordered a review of affirmative-action programs within the federal government. At the conclusion of this review, the administration declared that affirmative action was "still an effective and important tool to expand educational and economic opportunity to all Americans." Along the same lines, the administration opposed California's Proposition 209, which stated that the "state shall not discriminate against, or grant preferential treatment to, any individual or group on the basis of race, sex, color, ethnicity, or national origin in the operation of public employment, public education, or public contracting." While the language of the proposition sounded nondiscriminatory, the administration contended that the referendum perpetuated discrimination. After Proposition 209 passed, the president opposed similar efforts to eliminate affirmative-action programs in other jurisdictions.

While many conservatives opposed affirmative action, Clinton's support of it did not become a major issue in the **election of 1996**. Although Republican presidential candidate **Robert Dole** stated his opposition to affirmative action, he selected as his running mate **Jack Kemp**, one of the few prominent Republicans who held generally favorable views of affirmative action. Clinton's support of affirmative action did not cost him votes in California, which he carried easily in 1996, even though Proposition 209 passed at the same time. After the election, the Justice Department expressed its support for a suit seeking to block implementation of Proposition 209. (While the American Civil Liberties Union gained a temporary injunction against the proposition, the California State Supreme Court upheld the law as constitutional.)

While Ward Connerly, the author of Proposition 209, sought to get other states to enact similar measures, the more immediate threat to affirmative action came from the courts. Even though the Supreme Court upheld affirmative action in principle, the federal courts continued to narrow or limit the instances in which affirmative action could be used. In *Adarand Constructors* v. *Peña* (1995), in a 5–4 decision, the Supreme Court called for using the strictest scrutiny in implementing affirmative-action programs. The court ruled that to do so, the federal government had to show that affirmative-action plans met a "compelling governmental interest" and were tailored to address past discrimination. (Two of the justices, Clarence Thomas and Antonin Scalia, called for ending all forms of racial preferences.) This ruling, according to many legal experts, jeopardized numerous federal affirmative-action programs. The Supreme Court also refused to review a lower-court ruling in the suit of *Hopwood* v. *Texas*. In this suit, four white law-school applicants successfully challenged the University of Texas's affirmative-action program. They argued that the university admitted minority applicants with lower test scores and grades than they had and rejected their applications. While the *Hopwood* decision applied only to public universities in the federal lower court's jurisdiction—Texas, Louisiana, and Mississippi—it left other schools scrambling to make sure that they could withstand similar challenges.

In one further sign of the administration's pro-affirmative-action policy,

Clinton appointed an advisory board to conduct a dialogue or discussion on race in America. The advisory board sponsored public meetings and conducted an independent investigation of the state of race relations in America. In the fall of 1998, the board issued its final report. The report reiterated the administration's support of affirmative action.

Suggested Readings: "California Voters on Affirmative Action," *Historic Documents*, 1996, p. 759; "Supreme Court on Federal Affirmative Action Plans," *Historic Documents*, 1995, p. 307; "Working on Behalf of African Americans," http://www.clinton3.nara.gov/WH/Accomplishments.african.html.

Related Entry: African Americans.

AFRICAN AMERICANS. President Clinton took pride in his record toward African Americans. By the end of his presidency, he could cite a long list of gains that they had made since he took office. As the White House observed on its web page, African American unemployment reached a record low, falling from 14.2 percent in 1992 to 8 percent in 1999; median income, adjusted for **inflation**, for African American households rose to a new high, from $24,300 in 1993 to $29,404 in 1998, a 21 percent increase; **poverty** rates for African Americans declined, while homeownership rates increased. In addition, the administration touted its continuing support for **affirmative action**, its **President's Initiative on Race**, which promoted a national dialogue on race, and the racial diversity of the administration itself. In addition, in a symbolic speech at Tuskegee University in 1997, President Clinton offered the nation's formal apology to African Americans for the infamous syphilis studies of the midtwentieth century. Known as the Tuskegee Syphilis Experiment, this study, sponsored by the federal government during the 1930s, intentionally refused to treat black men infected with syphilis, so that the government could compare the effect of the disease on blacks and whites.

In the year 2000, three African Americans were members of the president's **cabinet**, Secretary of Transportation **Rodney Slater**, Secretary of Veterans Affairs Togo West, and Secretary of Labor **Alexis Herman**. Other African Americans had been members of the cabinet or had held other top administrative posts, including Clinton's original secretary of commerce, **Ron Brown**, and surgeon general, **Joycelyn Elders**. Moreover, several of Clinton's closest friends and advisers, most prominently **Vernon Jordan**, the former head of the National Urban League, were African Americans.

Some pundits even described Clinton as the first black president, meaning that he was the first president to fully understand the concerns of African Americans. Undoubtedly, civil rights leaders had greater access to the White House under Clinton than they had had during the previous administrations of Ronald Reagan and **George Bush**. Clinton's experience as a youth growing up in the South at the time of the struggle for civil rights added to his personal commitment to address the needs of African Americans. The fact that African Americans voted overwhelmingly for Clinton in 1992 and 1996 and for **Al Gore** in 2000 demonstrated their support for him and his policies. (Polls also showed that African Americans were Clinton's most loyal supporters during the **Monica Lewinsky** scandal and **impeachment** proceedings.)

Nonetheless, African Americans continued to suffer disproportionately from many of the ills that did not disappear in spite of the booming **economy**. While **crime** rates declined, African Americans continued to be the victims of a disproportionate number of crimes. Perhaps even more important, African Americans comprised a disproportionate share of the prison population, which skyrocketed during the 1990s. The number of African Americans on death row jumped as well, and the fact that Clinton supported the death penalty, which blacks were more likely to receive than whites, was not lost on some of the president's critics. The expanding economy, which benefited blacks, at the same time did little to close the gap between blacks and whites. For instance, while the administration undertook initiatives to help minorities buy homes, blacks continued to live disproportionately in poor inner-city neighborhoods. The nation did not undertake a war against poverty or a massive effort to renew its cities during Clinton's presidency. (Even if Clinton had proposed such a plan, the Republican-controlled Congress would not have enacted it.) Indeed, when Clinton signed **welfare reform** into law in 1996, critics warned that children, especially black children, would be harmed. Fortunately for the Clinton administration, the expanding economy allowed many welfare recipients to find work, and predictions of catastrophe proved unfounded.

Suggested Readings: http://clinton3.nara.gov/WH/Accomplishments/african.html; Dan Wycliff, "One of Ours," *Commonweal* 26:4 (February 26, 1999), pp. 14–15.

AGRICULTURE. While agriculture did not gain the attention that **high technology** or even the revived manufacturing sectors did, it remained an important segment of the **economy**. The Clinton administration undertook several initiatives that affected the farm economy and those who made a living off it. Shortly after taking office, Secretary of Agriculture **Mike Espy** unveiled a plan to reorganize the Department of Agriculture. The move to do so dovetailed with the administration's broader goal of "**reinventing**" **government**. Building on studies conducted by the **George Bush** administration, Espy proposed consolidating nearly all of the Department of Agriculture's numerous conservation agencies into one branch, the National Resources Conservation Service. After lengthy hearings in the **House** and **Senate**, which bogged down in part over differences over the power enjoyed by environmentalists, Congress passed this reorganization plan. On October 13, 1994, Clinton signed the plan into law.

More substantially, on April 4, 1996, President Clinton signed a farm bill that dramatically altered the federal government's relationship to farmers. "The new law," observed the *Congressional Quarterly Almanac*, "did away with the decades-old policies of issuing subsidies when market prices dropped and requiring farmers to plant the same commodities every year. Instead, it guaranteed farmers fixed, declining federal payments regardless of market prices." As Senate Agriculture Committee Chairman Richard Lugar declared, "Farmers will be producing for the market, rather than [being] restricted by federal government supply controls, for the first time since the Great Depression" ("Longstanding Farm Laws Rewritten," p. 3–15). The new law marked a triumph for free-market conservatives, particularly Lugar and House Majority Leader **Dick Armey**, and a defeat for farm-state Democrats who had historically supported subsidies. In many ways, Clinton's support for this measure was part of his strategy of triangulation, whereby he went against the wishes of many within his own party and stole the thunder from Republicans, leaving his political opponents with one less issue to rally around during the **election of 1996**. To appease critics within his own party, Clinton pledged to send proposals to Congress in 1997 that would enhance the "safety net" for small farmers but Congress did not act on said proposals.

The impact of this farm-reform bill was mixed. The long-term trend of hardship and difficulty making ends meet continued for small family farmers, particularly as commodity prices declined in the latter part of the decade. Yet at the same time, large agricultural producers seemed to benefit from the reform and from the globalization of the economy, which opened new markets for their products. Moreover, the overall economic expansion ameliorated somewhat the crisis faced by small farmers,

Madeleine Albright is sworn in as secretary of state, January 23, 1997. The White House.

as some turned to niche farming (producing exotic fruits, vegetables, and grains), or found employment in farm-related industries.

Suggested Readings: "Agriculture Secretary on 1996 Form B: 11, April 4, 1996," *Historic Documents*, 1996, p. 199; "Lawmakers 'Reinvent' Agriculture," *Congressional Quarterly Almanac*, 1994, p. 191; "Longstanding Farm Laws Rewritten," *Congressional Quarterly Almanac*, 1996, p. 3-15.

ALBRIGHT, MADELEINE KORBEL. (May 15, 1937, Prague, Czechoslovakia– .) U.S. Ambassador to the United Nations, 1993–1996; Secretary of State, 1997–2001.

On January 23, 1997, Madeleine Albright was sworn in as the first female secretary of state and the highest-ranking woman in government in U.S. history. She had already served as U.S. ambassador to the United Nations during Clinton's first term. Throughout his presidency, Albright was one of the administration's most important shapers of American **foreign policy**, often advocating a more active role than was favored by several of his other top advisers. Under her lead, the U.S. sent peacekeepers to **Bosnia and Herzegovina** and conducted an air war against Yugoslavia. While critics charged that the Clinton administration overextended its military and lacked a coherent foreign policy vision during Albright's tenure, her supporters countered that Albright correctly prodded the nation to meet its humanitarian obligations abroad without endangering national security at home.

Albright was born in Prague, Czechoslovakia, in 1937. Her father, a Czech diplomat, lived in exile in London during World War II. In 1948, following a Communist coup in Czechoslovakia, her family fled to the United States, where it was granted political asylum. Her father taught international relations at the University of Colorado and deeply influenced his daughter's view of the world. In particular, her father taught her never to forget the lesson of Munich, namely, never to appease tyrants; at the same time, he emphasized the need to defend basic human rights as much as possible. After graduating from Wellesley College in 1959, she married Joseph Albright, the heir of the Robert R. McCormick–Alicia Patterson newspaper chain. She bore three children and earned an M.A. in Russian studies from Columbia University. After her husband was hired as the Washington bureau chief for *Newsday* in 1968, she became increasingly active in politics. She also completed her Ph.D. in International Studies. In 1976, she went to work full-time for Maine senator Edmund Muskie as his chief legislative assistant. Two years later, she went to work for the National Security Council, headed by Zbigniew Brzezinski, one of her former teachers. During the Ronald Reagan and **George Bush** presidencies, Albright served as a research professor and director of the Women in Foreign Service Program at Georgetown University. She remained active in politics, advising Walter Mondale and Michael Dukakis during their respective bids for the presidency in 1984 and 1988. She played a prominent role in formulating the Democratic Party's foreign policy platform in 1992 and wrote foreign policy position papers for Bill Clinton during his presidential campaign.

Albright served as U.S. ambassador to the United Nations at a time when that body was becoming increasingly active around the globe. She promoted the UN's mission of preserving peace around the globe, from **Rwanda** to the republics of the former Yugoslavia. Often this entailed sending American forces, operating under the UN flag, abroad. As ambassador to the United Nations and then as secretary of state, Albright challenged the so-called Powell doctrine, named after Colin Powell, the head of the Joint Chiefs of Staff during the Persian Gulf War, which advocated limiting American military involvement to engagements with a clearly defined and "winnable" mission. Albright's pointed, often-pithy remarks gained her much public attention even before she became secretary of state. For example, while she was ambassador to the United Nations, she successfully won UN approval for a resolution condemning Cuba for shooting down two unarmed planes flown by Cuban exiles. When the Cuban pilot who shot down the two planes stated that he had shot the Cubans in the *cojones* (the Spanish word for testicles), Albright retorted that the pilot did not have "cojones" but rather was a coward.

During the **Monica Lewinsky** scandal, Albright remained loyal to the president and countered claims that the **impeachment** process endangered American credibility abroad. Along with the president, she sought to maintain stability in Asia in the wake of the region's financial crisis in 1998 and pursued peace in **Northern Ireland** and the **Middle East**. While the economic recovery of the former enhanced her reputation, the inability of the administration to nail down a final peace agreement between Israel and Palestine diminished the administration's ability to claim a crowning victory.

Suggested Readings: "Biography of Madeleine Korbel Albright," http://www.usis. usemb.se/cabbio/albright.htm; Michael Dobbs, *Madeleine Albright: A Twentieth-Century Odyssey*, (New York: Henry Holt and Co., 1999); *Current Biography Yearbook*, 2000 (New York: H. W. Wilson Co., 2000), p. 7; William Hyland, *Clinton's World*, (Westport, CT: Praeger, 1999).

Related Entries: China; Korea; Kosovo; North Atlantic Treaty Organization; Russia.

ALTMAN, ROGER CHARLES. (April 2, 1946, Boston, Massachusetts–   .) Deputy Treasury Secretary, 1993–1994.

On August 14, 1994, six months after he appeared before the Senate Banking Committee regarding the **Whitewater** affair, Roger Altman resigned as President Bill Clinton's deputy Treasury secretary. Part of the president's original economics team that gained passage of a controversial tax hike and budget package, as well as approval of **NAFTA**, Altman became a liability to the administration when questions about his testimony before the committee continued to surface. After conferring with Treasury Secretary **Lloyd Bentsen**, Altman decided to resign.

Altman was born and raised in Boston, Massachusetts. His father died when he was ten, and some referred to Altman's rise to the top as a real-life Horatio Alger story. After attending Boston Latin school in Boston, Altman earned his B.A. from Georgetown University in 1967 and his M.B.A. from the University of Chicago in 1969. At Georgetown, he befriended Bill Clinton. In 1977, after seven years of work as an investment banker on Wall Street for Lehman Brothers, he went to work in Washington, D.C., as assistant secretary of the Treasury in the Jimmy Carter administration. He played a key role in putting together the financial bailout of Chrysler, which produced one of the most remarkable corporate turnarounds in history. Returning to Lehman Brothers following Ronald Reagan's election, Altman remained active in Democratic Party politics throughout the 1980s. He served as an economic adviser to Michael Dukakis, the Democratic Party's presidential nominee in 1988.

Working with Treasury Secretary Lloyd Bentsen and other members of President Clinton's **domestic policy** team, Altman developed a strategy for enacting Clinton's deficit-reduction plan in 1993. He quickly gained a reputation as one of the administration's most effective spokespersons. For example, in a CNN interview, Altman repudiated Republican claims that Clinton's tax hike would hurt small businessmen and the middle class by noting that in fact, the plan would cost the average family only about one dollar a week. Altman maintained his combative stance when he appeared before the Senate Banking Committee, where he rebuffed Senator Alfonse D'Amato's attempt to uncover evidence of a White House cover-up of the Whitewater affair. Nonetheless, since his testimony conflicted with that of Jean Hansen and Joshua Steiner, two other Treasury Department officials, pressure developed for him to resign. Never indicted or convicted of any wrongdoing, Altman returned to private life in New York City, where he took pride in the economic accomplishments of the Clinton administration.

Suggested Readings: "Altman Resigns His Post amid Whitewater Clamor," *New York Times*, August 18, 1994, p. B10; Owen Ullman, "Who Killed Roger Altman?" *Washingtonian*, October 1994, p. 71; "Washington at Work," *New York Times*, August 1, 1993, sec. 1, p. 30.

Related Entry: Budget, Federal.

AMERICORPS. Perhaps Bill Clinton's favorite program enacted early in his presidency was AmeriCorps. Modeled in part after the Peace Corps and the Civilian Conservation Corps, two highly popular programs established by Presidents John F. Kennedy and Franklin D. Roosevelt, respectively, AmeriCorps enabled youths to work in communities performing a variety of services. More specifically, AmeriCorps was divided into three parts. First, there were state and national programs whereby national, state, and local nonprofit organizations sponsored, recruited, and trained AmeriCorps volunteers for specific services. Second, via the National Civilian Conservation Corps, volunteers who lived in AmeriCorps "camps" across the nation performed a variety of community services, such as helping the homeless. Third, through Volunteers in Service to America (VISTA), workers aided public and private nonprofit organizations in disadvantaged communities. AmeriCorps was distinct from the Job Corps, which sought to enhance the job skills of disadvantaged youths. Clinton argued that AmeriCorps benefited both the participants, who profited from the service they gave to their country, and the communities, which gained from the particular services that the AmeriCorps workers performed. AmeriCorps could trace its origins to the National and Community Service Act of 1990, which President **George Bush** signed into law. This act provided federal funding for national programs run by nonprofit organizations and colleges and universities aimed at youth-based service programs. During his 1992 presidential campaign, Bill Clinton pledged to expand on these efforts. In September 1993, he signed the National Community Service Trust Act, which created the Corporation for National Service. This corporation oversaw Ameri-Corps and two somewhat similar programs, Learn and Serve America and the National Senior Service Corps. Of the three, AmeriCorps received the lion's share of the federal funds and gained the greatest amount of public attention. In September 1994, the first class of AmeriCorps members, 20,000 young men and women, went to work in more than a thousand communities.

While conservatives tended to oppose AmeriCorps as a waste of taxpayer dollars, studies by foundations and a summit on volunteerism chaired by Colin Powell, the former chairman of the Joint Chiefs of Staff, added impetus to AmeriCorps. The booming **economy** helped as well. As a result, even though conservatives never endorsed the program, it was refunded and expanded by Congress. Between 1992 and 2000, nearly 100,000 young men and women served in AmeriCorps. Congress extended the life of the program in 2000 for four more years.

Suggested Readings: http://www.cns.gov/americorps/research/history.html; Kevin McCarron, "Jobs Corps, AmeriCorps, and Peace Corps: An Overview," *Occupational Outlook Quarterly* 44:3 (Fall 2000), p. 18.

ANGELOU, MAYA. (April 4, 1928, St. Louis, Missouri– .) Poet.

When Maya Angelou recited "On the Pulse of Morning" in Washington, D.C., on January 20, 1993, she became the first poet since Robert Frost to take part in a presidential inauguration. (Frost had taken part in John F. Kennedy's inauguration in 1961.) Bill Clinton's decision to invite Angelou, an **African American** woman, to deliver the poem displayed the administration's desire to appear inclusive and diverse. President-elect Clinton asked Angelou to write a special poem that would capture the tenor of the times. Before sequestering herself in a hotel room to write the poem, Angelou spent weeks reading the works of W.E.B. Du Bois, Frederick Douglass, and other prominent activists, writers, and scholars. Angelou's poem, which many considered the highlight of the ceremony, concluded with the powerful words "Good Morning, America."

Born in St. Louis on the eve of the Great Depression, Angelou experienced a very difficult childhood, including being raped by her mother's boyfriend. During the 1950s, 1960s, and 1970s, she worked as a dancer, actress, and writer. She published numerous books and collections of poetry, including *I Know Why the Caged Bird Sings* (1970). Yet it was not until she recited "On the Pulse of Morning" that Angelou became a household name. Overnight, *I Know Why the Caged Bird Sings* became a best-seller. Undaunted by her new fame, Angelou continued to write and teach at Wake Forest University in North Carolina.

Suggested Readings: Karima Heynes, "Maya Angelou: Prime-Time Poet," *Ebony* 48:6 (April 1993), p. 68; http://mayaangelou; Catherine S. Manegold, "An Afternoon with Maya Angelou," *New York Times*, January 20, 1993, p. C1.

APPROVAL RATING. Through much of his presidency, Bill Clinton retained a relatively high "approval rating." For decades, the Gallup Poll organization has surveyed American opinion of the president, asking the question, "Do you approve or disapprove of the way [name of president] is handling his job as president?" Of the ten presidents of the second half of the twentieth century, Clinton fell in the middle (Table 1).

Of this group, only two other than Clinton, Dwight Eisenhower and Ronald Reagan, completed two terms in office. Eisenhower ended his presidency with a 58 percent approval rating; Reagan ended his presidency with a 51 percent approval rating. Clinton ended his presidency with a 65 percent approval rating. Paradoxically, in the **election of 2000**, many voters stated that one of the reasons they supported **George W. Bush** was because of their dislike of Clinton. Clinton's highest job approval rating came in December 1998, ironically in the midst of the **im-**

Table 1
Approval Ratings of U.S. Presidents from Dwight Eisenhower to Bill Clinton

President	Average	High	Low
Kennedy	70%	83%	56%
Eisenhower	65	79	48
Bush	61	89	29
Johnson	55	79	35
Clinton	54	79	37
Reagan	53	65	35
Nixon	49	67	24
Ford	47	71	37
Carter	45	74	28

Source: The Gallup organization; http://www.gallup.com/poll/trends/ptjobapp.asp October 2000.

peachment process. These high poll numbers, according to many, influenced the **Senate**'s decision not to remove him from office. Clinton's lowest approval ratings came in June 1993 and in the fall of 1994, stemming from public opposition to his **health care reform** plan and his support of several controversial measures, such as **gays in the military**. Throughout much of his presidency, a very large percentage of the public expressed their approval of Clinton's handling of the **economy** but simultaneously expressed their low opinions of Clinton's character. For example, as he left office, 58 percent of the public felt that Clinton was not trustworthy, and 65 percent felt that he would be most remembered for his involvement in a personal scandal.

Suggested Readings: http://www.gallup.com; David W. Moore, "Clinton Leaves Office with Mixed Public Reaction," http://www.gallup.com/poll/releases/pr010112. asp.

ARAFAT, YASIR. *See* **Middle East.**

ARISTIDE, JEAN-BERTRAND. *See* **Haiti.**

ARMEY, RICHARD (DICK) KEITH. (July 7, 1940, Cando, North Dakota– .) Congressman from Texas, 1984– .

With the Republican Party's victory in the midterm **election of 1994**, Dick Armey, a former economist and teacher, became **House** majority leader and one of the most powerful persons in the United States. Born in 1940, the son of a farmer and grain dealer, Armey earned his B.A. from Jamestown College in North Dakota in 1963. Five years later, he was awarded his Ph.D. in economics by the University of Oklahoma. For the following sixteen years, he worked as a professor, first at Austin College in Sherman, Texas, and then at North Texas State University. With little political experience, he mounted a successful campaign against the incumbent Democratic congressman, Tom Vandergriff, for the seat from the Twenty-sixth District of Texas in 1984. Over the next ten years, he earned a reputation as a staunch conservative, leading a crusade to abolish the National Endowment for the Arts. In 1993 and 1994, Armey was one of President Clinton's fiercest opponents. He lambasted Clinton's health care proposals and termed his national service program "welfare" for "aspiring yuppies." By the time of the "Republican revolution" of 1994, Armey had risen to a leadership position within the party, and in 1995 he became the House majority leader. Together with Speaker **Newt Gingrich**, Armey promoted the **Contract with America**. Armey also became one of the best-known proponents of tax reform, proposing a flat tax rate, with no deductions, that, he argued, could be filed on "a form the size of a postcard." He made a brief bid for the Republican nomination for the presidency in 2000, but his campaign never got off the ground. While he was passed over as a successor to Gingrich following Gingrich's resignation as Speaker of the House in 1999, Armey remained one of the most powerful Republicans in Congress.

Suggested Readings: *CQ's Politics in America: The 106th Congress* (Washington, D.C.: Congressional Quarterly, Inc. 2000), p. 1355; *Current Biography Yearbook*, 1995, pp. 20–24.

Related Entries: Contract with America; Election of 1994; Election of 2000; Gingrich, Newt; House of Representatives, United States.

ASPIN, LESLIE (LES). (July 21, 1938, Milwaukee, Wisconsin–May 21, 1995, Washington, D.C.) Secretary of Defense, 1993–1994.

Following twenty-two years in the U.S. Congress, during which time he earned a reputation as an expert on military affairs, Les Aspin was sworn in as President Bill Clinton's first secretary of defense on January 23, 1993. In spite of his experience, Aspin encountered difficulties right from

Les Aspin, President Bill Clinton, and the Joint Chiefs of Staff, 1993. Library of Congress.

the start. Even before a serious heart ailment landed him in the hospital for several days in early February 1993, Aspin had to grapple with the subject of **gays in the military**. While still fending off criticism of the administration's "don't ask, don't tell" plan, Aspin became embroiled in another controversy, this one dealing with the administration's loosening of regulations that restricted the combat roles open to servicewomen. On a more substantive level, the end of the cold war and President Clinton's campaign promise to reduce defense spending prodded Aspin to initiate a "bottom-up review" of the military. This review culminated in a Defense Department budget for fiscal year 1994 that was approximately $12 billion less than that of the previous year. At the same time, Aspin warned the president that the nation's defense needs would compel the government to spend $1 trillion more over the next five years than initially projected by the administration. Aspin faced further difficulties because, like his immediate predecessors, he had the responsibility of carrying out and extending plans for closing various military bases. In U.S. actions abroad, Aspin oversaw the reinstatement of Jean-Bertrand Aristide as president of **Haiti** (an endeavor that he personally opposed), the establishment of the "Partnership for Peace" program, which aimed at enlarging the mission and membership of **NATO**, and ongoing actions in the Persian Gulf area and **Korea**. More important, Aspin presided over the expansion of America's role in **Somalia**, which culminated in a deadly attack on American troops and calls for his resignation by some members of Congress.

Aspin resigned on February 3, 1994. Most assumed that the various controversies that had dominated his tenure led President Clinton to ask to replace him with **William Perry**. Yet ill health clearly contributed to Aspin's decision to end his long and distinguished career in public life. In 1970, not long after completing his education—B.A., Yale, 1960; M.A., Oxford, 1962; Ph.D in economics, Massachusetts Institute of Technology, 1965—and military service, 1966–1968, Aspin successfully ran for a seat in the **House of Representatives**. He was reelected eleven times, rising to the post of chairman of the Armed Services Committee. A Rhodes scholar, like Clinton, Aspin died of a stroke on May 21, 1995, in Washington, D.C.

Suggested Readings: http://bioguide.congress.gov; http://www.defenselink.mil/specials/secdef-histories/bios/aspin.htm; *Current Biography Yearbook*, 1995, (New York: H. W. Wilson Co., 1995), p. 612.

Related Entry: Defense, Military.

ASSASSINATION ATTEMPTS. While President Bill Clinton's life was never seriously threatened by a would-be assassin, several attempts on his life were made during his presidency. Before dawn on September 12, 1994, Frank Eugene Corder, an unlicensed pilot with a history of mental illness, stole a small airplane and crashed it into the White House lawn. (Corder died in the crash.) The White House appeared to have been Corder's target. About a month later, on October 19, 1994, Francisco Martin Duran fired twenty-nine rounds from a semiautomatic rifle at the White House. He was tackled by two bystanders, arrested, and later convicted of attempted assassination. No one was hurt. On December 17, 1994, shots were fired at the White House from the Ellipse across the street. No one was apprehended. Several days later police shot and killed a homeless man who brandished a knife near the spot where the shots had been fired. On May 23, 1995, shortly after two blocks of Pennsylvania Avenue were closed across from the White House in response to the bombing of the federal building in **Oklahoma City**, Leland William Modjeski, a former pizza deliveryman, jumped the fence that surrounded the White House, declared, "I'm here to see the president," and rushed toward the

East Wing of the White House, gun in hand. Secret Service agents shot Modjeski in the arm and apprehended and arrested him.

Suggested Readings: Peter Castro, "Under Siege," *People*, June 5, 1995, p. 48; Donald Shelly Coolidge, "The Man Shot by the Secret Service," *Christian Science Monitor*, June 9, 1995, p. 2; "Clinton on the Closing of Pennsylvania Avenue, May 20, 1995," *Historic Documents*, 1995, p. 254; Michael Janofsky, "Man Convicted of Trying to Assassinate President," *New York Times*, April 5, 1995, p. A16.

B

BABBITT, BRUCE E. (June 27, 1938, Los Angeles, California– .) Secretary of the Interior, 1993–2001.

When President Bill Clinton announced Bruce Babbitt's nomination as secretary of the interior, many liberals responded with glee. After twelve years of what they saw as a period of neglect, they predicted that Babbitt's nomination would usher in a golden age for the **environment**. Not surprisingly, given Babbitt's long record of environmental activism, he never won the support of conservatives, who even initiated hearings into alleged acts of corruption by Babbitt and his associates. Yet, somewhat surprisingly, over the course of his tenure, Babbitt earned a good deal of criticism from many environmentalists, who lamented his willingness to compromise on numerous issues during his eight years as secretary of the interior.

A member of one of Arizona's most famous families, Babbitt grew up in Flagstaff on an enormous ranch, surrounded by Navajo and Hopi reservations, within easy reach of the Grand Canyon. He early came to appreciate the outdoors. He received his B.A. in geology from the University of Notre Dame, where he was elected student-body president. He attended graduate school at the University of Newcastle in England, during which time he spent some time traveling on the Amazon River, and earned his law degree from Harvard University. Upon returning to Arizona he became involved in politics, serving as attorney general (1975–1978) and then as governor (1978–1987). Early in his administration, President Clinton mentioned Babbitt as a potential **Supreme Court** nominee, but he never nominated Babbitt to the Court.

In 1988, Babbitt unsuccessfully sought the Democratic presidential nomination. In 1992, he actively campaigned for Clinton, especially in the West. As secretary of the interior, he helped formulate and enforce

Interior Secretary Bruce Babbitt and President Clinton commemorate the first annual National Park Week, May 23, 1994. AP/Wide World Photos.

the administration's policies toward land usage in the West. These included dismantling some dams to allow for a more natural flow of rivers and streams, and the creation of several new national parks and monuments, which increased federal protection of millions of acres of land. In July 1993, Babbitt announced a new forestry plan that reduced but did not restrict logging in the national forests. Somewhat typically, this plan satisfied neither environmentalists, who wanted to put an end to the destruction of old-growth trees, nor the loggers, who decried the new regulations as antibusiness. During the 2000 presidential campaign, Texas governor **George W. Bush** criticized the administration for allowing the national parks, which fell under Babbitt's purview, to deteriorate. Administration spokespersons countered that the Republican-controlled Congress had cut federal funding for the Department of the Interior and that it had done as well as it could with limited resources.

In the final days of his presidency, Bill Clinton issued new regulations that protected millions of acres of national forest. According to the *New York Times*, Clinton's regulations represented the "biggest conservation act in decades." While the new regulations were technically issued by the Department of Agriculture under the direction of Secretary **Dan Glick-**

man, they enhanced both the administration's and Babbitt's legacy as friends of the environment. Whether incoming president George W. Bush would allow the regulations, enacted by executive order, to stand remained to be seen.

Suggested Readings: "The (Bruised) Emperor of the Outdoors," *New York Times*, August 1, 1993, sec. 6, p. 21; "Clinton to Put New Restraints on U.S. Forests," *New York Times*, January 5, 2001, p. 1; "Environmentalists Get Their Wish," *Los Angeles Times*, December 25, 1992, p. 39.

BAILY, MARTIN N. (January 13, 1945–   .) Chairman, Council of Economic Advisers, 1999–2001.

Martin Baily chaired the Council of Economic Advisers (CEA) during President Bill Clinton's final two years in office. Hence he was in a position to take credit for the longest economic expansion in American history. At the same time, by the time he left office, the **economy** was beginning to slow, with some suggesting that by the time **George W. Bush** took office, it would be in a recession.

Baily earned his B.A. from Cambridge University, England, in 1967, and his Ph.D. in economics from Massachusetts Institute of Technology (MIT) in 1972. He taught at MIT, Yale University, and the University of Maryland and had experience as an economic adviser to numerous boards and agencies, including the Office of Technology Assessment and the Federal Reserve Board. Baily had been a member of the CEA from 1994 to 1996 and was a partner at McKinsey and Company when President Clinton nominated him to chair the CEA. One of his duties was to assemble the president's economic reports. Under his lead, the council also worked with the **President's Initiative on Race** to develop *Changing America: Indicators of Social and Economic Well-Being by Race and Hispanic Origin* (1998). This book documented the economic gains that minorities made while Clinton was president. At the same time, the study also detailed the persistent gaps that existed between whites and nonwhites in American society.

Suggested Reading: George Hager, "Former CEA Member Likely Pick for Chief," *Washington Post*, June 9, 1999, p. E2.

BAIRD, ZOË. (June 20, 1952, Brooklyn, New York–   .) Nominee for U.S. Attorney General, 1993.

President Bill Clinton hit a bump in the road very early in his presidency when he nominated Zoë Baird to the post of attorney general. Baird's name soon became synonymous with the term "nannygate." As an attorney in the public and private sectors, Baird had gained much praise. At forty years of age, Baird had risen to the position of senior vice president and general counsel of Aetna, one of the nation's largest insurance companies. Many career attorneys at the Justice Department also expressed their strong support for Baird when Clinton nominated her because they respected her record as an attorney in the public sector, including a stint at the Justice Department. In addition, many saw her nomination as a symbol of the breaking of the gender barrier in the legal world and of Clinton's commitment to opening up his administration to **women** and minorities.

However, shortly after Clinton nominated her, stories emerged that Baird had hired illegal immigrants as day-care providers for her children and had failed to pay Social Security taxes on their earnings. Rather than spend a great deal of political capital defending Baird from charges that she had broken the law—Baird testified that she had paid the back taxes on her employees and that she was not required to document whether they were legal immigrants at the time of their employment—the Clinton administration expressed its relief when Baird declared that she would withdraw her candidacy. Unfortunately, things got worse before they got better for the administration. Clinton's second nominee to the post of attorney general, **Kimba Wood**, suffered from similar nanny problems, and the administration withdrew her name from consideration as well.

Even though neither Baird nor Wood became attorney general, their nominations and the controversy surrounding them raised national awareness of the difficulties of obtaining adequate child care. After withdrawing her name from nomination, Baird returned to Aetna, taught briefly at Yale Law School, and accepted a position as the head of the Markle Foundation, a nonprofit organization dedicated to increasing access to **high technology**. Later during Clinton's presidency, Baird also served on the president's Foreign Intelligence Advisory Board.

Suggested Readings: Amy Harmon, "For Zoe Baird a New Opportunity for Public Service," *New York Times*, July 26, 1999, p. C4; Michael Kelly, "Setting In: The President's Day; Clinton Cancels Baird Nomination for Justice Dept.," *New York Times*, January 22, 1993, p. A1; Neil A. Lewis, "Clinton Completes Cabinet," *New York Times*, December 25, 1992, p. A1.

Related Entries: Cabinet; Reno, Janet.

BARSHEFSKY, CHARLENE. (c. 1951, Illinois.) U.S. Trade Representative, 1997–2001.

Charlene Barshefsky served as President Bill Clinton's chief trade negotiator through most of his administration. From May 1993 to April 1996, she was the deputy U.S. trade representative; from April 1996 to March 1997, she served as acting U.S. trade representative; and from March 1997 through January 2001, she was the U.S. trade representative. When she was sworn in to her final post, which made her a member of the **cabinet**, President Clinton described Barshefsky as a "brilliant negotiator" who had played an instrumental role in negotiating over 260 trade agreements. She promoted the president's economic program by encouraging regional trade agreements, expanding the markets open to American-made products, and protecting the intellectual property rights of U.S. producers. Even though the **trade deficit** increased to record heights during the Clinton years, the concurrent increase in exports and expansion of the **economy** kept Barshefsky, unlike some previous trade representatives, generally out of the spotlight.

Barshefsky received her B.A. from the University of Wisconsin in 1972 and her law degree from Catholic University in 1975. She rose to the level of partner at Steptoe and Johnson, one of Washington, D.C.'s most prestigious firms, developing a very successful international law practice. She succeeded **Mickey Kantor** as U.S. trade representative when Kantor became the new secretary of commerce upon **Ronald Brown**'s death.

Suggested Reading: *Current Biography Yearbook,* 2000 (New York: H. W. Wilson Co., 2000), p. 41; Kerry McIlroy, "Charlene Barshefsky," *George* 4:2 (February 1999), p. 24.

Related Entires: GATT; NAFTA.

BEGALA, PAUL. (1961–   .) Political adviser.

Paul Begala was one of Bill Clinton's top political advisers. In 1992, Begala teamed with **James Carville** to map out Clinton's successful campaign strategy. Some referred to the two as the dynamic duo, with Begala being Robin and Carville Batman. Following Clinton's election, Begala continued to serve as one of the president's top political advisers, although he did not take a position on the White House staff. Largely due to his dislike of **Dick Morris**, Begala did not play an active role in Clinton's bid for reelection in 1996. However, in 1997, Begala reemerged as a key adviser to the president. He was very visible throughout the **im-**

peachment battle, defending the president regularly on television. After the **Senate**'s vote on the **House**'s impeachment charges, Begala resigned his post with the White House to teach at Georgetown University and write a column for *George*, John F. Kennedy, Jr.'s magazine.

Begala traced his gift for translating broad political insights into specific and forceful messages to his youth in Missouri City, Texas, a suburb of Houston, where his family moved when he was in his teens. Working part-time at a local hardware store, he imbibed the community's pastime, talking politics. In high school and college, Begala got his first political experience, running for and being elected student-body president.

Begala and Carville began working together in 1984. While their candidate for the Senate in the state of Texas lost, over the next six years they earned a reputation as two of the most talented political consultants in the country. They helped Pennsylvania governor Robert Casey, New Jersey senator Frank Lautenberg, Georgia governor Zell Miller, and Pennsylvania senator Harris Wofford win hotly contested campaigns. Along with several other young political strategists, including **Stanley Greenberg** and **George Stephanopoulos**, Begala and Carville constituted the famous "war room" that responded to one crisis after another in the early months of Clinton's campaign for the presidency in 1992. **Dee Dee Myers**, Clinton's press secretary, observed that Begala made sure that Clinton stuck to his main message in spite of all of the distractions.

Suggested Readings: Lloyd Grove, "Nailing the Lid on the GOP," *Washington Post*, November 5, 1992, p. D1; John Harris, "Top Adviser to Clinton Announces Departure," *Washington Post*, February 25, 1999, p. A16.

Related Entry: Election of 1992.

BENNETT, ROBERT (BOB) S. (1939–   .) Personal attorney to President Clinton 1994–2001.

The brother of well-known conservative pundit and former Ronald Reagan and **George Bush** administration official William (Bill) Bennett, Bob Bennett served as Bill Clinton's personal attorney during much of his presidency. He oversaw the president's response to **Paula Jones**'s sexual harassment lawsuit and played a leading role in fending off the **impeachment** charges. In April 1998, Bennett won a major legal victory when he helped convince federal judge **Susan Webber Wright** to dismiss Paula Jones's lawsuit, although this victory did not end the president's legal travails, in general or with Jones. Bennett's brash style, including his willingness to challenge the credibility of numerous witnesses in the case, such as **Linda Tripp**, led some to blame him for many of Clinton's troubles. Harvard Law School professor Alan Dershowitz, for one, accused Bennett of having turned "a political problem into a legal nightmare," adding that the president was "subject to impeachment because of missteps by his attorney" (Grover, "A Jury of His Peers").

Bennett was raised in Brooklyn, New York, where he earned a reputation as an accomplished fighter, a background he would draw on later in life. He earned his B.A. from Georgetown University and a law degree from Harvard University. Before starting his own law firm, he worked at Hogan and Hartson in Washington, D.C., for five years. In 1990, he joined the high-powered Washington, D.C., firm of Skadden, Arps. He specialized in white-collar criminal defense work, representing former Defense Secretary Caspar Weinberger against charges developed by independent counsel Lawrence Walsh in the Iran-contra affair, and Democratic power brokers Clark Clifford and **Roger Altman** in the Bank of Commerce and Credit International (BCCI) case.

Bennett first went to work for the president at $475 an hour in 1994 to represent him in the so-called **travelgate** affair. With a reputation for keeping his clients out of court and maintaining the initiative in the court of public opinion, Bennett soon became embroiled in Paula Jones's lawsuit. Even though Bennett convinced Judge Wright to dismiss the case, he did so only after Clinton had been deposed by Paula Jones's attorneys. During his deposition, the president sought to finesse his way around questions regarding his relationship with **Monica Lewinsky** through questionable legal doublespeak. Bennett, who was present at the time, did not seek to get his client to clarify his answers in which he denied having had sex with Lewinsky according to the definition of sex presented by Jones's attorneys. At one point during Jones's lawsuit, Bennett sought to negotiate a settlement. The settlement, however, fell through, and the case grew in magnitude. Bennett played a less significant role following Clinton's impeachment by the **House of Representatives** than he had played before the impeachment.

Suggested Readings: Gerald S. Greenberg, ed., *Historical Encyclopedia of the U.S. Independent Counsel Investigations* (Westport, CT: Greenwood Press, 2000); Lloyd Grove, "A Jury of His Peers," *Washington Post*, January 28, 1998, p. D1; "Key Player: Robert S. Bennett," http://www.washingtonpost.com/wp-srv/politics/special/clinton/players/bennett.htm.

Related Entries: Filegate; Independent Counsel Law; White House Defense Team; Whitewater.

BENTSEN, LLOYD. (February 11, 1921, Mission, Texas– .) Secretary of the Treasury, 1993–1994.

Michael Dukakis's vice presidential running mate in 1988, Lloyd Bentsen was a popular choice to serve as President Bill Clinton's Treasury secretary. He enjoyed widespread support on Capitol Hill due, in part, to his long years of service as a congressman (1955–1970) and senator (1971–1993) from Texas and to his amiable personality. Bentsen's experience as chairman of the Senate Finance Committee, during which time he helped craft several budget deals with Presidents Ronald Reagan and **George Bush**, added to the support he garnered from both Democrats and Republicans. Indeed, the Senate Finance Committee listened to Bentsen's opening remarks and then confirmed his nomination without any further questions.

As Treasury secretary, Bentsen promoted President Clinton's economic program. He pushed for ratification of **NAFTA** and lobbied in favor of a tax increase and Clinton's economic stimulus plan. Bentsen's connections and long-standing ties in the Senate helped gain narrow passage of key aspects of the president's program. During his tenure, Bentsen had to grapple with the savings and loan crisis, left over from the Bush administration, the bailout or rebuilding of **Russia**'s economy, and several controversial federal law-enforcement incidents, most infamously the raid in **Waco**, Texas, which involved agents of the Bureau of Alcohol, Tobacco, and Firearms, which was part of the Department of the Treasury, as well as the FBI.

When Bentsen resigned on December 6, 1994, the **economy** was in the process of recovering from the recession of the early 1990s. Nonetheless, at the time, few realized that the economic expansion would prove so long-lasting. As a result, while Bentsen's tenure as Treasury secretary garnered him praise from many Democrats, **Robert Rubin**, who succeeded him, ultimately won more accolades and credit for the economic expansion of the Clinton years than did the onetime senator from Texas.

Suggested Readings: *Current Biography Yearbook*, 1993, p. 48; Peter B. Levy, *Encyclopedia of the Reagan-Bush Years* (Westport, CT: Greenwood Press, 1996), p. 37.

Related Entries: Budget, Federal; Domestic Policy.

BERGER, SAMUEL (SANDY) R. (October 28, 1945, Sharon, Connecticut– .) Deputy Assistant to the President for National Security Affairs, 1993–1996; National Security Adviser, 1997–2001.

Following President Bill Clinton's reelection in 1996, Sandy Berger became the national security adviser, succeeding **Anthony Lake**, as part of a broader shake-up of Clinton's **foreign policy** team. Prior to his elevation to this cabinet-level post, Berger had served as the deputy assistant to the president for national security affairs. During the 1992 campaign, Berger advised Clinton on foreign policy matters. He also played a key role on Clinton's transition team.

Berger and Clinton were longtime friends, going back to their work together for George McGovern's presidential campaign in 1972. Some pundits described Berger as the most important National Security Agency (NSA) head since Henry Kissinger. Unlike Kissinger, however, Berger was more of a political and less of a strategic thinker. Perhaps Berger's chief attribute was his ability to judge the political impact of a particular foreign policy decision. This has led some to argue that the president's foreign policy was dictated by the polls rather than by a coherent vision. A tireless worker who got along personally with nearly everyone, Berger jumped from one crisis and/or scandal to another through much of his tenure. Meeting regularly with Secretary of State **Madeleine Albright** and Secretary of Defense **William Cohen**, Berger helped map out the administration's foreign policy during Clinton's second term in office. The three of them were known as the ABC club. Even during President Clinton's most trying times, Berger remained loyal to him and vice versa. Berger received much criticism for allegedly reacting too slowly to the reports of espionage by the Chinese of American nuclear secrets. He also had to defend the president's decision to go to war in **Kosovo**, which initially was much criticized by both conservatives and liberals.

Responding to criticism that the Clinton administration's foreign policy was haphazard and lacked a coherent vision, Berger retorted that most "grand strategies" were, in fact, rationales given to decisions made on an ad hoc basis in the first place. The bumpiness of the administration's policy also reflected the views and personalities of Clinton and Berger. Both men were essentially pragmatists. Berger was trained as a trade lawyer, accustomed to cutting deals and making compromises. Like Clinton, he felt comfortable with the art of the possible. The lack of a clear public consensus on the direction that U.S. foreign policy should take in the post-cold-war era also affected the decisions that Clinton and Berger made.

Berger was born in Sharon, Connecticut, and was raised in a small dairy community outside Poughkeepsie, New York. His father died when he was eight, and he grew accustomed to long hours of work, which became one of his trademarks. He received his B.A. from Cornell University in 1967 and a law degree from Harvard University in 1971. He went to work in Washington, D.C., after law school, becoming a speech writer for Senator George McGovern in 1972. While he strongly opposed the **Vietnam** War, Berger always maintained a conservative manner and was attracted to McGovern's attempt to end the war through traditional politics rather than protest. After McGovern lost, Berger worked for a while for New York City mayor John Lindsay and then practiced law with the firm of Hogan and Hartson in Washington, D.C. He served as deputy director of policy planning in the State Department during the Jimmy Carter administration, where his boss was Anthony Lake. During the Ronald Reagan and **George Bush** years, Berger returned to private law practice. From early on, he was one of Clinton's chief supporters and advisers.

Suggested Readings: R. W. Apple, Jr., "A Domestic Sort with Global Worries," *New York Times*, August 25, 1999, p. A1; *Current Biography Yearbook*, 1998, pp. 53–56.

Related Entries: China; Christopher, Warren; Defense, Military; Talbott, Strobe.

BLUMENTHAL, SIDNEY. (November 6, 1948, Chicago, Illinois–   .) Assistant to the President, 1997–2001.

A prominent liberal writer who authored numerous favorable stories on the Clintons for the *New Republic* and the *New Yorker*, Sidney Blumenthal accepted a post within the White House in June 1997. During the **impeachment** hearings in the **House of Representatives**, Blumenthal played a particularly public role, becoming embroiled in Clinton's trial itself as an alleged accomplice.

Raised in Chicago, Blumenthal got his first taste of politics at an early age, working for the Democratic Party machine in his preteens. He received his B.A. from Brandeis University in 1969 and then embarked on a successful career as a journalist, writing five books, including *The Permanent Campaign* (1980) and *Pledging Allegiance: The Last Campaign of the Cold War* (1989). During the same time period, he wrote for the *New Republic*, forging a distinctive style of political advocacy journalism. In January 1992, he penned a cover story for the *New Republic*, "The Anointed," which portrayed the Arkansas governor, whom Blumenthal had met four years earlier, in a very favorable light, in spite of rumors circulating regarding Clinton's personal life. After the election, Blumenthal remained one of Clinton's most vocal supporters. He dismissed **Whitewater** as a bogus scandal and attacked **Paula Jones** and her conservative backers as hacks.

During the mid-1990s, Blumenthal's open bias in favor of Clinton, along with his and his wife's personal ties to **Hillary Clinton** (Blumenthal's wife ran the White House fellows program), created a rift with the *New Republic*'s new editor, Michael Kelly, a critic of the president. When Blumenthal accepted a post within the White House, one journalist quipped that now he would get paid for his boosterism. Blumenthal garnered even further notoriety when fellow journalist Christopher Hitchens accused him of being part of Clinton's attack team (Grove, "The Lunch"). More precisely, Hitchens signed an affidavit that challenged Blumenthal's testimony before a grand jury in which Blumenthal had stated that he had no knowledge of any White House effort to paint **Monica Lewinsky** as a "stalker." Hitchens argued that Blumenthal had described Lewinsky as a "stalker" in a conversation they had had. In response to Hitchens's accusations, House Judiciary Committee chair Henry Hyde, among others, called for taking legal action against Blumenthal. Blumenthal defended himself from this charge, and no legal action was ever taken against him.

Suggested Readings: Lloyd Grove, "The Lunch That Sticks in Capital's Craw," *Washington Post*, February 9, 1999, p. C1; http://washingtonpost.com/wp-srv/politics/special/clinton/players/blumenthal.htm; Al Kamen, "Friend Questions Blumenthal Testimony," *Washington Post*, February 7, 1999, p. A10; Howard Kurtz, "The Clintons' Pen Pal," *Washington Post*, June 16, 1997, p. C1.

BOSNIA AND HERZEGOVINA. During the 1992 presidential campaign, Bill Clinton criticized President **George Bush** for his reluctance to intervene more forcefully to stop the conflict in Bosnia and Herzegovina. In 1992, war erupted in this state of the former Republic of Yugoslavia shortly after its Muslim-led government declared independence from the Serb-dominated central government headed by **Slobodan Milosevic**, an extreme nationalist. (In the summer of 1991, Croatia and Slovenia declared their independence.) In February 1992, Serbs living inside Bosnia announced that they had formed their own independent state; a couple of months later, they initiated a brutal siege against Sarajevo, the capital of Bosnia. Backed by Milosevic, Serb forces in Bosnia took control of much of Bosnia and commenced removing non-Serbs from Serb-

Secretary of Defense William Cohen greets soldiers in Bosnia and Herzegovina. Department of Defense.

controlled villages, an act the international community referred to as "ethnic cleansing." Reports of atrocities against Muslims and Croatians committed by the Serbs, as well as coverage of the siege and bombardment of Sarajevo, horrified Europeans and many Americans. Not wanting to directly involve the United States in the fighting in the region, President Bush supported tepid United Nations attempts to restore the peace. Bill Clinton suggested that he would adopt a more aggressive posture.

When Clinton became president, however, his policy toward Bosnia and Herzegovina remained essentially the same as President Bush's, at least for the first couple of years of his presidency. Even though Clinton decried human rights violations in the region and supported UN efforts to maintain certain so-called safe havens from Serb aggression, his focus on domestic affairs and his reluctance to commit U.S. troops to the region resulted in little real change. Beginning in May 1994, **NATO** warplanes, under the direction of the United Nations, conducted air strikes against Serb forces, although with minimal affect. In December 1994, former President Jimmy Carter negotiated a cease-fire in the region, which began to break apart the following spring. Renewed fighting convinced the Clinton administration that it needed to become more directly involved.

Hence, beginning on November 1, 1995, the Clinton administration sponsored peace talks in Dayton, Ohio, including the leaders of Bosnia, Croatia, and Serbia.

After three weeks of negotiations, the parties emerged with a tentative agreement known as the Dayton Agreement or Accords. On December 14, 1995, the accords were formally signed in Paris. While officially recognizing Bosnia-Herzegovina as a single nation, the accords split the country into separate districts, one controlled by Serbs and the other by Bosnian Muslims and Croatians. NATO agreed to commit 60,000 troops to the region, including about 20,000 U.S. troops. To gain support for the plan, President Clinton pledged that the mission would be "limited, focussed, and under the command of an American general" (*Historic Documents*). Clinton defended U.S. involvement by arguing that the United States, as the leader of the free world, had the responsibility to "defend our fundamental values as a people and serve our most basic, strategic interests." Many Republicans criticized the action, questioning the use of U.S. troops under UN command and wondering about the specific objectives of the mission. Nonetheless, with most Democrats rallying behind the president, Congress enacted a resolution in support of U.S. troops; the resolution neither endorsed nor repudiated the mission.

For the rest of Clinton's presidency U.S. troops remained in Bosnia. (3,350 American personnel were in the region as of April, 2001.) The administration argued that their presence helped establish a lasting peace in the region. In July 1999, Clinton traveled to formerly war-torn Sarajevo to mark the anniversary of the signing of the Dayton Accords. The administration claimed that ethnic reconciliation had begun and contrasted the peace, stability, and economic vibrancy of the state to the ethnic warfare and economic turmoil in **Kosovo** and Serbia. Conservatives, however, continued to question the administration's policy in the region, noting that American troops had stayed long past the initial deadline and that Bosnia and Herzegovina had been divided into de facto separate nations.

Suggested Readings: Wayne Bert, *The Reluctant Superpower: United States Policy in Bosnia, 1991–95* (Basingstoke: Macmillan, 1997); "Clinton on U.S. Role in Bosnia Peacekeeping Mission," *Historic Documents*, 1995, p. 717; Jane Perez, "Powell Joins Europeans and Russians in Talks About Balkans," *New York Times*, April 12, 2001, p. A9; "What Is the OSCE Mission to Bosnia and Herzogovinia?" http://www.oscebih.org/missionoverview/overview.htm.

Related Entry: Foreign Policy.

BOWLES, ERSKINE. (August 8, 1945, Greensboro, North Carolina–   .) Director of Small Business Administration, 1993–1994; Deputy Chief of Staff, 1994–1995; Chief of Staff, 1997–1998.

Erskine Bowles, a North Carolina businessman with a reputation as a sound manager and leader, served in the Clinton administration for about six years, most importantly as the president's chief of staff in 1997 and 1998. While Clinton's first chief of staff, **Thomas "Mack" McLarty**, was a lifelong friend who had difficulty mastering the art of managing the White House office, Bowles, who became very close to the president after the **election of 1992** departed in 1998 with a reputation of having performed an excellent job in an often-overlooked but crucial role.

Born in Greensboro, North Carolina, Bowles earned his B.S. from the University of North Carolina at Chapel Hill in 1967 and his M.B.A. from Columbia University in 1969. He worked briefly on Wall Street for Morgan Stanley and then returned to North Carolina to work for his wife's investment banking firm. In 1975, he started his own firm, Bowles Hollowell Conner and Company, which grew into a multimillion-dollar enterprise. Both his family and his in-laws were involved in politics. His father unsuccessfully ran for governor in 1972, and his sister-in-law lost to South Carolina senator Strom Thurmond in 1996.

Bowles first met Bill Clinton in 1992, raising over $1 million for his presidential campaign. The two shared a passion for golf and often played together on the links. About the same age and with similar political temperaments, they quickly developed a close relationship. One of the issues that cemented Bowles's support for Clinton was **George Bush**'s support for a ban on using fetal tissue in scientific research. Bowles, who was president of the Juvenile Diabetes Foundation, contended that this politically motivated ban hurt efforts to find a cure for juvenile diabetes.

After Clinton defeated George Bush, Bowles helped orchestrate Clinton's preinauguration economic summit in Little Rock, Arkansas, and accepted a post as director of the Small Business Administration (SBA) shortly thereafter. In 1994, he left the SBA to serve as Clinton's deputy chief of staff under **Leon Panetta**, who had replaced Mack McLarty. In addition to shaping the president's battle over the budget with Congress, Bowles often played golf with Clinton during this period, enhancing their personal relationship in the process. Citing a desire to spend more time with his family, Bowles returned to North Carolina at the end of 1995. However, when Panetta resigned following Clinton's reelection, the president turned to Bowles to become his third chief of staff. Bowles accepted Clinton's offer but publicly stated that he would remain in Washington,

D.C., for only a short period because of his desire to continue to spend more time with his family. Among Bowles's proudest accomplishments was promoting the **President's Initiative on Race**.

Bowles was Clinton's chief of staff when the **Monica Lewinsky** matter erupted and during the House Judiciary Committee's **impeachment** hearings. By and large he remained above the fray, testifying before the grand jury that he had no knowledge of any attempt to bribe **Webster Hubbell** not to testify against the president. Indeed, Bowles probably would have returned to North Carolina earlier than he did if it had not been for the Lewinsky scandal. Not wanting to leave the president in the midst of the crisis, he chose to stay on as chief of staff until it became clear that the **U.S. Senate** would lack the votes to convict the president. Bowles was succeeded by his deputy, **John Podesta**.

Suggested Readings: *Current Biography Yearbook*, 1998, p. 64; Todd Perdum, "After the Election: The Players," *New York Times*, November 9, 1996, p. 1.

BRADY BILL. President Clinton signed the Brady bill on November 30, 1993. The law instituted a five-day waiting period before one could purchase a handgun, raised licensing fees on gun dealers, and increased regulation of multiple gun purchases. The law allowed for the phasing out of the waiting period once an instant background check was feasible. The Brady bill was the first **gun-control** measure enacted by Congress since 1968.

Seven years in the making, the law was named after James Brady, President Ronald Reagan's press secretary, who was shot at the same time Reagan was by a would-be assassin. Following his recovery from the incident, Brady and his wife Sarah, although they were Republicans, championed the call to regulate the purchase of handguns, particularly so-called Saturday-night specials. Several times the so-called Brady bill died in committee or in conference after the **House** and **Senate** enacted different versions of the measure. During the 1992 presidential campaign, Bill Clinton promised to sign the bill into law. President **George Bush** opposed the bill. Clinton included the Brady bill as part of a larger anti-crime package in 1993. For tactical reasons, however, it was voted on separately. Differences between Senate and House Democratic leaders threatened to kill the Brady bill, as did fierce opposition from the National Rifle Association. Yet in a spurt of activity, both the House and the Senate enacted similar versions of the Brady bill, with Democrats and

Stephen Breyer. Supreme Court Historical Society.

Republicans largely voting along party lines. Subsequently, Clinton and his supporters touted the Brady bill as an effective means for keeping guns out of the hands of criminals and pointed to it to build support for further gun-control measures. Critics questioned the effectiveness of the law and argued that no further measures should be enacted, particularly since the Justice Department had proved reluctant to prosecute violators of the gun-control laws that already existed. Just as important, in 1994, the National Rifle Association and other conservative groups targeted key Democratic politicians who had supported the bill. Their efforts helped Republicans gain control of both houses of Congress for the first time in decades.

Suggested Readings: "An Assault on Gun Control," *America*, April 29, 1995, p. 3; "President Signs 'Brady' Control Law," *Congressional Quarterly Almanac*, 1993, p. 300.

BRANCH DAVIDIANS. *See* **Waco**.

BREYER, STEPHEN G. (August 15, 1938, San Francisco, California– .) Associate Justice of the U.S. Supreme Court, 1994– .

Stephen G. Breyer easily won **Senate** confirmation as President Bill

Clinton's second nominee to the U.S. **Supreme Court** in 1994. His strong credentials and moderate record allowed him to avoid much of the contentiousness that had characterized many recent confirmation hearings. He maintained his moderate reputation while on the Court.

Breyer was born in San Francisco, California, into a well-educated and middle-class Jewish family. Both of his parents were active in civic life, his father as legal counsel to the San Francisco Board of Education and his mother in the League of Women Voters. Voted the most likely to succeed by his classmates at Lowell High School, Breyer, an Eagle Scout, received his A.B. from Stanford University in 1959 and his law degree from Harvard University in 1964. He excelled academically at both institutions, being chosen for Phi Beta Kappa at Stanford and serving as an editor for the *Harvard Law Review*.

After clerking for Supreme Court justice Arthur Goldberg and working for the Justice Department, Breyer joined the Harvard Law School faculty in 1967. In the early 1970s, he worked for the Justice Department and as a special counsel to the Senate Judiciary Committee during President Richard Nixon's impeachment hearings. In the latter half of the 1970s, Breyer continued to lecture at Harvard and served as the chief counsel of the Senate Judiciary Committee. Shortly before Ronald Reagan was inaugurated, Breyer was confirmed as a judge on the U.S. Court of Appeals for the First Circuit. Throughout the 1980s, he earned a reputation as a judicial moderate, favoring flexible sentencing guidelines and upholding environmental regulations and laws requiring that minors receive parental consent to obtain an abortion.

While Clinton passed over Breyer in favor of **Ruth Bader Ginsburg** in 1993, he nominated Breyer to replace Justice Harry Blackmun in 1994. Clinton recognized that Breyer, who had won the support of both Senators Ted Kennedy and Strom Thurmond, the senior Democratic and Republican members of the Senate Judiciary Committee, in 1980, would be able to gain confirmation much more easily than several other possible nominees, most prominently Secretary of the Interior **Bruce Babbitt**.

Known for the eloquence of his writing, Breyer often joined with Ginsburg, Clinton's other Supreme Court nominee, and John Paul Stevens and David Souter in writing dissenting opinions in a number of divided Court decisions. He opposed the Court's 5–4 decisions in *Seminole Tribe of Florida* v. *Florida* (1996) and *U.S.* v. *Lopez* (1995), both of which struck down federal laws as a violation of states' rights (as protected by the little-used Eleventh Amendment). Breyer, however, was not always in the minority. Particularly in several key First Amendment cases, he stood with the majority. Breyer was sharply critical of the majority's reasoning in *Bush* v. *Gore* (2000) in which the Supreme Court stopped the vote recount in the state of Florida, insuring that **George W. Bush** would become president.

Suggested Readings: *Current Biography Yearbook*, 1996, pp. 52–56; Gwen Ifill, "The Supreme Court: President Chooses Breyer," *New York Times*, May 14, 1994, sec. 1, p. 1.

Related Entry: Election of 2000.

BRIDGE TO THE TWENTY-FIRST CENTURY. During the 1996 campaign for the presidency, Republican nominee **Robert Dole**, who sought to emphasize the themes of traditional values and character, promised to be a "bridge to the past" if elected president. The Democratic Party, in general, and President Clinton, in particular, picked up on this phrase to cast Dole and the Republicans as reactionaries who sought to turn back the clock on the progress that the nation had made over the course of the past several decades. In his acceptance speech at the Democratic National Convention, Bill Clinton explicitly focussed on this theme by promising to "build a bridge to the twenty-first century." Even before Clinton uttered this specific retort, other Democrats had made it clear that this would be one of the main themes of the **election of 1996**. Georgia's popular governor, Zell Miller, for example, declared in one of the keynote addresses, "We choose progress. They offer reaction." (*CQ Almanac*, 1996). On the campaign trail after the convention, Clinton and **Al Gore** repeatedly exhorted their audiences to build a "bridge to the future."

Suggested Readings: "Democratic Convention Day-by-Day," *Congressional Quarterly Almanac*, 1996, p. 11–10; Evan Thomas, *Back from the Dead: How Clinton Survived the Republican Revolution* (New York: Atlantic Monthly Press, 1997).

BROADDRICK, JUANITA. Sex-scandal figure.

One of the more damning charges against President Bill Clinton came from Juanita Broaddrick, who accused him of having sexually assaulted her in a hotel room in 1978 during Clinton's first campaign for governor. Long before he ran for president, in fact, stories about Clinton's alleged sexual assault on Broaddrick circulated in Arkansas. Yet neither then nor during the 1992 presidential campaign did they gather much credence.

In 1997, Broaddrick signed an affidavit in the **Paula Jones** lawsuit in which she denied that Clinton had ever sexually assaulted her. However, in testimony before independent counsel **Kenneth Starr**, Broaddrick recanted her original denial, stating that she had lied in the first place because she did not want to become involved in the Paula Jones case and because she did not believe that anyone would believe her. In his report to Congress, Starr included her accusations against the president in a footnote, officially referring to her as Jane Doe No. 5. In violation of Judge **Susan Webber Wright**'s orders, Paula Jones's attorneys used Broaddrick's real name in their reply to Clinton's defense team's summary-judgment motion. Wright subsequently dismissed Jones's suit. Following the **Senate impeachment** trial, the *Wall Street Journal* described Broaddrick's charges in an article on its opinion page. Other newspapers quickly pounced on the story. By this time, Clinton had already been acquitted of all impeachment charges by the U.S. Senate. Moreover, Broaddrick had so little evidence to substantiate her allegations that nothing else came of the charges. Clinton's defenders added that Broaddrick's claim did not fit the pattern of Clinton's alleged womanizing, which at least in the cases of **Monica Lewinsky** and **Gennifer Flowers** had been between two consenting adults. Moreover, the fact that Broaddrick never filed criminal or civil charges against Clinton cast further doubt on the veracity of her accusation.

Suggested Readings: Luis Romano, Peter Baker, "Jane Doe #5 Tells Story of Alleged 1978 Assault," *Washington Post*, February 20, 1999, p. A1.; Howard Kurtz, "Key Player: Juanita Broaddrick," http://www.washingtonpost.com/wp-srv/politics/special/clinton/players/broaddrick.htm; "Long Simmering Story Goes Mainstream," *Washington Post*, February 20, 1999, p. A9; Jeffrey Toobin, *A Vast Conspiracy* (New York: Random House, 1999).

BROWN, RONALD H. (August 1, 1941, New York, NY–April 13, 1996, Croatia.) Secretary of Commerce, 1993–1996.

Ronald Brown, President Clinton's secretary of commerce and one of the highest-ranking **African American** officials in the United States, died in a tragic airplane crash in Croatia along with thirty-two other Americans and two Croatians on April 3, 1996. Brown had helped unify the Democrats as their party chairman from 1989 to 1993. From 1993 until his death, Brown was one of Clinton's most prominent **cabinet** members. He died in the midst of an independent counsel's investigation into his alleged misuse of office. The investigation was ended with his death, and

Secretary of Commerce Ron Brown, right, Secretary of State Warren Christopher, left, and Jordan Crown Prince Hassan at Jordan Mideast Summit, October 29, 1995. AP/Wide World Photos.

no one was charged with or convicted of any crimes stemming from the investigation.

Brown was born in New York City, the son of a prominent black family that owned a famous Harlem hotel. He received his B.A. from Middlebury College and his law degree from St. John's University. He worked for the National Urban League for a little more than a decade and then for the **U.S. Senate**, first as chief counsel to the Senate Judiciary Committee and then as one of Senator Edward Kennedy's top aides. Later he became a partner at the prestigious law firm of Patton, Boggs and Blow and a prominent corporate lobbyist.

As secretary of commerce, Brown aggressively promoted the Clinton administration's goal of expanding trade. Some conservatives contended, largely after Brown's death, that the secretary had jeopardized national security interests in exchange for trade with **China**. Indeed, Brown saw foreign trade as a key to allowing those with large investments in defense-related technology to survive in the post-cold-war **economy**. Upon his nomination, some questioned Brown's qualifications for the post, since he was a lawyer rather than a businessman, and worried about his close ties to several controversial clients. Yet the expansion of the economy and favorable relations with many prominent corporate leaders quieted these criticisms during his tenure in office.

Suggested Readings: Jill Dutt, "Profiles of the New Appointees," *Newsday*, December 13, 1992, p. 22; Joyce Jones, "The Best Commerce Secretary Ever," *Black Enterprise*, June 1996, p. 90; Marc Lacey, "In Sadness, U.S. Receives 33 Caskets," *Los Angeles Times*, April 7, 1996, p. A1.

Related Entries: Domestic Policy; Trade Deficit.

BROWNER, CAROL M. (December 16, 1955, Miami, Florida–   .) Director of the Environmental Protection Agency, 1993–2001.

Throughout Bill Clinton's presidency, Carol M. Browner headed the Environmental Protection Agency (EPA), one of the most significant independent federal regulatory bodies. Under her lead, the EPA sped up the cleanup of toxic-waste sites, issued stricter clean-air rules, and enacted new food-safety laws. While conservatives claimed that the EPA often implemented regulations without regard to their cost or their impact on the **economy**, Browner steadfastly sought to fulfill her mandate of protecting the **environment** and preventing further pollution.

Born and raised in Florida, Browner earned her B.A. and law degrees from the University of Florida in 1977 and 1979, respectively. Prior to becoming the director of the EPA, she worked as a legislative aide for Florida senator Lawton Chiles, as the counsel for the Senate Committee on Energy and Natural Resources, as Senator **Al Gore**'s legislative director, and as secretary of the Department of Environmental Regulations for the state of Florida. Like President Clinton, she contended that economic growth and environmentalism need not conflict with one another. The ability of the Clinton administration to create millions of new jobs while simultaneously enacting stricter environmental regulations lent weight to this claim.

Perhaps the most important regulation enacted under Browner's tenure came in 1997. Against the strong objections of conservatives, the EPA issued new clean-air rules that significantly restricted auto emissions and other sources of air pollution, including charcoal barbecue grills in certain areas. Even some Democrats complained that Browner had overstepped her authority in issuing these regulations. The National Association of Manufacturers and the American Petroleum Institute, among others, lambasted the new rules as a threat to American industry and argued that they were based on bad science. But Browner persevered, contending that the EPA was required to frame regulations without regard to costs and that a great deal of scientific evidence existed that showed that stricter rules were necessary.

Suggested Readings: "The Queen of Clean Air," http://www.cnn.com/ALLPOLITICS/ 1997/06/30/time/browner.html; "A Victory for Cleaner Air," *New York Times*, September 29, 1998, A24.

BUDGET, FEDERAL (DEFICIT REDUCTION). When Bill Clinton became president, the federal budget deficit was one of the top problems facing the nation. Throughout the 1992 presidential campaign, independent candidate **H. Ross Perot** focussed on the danger of persistently high federal deficits and ever-increasing debt. He gained much attention and a considerable portion of the vote in the process. Other candidates, such as Democratic challenger **Paul Tsongas**, similarly emphasized the need to address the budget deficit. As Perot and others observed, the federal government had not balanced its budget since 1969, in spite of a number of budget deals enacted by Congress and signed by Presidents Ronald Reagan and **George Bush**. For example, the much-heralded Gramm-Rudman-Hollings Act of 1985, a bipartisan bill signed by President Reagan, promised to balance the budget by the year 1990. Instead, the federal deficit more than doubled, from $149.7 billion in 1987 to $290 billion in 1992. While President George Bush reneged on his "no new taxes" pledge in order to address the growing deficit, the recession of the early 1990s and the savings and loan crisis actually resulted in record budget deficits.

Convinced that the Democratic-controlled Congress was incapable of acting in a fiscally responsible way, Republicans proposed enacting a balanced-budget amendment to the U.S. Constitution. Only by making budget deficits a violation of the Constitution, they argued, would law-makers be compelled to balance the budget. The pledge to pass such an amendment was part of the Republican Party's **"Contract with America"** in 1994 and remained on the agenda of many leading conservatives through the mid-1990s. In 1995, the Republican-controlled **U.S. House of Representatives** passed the balanced-budget amendment to the U.S. Constitution. However, the amendment fell two votes short of passage in the **U.S. Senate**.

During the 1992 campaign and afterwards, President Clinton opposed a balanced-budget amendment. Instead, he pledged to cut the budget deficit in half by 1996 through prudent fiscal management—targeted tax increases, reduced government and waste, and stimulating the **economy**. Few pundits expected his plan to work, which was one of the reasons the Republicans persisted in calling for a balanced-budget amendment.

Without a doubt, one of the major achievements of the Clinton years was the eradication of the federal budget deficit and the creation of a sizeable budget surplus. From a high of $290 billion in 1992, the deficit fell steadily, to $107 billion in 1996 and $22 billion in 1997 (see Table 2). The speed with which the deficit declined made moot the conflict over the balanced-budget amendment and gave way to new debates over what to do with the surplus. Indeed, the economy grew at such a steady rate in the latter half of the 1990s that revenues repeatedly exceeded expectations. The president proclaimed that the budget was balanced in 1998. Subsequently, he and others forecast large surpluses, in the trillions of dollars over the long term. Shortly before he left office, Clinton an-nounced that the budget surplus had reached $211 billion dollars. The reduction in the deficit allowed first for a much-reduced rate in the growth of the federal debt and ultimately to a discussion about actually paying off the entire debt in the not-so-distant future. As a percentage of the gross domestic product, arguably the most meaningful statistic, the federal debt continuously declined from a high of 68.6 percent of the GDP in 1996 to about 60 percent in 2000. Moreover, the president and

Figure 1
Gross Federal Debt as Percentage of Gross Domestic Product (GDP)

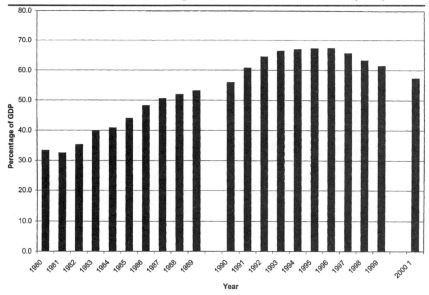

Source: *Economic Report of the President, 2000.*

Figure 2
Federal Budget Deficits and Supluses

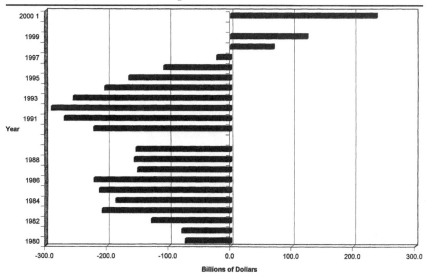

Source: *Economic Report of the President, 2000.*

Table 2
The Federal Budget (In Millions of Dollars)

Year	Receipts	Outlays	Surplus or Deficit (−)	Outlays as percentage of GDP	Gross Federal Debt	As percentage of GDP
1980	517,112	590,947	−73,835	21.7	909,050	33.4
1985	734,088	946,423	−212,334	23.1	1,817,521	44.3
1990	1,031,969	1,253,163	−221,194	22.0	3,206,564	56.4
1991	1,055,041	1,324,400	−269,359	22.6	3,598,498	61.4
1992	1,091,279	1,381,681	−290,402	22.5	4,002,136	65.1
1993	1,154,401	1,409,414	−255,013	21.8	4,351,416	67.2
1994	1,258,627	1,461,731	−203,104	21.4	4,643,705	67.8
1995	1,351,830	1,515,729	−163,899	21.1	4,921,018	68.4
1996	1,453,062	1,560,512	−107,450	20.7	5,181,934	68.6
1997	1,579,292	1,601,232	−21,940	19.7	5,369,707	67.2
1998	1,721,798	1,652,552	69,246	19.7	5,478,724	65.2
1999	1,827,454	1,703,042	124,412	18.7	5,606,087	61.4
2000*	2,025,200	1,789,000	263,200	18.2	5,629,009	57.3

*Estimated.

Source: Council of Economic Advisers, *Economic Report of the President*, 2001 (Washington, D.C.: GPO, 2001).

Vice President **Al Gore** promised that they could retire the debt in ten years, something Clinton observed had not been done since the days of President Andrew Jackson.

The eradication of the federal deficit left several major questions unanswered. First, how much credit did President Clinton deserve? Second, to what extent was the balanced budget due to accounting tricks that allowed the federal government to count **Social Security** off budget? Third, should the surplus primarily be returned to the people via an across-the-board tax cut, the position favored by most Republicans, or used to guarantee and expand key federal programs, the position advocated by President Clinton? No consensus was reached on any of these questions, although to some extent the presidential **election of 2000** indicated the public's preference for tax cuts.

Clinton's supporters emphasized that the economic policies he pursued in his first year in office played a seminal role in reducing the federal deficit. Clinton's first budget, incorporated in the Omnibus Budget-Reconciliation Act, HR 2264, included a tax hike on upper-income taxpayers and spending cuts (or at least a reduction in projected spending) for several large-ticket items, particularly defense. The **House of Repre-**

sentatives passed this bill by a single vote. In the **Senate**, Vice President Al Gore broke a tie vote in favor of Clinton's package. Not a single Republican in either the House or the Senate voted for the measure. (The administration's economic stimulus package failed to win congressional approval.) The tax hike and budget cuts, Clinton's supporters contended, sent a message to financial markets and the Federal Reserve Board that the federal government was serious about reducing its deficit. As a result, interest rates remained low, which in turn produced sustained economic growth. Economic growth, in turn, produced more revenues. Prudent fiscal management by Treasury Secretaries **Lloyd Bentsen** and **Robert Rubin** maintained this virtuous cycle that allowed the Clinton administration to cut the federal deficit even faster than nearly anyone predicted in 1993.

Critics of President Clinton countered that the economy had already begun to recover before the Omnibus Budget-Reconciliation Act was enacted. They added that the fiscal responsibility of Republicans, who took control of Congress in 1994 for the first time in two generations, not Clinton, led to reduced federal spending. Lastly, they gave Federal Reserve Board Chairman **Alan Greenspan** the lion's share of the credit for the economic expansion of the 1990s that created the revenues that allowed Clinton to take credit for balancing the budget. Regardless of which interpretation is right, the Clinton administration could point with pride at the final results.

Suggested Readings: "Balanced-Budget Amendment Fails," *Congressional Quarterly Almanac*, 1997, p. 2–66; "Budget Amendment Sinks in Senate," *Congressional Quarterly Almanac*, 1995, p. 2–34; "Budget Resolution Embraces Clinton Plan," *Congressional Quarterly Almanac*, 1993, p. 102; "Clinton and Gingrich on Balanced Budget Agreement," August 5, 1997, *Historic Documents*, 1997, p. 602; Council of Economic Advisers, *Economic Report of the President*, 2001 (Washington D.C.: GPO, 2001); "Pact Aims to Erase Deficit by 2002," *Congressional Quarterly Almanac*, 1997, p. 2–18; "President Clinton and Vice President Gore: A Remarkable Moment of Progress and Prosperity," http://www.clinton6.nara.gov/2000/08/2000–08–15.fact-sheet-on-a-remarkable-moment-of-progress-and-prosperity.html; "Rosy Surplus Numbers Energize Clinton, Congress to Sign Omnibus Bill," *Congressional Quarterly Almanac*, 1998, p. 2–112.

BUDGET-RECONCILIATION BILLS OF 1997. On August 5, 1997, President Bill Clinton signed two interrelated bills that Congress and the president declared would produce a balanced federal **budget** by the year 2002. After decades of budget deficits and budget bills that had been signed with similar fanfare, there was reason to be skeptical that the budget-reconciliation bills of 1997 would achieve their declared ends. For instance, the Gramm-Rudman-Hollings Act of 1985, signed by President Ronald Reagan, had committed the federal government to achieving a balanced budget by the year 1990. Yet when 1990 came, the budget deficit stood at $200 billion and government finances appeared out of control. By 1997, however, the booming **economy**, in combination with the relative fiscal restraint of the federal government, made a real balanced budget feasible. Indeed, not only did the Clinton administration achieve a balanced budget, it achieved a balanced budget ahead of schedule and the first budget surplus in memory.

Specifically, Clinton signed two bills on August 5, 1997, the Balanced Budget Act of 1997 and the Taxpayer Relief Act of 1997. These two bills displayed the degree to which Clinton and the Republican-controlled Congress had rejected the tactics of confrontation, which had dominated in 1994 and 1995, in favor of accommodation and compromise. Taken together, the two bills contained several items long desired by both sides. The Balanced Budget Act, for example, which extended caps on discretionary spending, a Republican goal, also included spending for the new **Children's Health Insurance Program (CHIP)**. The bill also modified **welfare reforms** that had been enacted in 1996, namely, by restoring funding for benefits for legal immigrants, another priority for the Clinton administration. The Taxpayer Relief Act included a tax credit of $500 per child for millions of middle-class families, a cut in the tax rate on capital gains from 28 to 20 percent for investments held more than eighteen months, and the so-called Roth IRA, which provided incentives to invest in retirement accounts. A capital-gains tax cut had been on the Republican agenda for years, and the targeted tax credit for children represented a victory for Democrats, who sought to resist an across-the-board cut that would primarily benefit the wealthy.

The enactment of the budget-reconciliation bills of 1997 represented a strange moment in the Clinton presidency. One of the overarching themes of his eight years in office was partisan acrimony. During and after the **election of 1994**, Republicans rallied around the "**Contract with America**," which they sought to push through in spite of Clinton's adamant opposition to many of its provisions. Less than six months after Clinton signed the 1997 budget bill, Republicans would be demanding his resignation due to allegations stemming from the **Monica Lewinsky** scandal. Yet in 1997, Clinton and Republican leaders found common ground.

Suggested Readings: "Reconciliation Package: An Overview," *Congressional Quarterly Almanac*, 1997, p. 2–27; Alexis Simendinger, "White House Notebook," *National Journal*, September 20, 1997, p. 1844; "White House: And Now for My Next Act," *Time*, August 25, 1997, p. 36.

BUSH, GEORGE HERBERT WALKER. (June 12, 1924, Milton, Massachusetts–   .) Forty-first President of the United States, 1989–1993.

On January 20, 1993, George Bush departed the White House to witness the swearing in of his political rival William (Bill) Jefferson Clinton to the presidency. In the November 1992 presidential election, he gained only 38 percent of the popular vote, one of the worst Republican showings in years. After departing the White House, he and his wife, Barbara, moved from Washington, D.C., to their new home in Dallas, Texas. It was one of the low points in what otherwise was a remarkable career. The success of his son, **George W. Bush**, who was elected governor of Texas in 1994 and president of the United States in 2000, lent him some degree of vindication. Indeed, many of his son's **cabinet** members, as well as his vice president, Dick Cheney, had once been part of his cabinet.

Born in Massachusetts, George Herbert Walker Bush spent most of his youth in Greenwich, Connecticut. His father, Prescott Bush, was a Wall Street banker and a U.S. senator. When World War II broke out, George Bush enlisted in the navy and served as a fighter pilot, for which he received the Distinguished Flying Cross. After being shot down over the Pacific and rescued, he married Barbara Pierce. He earned his B.A. from Yale University in 1948 and then moved to Texas to start his own business. He had six children (one died in childhood) and made millions of dollars in the oil industry.

In 1964, Bush began his career in politics, running unsuccessfully for the **U.S. Senate**. Two years later, he won a seat in the **U.S. House of Representatives**. In 1970, he ran for the U.S. Senate again, losing this time to **Lloyd Bentsen**, who would later be Michael Dukakis's running mate and serve as President Clinton's first secretary of the Treasury. After Bush lost to Bentsen, President Richard Nixon nominated him to serve as the U.S. ambassador to the United Nations. After two years at this post, Bush became chairman of the Republican Party (1973–1974), chief liaison officer in Beijing, **China** (1974–1975), and director of the Central Intelligence Agency (1976–1977). After losing to Ronald Reagan in the 1980 campaign for the Republican presidential nomination, he accepted Reagan's offer to serve as his running mate. After eight years as vice president, Bush successfully ran for president, defeating Massachusetts governor Michael Dukakis in 1988.

While Bush's presidency was marked by the collapse of communism in Eastern Europe and **Russia** and victory in the Persian Gulf War, several economic developments cost him dearly. The savings and loan crisis turned already-large deficits into enormous ones. To stabilize the deficit, Bush broke his campaign pledge and raised taxes, an action that infuriated conservatives within the Republican Party. To make matters worse, the **economy** went into a recession. As it did so, public confidence in Bush's leadership dwindled, in part because he was slow to react to the economic downturn. Even before 1992, many expressed doubts about Bush's leadership capabilities. The recession, coupled with a race riot in Los Angeles, reignited such concerns. The decision of **H. Ross Perot**, a Texas businessman, to run for president as an independent further eroded Bush's support. Nonetheless, Bush left office proud of his record, especially in **foreign policy**. While the Democrats took and received the lion's share of the credit for the economic expansion of the 1990s, Bush's supporters noted that the recovery began while Bush was still in office.

Suggested Readings: Colin Campbell and Bert A. Rockman, eds., *The Bush Presidency* (Chatham, NJ: Chatham House, 1991); Dilys M. Hill and Phil Williams, eds., *The Bush Presidency* (New York: St. Martin's Press, 1994); Herbert S. Parmet, *George Bush: The Life of a Lone Star Yankee* (New York: Scribner, 1997).

Related Entries: Election of 1992; Election of 2000.

BUSH, GEORGE W. (July 6, 1946, New Haven, Connecticut–   .) Governor of Texas, 1994–2000; Forty-third President of the United States, 2001–   .

The son of President **George Herbert Walker Bush**, George W. Bush served as the governor of Texas from 1994–2000 and won the Republican nomination for the presidency in 2000. Casting himself as a "compassionate conservative," George W. Bush ran a hard-fought campaign against Bill Clinton's vice president **Al Gore**. During the Republican convention and after, Bush sought to focus the public's attention on Bill Clinton's moral lapses, suggesting that Al Gore's character and leadership capabilities were significantly compromised by his long-term relationship with and unwavering support for the president. Like other Republicans, Bush promised to cut taxes and decrease the role of the federal government, but at the same time, he tended to disassociate himself from conservative Republicans identified with the **"Contract with America"** and the **impeachment** of President Clinton. In the final days of the campaign, polls showed Bush and Gore in a virtual tie. More remarkably, on the day after the election, no one was declared a winner because of the tightness of the race. Only on December 13, 2000, over a month after the vote, the day after the **Supreme Court** ordered a halt to a recount of votes in Florida, did Al Gore concede. George W. Bush became the first president since Benjamin Harrison in 1888 to lose the popular vote but win the presidency by winning a majority of the electoral college vote, 271 to 266.

In many ways, George Walker Bush modeled his life after his father. While he was born in Connecticut, he spent most of his childhood in Midland, Texas, but like his father, he attended private high school in New England and Yale University, earning his B.A. in 1968. Rather than fighting in Vietnam, Bush enlisted in the Texas Air National Guard. After earning an M.B.A. from Harvard Business School, he returned to Midland to establish his own oil and gas company, Bush Exploration. Like his father, he did quite well. In 1978, George W. Bush ran unsuccessfully for Congress. Hence, rather than enter public service, he continued to focus on business. After a brief stint in Washington, D.C., where he served as one of his father's top political advisers, Bush returned to Texas and became part owner of the Texas Rangers baseball team.

In 1994, Bush successfully ran for governor in the state of Texas, defeating Ann W. Richards, the Democratic incumbent. He was only the second Republican since Reconstruction to win the top post in the Lone Star State. His brother, Jeb Bush, was elected governor of Florida as well. Even though the Democrats controlled both houses of the state legislature, George W. Bush won passage of many of his campaign promises, including educational and **welfare reform**. In 1997, with his public approval rating standing very high, he took the political risk of calling for tax reform in Texas. He was reelected the following year. Building on his record as governor, his prominent name, the Bush family's political connections, and a hefty campaign treasury, Bush defeated all comers for the Republican presidential nomination in 2000. A week before the Republican convention, he named Dick Cheney, his father's secretary of defense and President Gerald Ford's chief of staff, to be his running mate. Among the other veterans from his father's administration he appointed to his cabinet was Colin Powell. Powell, who had served as the chairman of the Joint Chiefs of Staff under George Herbert Walker Bush, became George W. Bush's secretary of state.

Suggested Readings: George W. Bush and Karen Hughes, *A Charge to Keep* (New York: William Morrow, 1999); *Current Biography Yearbook*, 1997, p. 70; Bill Minutaglio, *First Son: George W. Bush and the Bush Family Dynasty* (New York: Times Books, 1999).

Related Entry: Election of 2000.

C

CABINET. Twenty-eight different men and **women** served in President Clinton's cabinet. Four of them served the entire eight years: **Janet Reno**, **Donna Shalala**, **Bruce Babbitt**, and **Richard Riley**. Although twenty-three of the twenty-eight who served were men, Clinton received credit for advancing women and minorities to high positions of power in the government. He did so in part because two of his cabinet members, **Madeleine Albright** and Janet Reno, were the first women to serve as secretary of state and attorney general, respectively, two of the highest-ranking cabinet posts. In addition, nearly one-third of all the men and women who served in the cabinet were nonwhite. One Republican, **William Cohen**, served in Clinton's cabinet. Norman Minetta, Clinton's third secretary of commerce, was nominated by **George W. Bush** to serve as secretary of transportation.

Department, Secretaries, and Date of Service

Agriculture

  Mike Espy, 1993–1994

  Dan Glickman, 1995–2001

Commerce

  Ronald Brown, 1993–1996

  William Daley, 1997–2000

  Mickey Kantor, 1996–1997

  Norman Mineta, 2000–2001

Defense

  Les Aspin, 1993–1994

  William Perry, 1994–1997

  William Cohen, 1997–2001

Clinton's first cabinet, 1993.

Education

Richard Riley, 1993–2001

Energy

Hazel O'Leary, 1993–1997

Federico Peña, 1997–1998

William Richardson, 1998–2001

Health and Human Services

Donna Shalala, 1993–2001

Housing and Urban Development

Henry Cisneros, 1993–1997

Andrew Cuomo, 1997–2001

Interior

Bruce Babbitt, 1993–2001

Justice (Attorney General)

Janet Reno, 1993–2001

Labor

Robert Reich, 1993–1997

Alexis Herman, 1997–2001

State

Warren Christopher, 1993–1997

Madeleine Albright, 1997–2001

Transportation

Federico Peña, 1993–1997

Rodney Slater, 1997–2001

Treasury

Lloyd Bentsen, 1993–1994

Robert Rubin, 1995–1999

Lawrence Summers, 1999–2001

Veterans Affairs

Jesse Brown, 1993–1997

Togo West,1998–2000

Hershel Gober, 2000–2001

CAMPAIGN FINANCE REFORM. One of the main issues of the 1990s was campaign finance reform. While many political pundits expressed their support for reform and public opinion polls displayed a distrust of politicians and the influence enjoyed by "big money" and special interests, all attempts to enact specific campaign finance reform failed in Congress. Efforts to alter the campaign finance system had originated in the early 1980s. In 1992, this movement received a shot of adrenalin from **H. Ross Perot**, who railed at the corruption of Washington. Somewhat similarly, as a presidential candidate, Bill Clinton claimed to represent a new commitment to honest government. After becoming president, he helped convince both houses of Congress to pass different versions of a campaign finance reform bill, but a Republican-led filibuster in the **Senate** in 1994 kept a reconciliation measure from coming to a vote, thus killing the proposal.

While both President Clinton and Republican **House** leader **Newt Gingrich** declared their support for campaign finance reform after this initial attempt failed, no new bills got to the floor until 1996, when the McCain-Feingold bill, named after its cosponsors, Republican senator John McCain and Democratic congressman Russell Feingold, gained bipartisan backing for limitations on political action committees. Again, Republican-led filibusters in the Senate blocked the measure. The same thing happened in 1997 and 1998. As the *Congressional Quarterly Almanac* put it, in 1998 the McCain-Feingold bill proved "dead on arrival." During the 2000 campaign for the Republican nomination for president, John McCain gained a great deal of attention and won a few primaries to a large degree by emphasizing his support for campaign finance reform and the need to clean up Washington, but he failed to ride the issue to an upset over the heavily favored **George W. Bush**, who had amassed a record campaign treasury before the primaries began.

Throughout, opponents of the proposed reforms, most prominently Senator Mitch McConnell of Kentucky, argued that the reforms would accomplish the exact opposite of what they sought to achieve. By limiting free speech, McConnell declared, the reforms would narrow rather than enhance political debate. McConnell and others also opposed the McCain-Feingold bill because it banned "soft-money" contributions from political action committees but not from unions. Some argued that President Clinton, who was able to raise record sums of money, really did not want to spend political capital on campaign finance reform. Clinton's and Vice President **Al Gore**'s entanglements with possible violations of existing campaign finance laws in 1996 diminished their credibility as torchbearers for the campaign finance reform movement, making them appear as part of the problem rather than part of the solution.

The inability of McCain to secure the Republican nomination for President in 2000 suggested that the public's dissatisfaction with the political system was overdrawn by the press in the first place. While the media and scholars liked to harp on the need for campaign finance reform, the public remained much more concerned with issues that directly affected their pocketbooks. Another possibility was, as Perot and others argued, that the "establishment" so controlled the system that no serious campaign finance reform bill would ever be enacted.

Suggested Readings: "Filibuster Halts Campaign Finance Bill," *Congressional Quarterly Almanac*, 1997, p. 1-26; Thomas Mann, *The New Campaign Finance Sourcebook* (Washington: Brookings Institution, 2000); "McCain-Feingold Campaign Finance Bill Proves Dead on Revival," *Congressional Quarterly Almanac*, 1998, p. 18-3.

Related Entry: Chinagate.

CARVILLE, JAMES. (October 25, 1944, Fort Benning, Texas–   .) Political consultant, 1992.

James Carville, one of Bill Clinton's political advisers, was considered by many to be the brains behind Bill Clinton's successful run for the presidency in 1992. Carville responded quickly and effectively to attacks on Clinton's character while at the same time keeping the Democratic candidate focussed on the main task, winning the votes of middle-class suburban voters. After the election, many expected Carville to take a top post within the Clinton administration. Instead, Carville remained in the private sector as a political consultant, although he continued to serve as Clinton's unofficial political adviser. In late 1993, in one of the stranger turns in modern political history, Carville married Mary Matalin, President **George Bush**'s top political adviser and Carville's main adversary in 1992. Together, they toured the nation and cowrote a book, *All's Fair: Love, War, and Running for President* (1994). While Clinton tended to rely more on the advice of **Dick Morris** following the Republican capture of Congress in 1994, Carville and Clinton remained close friends, and Carville staunchly defended Clinton during the **Monica Lewinsky** scandal and **impeachment** proceedings. His book *Stickin': The Case for Loyalty* (2000) defended the president and lambasted conservatives for their scandalous behavior.

Although Carville was born in Texas, he spent most of his youth in Carville, Louisiana, in the heart of Cajun country. After serving a term in the marines, Carville enrolled at Louisiana State University, from which he had been expelled in the early 1960s. He earned his B.A. in 1970 and his law degree three years later. After passing the bar examination, Car-

James Carville at a roast by Independent Action in his honor in Washington, D.C., June 16, 1993. AP/Wide World Photos.

ville practiced law in Louisiana, but his real love was politics, and in 1980 he began working full-time as a political consultant. Beginning with Robert Casey's successful campaign to be governor of Pennsylvania in 1986, Carville enjoyed a string of victories that gained him fame and recognition as an extremely talented political strategist. Among the campaigns Carville helped direct were those of Frank Lautenberg, who defeated Pete Dawkins, a football star and army general, in the 1988 senatorial race in New Jersey, Zell Miller, who became governor of Georgia in 1990, and Harris Wofford, who upset George Bush's former attorney general Richard Thornburgh in a special election for the **U.S. Senate** in Pennsylvania in 1991. Along the way, he joined with **Paul Begala** to form the political consulting firm of Carville and Begala. Courted by two other contenders for the Democratic presidential nomination, Senators Bob Kerrey and Tom Harkin, Carville and Begala agreed to head Bill Clinton's campaign team in December 1991.

Operating out of the so-called war room, Carville crafted responses to a series of crises, including **Gennifer Flowers**'s claim that she had had an affair with Clinton and rumors that Clinton had smoked marijuana and dodged the draft during the 1960s. Often credited with coining the phrase **"it's the economy, stupid,"** Carville kept the campaign focussed on its main message, allowing it to overcome such scandals. Carville's down-home Cajun style and twang added to the populist aura of the 1992 Clinton bid and probably helped the Arkansas governor compete for the votes of Democrats who had voted for Ronald Reagan and George Bush in 1980, 1984, and 1988. Carville's combative spirit also flavored Clinton's campaign, as the candidate and his aides responded vigorously to every accusation that appeared in the press. (This contrasted with the history of the 1988 Michael Dukakis campaign, which allowed many sharp charges to go unanswered.)

Carville, who appeared regularly as a guest on televised news programs, was somewhat critical of **Al Gore**'s campaign strategy in 2000. Carville felt that Gore should have run much more openly on Clinton's legacy of having revived the **economy**. Carville even suggested before the Democratic convention that Gore should nominate **Robert Rubin** as his running mate to drive home the point that the Clinton-Gore administration had been about the economy. Still, during the postelection battle over the votes in Florida, Carville publicly defended Gore's call for a recount.

Suggested Readings: James Carville, *We're Right, They're Wrong* (New York: Random House, 1996); James Carville, *Stickin': The Case for Loyalty* (New York: Simon & Schuster, 2000); *Current Biography Yearbook*, 1993, p. 105; Lloyd Grove, "The Double-Fidget Campaign Whiz," *Washington Post*, January 23, 1992, p. D1; Howard Kurtz, "In the Pit Bully Pulpit," *Washington Post*, January 14, 1999, p. C1; Mary Matalin and James Carville, *All's Fair: Love, War, and Running for President* (New York: Random House, 1994).

Related Entries: Election of 1992; Election of 1996; Election of 2000.

CHEMICAL WEAPONS CONVENTION. On April 24, 1997, the **U.S. Senate** ratified a treaty negotiated by the Ronald Reagan and **George Bush** administrations that banned the production, sale, use, and stockpiling of chemical weapons. George Bush had signed the treaty in the waning days of his presidency. However, Congress failed to enact legislation necessary to implement all of the treaty prior to adjourning in 1993. This left President Bill Clinton the task of convincing Congress to enact the measures necessary to enforce the international agreement. In his way stood Jesse Helms of North Carolina, the conservative Republican chairman of the Senate Foreign Relations Committee. Helms tied support for the chemical weapons treaty to concessions on collateral issues. For several years the measure got nowhere. **Robert Dole**, the Senate majority leader and Republican nominee for president in 1996, held up the treaty as well. Following the presidential **election of 1996** and **Trent Lott**'s ascendancy to the post of Senate majority leader, the bill was revived. Lott won Republican support for the treaty in exchange for concessions from the president on other **foreign policy** matters. Subsequently, conservative criticism of Lott's deal with the Clinton administration on the chemical-weapons-ban treaty prompted him to block ratification of the Comprehensive Nuclear Test-Ban Treaty. Clinton's failure to gain passage of this nuclear pact was considered to be one of his more significant setbacks during his second term in office.

Suggested Readings: "Senate Ratifies Chemical Arms Pact," *Congressional Quarterly Almanac*, 1997, p. 8-13; Eric Schmitt, "Why Clinton Plea on Pact Left Lott Unmoved," *New York Times*, October 15, 1999, p. A13.

Related Entry: Nuclear Nonproliferation.

CHILDREN'S HEALTH INSURANCE PROGRAM (CHIP). While Congress blocked the Clinton administration's attempt to establish a national health insurance program, President Bill Clinton successfully convinced it to enact a more limited effort to make medical coverage available to children. In his 1997 State of the Union Address, President Clinton made extending health care coverage to uninsured children one of his top priorities. Working with the president, Congress enacted the Children's Health Insurance Program (CHIP) in the fall of 1997 as part of the Balanced Budget Act of 1997. The plan provided for $24 billion of federal funds to cover up to five million children of working families who earned too much to qualify for Medicaid but could not afford private coverage. The program was administered on the state level. A year after the law was enacted, President Clinton reported that four out of every five states were participating in the program and that the other states were in the process of developing proposals to do so. Subsequent reports, however, suggested that forty out of the fifty states did not use their full allotment of federal funds and that a sizeable number of children in these states remained uninsured. In the 1998 and 2000 elections, Democratic candidates pledged to expand CHIP. **Al Gore** criticized Republican presidential nominee Governor **George W. Bush** for not fully utilizing the CHIP program as governor of Texas. In arguing for expanded coverage, the Clinton administration claimed that spending money to insure children was a cost-effective way of limiting medical costs. Children who regularly had checkups and received prompt attention for ear infections and other minor problems avoided more expensive complications.

Suggested Readings: Robert Pear, "40 States Forfeit Health Care Funds for Poor Children," *New York Times*, September 24, 2000, p. 1; "Statement by the President: The Children's Health Insurance Program One Year Anniversary," http:// www.hcfa.gov/init/wh%2Dchip-9.htm.

Related Entries: Health Care Reform; Health Insurance Portability and Accountability Act of 1996 (HIPAA).

CHINA. During Bill Clinton's presidency, one could argue that China replaced **Russia** as the single most important nation in the area of U.S. **foreign policy**. The collapse of communism in the Soviet Union, China's growing economic and military power, and the stillbirth of democracy in this nation of close to one billion people all played a part in China's increasing prominence. In one of his few major speeches on foreign policy during his 1992 presidential campaign, Clinton contended that the **George Bush** administration continued to "coddle China, despite its crackdown on democratic reforms, brutal subjugation of Tibet, its irresponsible exports of nuclear and missile technology . . . and its abusive trade practices" (Hyland, *Clinton's World*). Exactly what Clinton proposed to do differently once he was in office, however, remained unclear. Indeed, by the end of his presidency, Clinton's foreign policy toward China differed little from that of the Bush administration. Some conservatives even argued that the Clinton administration, motivated by political campaign contributions from the Chinese, did far more than coddle China, that the administration jeopardized U.S. national security by allowing China to develop its military potential using American technology.

In an assessment of the Clinton administration's overall foreign policy, *New York Times* reporter David Sanger more accurately captured the main theme of the administration's policy toward China. Even though Clinton initially criticized George Bush for putting commerce ahead of human rights, Sanger observed, over time, Clinton, even more than Bush, came to promote commerce or open trade with China. He did so because he came to see free trade as the key to spreading democracy in China

President Clinton, the First Lady, and daughter Chelsea in the Forbidden City, June 28, 1998, in Beijing. AP/Wide World Photos.

and other nations. Or, as Sanger stated, "For his part, Mr. Clinton wants to be remembered as the man who pushed China toward capitalism" ("Economic Engine," p. 1). To this end, President Clinton appointed Winston Lord as his first ambassador to China. During confirmation hearings, Lord made it clear that he favored a "nuanced" policy toward China, suggesting that he opposed imposing trade sanctions on the world's largest nation over human rights abuses. In 1993, President Clinton granted China most-favored-nation status on a conditional basis, against the wishes of some liberal Democrats who wanted to punish China for its poor human rights record. Several years later, Clinton acknowledged that his earlier criticism of the Bush administration had been "simply not right." Over the course of the remainder of the 1990s, Clinton pushed for further expanding trade with China. In 1999, China and the United States signed an accord whereby China agreed to open its markets to foreign imports in exchange for entry into the World Trade Organization (WTO). On October 10, 2000, President Clinton signed into law the China Relations Act of 2000, which granted permanent normal trade relations to China. In a major victory for the Clinton administration, the **Senate** and **House** voted overwhelmingly in favor of this act. In September 2000, President Clinton summarized the positive steps the administration had made with China, emphasizing agreements made on **nuclear nonproliferation**, chemical weapons, and, most important, trade. By prodding China to join the WTO, Clinton asserted, the United States "will entangle China more deeply in a rules-based international system and change China internally" (Clinton, "China's Opportunities").

President Clinton also took credit for maintaining "peace in the Taiwan Straits" and working with China "to maintain stability on the Korean Peninsula." With regard to Taiwan, many conservatives assessed the record of the administration differently. In 1996, the United States stationed a flotilla of naval warships in the Taiwan Straits as a display of its commitment to defend Taiwan from an attack from the mainland. This move was prompted by the rise of an ardent nationalist leader in Taiwan and China's rhetorical criticism of nationalist sentiment in Taiwan. In spite of this particular show of force, conservatives argued that the administration left Taiwan in a more precarious situation than it had found it in 1992. By committing U.S. forces to various peacekeeping efforts around the globe, conservatives contended, the administration made the United States less able to live up to its commitment to protect Taiwan in the future. This argument was coupled with a criticism of the administration's defense policy. Whether **George W. Bush** would significantly alter America's policy toward China, however, remained to be seen.

Suggested Readings: William Jefferson Clinton, "China's Opportunities and Ours," *New York Times*, September 24, 2000, sec. 4, p. 15; William G. Hyland, *Clinton's World* (Westport, CT: Praeger, 1999), pp. 109–26; David Sanger, "Economic Engine for Foreign Policy," *New York Times*, December 28, 2000, p. 1; White House, Office of the Press Secretary (Omaha, Nebraska), "Fact Sheet: A Foreign Policy for the Global Age," December 8, 2000, http://clinton6.nara.gov/2000/12/2000–12–08-fact-sheet-on-a-foreign-policy-for-the-global-age.html.

Related Entries: Campaign Finance Reform; Chinagate; Chung, Johnny.

CHINAGATE. The team "Chinagate" described a variety of scandals involving the Clinton administration and **China**. Most specifically, it referred to alleged ties between campaign donations from Chinese businessmen and the Clinton administration's policy toward China. The term "Chinagate" was also used to describe allegations of nuclear espionage by China, particularly at the Los Alamos National Laboratory in New Mexico.

While the Chinagate scandal first surfaced in 1996 prior to the presidential election, it did not receive a great deal of attention from the mainstream press until after Bill Clinton was reelected. In May 1997, the *New York Times* and other newspapers reported that California businessman **Johnny Chung** had admitted that he had contributed approximately $100,000 to the Democratic Party. Chung stated that he had received $300,000 from Lt. Col. Liu Chaoying, an executive with the China Aerospace Corporation and a relative of one of China's military commanders. In addition to contributing $100,000 to the Democratic National Committee (presumably Chung kept the rest), Chung arranged for Liu to be photographed with the president. The *New York Times* story lent credibility to broader charges of Chinese influence on the Clinton administration that Senator Fred Thompson and other conservatives had been leveling at the administration and investigating for nearly a year. Among the leads that the Senate Governmental Affairs Committee, chaired by Thompson, pursued was the charge that the Lippo Group, which was owned by a wealthy Indonesian family, had curried favors from the Clinton administration by supporting Clinton's campaigns for office as far back as some of his early runs for governor. One of the key figures in this allegation was John Huang, a Lippo employee, who was appointed to a post in the Commerce Department shortly after Clinton became president, and then worked as a fund-raiser for the Democratic Party. After investigating this and other leads, the Senate Governmental Affairs Committee found "strong circumstantial evidence" of Chinese attempts to influence the **election of 1996**. Based on the committee's finding and the *New York Times* report, many Republicans called for the appointment of another independent counsel.

The administration not only rejected the findings of Thompson's committee, it argued that there was no proof that it knew of the origins of the funds Chung had contributed to the Democratic Party. It also denied that there was any quid pro quo agreement to allow for the transfer of technology to China in exchange for campaign funds. In spite of Republican demands, in October 1997 the Justice Department concluded that President Clinton had not violated any law, and Attorney General **Janet Reno** refused to request the appointment of another independent counsel because her office found that insufficient evidence existed to appoint one. Reno's decision perpetuated the conservative claim of a cover-up. For instance, **George W. Bush** insinuated that **Al Gore** had acted illegally by raising funds from the Chinese American community. Gore's alleged impropriety was that he had used White House telephones to solicit donations.

Chinagate regained attention in 1998 and 1999 when the media began to release stories of alleged espionage by the Chinese at American nuclear facilities. In May 1999, in the wake of President Clinton's **impeachment** and acquittal, the Cox Committee, the Select Committee on U.S. National Security, headed by Republican congressman Christopher Cox of California, reported that there was evidence of a long-term effort by the Chinese to obtain nuclear and military secrets. Security lapses by the federal government, going back to Ronald Reagan's presidency, the report continued, had allowed China to secure top-secret nuclear technology. While the Clinton administration -disagreed with some of the specific conclusions of the committee, it agreed to take "aggressive action to deal with the problem." Nonetheless, a number of conservatives felt that the administration had been treated too lightly. They complained that the Cox committee and the liberal media covered up illegal actions and demanded further investigation. In early 2000, a Chinese American scientist, Wen Ho Lee, an employee at Los Alamos National Laboratory, was arrested and charged with espionage. The charges were later dropped in exchange for a lesser plea. While Attorney General Janet Reno defended the initial accusations, the judge in the case argued that a poisoned political atmosphere combined with overzealousness on the Justice Department's part led to an abuse of the defendant's rights. Ironically, in response to the judge's findings, conservatives accused liberals of rushing to judgment.

As with many of the other scandals of the Clinton years, the final tally resulted in no criminal indictments or convictions of the president or other top officials. Nonetheless, the cumulative impact of the charges left many with a poor view of Clinton's character and a distaste for the hyperpartisan politics that seemed to characterize Washington, D.C., during the Clinton years.

Suggested Readings: Lucinda Fleeson, "Rush to Judgment," *American Journalism Review* 22:9 (November 2000), p. 20; William Greider, "Does Whitewater + Hubbellgate + Chinagate = Watergate?" *Rolling Stone*, June 12, 1997, p. 45; James Inhofe, "End Chinagate Cover-Up," *Human Events*, July 10, 1999, p. 1.

Related Entries: Campaign Finance Reform; Whitewater.

CHRISTOPHER, WARREN M. (October 27, 1925, Scranton, North Dakota– .) Secretary of State, 1993–1996.

A longtime Democratic power broker and diplomat, Warren Christopher was the secretary of state during Bill Clinton's first term as president. Christopher's low-key approach contrasted sharply to that of better-known secretaries of state, such as Henry Kissinger and Christopher's successor, **Madeleine Albright**, and reflected the Clinton's administration's emphasis on domestic rather than foreign affairs, particularly during Clinton's first term as president. Unlike several of Clinton's other **cabinet** members and advisers, Christopher left office without any hint of scandal. Yet his tenure as secretary of state, according to many, was relatively undistinguished. Experts complained about the inconsistency of the administration's **foreign policy**, particularly in Eastern Europe, and the mishandling of America's intervention in **Somalia**. Christopher's and Clinton's defenders, in contrast, argued that the United States successfully navigated its way though several global crises, maintained cooperative relations with **Russia**, and resisted the temptation to retreat to an isolationist position, a position favored by much of the public if not the foreign policy elite.

Born on the northern plains, Christopher moved to southern California following his father's death in 1939. He attended the University of Redlands for a year and then transferred to the University of Southern California, where he earned his B.A. in 1945. While serving in the naval reserve, he went to Stanford University Law School, from which he graduated in 1949. He clerked for U.S. **Supreme Court** Justice William O. Douglas and then joined the firm of O'Melveny and Myers in Los Angeles. In spite of the conservative reputation of the firm, Christopher became active in Democratic Party politics, working as the special counsel for California's governor Pat Brown and serving on the McCone Commission, which was established to investigate the causes of the Watts riots of 1965. During Jimmy Carter's presidency, Christopher served as the deputy secretary of state under Cyrus Vance. He played a very prominent role during the Iran hostage crisis, successfully negotiating the release of the American hostages on the day that Ronald Reagan was sworn in to succeed Carter as president.

During the Reagan and **George Bush** presidencies, Christopher returned to Los Angeles to practice law. In the early 1990s, Mayor Tom Bradley appointed him to head a commission to investigate the beating of Rodney King by Los Angeles police. The Christopher Commission's report was sharply critical of police chief Daryl Gates and the record of the Los Angeles police in general. In 1992, Christopher recommended that Clinton select Senator **Al Gore** as his running mate. Partly out of respect for this advice and for his years of experience within the Democratic Party, following his election, Clinton chose Christopher to head his transition team, which was responsible for assembling Clinton's cabinet and top advisers. On December 22, 1992, Clinton announced that he would nominate Christopher to serve as his secretary of state. Christopher called the nomination a "dream come true" and promised to build on the Bush administration's efforts to achieve peace in the **Middle East** and restore order in Somalia. Christopher won confirmation with relative ease, notwithstanding charges brought forth by Senator Jesse Helms of North Carolina that Christopher had known about and authorized the army's illegal spying on antiwar protesters during the 1960s.

As secretary of state, Christopher worked to resolve the crisis in **Haiti**, inherited from the Bush administration, to develop a solution to the ongoing war in **Bosnia and Herzegovina**, and to maintain the peace process in the Middle East. Christopher also had to deal with crises involving North Korea and recurrent problems with Iraqi leader Sadam Hussein, as well as enhancing America's relationship with the former Soviet Union, the European Union, **China**, and Japan. As noted above, critics emphasized that the Clinton administration failed to resolve the crisis in the Balkans during Christopher's tenure and that Christopher did not develop a coherent and consistent policy toward China or other nations in the Far East. Hence, Christopher left office with few major accomplishments, and the overall policy of the Clinton administration was still in flux.

Christopher reemerged as a prominent figure on the morning after the **election of 2000**. He headed the official Gore challenge to the vote in Florida, squaring off against James Baker, President Bush's secretary of state. Yet by the end of the extended legal battle, Christopher had assumed a lesser role, giving way to David Boies, Gore's lead attorney.

Suggested Readings: *Current Biography Yearbook*, 1995, p. 96; William G. Hyland, *Clinton's World: Remaking American Foreign Policy* (Westport, CT: Praeger, 1999); Robert Scheer, "Clinton's Globe-Trotter," *Los Angeles Times*, February 21, 1993, Magazine, p. 18.

Related Entries: Bosnia and Herzegovina; Iraq; NATO.

CHUNG, JOHNNY. (Taiwan.) Chinagate defendant.

Johnny Chung, a Taiwanese-born U.S. citizen and businessman, was one of the most prominent individuals associated with the **Chinagate** scandal. On December 15, 1998, he was sentenced to five years' probation for funneling illegal contributions to the Democratic Party. Between 1994 and 1996, Chung contributed about $400,000 to the Democratic Party. He visited the White House nearly fifty times, often accompanied by other prominent Asian businessmen who sought to gain access to President Clinton. On one occasion, he delivered a $50,000 check to **Hillary Rodham Clinton**'s chief of staff, **Margaret Williams**. On a separate occasion, he was photographed with President Clinton at a Los Angeles fund-raiser. Federal election laws prohibit nonresident foreigners from donating more than $2,000 to a single campaign, and investigators suspected that Chung was funneling the contributions of foreigners into the Clinton campaign.

At the time of the sentencing, U.S. District Judge Manuel L. Real criticized Attorney General **Janet Reno** for refusing to appoint a special prosecutor to investigate Chung and the campaign-funding scandal. Many conservative Republicans accused Reno of covering up the president's illegal involvement with foreign contributors, suggesting that the administration gave away classified information to **China** and to other Asian firms in exchange for campaign contributions. After the scandal broke, the Democratic Party returned the contributions to Chung and denied that any illegal bargains had been made. Chung negotiated a deal with the Justice Department, agreeing to cooperate with its investigation in exchange for a lighter sentence. In May 1999, Chung testified as a friendly witness before the House Committee on Government Reform and Operations, which was investigating the campaign finance scandal. His testimony did not produce any new revelations that tied the president or Vice President **Al Gore** directly to the illegal gifts, nor did it produce evidence of any specific exchange of technology or favors for campaign contributions.

Suggested Readings: "Campaign Finance Key Player: Johnny Chung," http://www. jobs.washingtonpost.com/wp-srv/national/longterm/campfin/players/chung.htm; "Democratic Fund-Raiser Chung Sentenced to Five Years Probation," *Washington Post*, December 15, 1998, p. A8.

Related Entries: Campaign Finance Reform; Impeachment; Travelgate; Whitewater.

CISNEROS, HENRY G. (June 11, 1947, San Antonio, Texas– .) Secretary of Housing and Urban Development, 1993–1997.

The political career of Henry Cisneros, perhaps the most prominent Hispanic leader in the United States, was like a roller coaster, enjoying highs and lows in rapid succession. In 1981, Cisneros became the first Hispanic mayor of a major city in the United States when he was elected mayor of San Antonio, Texas, a post he held for four terms, 1981 to 1989. In 1985, he was elected president of the National League of Cities. His age, ethnicity, and charisma made him one of the rising stars within the Democratic Party. Some even floated his name as a possible vice presidential nominee. Revelations that he had had an extramarital affair with Linda Jones (formerly Medlar), however, quickly changed his fortunes. He quit politics, moved in with Jones, and convinced her to file for divorce. A year later, they ended their affair, and Cisneros moved back in with his wife. In 1993, President Bill Clinton nominated him to be the secretary of housing and urban development (HUD).

Cisneros inherited an agency that had fallen on hard times. Founded in 1965 as part of President Lyndon Johnson's Great Society, HUD watched its budget shrink and obligations grow during the Ronald Reagan years. To make matters worse, in the late 1980s, eleven high-level Reagan appointees at HUD were indicted and convicted for influence peddling. Seeing HUD as key to addressing the nation's problems, Cisneros labored to rejuvenate the agency. By the end of Clinton's first term, he could point to several major achievements, including the enactment of the **Empowerment Zone** and Enterprise Community programs, aimed at sparking growth in impoverished urban areas and at restructuring of public housing. This included a rent-subsidy program that sought to locate poor tenants outside of the inner city. But then an old scandal re-emerged, compelling him to resign.

During a routine background check after his nomination, Cisneros informed federal agents that he had made payments to his former lover, Linda Jones. Investigations, however, revealed that he had understated the amount of the payments by $30,000. Further controversy arose in part because Cisneros had stopped paying Jones in 1993, largely for financial reasons, including the cost of paying for medical care for their son, John Paul, who was born with a heart defect. Jones herself fell into financial difficulty, sued Cisneros for "breach of contract," and simultaneously sold her story to the television tabloid *Inside Edition*. While Cisneros had not committed a crime by paying Jones or stopping the payments, he had broken the law by lying about the payments to the FBI. In March 1995, **Janet Reno** appointed an independent counsel to investigate the scandal. Cisneros denied any wrongdoing but chose to step down after Clinton was reelected. Ultimately, after being charged with crimes that could have landed him in jail for ninety years if convicted, Cisneros pled guilty to committing a minor misdemeanor. He paid a $10,000 fine for lying to the FBI. Special prosecutor David Barrett spent upwards of $3 million investigating the case.

Cisneros was born and raised in San Antonio, Texas. He earned his B.A. and M.A. from Texas A&M University in urban and regional planning, an M.A. in public administration from the John F. Kennedy School of Government at Harvard University, and a Ph.D. in public administration from George Washington University. In addition to serving as mayor of San Antonio, Cisneros briefly worked as the deputy chairman of the Federal Reserve Board in Dallas, Texas, headed the Cisneros Asset Management Company, and hosted *Adelante*, a one-hour show that appeared regularly on Spanish-language television and radio.

Suggested Readings: "Henry Cisneros and the Starr Syndrome," *Salon.com*, June 25, 1999; Marcelo Rodriguez, "Henry Cisneros and the Politics of Ambivalence," *Los Angeles Times*, February 27, 1994, p. 20.

Related Entries: Domestic Policy; Independent Counsel Law.

CIVIL RIGHTS. *See* **Affirmative Action**; **African Americans**; **President's Initiative on Race**.

CLARK, WESLEY K. (December 23, 1944, Chicago, Illinois–   .) Supreme Allied Commander in Europe.

General Wesley Clark's direction of NATO forces during the Kosovo "war" marked a high point in his career as a military officer. Ironically, on August 2, 1999, a little more than a month after traveling to Kosovo as NATO's victorious supreme commander, he learned that his tenure as America's top commander in Europe was to come to an early end because of differences he had with top Pentagon officials, particularly its opposition to the use of helicopters or ground forces. In *Waging Modern War* (2001), he aired his criticism of the Defense Department's top brass and its reluctance to fight.

After graduating first in his class at the U.S. Military Academy at West Point in 1966, Clark was a Rhodes scholar at Oxford University in England, where he earned his M.A. in philosophy, politics, and economics. He also graduated from the National War College and the Command and General Staff College and served as a White House fellow. His field experience included commanding the 1st Cavalry Division, the 4th Infantry Division, and three companies of infantry in Vietnam. For five years, he trained soldiers at the National Training Center, many of whom saw combat in Operation Desert Storm in the Persian Gulf. Prior to being appointed the supreme allied commander in Europe, he served as commander in chief of the U.S. Southern Command, where he was responsible for most of the armed forces' activities in Latin America and the Caribbean. He also participated in the Bosnian peace talks in Dayton, Ohio.

During the Kosovo war, Clark called for putting maximum pressure on Yugoslavian leader Slobodan Milosevic. In addition to sustained attacks by NATO's bombers and fighter planes, he requested deployment of U.S. Army Apache helicopters. Although this request was granted, the helicopters were never used, presumably because of fears that they would have increased the chance of heavy casualties, which would have decreased public support for the military campaign. In the early stages of the fighting, Clark was criticized when Milosevic did not back down. Opponents of Clinton's policy warned that the attacks would lead to a prolonged military engagement in the Balkans and that air attacks alone would not work. Ironically, after the seventy-eight-day bombing campaign convinced Milosevic to withdraw his forces from Kosovo, with a bare minimum of American casualties, other criticisms of Clark began to surface. Most important, stories appeared stating that he had clashed with Lieutenant General Mike Jackson, NATO's commander in Kosovo. In addition, some reported that the air strikes had been less effective than Clark claimed. Clark was succeeded by General Joseph Ralston.

Hillary Clinton.
The White House.

Suggested Readings: *Current Biography,* 1999 (New York: H. W. Wilson Co., 1999), p. 135; Martin Fletcher, "General Tells of Kosovo Fight with Pentagon," *The Times (London),* May 22, 2001; Alexander Nicoll, "A Victim of War," *Financial Times of London,* August 3, 1999, p. 16.

Related Entries: Defense, Military; Foreign Policy.

CLINTON, HILLARY RODHAM. (October 26, 1947, Chicago, Illinois–   .) First Lady.

One of the most active and controversial first ladies in American history and the first to have had a distinguished career of her own independent of her husband, Hillary Diane Rodham was born in Chicago in 1947. The oldest child of Dorothy and Hugh Rodham, a successful businessman, she grew up in the suburb of Park Ridge, Illinois, and attended Eugene Field Elementary School, Emerson Junior High, and Maine East and Maine South high schools. She excelled in school and was active in extracurricular activities. As early as high school, Hillary Rodham displayed a penchant for social activism, organizing a food drive for migrant workers. Nonetheless, coming from a Republican family, she campaigned for the conservative Barry Goldwater for president in 1964.

Rodham graduated from Wellesley College with a degree in political science in 1968. A photograph of her delivering a commencement address appeared in *Life* magazine. In the address, Rodham asserted that her generation was searching for "more immediate, ecstatic, and penetrating modes of living" (*Current Biography, 1993*, p. 117). After college, she enrolled at Yale Law School, where she served on the editorial board of the *Yale Review of Law and Social Action* and met her future husband, Bill Clinton. Both of them became involved in various political crusades. One summer while she was still in law school, she worked in Washington, D.C., for Marian Wright Edelman's Washington Research Project, which later became the Children's Defense Fund. After receiving her law degree in 1972, Rodham joined the Children's Defense Fund and then became one of forty-three lawyers on the House Judiciary Committee staff that was busy readying impeachment charges against President Richard Nixon. Meanwhile, she kept up her courtship with Bill Clinton. In 1974, much to the dismay of many of her friends, she turned down offers to work at several prestigious East Coast firms and accepted a position on the University of Arkansas Law School faculty. She and Bill Clinton were married the following year.

Rodham held a variety of jobs before accepting a post with the Rose Law Firm, where she was made a partner in 1980, the same year she gave birth to her first and only child, Chelsea. In 1984, she was named Arkansas woman of the year in recognition of her professional accomplishments. She was also named one of the best business-litigation attorneys in the state by the *National Law Journal*. Rodham played a seminal role in almost all of her husband's political campaigns, and he frequently consulted her before making important policy decisions. Her defense of their marriage in the wake of claims that he had had an affair with **Gennifer Flowers** helped save his campaign for the presidency in 1992. As the election approached, some of Clinton's opponents tried to win voter support by contrasting **George Bush**'s popular wife, Barbara, with Hillary. They did so by casting Hillary as a radical feminist and antifamily and Barbara as a symbol of family values. In fact, pundits began to speak of a so-called Hillary problem or Hillary factor. One possible cause of this was that Bill Clinton made it clear that his wife would play a leading role in his administration rather than just a ceremonial one.

Indeed, Hillary Clinton did play a very active role in Bill Clinton's administration right from the start. Most important, Clinton put her in charge of developing viable **health care reform**. As the unofficial head of the Task Force on National Health Care Reform, she met with experts, testified before Congress, and appeared frequently as an advocate for national health insurance. Conservative criticism, however, killed the plan and suggested that the "Hillary problem" was a real one for the administration. As a result, in 1996, Hillary Clinton played a far less prominent role in Clinton's campaign than she had in the past. Nonetheless, she remained extremely popular among a significant segment of the population, especially liberal **women** who saw her as an unfair victim of the New Right's attack on feminism.

In 1996, Rodham wrote *It Takes a Village and Other Lessons Children Teach Us*, a book that argued that the health of children, and ultimately of society, depended on parents and the broader society. This was a theme she stressed in her weekly syndicated newspaper column, "Talking It Over," and in countless speeches. Following Clinton's reelection, she focussed much of her attention on children, playing an active role in the White House Conference on Early Childhood Development and Learning and the White House Conference on Child Care. She also traveled abroad extensively, advocating women's rights and health and **education** reform.

Ironically, her approval ratings improved considerably during the **Monica Lewinsky** and **impeachment** scandal. In spite of Bill Clinton's obvious marital infidelity, she continued to defend her husband. In one televised appearance prior to the president's public acknowledgment that he had had an affair with Lewinsky, she proclaimed that she and her husband were the victims of a vast right-wing conspiracy. As Clinton's term drew to a close, she readied her own bid for a seat in the **U.S. Senate** from the state of New York. Initially, this pitted her against Rudolph Giuliani, the Republican mayor of New York City. Health problems and revelations of his own marital infidelity, however, compelled him to withdraw from the race. Hillary's Senate campaign took on special significance, with some casting it as a referendum on the Clinton administration. On election day, she easily defeated her Republican opponent, Congressman Rick Lazio. Shortly before Bill Clinton's presidency came to an end, he had the unique privilege of sitting in the Senate gallery with Chelsea as spectators as Hillary was sworn in as a senator. Some Clinton diehards even quietly talked about the possibility of Hillary retaking the White House in 2004.

Suggested Readings: *Current Biography, 1993* (New York: H. W. Wilson Co., 1999), pp. 116–117; Joyce Milton, *The First Partner* (New York: HarperTrade,

William Jefferson Clinton. The White House.

2000); Meredith Oakley, *On the Make: The Rise of Bill Clinton* (Washington, DC: Regnery Publishing, 1994); Gail Sheehy, *Hillary's Choice* (New York: Ballantine, 2000).

Related Entry: William Jefferson Clinton.

CLINTON, WILLIAM JEFFERSON [BLYTHE]. (August 19, 1946, Hope, Arkansas– .) Forty-second President of the United States, 1993–2001.

Born in Hope, Arkansas, a farming community near the borders of Louisiana and Texas, in 1946, Bill Clinton was the first "baby boomer" to become president. Given his inauspicious origins, few would have suspected that he would become the first to represent his generation in the White House.

In contrast to his predecessor, **George Bush**, the son of a senator and the heir to a fortune, Bill Clinton began his life at the bottom of the social ladder and experienced a very turbulent childhood. His father, William Jefferson Blythe III, a traveling salesman, died in a car accident several months before his birth. His mother, Virginia Kelly, left him to be raised by her parents so that she could study to become a nurse-anesthetist in New Orleans. When he was four, his mother married Roger Clinton, a car dealer and alcoholic who occasionally beat his wife. When he was seven, the Clinton family moved to Hot Springs, Arkansas. In 1956, when he was ten, his brother Roger was born. Throughout his youth, his mother and stepfather had a tempestuous relationship that led to several separations, a divorce, and remarriage. At one point in their life, at age fourteen, Bill Clinton physically had to protect his mother from his stepfather. Two weeks after one of these reconciliations between his mother and stepfather, Roger Clinton died from cancer. His mother remarried several times. Her third husband, Jeff Dwire, died of a heart ailment in 1974. She died in 1994 while Clinton was president.

First at St. John's, a private Catholic elementary school—Clinton was a Southern Baptist—and subsequently at public elementary, junior, and high schools, Clinton excelled as a student, both in and out of the classroom. He spent much of his time playing the saxophone and participating in various youth organizations. He was the junior-class president at Hot Springs High School, although he lost in his bid to become senior-class secretary. He graduated fourth in his class of 323 in 1964 and enrolled at Georgetown University in Washington, D.C., the following fall. One reason he chose to attend Georgetown was his interest in politics. In the summer of 1963, he served as Arkansas's delegate to Boys' Nation (a national convention of representatives from each state, affiliated with the American Legion) in Washington, D.C. In the nation's capital, he met Arkansas senator J. William Fulbright, who would become one of the most prominent critics of the **Vietnam** War, and had his picture taken shaking the hand of President John F. Kennedy. Over the course of the next few years, while still in college, Clinton spent a good deal of time working for various political candidates and officials, including a post with Senator Fulbright. He also was elected freshman-class president at Georgetown.

As in high school, Clinton excelled as a college student. Upon graduating, he was awarded a Rhodes scholarship, which allowed him to study at Oxford University in England. The Vietnam War was raging during this period, and Clinton initially accepted a draft deferment through the first year of his Rhodes scholarship. Presumably because of his interest in politics, however, Clinton agreed to enroll in the ROTC program at the University of Arkansas Law School, beginning in the summer of 1969. Apparently, only after he received a high draft-lottery number did Clinton rescind his decision to join ROTC and decide to complete his two-year program at Oxford. During the 1992 presidential campaign, many accused Clinton of having dodged the draft. Clinton took part in some antiwar demonstrations while he was abroad but never played a leading role in the antiwar movement.

In 1970, Clinton enrolled at Yale Law School, where he met his future wife, Hillary Rodham. They were married in 1975. Together they worked on George McGovern's unsuccessful campaign for the presidency in 1972. After earning his law degree in 1973, he worked briefly in Washington, D.C., and then joined the faculty of the University of Arkansas Law School. In 1974 he ran for Congress. Even though he lost to incumbent Republican John Paul Hammerschmidt, he did well enough (he lost by only 4 percent of the vote) to keep his political aspirations alive. Two years later, he was elected attorney general of the state of Arkansas. In 1978, he ran successfully for governor, becoming the youngest governor (he was thirty-two) in the United States. Two years later, however, he was narrowly defeated by Frank White, who criticized Clinton for raising taxes and linked him to the unpopular president, Jimmy Carter.

Years later, pundits would refer to Clinton as the "comeback kid" because of his ability to overcome political adversity. The first example of such a comeback occurred in 1982, when Clinton retook the governorship by defeating Frank White, 55 to 45 percent. He was reelected in 1984 and 1988 (the governor's term was changed to four years), building a reputation as an advocate of educational reform. He also began to align himself with centrist Democrats, many of whom were associated with the **Democratic Leadership Council**, which sought to overcome the Republican Party's grip on the presidency. He considered running for the presidency in 1988 but decided not to for family reasons—his daughter, Chelsea, was only seven at the time. At the 1988 Democratic convention, he gained national exposure by nominating Massachusetts governor Michael Dukakis for president.

On October 3, 1991, Bill Clinton formally announced his candidacy for the presidency. Shortly before the first primary in New Hampshire, however, his campaign was rocked by a series of scandals over his dodging of the draft, use of **drugs** while a youth, and marital infidelity. Most important, **Gennifer Flowers** alleged that she and Clinton had had a long affair. Appearing with his wife, Hillary, on the popular television show *60 Minutes*, Clinton responded to questions regarding his marriage. His answers on the news program helped quash rumors about his character, allowing him to string together a series of victories in the primaries and to win the Democratic nomination. In the general election, he focussed on the economic doldrums that characterized the Bush presidency and promised to create millions of new jobs.

Clinton was inaugurated as the forty-second president on January 20, 1993. Giving top priority to domestic issues, he enacted an economic reform package that included a tax hike, pushed for ratification of **NAFTA**, and advocated **health care reform**. The latter position, which initially looked like one of his politically most attractive ones, unleashed an avalanche of criticism. On top of this, several new scandals, one involving his involvement in the **Whitewater** investment scheme and another revolving around his alleged sexual harassment of **Paula Jones** prior to his presidency, pushed his poll numbers down. In the general **election of 1994**, the Democrats suffered a resounding defeat, and the Republicans took control of both houses of Congress for the first time in decades. In the wake of the election, many predicted that Clinton would become another one-term president, but again displaying his ability to come back from political adversity, Clinton easily defeated Republican senator **Robert Dole** and Reform Party candidate **H. Ross Perot** in November 1996, thus becoming the first Democratic president to be reelected since Franklin D. Roosevelt.

Clinton's second term was characterized by countervailing themes, political scandal and economic prosperity. Several of the scandals that had emerged during his first term did not go away, and while independent counsel **Kenneth Starr** failed to uncover evidence of illegal activities in the president's involvement in Whitewater (the original reason for the creation of Starr's post), he did uncover evidence that Clinton had lied in order to cover up his affair with White House intern **Monica Lewinsky**. In turn, this led to Clinton's **impeachment** by the **U.S. House of Representatives** and acquittal by the **U.S. Senate**. Simultaneously, the **economy**, which had begun to rebound shortly before he assumed office, continued to expand. The **stock market** enjoyed a boom as well. While Clinton turned more of his attention to **foreign policy** than he had during his first term, the two themes of scandal and economic expansion continued to dominate the public's views of him.

Most likely, Clinton's historical legacy will be an ambiguous one. Along with Andrew Johnson, he is the only president to have been impeached. At the same time, the United States experienced the longest sustained economic expansion ever during his tenure in office. Symbolically, the federal budget deficit, which seemed a permanent threat to the nation's prosperity when he became president, was wiped out, and he left his successor with an unprecedented budget surplus. As one of the youngest presidents in American history, Clinton likely will spend a good deal of time trying to shape his legacy.

Suggested Readings: Elizabeth Drew, *On the Edge: The Clinton Presidency* (New York: Simon & Schuster, 1994); David Maraniss, *First in His Class: A Biography of Bill Clinton* (New York: Simon & Schuster, 1995); R. Emmett Tyrrell, Jr., *Boy Clinton: The Political Biography* (Washington, DC: Regnery Publishing, 1996).

Related Entry: Hillary Rodham Clinton.

COHEN, WILLIAM S. (August 28, 1940, Bangor, Maine– .) Secretary of Defense, 1997–2001.

Shortly after being reelected in 1996, President Bill Clinton nominated William Cohen, a Republican senator from Maine, to serve as his secretary of defense. The Clinton administration hoped that Cohen's appointment would result in bipartisan support for its defense policies. Cohen was unanimously confirmed by the **U.S. Senate**. Nonetheless, his tenure in office was not without its difficulties. While Cohen himself was not a primary target of Republican criticism, during the 2000 presidential campaign, Texas governor **George W. Bush** and his running mate, former secretary of defense Dick Cheney, contended that the military had weakened during Clinton's presidency.

In addition to promoting the controversial decision to attack Yugoslavia during the **Kosovo** "war," Cohen had to grapple with the ongoing controversy over **gays in the military** and charges of sexual harassment against female military personnel. While he became the target of some conservative barbs for his positions on these issues, conservatives were even more critical of his refusal to resign during the **Monica Lewinsky** scandal and **impeachment** proceedings. Among Cohen's other priorities were the continued expansion of **NATO** to include several former members of the Warsaw Pact and, during his final year in office, increased defense spending to enable the United States to engage in two regional conflicts simultaneously. Ironically, Cohen's call for increased spending

Secretary of Defense William S. Cohen and General Henry Shelton. Department of Defense.

provided some support to the Republican argument that Clinton and **Al Gore** had left the United States unprepared to meet its commitments abroad. The healthy **economy** and, according to some, Clinton's less-than-stellar character contributed to the military's allegedly declining morale. Nonetheless, both Clinton and Cohen insisted that the military was stronger, in relative terms, and America more secure at the end of the 1990s than at any other time in U.S. history.

The son of a Russian Jewish immigrant and an Irish Protestant, Cohen was born and raised in Bangor, Maine. His position as an outsider, both among Jewish and Christian children, helped forge his independent spirit, which would remain the trademark of his career as a politician. A star basketball player, he earned his B.A. from Bowdoin College in 1962 and his law degree from Boston University in 1965. After being elected as Bangor's mayor in 1971, he ran successfully for the **House of Representatives** in 1972. He quickly gained a reputation as a moderate and independent Republican, partly due to his vote to bring impeachment charges against President Richard Nixon. He was elected to the Senate in 1978, where he quickly became an expert on defense policy. While he supported the arms buildup of the 1980s, Cohen gained notoriety during the Iran-contra hearings. He was one of only three Republicans to sign a report criticizing President Ronald Reagan for the affair.

A supporter of the Persian Gulf War, Cohen displayed his independence from the Republican Party on social and environmental issues during the late 1980s and early 1990s. In spite of his popularity in Maine, he chose not to seek reelection in 1996, making him available for the post of secretary of Defense following Clinton's reelection. At times Cohen differed with Secretary of State **Madeleine Albright** over U.S. policy in the Balkans, with the latter proving more amenable to deploying troops than Cohen. Nonetheless, Cohen supported the Kosovo war and attacks on **Sudan** for its alleged involvement in **terrorism**. Among Cohen's most controversial actions was his decision to support General Joseph Ralston's nomination to become the chairman of the Joint Chiefs of Staff even after the media reported, and Ralston admitted, that he had had an adulterous affair with a civilian. Ironically, Ralston had forced a subordinate general to resign because of the subordinate's sexual impropriety. Ultimately, Ralston withdrew his name from consideration for the post. Cohen was the first secretary of defense to travel to **Vietnam** since the end of the Vietnam War. Throughout his tenure, Cohen also pushed for reforming the mission and capabilities of the military, enhancing U.S. ability to rapidly deploy forces around the globe.

Cohen has written eight books, including works of poetry, fiction, and nonfiction. His autobiography *Roll Call* (1981) was republished in paperback as *Power and Privilege*.

Suggested Readings: *Current Biography Yearbook*, 1998, p. 113; http://www.defenselink.mil/specials/secdef_histories/bios/cohen.htm; Dana Priest, "An 'Outsider' Set to Take Over the Pentagon," *Washington Post*, January 22, 1997, p. A21.

Related Entries: Cabinet; Defense, Military; Election of 2000; Foreign Policy.

"CONTRACT WITH AMERICA." On September 27, 1994, over three hundred Republican candidates for the **U.S. House of Representatives** signed a document entitled the "Contract with America" in a ceremony on the steps of the U.S. Capitol. The contract listed ten specific items that the candidates pledged to bring to a vote if they were elected that fall during the first hundred days of the next session of Congress. Congressman **Newt Gingrich**, a conservative Republican from Georgia, sought to use the contract as a means toward galvanizing public support for Republican candidates and conservative causes. While pundits expected the Republicans to make gains in the off-year **election of 1994**, few expected them to gain a majority in the House of Representatives for the first time in decades. Yet the contract served as a very effective rallying tool against the Clinton administration, and the Republicans gained a 230–204 majority in the House and a 53–47 majority in the **U.S. Senate**. In addition, Newt Gingrich was elected the new Speaker of the House. Table 3 lists the specific pledges and the actions taken and results of those actions during the term of the 104th Congress, which served from 1995 to 1997. The "contract" also promised to amend the House rules so that Congress's exemption from safety and workplace laws that affected the private sector would be ended and limits would be placed on the terms of committee chairmen. The rules changes also demanded a three-fifths majority to increase taxes. These rules changes were adopted.

Although Republicans profited from the "Contract with America," they proved less enthusiastic about rallying around another such contract in subsequent years. In 1999, after resigning from the House of Representatives, Gingrich called for a new contract that would include reforming Social Security. While many Republicans campaigned on some of the issues in this new contract, the party as a whole did not unite behind it.

Suggested Readings: "'Contract with America' Scorecard," *Congressional Quarterly Almanac*, 1995, p. 1-10; "House Republican 'Contract with America,'" *Historic Documents*, 1994, p. 374; Gabe Martinez, "Republicans Reach a Crossroads," *CQ Weekly*, April 17, 1999, p. 886.

Related Entries: Deregulation; Government Shutdown; Tort Reform.

Table 3
Pledges of the "Contract with America"

Pledge and Description	House Approved	Senate Approved	Enacted or Vetoed
1. *The Fiscal Responsibility Act*: Balanced budget Amendment	Passed	Defeated	
line-item veto	Passed	Passed	Enacted
2. *Taking Back Our Streets Act*: Increase victims' rights and prison spending; limit death-row appeals	Modified	Passed	Modified version enacted
3. *Personal Responsibility Act*: **Welfare reform**, limiting aid and imposing other restrictions	Passed	Passed	Enacted
4. *Family Reinforcement Act*: Enhance child-support laws, strengthen child-pornography laws, and extend child tax credits	Passed	Passed	Enacted
5. *American Dream Restoration Act*: $500 tax credit per child, repeal of marriage tax, expansion of individual retirement accounts (IRAs)	Passed	Passed	Enacted with some modification
6. *National Security Restoration Act*: Bars U.S. troops from taking part in United Nation missions and cuts U.S. funding for UN; also develops missile defense system	Passed		
7. *Senior Citizens Fairness Act*: Repeal 1993 tax on **Social Security** benefits and develop incentives to buy long-term-care insurance	Passed	Modified	Modified version enacted
8. *Job Creation and Wage Enhancement Act*: Capital-gains tax cut and regulatory reform	Passed	Passed	Modified version enacted
9. *Common Sense Legal Reform Act*: Limit punitive damages on product liability and make it more difficult or risky to sue corporations	Passed	Passed	Vetoed
10. *Citizens Legislature Act*: Set **term limits** for federal lawmakers	Defeated	Defeated	

Source: Congressional Quarterly Almanac, 1995, p. 1-10.

House Minority Whip Gingrich addresses Republican congressional candidates on September 27, 1994. AP/Wide World Photos.

COUNCIL OF ECONOMIC ADVISERS. *See* **National Economic Council**.

CRIME. Since at least the mid-1960s, crime has stood as one of the most prominent political issues. Republicans gained support by arguing that they favored "law and order" while Democrats coddled criminals. Rising crime rates as well as the Democratic Party's general commitment to ending or at least limiting the death penalty, along with a string of legal rulings by the Warren Court, the name given to the **Supreme Court** during the 1960s, that expanded the rights of the accused, lent weight to this charge. Studies by political scientists demonstrated that crime was one of the main "wedge" issues whereby Republicans, especially on the national level, prodded voters who traditionally supported the Democratic Party to support Republican candidates. For example, in 1988, Vice President **George Bush** attacked Governor Michael Dukakis of Massachusetts via the famous Willie Horton television commercial, which held Dukakis responsible for the release of a convicted murderer and rapist who committed a series of horrific crimes upon his release. In the **election**

Figure 3
Murder Rate

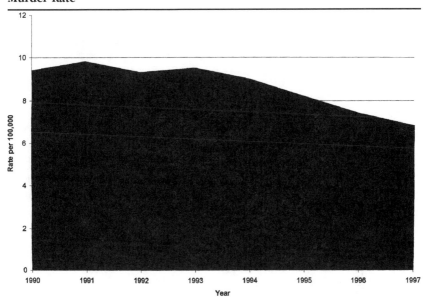

Source: U.S. Department of Justice, "Violent Crime Rates."

of 1992, Bill Clinton sought to overcome this stereotype. He did so in part by pointing to his stance and record in favor of the death penalty.

In 1994, Clinton made enacting a new anticrime bill one of his top priorities. Most Republicans opposed key aspects of his proposal, particularly a ban on assault weapons and certain preventive measures, such as a "midnight-basketball" program, which aimed at providing at-risk youths with an alternative to hanging out on the streets. Nonetheless, Clinton won passage of his plan. Specifically, the Omnibus Crime Act of 1994 appropriated millions of dollars to help communities hire up to 100,000 new police officers. It also allocated funds for prison construction, expanded the number of federal crimes for which one could be sentenced to death, and established the so called three-strikes-and-you're-out rule. According to this rule, life imprisonment became the mandatory sentence for an individual convicted of a third violent felony.

Even though he opposed several parts of the Republicans' **"Contract with America,"** President Clinton signed bills associated with the contract that had to do with crime, including one that limited the number of appeals available to death-row inmates and another that established

Table 4
Crime Statistics, 1990–1999

	1990	1995	1997	1998	1999
Violent crimes per 100,000 people	732	685	611	568	325
Murders, manslaughters (1,000)	23.4	21.6	18.2	17.0	15.1
Prisoners (1,000)	740	1,085	1,195	1,253	1,277

Source: http://www.ojp.usdoj.gov/bjs/dtdata.htm#crime

certain victims' rights. In 1996, Clinton signed the Interstate Stalking Punishment and Prevention Act, which made it a federal crime to cross state lines with the intention of injuring or harassing someone. Throughout his second term, Clinton continued to push for a slew of other anticrime measures, including new **hate-crime** and domestic-violence laws. Following the incident at Columbine High School, where thirteen students were killed by two of their classmates, President Clinton also demanded more stringent **gun-control** measures.

In the **election of 1996** and throughout his second term, President Clinton touted his record on crime. Most important, he and his supporters pointed to a sustained drop in the crime rate as evidence of the effectiveness of the administration's measures. Violent crimes declined nearly 30 percent between 1993 and 1999 to their lowest level in over twenty-five years (see Table 4). Homicides, which peaked at 10.7 per 100,000 in 1980 and stood at 10.5 per 100,000 in 1991, fell to below 7 per 100,000 for the first time since the mid-1960s. The rate of nearly every other type of crime fell as well.

As with many of Clinton's other "accomplishments," however, some scholars and conservatives questioned the relationship between the president's policy and the outcome, seeing more of a correlation between the two than direct causation. The rebounding **economy**, demographic shifts, particularly a decrease in the proportion of young males in the population, and stiffer enforcement and penalties on the state and local levels were responsible for the declining crime rate, they argued, not Clinton's measures. At the same time, conservatives often expressed exasperation over the fact that Clinton was getting credit for measures that conservatives had long demanded. Regardless of who got the credit, for the first time in a generation, the "war against crime" seemed to be working.

Paradoxically, the war against crime produced a new set of problems.

Concerns arose over the disproportionate number of **African Americans** who received the death penalty. In Clinton's last year in office, revelations about the execution or near execution of individuals wrongfully convicted of murder prompted the governor of Illinois to place a moratorium on executions. The booming prison population, disproportionately black and comprised of men and women convicted on **drug** charges, prompted some to question the mandatory sentencing laws that had been put in place in reaction to the growing fear about crime. In addition, several sensational cases of police brutality, particularly in New York City, decreased public support for some of the most aggressive anticrime tactics.

Suggested Readings: http://www.census.gov/statab/www/part2.html; "Lawmakers Enact $30.2 Billion Anti-Crime Bill," *Congressional Quarterly Almanac*, 1994, p. 273; "A Nation Transformed: Crime and Drugs: Lowest Rates in 25 Years," http://clinton3.nara.gov/WH/Accomplishments.crime.html; U.S. Department of Justice, "Violent Crime Rates," http://www.ojp.usdoj.gov/bjs/glance.htm.

Related Entry: Terrorism.

CUOMO, ANDREW M. (Queens, New York, December 6, 1957–   .) Secretary of Housing and Urban Development, 1997–2001.

The son of Mario Cuomo, the well-known governor of New York during the 1980s, Andrew Cuomo served in the Clinton administration throughout Bill Clinton's tenure, first as assistant secretary of housing and urban development (HUD) and then as secretary of HUD. Cuomo brought with him to Washington, D.C., years of experience, having headed a nonprofit company that constructed housing for the homeless in New York. As secretary of HUD, Cuomo helped revive one of the most troubled federal agencies. Years of building large public housing projects, which came into disfavor during the 1980s, along with recurrent scandals involving top officials during the Ronald Reagan and **George Bush** years, left HUD grasping for life. To overcome its reputation for corruption, Cuomo set out to reform the agency. He upgraded the agency's outmoded computer system, cracked down on housing discrimination and abusive landlords, rescued an unpopular Section 8 rent-subsidy program, and worked diligently to reduce waste and fraud within HUD. Even conservative Republicans like Jerry Lewis, who chaired the housing panel of the House Appropriations Committee, gave Cuomo high marks for his efforts. A near doubling of HUD's budget during Cuomo's tenure testified to the respect he gained from a Republican Congress otherwise reluctant to support large federal programs.

Cuomo was raised in Queens in a world immersed in Democratic politics. At age seventeen, he worked on his father's successful bid for the post of lieutenant governor and again for his father's bid to become mayor of New York in 1977. Andrew Cuomo earned his B.A. from Fordham University in 1979 and his J.D. from Albany Law School in 1982. Somewhat reluctantly, he headed his father's successful campaign for governor in 1982 and then became his special assistant. In 1984, he accepted a position at the district attorney's office in New York City. Unexpectedly, in 1986 he shifted career interests, founding and then directing HELP, a nonprofit agency that sought to build homes for the homeless. By the time Clinton nominated him to become assistant secretary of HUD, HELP had become one of the largest nonprofit developers and operators of housing for the homeless in the nation.

Along with his wife, Kerry Kennedy, the daughter of Robert F. Kennedy, Andrew Cuomo gained a reputation as one of the more powerful young politicians in Washington, D.C. When **Henry Cisneros** resigned in the face of a scandal, Cuomo was the obvious choice to replace him. He was unanimously confirmed by the **U.S. Senate**. By working exceptionally long hours, he overcame the criticism that he was appointed to the **cabinet** simply because he was Mario Cuomo's son. Some commentators even suggested that he was one of Clinton's most influential political advisers; others floated his name as a possible running mate with **Al Gore**.

Suggested Readings: Lizette Alvarez, "It's Andrew Cuomo's Turn at Bat, and Some See Makings of a Slugger," *New York Times*, January 4, 1998, p. 1; *Current Biography Yearbook*, 1998, p. 137.

Related Entry: Domestic Policy.

CURRIE, BETTY. (1941– .) Personal secretary to President Clinton, 1993–2001.

Until the **Monica Lewinsky** scandal broke, Betty Currie, President Bill Clinton's personal secretary, was virtually unknown except to those who either worked at the White House or covered it for the press. Once the scandal erupted, she became one of the most widely known persons in the United States, with some believing that she held the key to determining whether President Clinton had actually had an affair with Lewinsky and if he had conspired with Lewinsky to lie in their depositions in the **Paula Jones** case.

Currie grew up in Illinois and moved to Washington, D.C., shortly after she graduated from high school in 1957. Over the course of thirty years, she held a variety of jobs, working as a secretary for the Navy Department, the Agency for International Development (AID), and the Peace Corps. She also worked on a number of political campaigns, including those of Geraldine Ferraro, Gary Hart, and Michael Dukakis, during the 1980s in their quests for the **U.S. Senate** and presidency. She became part of the Clinton campaign team in 1992, working as an office manager in the "war room" in Little Rock, Arkansas. After Clinton's election, she served as **Warren Christopher**'s secretary on the transition team, first in Arkansas and later in Washington, D.C. She then became the president's personal secretary, his unofficial gatekeeper and confidante. Nearly all who encountered her praised her professionalism and described her as a delightful person.

Currie befriended Lewinsky during Lewinsky's service as an intern and employee at the White House. She remained close with Lewinsky afterwards. When the Lewinsky scandal broke, both the media and the independent counsel's office saw Currie as a key player in determining the extent of President Clinton's relationship with Lewinsky and whether the two had conspired to cover up their affair. Lewinsky entered the White House after hours on Currie's authorization. Currie's office was within earshot of the president's office. When President Clinton learned that Lewinsky had been subpoenaed to testify in the Paula Jones case, Currie picked up a package of gifts that Clinton had previously given to Lewinsky and brought them to her own home. These actions and others led independent counsel **Kenneth Starr** to describe Currie as an "enabler."

A crucial point in the scandal came with Currie's testimony to the grand jury. According to Starr's report, which drew on this testimony, Clinton sought to tamper with a potential witness by improperly attempting to corrupt the testimony of Currie, an impeachable offense according to the independent counsel's office. Surprisingly, the **House impeachment managers** who presented the case for **impeachment** to the U.S. Senate chose not to call Currie as a witness. The *Washington Post* and others speculated that House managers chose not to call Currie because they felt that she would present conflicting evidence, some of which would support their contention that the president had engaged in a cover-up and some of which might clear the president of these charges. In addition, news analysts conjectured that since Currie was a likeable person, and a middle-aged, African American woman, House prosecutors determined that an aggressive examination of her would produce no new evidence but might result in a public backlash against them.

Suggested Readings: "Betty Currie: Innocent or Enabler?" BBC News Profiles, February 10, 1998; "Clinton's Right-Hand Woman," January 23, 1998, http://www. ABCNEWS.com; Amy Goldstein, "Summons Thrusts President's Gatekeeper into View," *Washington Post*, January 23, 1998, p. A20; Ruth Marcus, "For Prosecutors, Tough Trade-Offs," *Washington Post*, January 27, 1999, p. A1.

D

DALEY, WILLIAM M. (August 19, 1948, Chicago, Illinois–   .) Secretary of Commerce, 1997–2000; Campaign Manager for Al Gore, 2000.

The son of one of the most prominent Democratic politicians of the twentieth century, William Daley developed his own reputation as a power broker within the Democratic Party in the 1980s and even more so as an adviser and then **cabinet** member in the Clinton administration during the 1990s. Daley's father, Richard J. Daley, served as Chicago's mayor and headed one of the most powerful political machines in the United States throughout William Daley's youth and early adult years. In spite of his father's prominence, William and his three brothers and sisters grew up in the working-class neighborhood of Bridgeport, where they dined with their father every night.

In contrast to two of his brothers, Richard M., who was elected mayor of Chicago in 1989, and John, who served as a state senator before being elected Cook County commissioner, William Daley's involvement in politics was largely behind the scenes. After graduating from Loyola University in Chicago in 1970 with a degree in political science and from John Marshall Law School in 1975, William became a prominent lawyer and businessman in Chicago. In 1990, he was named chief operating officer of the Amalgamated Bank of Chicago. Before and after holding this post, he was a law partner at Mayer, Brown and Platt.

In addition to serving as an unofficial adviser to his brother Richard, William Daley worked on the presidential campaigns of Walter Mondale in 1984 and Michael Dukakis in 1988. In 1992, he headed Bill Clinton's campaign in the state of Illinois. During Clinton's first term, Daley served as a special counsel on **NAFTA**, successfully shepherding it through Congress. In 1996, Daley cochaired the Democratic convention, which was held in Chicago for the first time since 1968. In 1997, Clinton nominated Daley to become the new secretary of commerce.

Prior to this, conservative Republicans had called for the abolition of the Department of Commerce, charging that it was an example of wasteful government spending and a source of government fraud and corruption. Daley worked to restore the department's reputation by streamlining the agency and focusing on the mission of promoting trade and economic growth. During his tenure, Daley oversaw the modernization of the National Weather Service and prepared for the 2000 census. He also focussed much energy on promoting e-commerce, which took off in the late 1990s.

On June 15, 2000, Daley announced that he would leave Clinton's cabinet to act as the chairman of **Al Gore**'s presidential campaign. While Daley gained little notoriety during the campaign itself, he was thrust into the spotlight on the morning after the election. When the results in the state of Florida produced no clear winner, Gore chose Daley to play a leading role in the campaign's challenge to the final vote, which showed Governor **George W. Bush** winning by a narrow margin. He has been credited by some as an effective spokesman for Vice President Gore during this difficult and tense period in American history.

Suggested Readings: "Biography of Secretary of Commerce William M. Daley," http://www.commerce.gov; *Current Biography Yearbook*, 1998, p. 145; Edward Walsh, "William Daley," *Washington Post*, December 14, 1996, p. A1.

Related Entries: Domestic Policy; Election of 1996; Election of 2000.

DASCHLE, THOMAS. (December 9, 1947, Aberdeen, South Dakota–   .) U.S. Senate Minority Leader, 1995–2001.

Thomas Daschle was one of the leading Democrats in the United States during the 1990s. He served as the minority leader in the **U.S. Senate** from 1995 until 2001. In this role, he did his best to promote President Bill Clinton's agenda in a Republican-controlled Congress. Daschle also played a crucial role during the **impeachment** process, uniting Democrats in the Senate in opposition to convicting the president on either of the two articles of impeachment approved by the **House of Representatives**.

Born and raised in South Dakota, Thomas Daschle earned a B.A. from South Dakota State University in 1969 and then joined the U.S. Air Force, rising to the rank of first lieutenant. After leaving the service in 1973, he went to work in Washington, D.C., as the legislative aide to Democratic senator James Abourezk. Daschle also worked on George McGovern's senatorial reelection campaign in 1974 and as a lobbyist. In 1978, he ran for and won a seat as one of South Dakota's two congressmen in the House of Representatives. Daschle barely defeated his opponent, Leo Thorsness, in 1978, but he was easily reelected in 1980, 1982, and 1984. In 1986, he decided to run for the U.S. Senate and, after a hard-fought campaign, barely defeated Republican Incumbent James Abdnor. He was easily reelected to the Senate in 1992 and 1998.

As a member of the House and Senate, Daschle focussed much of his time and energy on serving the needs of his constituents, promoting farm aid, alternative uses of grain, such as ethanol, and enhanced veterans' benefits. He established a record as a moderate on social issues. For example, he supported abortion rights, establishing a Department of Education, and the equal-rights amendment. He also gained a reputation as a congenial and loyal colleague, nurturing relationships with several of the Democratic leaders, including Robert Byrd and **George Mitchell**, both of whom served as Senate majority leaders. In 1994, when Mitchell announced that he would not run for reelection, Daschle campaigned behind the scenes to succeed him. While he was successful in winning the support of the majority of Democrats in the Senate, the Republican Party's victory in the general election relegated him to the post of minority rather than majority leader. As minority leader, he sought to hold Democrats together in the face of the Republican Party's attacks on numerous liberal programs and the Clinton administration. By promoting a solid Democratic front in the Senate, Daschle made it clear that the House's impeachment charges against President Clinton would not produce a conviction. On several controversial social and economic measures, such as **welfare reform**, he was less successful in uniting his party behind the president and/or defeating the Republicans. One of Daschle's more controversial votes came in 1995 on the Republican proposal to enact a balanced-budget amendment to the U.S. Constitution. For some time, Daschle had supported such a proposal, but in 1995, following the Republican takeover of Congress, he changed his position, allowing the proposal to be defeated by one vote. In its place, Daschle helped gain passage of a plan that would commit the government to balancing the budget by the year 2002. In fact, the booming **economy** ended budget deficits long before the target date and produced unprecedented budget surpluses instead.

In the **election of 2000**, the Democratic Party surprisingly gained more seats than many expected, leaving it with fifty seats in the Senate and the Republican Party with fifty seats. Since **George W. Bush** won the presidency and since the vice president can cast the deciding vote in case of a tie in the Senate, this left the Republicans effectively in control of the Senate. Nonetheless, Daschle and Senate Majority Leader **Trent Lott** crafted a power-sharing deal whereby both parties would have equal representation on Senate committees and staffs of the same size. How well this power-sharing scheme would work remained to be seen.

Suggested Readings: *CQ's Politics in America: The 106th Congress* (Washington, D.C.: Congressional Quarterly, Inc., 2000), p. 1244; *Current Biography Yearbook*, 1995, pp. 111–15.

Related Entries: Budget, Federal; Domestic Policy.

DAYTON AGREEMENT. *See* **Bosnia and Herzegovina**.

DEBT, FEDERAL. *See* **Budget, Federal**.

DEFENSE, MILITARY. One of the most controversial aspects of Bill Clinton's presidency was his defense policy. After the Republicans took control of Congress in the **election of 1994**, they sought to increase defense expenditures. While Clinton sought to allocate less for the military than did the Republicans, he gradually met their demands, especially during his final years in office. Nonetheless, during the 2000 presidential campaign, Republican presidential nominee **George W. Bush** and his running mate, Dick Cheney, claimed that the Clinton administration had left the U.S. military in a sad state. According to the Republican candidates, Clinton and **Al Gore** had weakened the military by decreasing its expenditures while at the same time expanding its commitments. To strengthen their critique of the Clinton-Gore defense record, Bush and Cheney asserted that some active commanders bemoaned the shortage of spare parts and the difficulty of recruiting and retraining qualified servicemen and women. Numerous Republicans also argued that Clinton's moral shortcomings, from allegedly avoiding the draft during the **Vietnam** War to the **Monica Lewinsky** scandal, undermined his credibility with America's troops. Moreover, conservatives decried the president's policies toward **gays in the military**.

Table 5
Defense Spending, 1985–2005 (Millions of Dollars)

Year	Total Spending	As Percentage of Federal Outlays	As Percentage of GDP
1985	252,748	26.7	6.1
1986	273,375	27.6	6.2
1987	281,999	28.1	6.1
1988	290,361	27.3	5.8
1989	303,559	26.5	5.6
1990	299,331	23.9	5.2
1991	273,292	20.6	4.6
1992	298,350	21.6	4.8
1993	291,086	20.7	4.4
1994	281,642	19.3	4.1
1995	272,066	17.9	3.7
1996	265,753	17.0	3.5
1997	270,505	16.9	3.3
1998	268,456	16.2	3.1
1999	274,873	16.1	3.0
2000 (est.)	290,636	16.2	3.0
2001 (est.)	291,202	15.9	2.9
2002 (est.)	298,390	15.7	2.8
2003 (est.)	307,363	15.7	2.8
2004 (est.)	316,517	15.7	2.8
2005 (est.)	330,742	15.6	2.7

Source: The Budget for Fiscal Year 2001, Historical Tables, http://www.gpo.gov.

Yet a careful look at the Clinton administration's defense record reveals that in many ways, Clinton's policy resembled that of his predecessor, **George Bush**. President Clinton inherited a military that President George Bush and his secretary of defense Dick Cheney had already begun to shrink and reorganize due to the end of the cold war. Federal spending on national defense decreased from a peak of $304 billion in 1989 to $291 billion in 1993 (see Table 5). This trend of downsizing continued after Clinton took office. As a result, military spending fell to a low of $265.7 billion in 1996. Yet the defense budgets of Clinton's second term increased at nearly the same rate that they fell during his first term in office.

Moreover, in terms of particular weapons systems and military policies, Clinton was hardly a dove. Throughout the 1990s, the Clinton administration supported research into a missile defense program, sometimes known as "Star Wars." Originally proposed by President Ronald Reagan, this ambitious and expensive endeavor aimed at constructing a space-based shield against a missile attack on the United States. While Clinton left the decision over whether to deploy such a system to his successor, it is problematic whether a Republican president would have pushed for deployment any faster than Clinton did. Clinton sent troops to **Haiti**, commanded an air war on Yugoslavia, ordered the bombing of **Iraq**, Sudan, and Afghanistan, and significantly increased the U.S. commitment to **NATO**. Even Clinton's record on gays in the military was not as liberal as it was often perceived, as he ultimately adopted a "don't ask, don't tell" standard, rather than allowing for gays in the military to be open about their sexual preference.

Further proof of Clinton's moderate record on defense lay in his nomination of **William S. Cohen**, a lifelong Republican, as secretary of defense in 1997. Under Cohen's leadership, funding for the Defense Department rose 2 percent per year, and the administration proposed even higher levels of spending in its final budget. Cohen supported Clinton's decision to attack Yugoslavia. When the aerial attack initially failed to dislodge Yugoslavian forces from **Kosovo**, Cohen defended the administration's strategy and denied claims that Kosovo would turn into another Vietnam. Throughout his tenure, Cohen also pushed for reforming the mission and capabilities of the military, enhancing U.S. ability to rapidly deploy forces around the world.

Undoubtedly, the downsizing of the military, which included a 25 percent cut of annual defense budgets and a 36 percent decrease in personnel over ten years, created strains for the military and defense-related industries. (These cuts began during the Bush administration.) The need for the United States to rethink its overall military strategy in the post-cold-war world added to these strains. Yet the strains did not add up to a military crisis, and the alleged crisis may end up looking a lot like the so-called missile gap of the 1960 presidential campaign, more fiction than fact, more political ploy than military reality. Indeed, in spite of conservative criticism of the administration's defense record, history may show that when Clinton left office, the United States was more dominant in terms of military strength than any other nation in world history. As Gregg Easterbrook, an analyst for the *New Republic*, observed, at the end of Clinton's presidency the United States was "stronger, relative to the rest of the world, than it has been at any point since the United States' brief atomic monopoly in the late 40s" (*New Republic*, p. 22). The United States still spent three times as much on defense as **Russia** and **China** combined and more than the next twelve highest-spending nations put together.

Hence the real question that may be posed as time passes is not whether the Clinton administration degraded America's fighting capabilities, but rather whether the United States responded properly to the end of the cold war. Did it still need such a large traditional army? Did its military preserve national security and bolster or undermine its ability to live up to its ideals at home and around the globe? By and large the nation avoided debating such topics during Clinton's presidency. President Clinton displayed little inclination to risk initiating such a debate, and conservative made it clear that they would attempt to punish him politically if he did.

Suggested Readings: Tom Bowman, "Military Distresses Provoke Campaign War of Words," *Baltimore Sun*, September 8, 2000, p. 1; Gregg Easterbrook, "Apocryphal Now: The Myth of the Hollow Military," *New Republic*, September 11, 2000, p. 22; http://www.defenselink.mil/pub/dod/101/budget.html; "Republicans Succeed in Shoring Up Funds for Anti-Missile Defenses," *Congressional Quarterly Almanac*, 1998, p. 8-17.

DEFENSE OF MARRIAGE ACT. On September 21, 1996, President Bill Clinton signed the Defense of Marriage Act. The law, introduced in the **U.S. House of Representatives** by Bob Barr, a conservative Republican from Georgia, grew out of a reaction to the possibility that Hawaii and a few other states might legalize same-sex marriages or civil unions. In general, marriages conducted in one state were recognized as legal by other states. The Defense of Marriage Act allowed states to determine whether they would recognize same-sex marriages sanctioned in other states or not.

Clinton had come into office with a reputation as a friend of gays and lesbians. However, criticisms of his support for allowing gays to serve in the military prodded him to back away from advocating gay rights. Clinton's decision to sign the Republican-sponsored bill also stemmed from his desire to co-opt certain conservative causes in advance of the presidential **election of 1996**. However, by the end of the 1990s, the agenda of the gay and lesbian community had expanded to the point that legalizing gay marriage, once a somewhat radical objective, assumed greater importance. Even though Clinton signed the Defense of Marriage Act, the concept of gay marriage gained increasing support around the country, arguably in part because of the president's more tolerant views of gay rights in general. For instance, in Vermont, the courts ruled same-sex civil unions legal, and voters upheld the decision in a statewide referendum in the **election of 2000**. Vice presidential candidate Dick Cheney in his debate with **Al Gore**'s running mate Joe Lieberman, expressed guarded support for greater toleration of diverse lifestyles than previous Republican candidates for higher office.

Suggested Readings: Mitchell Alison, "Clinton Signs Bill Denying Gay Couples U.S. Benefits," *New York Times*, September 21, 1996, p. 8; http://lambdalegal.org.

Related Entry: Gays in the Military.

DEFICIT. *See* **Budget, Federal**.

DEMOCRATIC LEADERSHIP COUNCIL. Founded in 1985, the Democratic Leadership Council (DLC) sought to remake the Democratic Party into a more centrist party than it had been in the recent past. Under the direction of its president and cofounder, **Al From**, the DLC attracted numerous moderate Democrats to its fold in the 1980s, including Bill Clinton, then Senator **Al Gore**, and Senator Joe Lieberman. Other prominent DLC members were Georgia senator Sam Nunn, Louisiana senator John Breaux, and Missouri congressman **Richard Gephardt**. The DLC published a bimonthly magazine, *The New Democrat*, and was affiliated with the Progressive Policy Institute. The DLC championed the notion of a "third way" in politics, opposed to the traditional liberal and conservative philosophies. This third-way philosophy, according to the DLC, aimed at "adapting enduring progressive values to the new challenges" of the post-industrial world (DLC web site). Most politicians associated with the DLC sought to distance themselves from several "wedge" issues that Republicans had used with great success against liberal Democrats in the 1980s. For instance, Bill Clinton supported the death penalty and **welfare reform**, two Republican issues of the 1980s.

Clinton's election as president solidified the DLC's position as a key player on the political scene. During the 1990s, several other DLC adherents outside of the United States won national elections, adding to the DLC's prominence. Calling for a third-way agenda in Great Britain, Tony Blair became the first Labour Party candidate to serve as prime minister in years. Similarly, Gerhard Schröder and the Social Democrats gained control in Germany by running on a third-way platform. The degree to which these three leaders, particularly Clinton, truly stuck to the DLC's agenda, however, was debatable. At times, Clinton appeared to drift to the left. Yet particularly after the Republican victory in the **election of 1994**, Clinton tended to reemphasize the need for a new Democratic approach. Ironically, while the nomination of Al Gore and Joe Lieberman in the **election of 2000** appeared to signal the victory of the DLC against more liberal blocs within the Democratic Party, Gore and Lieberman's decision to campaign as populists and oppose reforming **Social Security** and school vouchers, two goals the DLC favored implementing, suggested that even some of the DLC's original members had turned away from the third-way vision upon which the DLC was founded.

Suggested Readings: Jonathan Cole, "The Old New Thing," *New Republic*, April 17, 2000, p. 38; http://www.ndol.org/; John Nichols, "Behind the DLC Takeover," *Progressive* 64:10 (October 2000), p. 28.

DEREGULATION. Part of the Republicans' **"Contract with America"** was a pledge to enact sweeping deregulatory legislation that would require the government to assess the economic cost of federally mandated regulations. Based on this pledge, the **U.S. House of Representatives** passed legislation in the early spring of 1995 that required federal agencies to conduct a cost-benefit analysis of regulations that affected more than 100 people and cost more than $1 million. The aim of this bill, according to its sponsors, was to limit the proliferation of federal regulations and provide relief to small businesses, who, conservatives argued, were overburdened by the multitude of federal restrictions. Senate Majority Leader **Robert Dole** sought to push similar legislation through the **U.S. Senate**. However, Democrats, who in general opposed such deregulatory legislation on the grounds that it undermined necessary protections of the **environment** and the workplace, were able to defeat a cloture vote that would have stopped their filibuster against Dole's deregulatory proposals. As a result, Republicans were unable to deliver on their pledge to pass deregulation in 1995. In 1996, following the **government shutdown**, conservatives were even less able to push through significant deregulatory laws. Although Republicans won some concessions on **tort reform** and **unfunded mandates**, they failed to enact measures that fulfilled the promises embodied in the "Contract with America." Furthermore, in his final months in office, President Clinton issued thousands of pages of new regulations. These new regulations further protected the nation's forests, expanded the power of Occupational Safety and Health Administration, which was responsible for workplace safety, and broadened health care rights. While President-elect **George W. Bush** pledged that his administration would carefully review these "midnight" regulations, it was unclear if he would be unable to undo them, even if he saw fit to do so.

Suggested Readings: "Republicans Narrow Focus of Deregulatory Agenda," *Congressional Quarterly Almanac*, 1996, p. 3-3; "Senate Filibuster Derails Efforts to Limit Federal Regulations," *Congressional Quarterly Almanac*, 1995, p. 3-3.

DOLE, ROBERT (BOB) JOSEPH. (July 23, 1923, Russell, Kansas–   .) U.S. Senator, 1968–1996; Senate Majority Leader, 1984–1986; Senate Minority Leader, 1987–1996; Republican candidate for President, 1996.

One of the most prominent senators of the last third of the twentieth century, Robert Dole was the Republican candidate for president in 1996. Emphasizing his years of public service, including his heroic record as a World War II soldier, Dole pledged to cut taxes and enact numerous conservative measures delineated by the **"Contract with America."** Yet Dole failed to generate much enthusiasm among the Republican faithful who had driven the Republicans to victory in the midterm **election of 1994**. Moreover, by stressing his record as president, including the expansion of the **economy** and the enactment of **welfare reform**, Bill Clinton was able to win the support of the majority of independent voters and the election. He defeated Dole by a margin of 49.2 to 40.8 percent of the popular vote and won the electoral college by more than a two-to-one margin.

Born and raised in Russell, Kansas, Robert Dole left college to join the military when World War II began. During the fighting in Italy, he was severely wounded. After the war, he returned to college, earning his A.B. from Washburn Municipal University (1952) and his law degree from the same university in Topeka, Kansas, also in 1952. First elected to the Kansas state legislature in 1950, he was elected to the **U.S. House of Representatives** in 1960. Eight years later, he won a seat in the **U.S. Senate**. In 1976, Dole was President Gerald Ford's running mate against Jimmy Carter and Walter Mondale. He unsuccessfully sought the Republican presidential nomination in 1980 and 1988.

Dole was one of the most prominent Republicans in the Senate. He became the Senate majority leader in 1984, although he had to relinquish this position when the Democrats regained the majority of seats in the

Senate in 1987. As minority leader of the Senate, Dole played a key role in defeating President Clinton's **health care reform** proposals. He also opposed the administration's economic stimulus package. Yet Dole supported ratification of **NAFTA** and welfare reform. When the Republicans regained the majority of seats in 1994, Dole again became Senate majority leader. In 1996, he stepped down from this post and announced that he would leave the Senate to focus on his campaign for the presidency. After his retirement, Dole became a spokesman for the drug Viagra, which was prescribed to overcome male impotence. Dole's second wife, Elizabeth Hanford Dole, is also a prominent Republican politician. She served in both Presidents Ronald Reagan's and **George Bush**'s cabinets and made a brief bid for the presidency in the year 2000.

Suggested Readings: Stanley Hilton, *Senator for Sale: An Unauthorized Biography of Senator Bob Dole* (New York: St. Martin's Press, 1995); Jake Thompson, *Bob Dole: The Republicans' Man for All Seasons* (New York: D. I. Fine, 1994).

Related Entry: Election of 1996.

DOMESTIC POLICY. During his campaign for the presidency and after the **election of 1992**, Bill Clinton made it clear that he would focus on domestic rather than foreign affairs. Moreover, several of his main **foreign policy** objectives, **NAFTA, GATT**, and maintaining stability in Asia and Eastern Europe, were intertwined with his primary goals on the home front. While some foreign policy experts criticized Clinton for emphasizing domestic policy at the expense of foreign affairs, the American public appeared to approve of the president's priorities. Only during the final years of his presidency did Clinton tend to shift his attention away from the home front, seeking to cement his legacy by promoting major peace initiatives in the **Middle East** and **Northern Ireland** and by traveling to Africa, Latin America, and Southeast Asia.

At the center of Clinton's domestic agenda was his plan to cut the **federal budget** deficit and jump-start the **economy**. Less than a month after he was sworn in as president, Clinton laid out this plan in a dramatic speech before a joint session of Congress. To reduce the deficit, he called for a mixture of tax reform and spending cuts. These were to be accompanied by an economic stimulus package.

Specifically, Clinton's tax plan called for increasing the tax rate on the top income brackets—the new rate was 39.6 percent for earnings above $250,000. The administration also proposed boosting the taxes that people who were in the upper-income tax brackets paid on income they received from **Social Security**. Clinton also sought a new energy or BTU tax. In addition, the Clinton administration favored increasing the earned-income tax credit. To stimulate the economy, the plan called for increasing public spending and investments in education and job retraining. Part of this included a national service program that would allow college students to borrow money for college in exchange for work in their communities following graduation. Smaller spending proposals sought to enhance the growth of **high technology** and spur the development of renewable energy. Lastly, Clinton's plan called for rebuilding economically disadvantaged areas by providing tax incentives to corporations that invested in them.

In addition to raising revenues through tax hikes and stimulating the economy through tax incentives, Clinton's domestic programs called for modest spending cuts, nearly all of which came from the Department of Defense and from entitlement programs. The latter cuts were achieved largely by reducing payments to doctors and extending premium increases that the government had enacted before he became president, rather than actually shrinking benefits to medicare recipients. Otherwise, Clinton did not propose major reductions in nondiscretionary spending, although, as some experts observed, he did display fiscal discipline by not increasing spending on numerous federal programs that had seen their budgets cut during Ronald Reagan's presidency.

Republicans immediately objected to Clinton's agenda, voting unanimously against a budget resolution that established the parameters of Clinton's spending and taxing plans. In the face of strong opposition, Clinton and his aides lobbied furiously for the president's programs, especially the tax reforms. In a dramatic vote, Vice President **Al Gore** had to break a tie vote in the **U.S. Senate** to enact Clinton's tax proposals. The **House** had already narrowly passed the bill, splitting along partisan lines. Indeed, with Republican leader **Robert Dole** decrying Clinton's proposal as "the largest tax increase in the history of the world" (cited in "Clinton's Five-Year Economic Plan," p. 181), not a single Republican voted for the bill. President Clinton proved less successful in gaining passage of his economic stimulus plan. Republican filibusters in the Senate compelled Democratic leader **George Mitchell** to withdraw it in late April 1993. Some of its measures were approved in separate votes, in a piecemeal fashion. But the essence of his domestic program for 1993 lay in his tax reforms and spending cuts, both of which aimed at cutting the federal budget deficit.

With this part of his domestic agenda fulfilled, Clinton turned his attention and energy toward enacting sweeping **health care reform**, another one of his major campaign pledges. With **Hillary Clinton** taking the lead, the administration submitted a complicated plan to stem the rise in health care costs and increase the number of Americans who were covered by health insurance. Once again, Republicans rallied against the president's proposals. This time they were more successful in dealing the administration a defeat. By the fall of 1994, health care reform lay dead, and both the Clinton administration and the Democratic Party were on the defensive. Pledging to support the **"Contract with America,"** Republicans gained control of both the House and Senate for the first time in decades in the **election of 1994**. They quickly set about seeking to undo Clinton's tax reforms of 1993 and enacting sweeping **welfare reform**, which Clinton had supported during the 1992 campaign but had opposed since. In the short term, the Republican commitment to these and several other objectives set them on a crash course with President Clinton. Remarkably, the two parties clashed little on foreign affairs. Instead, they clashed over the specific direction the nation should take on the home front.

This conflict between Clinton and Republicans, particularly those led by **Newt Gingrich** in the House of Representatives, culminated with a series of **government shutdowns** in late 1995 and early 1996. Much to the consternation of conservatives, public opinion polls suggested that the majority of Americans blamed the Republican Party for these shutdowns. With the political momentum shifting back in his direction, a rejuvenated Clinton, following the advice of one of his longtime political strategists, **Dick Morris**, crafted a sophisticated domestic policy known as triangulation that involved supporting some of the Republican programs while refusing to budge or give in on others. By the time the **election of 1996** took place, President Clinton enacted welfare reform, cut capital-gains taxes, and established tougher federal criminal statues, all issues that Republicans favored. Yet he simultaneously refused to further decrease spending for entitlement programs, such as Medicare, vetoed measures that would have weakened product-liability laws, and stuck to his original tax hikes on the well-off. This tactic of triangulation, in combination with the growing economy and shrinking budget deficit, allowed him to easily defeat Bob Dole in the election of 1996.

President Clinton's domestic policy record during his second term was more muddled than during his first term. Sounding somewhat like an old-fashioned liberal, he proposed increasing the federal government's commitment to improving schools, including federal funding for construction, wiring schools to the Internet, and reducing class size. Yet, faced with a Republican Congress that was reluctant to increase federal spending, Clinton could take credit only for incremental or piecemeal reforms rather than major initiatives. Indeed, based upon his disastrous experience with health care reform, he tended to avoid calling for new sweeping reforms. For example, while he had once supported reforming Social Security and had appointed a bipartisan commission to study the issue, he ultimately favored using the projected budget surplus to save Social Security rather than overhauling the popular federal program. In some ways, his domestic policy during his second term was one of turning back Republican programs rather than pushing through his own. He vetoed Republican bills to repeal the estate tax and ban partial birth **abortion**. At the same time, he signed into law measures that extended health care for children and offered tax credits to pay for college **education**. Undoubtedly, the **Monica Lewinsky** scandal and **impeachment** battle cut into his ability to foster reform as well.

Nonetheless, as his second term came to a close, President Clinton proudly pointed to a long list of accomplishments on the domestic front, most prominently the creation of over twenty million new jobs, the elimination of the federal budget deficit, the creation of the first federal budget surplus in decades, the highest home-ownership rate in American history, the lowest unemployment and **crime** rates in twenty-five years, and a drastic reduction in the welfare rolls. Even though he enjoyed few major legislative victories during his second term, Clinton can be credited with transforming the nature of the debate over domestic policy. In the **election of 2000**, Al Gore and **George W. Bush** clashed over what to do with the budget surplus, and both agreed that the federal government needed to help enhance education and provide prescription drugs for the elderly. This was a far cry from the clash that took place between Clinton and Republicans in the mid-1990s.

Suggested Readings: "Clinton's Five-Year Economic Plan," *Historic Documents, 1993*, p. 181; "The Democrats' Economic Agenda," *Congressional Quarterly Almanac*, 1993, p. 81; Michael Genovese, *The Presidency and Domestic Policy: Comparing Leadership Styles, FDR to Clinton* (Washington, DC: Congressional Quarterly Press, 2000); Paul C. Light, "Domestic Policy Making," *Presidential Studies Quarterly* 30:1 (March 2000), p. 109; "A Nation Transformed," http://clinton3.nara.gov/WH/Accomplishments/issues.html.

"DON'T ASK, DON'T TELL." *See* **Gays in the Military**.

Table 6
Federal Drug-Control Spending by Function (Millions of Dollars)

	FY1981	FY1989	FY1992	FY1996	FY1999
Total	1,532.8	6,663.7	11,910.1	13,454.0	17,886.2
Drug treatment	513.8	1,148.2	2,204.7	2,553.8	3,193.3
Drug prevention	86.4	752.4	1,538.7	1,400.7	2,153.8
Criminal justice system	415.6	2,761.4	4,943.0	7,164.9	8,455.1
International	66.8	304.0	660.4	289.8	559.2
Interdiction	349.7	1,440.7	1,960.2	1,321.0	1,803.9
Research	76.5	230.5	504.5	609.3	771.8
Intelligence	32.1	53.4	98.6	114.5	254.9

Source: http://www.whitehousedrugpolicy.gov.

DRUGS. Throughout the 1990s, the Clinton administration continued the "war on drugs" launched by the Ronald Reagan and **George Bush** administrations. This "war" entailed massive federal spending, the lion's share going to prosecute drug offenders and to combating the flow of illegal drugs into the United States. For the second half of Clinton's presidency, the "war on drugs" was headed by **Barry R. McCaffrey**, a former four-star general who had played a key role during the Persian Gulf War. As director of the White House Office of National Drug Control Policy, better known as the drug czar, McCaffrey oversaw a substantial increase in federal funds committed to decreasing drug use in the United States (Table 6). Some of the new funds went toward enhancing drug treatment programs, an item traditionally low on the list of priorities of Republicans. Yet a larger share went to vastly increasing military aid to Colombia, the largest supplier of illegal drugs to the United States, to help it clamp down on drug producers inside that nation.

Over a ten-year period, 1988 to 1997, over 12.5 million drug-related arrests were made by law-enforcement officials. In both state and federal prisons, drug offenders comprised an increasing proportion of the inmates. In 1980, 6 percent of all state prisoners were drug offenders. By 1996, drug offenders made up nearly one-fourth of the entire state prison population. In federal prisons, the proportion jumped from 25 percent in 1980 to 60 percent in 1997. During the same time period, the total number of prisoners skyrocketed and drug penalties were stiffened. The average incarceration rate for federal drug offenders nearly doubled, from 47 months in 1980 to 85 months in 1995. During the same time frame, the amount of drugs seized by federal and state authorities increased. In spite of the massive sums of money spent on combating drugs and the vast increase in arrests, convictions, and incarcerations, the efficacy of the war on drugs was problematic. The Clinton administration claimed that it was winning the war, noting that the **crime** rate, which many assumed was directly linked to drug use and trafficking, was down. Both government and nongovernment officials also noted that surveys suggested that the number of drug users, particularly of cocaine, decreased over the 1990s. Yet other studies suggested an alarming revival of heroin usage and the appearance of new synthetic drugs, such as ecstasy.

Nonetheless, political support for the war on drugs remained high. Although some conservatives and liberals called for the decriminalization of drugs, most politicians did not. Numerous **African American** leaders criticized the emphasis on enforcement and mandatory sentences for drug offenders, as opposed to drug treatment and prevention. They noted that a disproportionate number of those arrested for drug-related crimes were African Americans. Several prominent federal judges questioned mandatory sentencing rules that compelled them to incarcerate nonviolent offenders. Still, Congress showed few signs of changing the drug laws.

Drugs were also an issue during the 1992 and 1996 presidential campaigns. Given Bill Clinton's acknowledgment that he had once tried marijuana as a youth, Republicans questioned his ability to lead the war on drugs. Pointing to statistics that showed that drug use among youths was on the rise, Senator **Robert Dole** revived this attack in 1996. While Clinton admitted smoking marijuana, he claimed that he had not inhaled it, a statement that many found improbable.

Suggested Readings: "Drug Data Summary," http://www.whitehousedrugpolicy. gov; "A New War," *Economist*, January 15, 2000, p. 34; Oliver North, "Narco-Terrorists Are Winning in Columbia," *Human Events*, August 27, 1999, p. 12.

E

ECONOMIC POLICY. *See* **Budget, Federal; Domestic Policy.**

ECONOMY. Economic renewal stood at the center of Bill Clinton's campaign for the presidency in 1992. A recession that began in the third quarter of 1990 and lasted through the spring of 1991 created the opening for him to run against President **George Bush** in the first place. When the economy remained anemic and the **federal budget** deficit rose to record levels in 1992, Clinton honed his economic message, pledging to create millions of new jobs and to halve the deficit by 1996. Sustained economic growth, the longest in American history, greater in magnitude and length than many of Clinton's top economic advisers ever forecast, was without doubt one of the greatest accomplishments of Clinton's presidency. Clinton's Internet home page forthrightly declared that it was "the strongest economy in a generation." Put somewhat differently, as **James Carville** stated, Clinton's allure in 1992 and high ratings in the polls in 2000 were simple to understand: **"It's the economy, stupid."**

Nearly every economic indicator showed marked improvement during Clinton's presidency. The gross domestic product, home-ownership rates, hourly wages, corporate profits, and productivity all rose. Unemployment, the federal budget deficit, and overall and child **poverty** rates declined. **Inflation**, which Clinton's opponents warned would revert to the double-digit levels America experienced during the Jimmy Carter years, remained in check. In spite of dire warnings that Clinton's tax hike of 1993 would discourage investment and jeopardize the nation's recovery, the economy soared to new heights. Unemployment fell from 7.5 percent in 1992 to under 4 percent for the first time in thirty years in the spring of 2000. The federal budget deficit, which had quadrupled during the Ronald Reagan and George Bush years, disappeared, leaving Clinton's successors with a record federal budget surplus. During the same time period, the economy created more than 22 million new jobs, an average of 255,000 per month, compared to 52,000 per month under Bush and 167,000 per month under Reagan. The **stock market** experienced its greatest run ever, making hundreds of millions of dollars for some of the initial investors in several **high-technology** firms and hefty gains for a broad base of Americans. Over a year before he stepped down, Clinton proudly announced that the economic expansion was the longest in history.

Perhaps the most significant achievement of the economy during the Clinton presidency was an improvement in productivity, upon which an increase in the standard of living depends. Historically the United States had enjoyed about 3 percent real growth, but in the 1970s the rate of growth fell to a snail's pace. As a result, some pundits predicted that members of the generation that came of age in the late 1980s and early 1990s would be the first not to enjoy a better standard of living than their parents. When Clinton left office, he could proudly declare that the economy was beginning to return to its historic rate of improved productivity, averaging about 2.5–3 percent per year (see Table 7). One byproduct of this was that the real wages of average workers, rather than just the incomes of the wealthy, improved. After declining 4.3 percent during the Reagan and Bush presidencies, real wages rose 6.5 percent between 1994 and 2000. About the only negative news was that the **trade deficit** remained high and the personal savings rate low. Yet dire warnings that the relaxation of trade restrictions would produce a massive loss of jobs to foreign countries proved wrong—**H. Ross Perot** and Pat Buchanan, a prominent conservative spokesperson and candidate for the presidency, in particular, lambasted free trade as a threat to American jobs.

Indeed, the performance of the economy was so amazing during Clinton's presidency that few Republicans tried to shift the nation's attention to other subjects in the **election of 1996** and the **election of 2000**. Instead, they questioned how much credit Clinton deserved for the economic growth of the 1990s. An alternative explanation for the economic expansion lay, they argued, with the wise leadership of Federal Reserve Board Chairman **Alan Greenspan**, whom Ronald Reagan originally nominated in 1987, and with the probusiness policies instituted by Reagan himself. In addition, Clinton's critics tended to credit the policies pursued by the Republican-controlled Congress, which limited the growth of government and cut capital-gains taxes, for the decline in the federal

Figure 4
Economic Growth Rate, 1970–1999

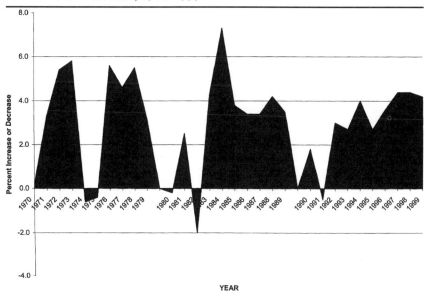

Source: *Economic Report of the President, 2000.*

Figure 5
Comparative Economic Growth Rate, United States and Other Industrial Nations

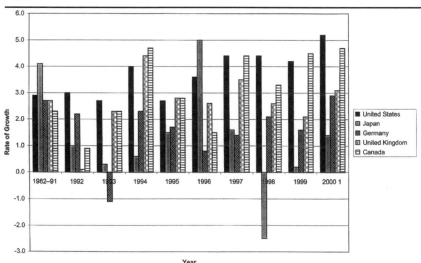

Source: *Economic Report of the President, 2000.*

Figure 6
Unemployment Rate

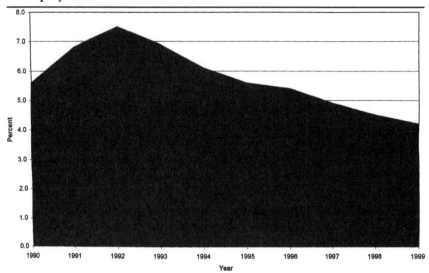

Source: *Economic Report of the President, 2000*.

Figure 7
Productivity, 1970–1999

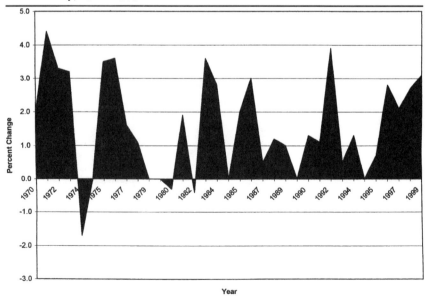

Source: *Economic Report of the President, 2000*.

Figure 8
Real Gross Domestic Product

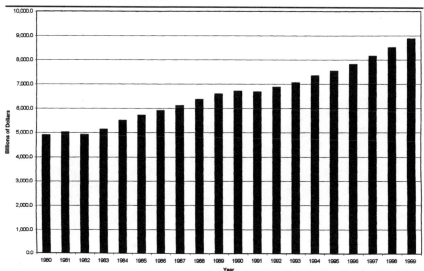

Source: Economic Report of the President, 2000.

budget deficit and the rise in corporate profits, productivity, and the
stock market.

While Clinton and his supporters heralded Greenspan for his adept
managing of the money supply (Clinton renominated him twice) and
agreed that the nation was experiencing a technological revolution, they
insisted that the economic expansion of the Clinton years was no coin-
cidence. Rather, they emphasized that the domestic policies pursued by
the administration in 1993, without Republican support, showed Greenspan and the financial markets that the Clinton administration was ear-
nest about cutting the federal budget deficit. This allowed Greenspan to
keep interest rates low and encouraged businesses to invest in new plants
and technologies. The administration's support for **education**, high technology, job training, and targeted tax cuts reinforced the financial community's trust of Clinton. His nomination and appointment of respected
businessmen and economists, especially **Robert Rubin**, the former head
of Goldman Sachs, augmented Clinton's reputation as a sound economic
leader. In fact, Clinton turned the tables in 1996, arguing that the sharp
tax cut proposed by Republican presidential candidate **Robert Dole**
risked increasing the deficit and stalling the economic expansion. As the

Table 7
Economic Indicators

Year	GDP (Billions of Dollars)	Real Rate of Growth	Civilian Labor Force (1,000s)	Productivity Percentage Increase	Inflation Rate	NYSE Index[†]
1990	5,803.2	1.8	125,840	1.3	6.1	183.46
1991	5,986.2	−0.5	126,346	1.1	3.1	206.33
1992	6,318.9	3.0	128,105	3.9	2.9	229.01
1993	6,642.3	2.7	129,200	.5	2.7	249.58
1994	7,054.3	4.0	131,056	1.3	2.7	254.12
1995	7,400.5	2.7	132,304	.7	2.5	291.15
1996	7,813.2	3.6	133,943	2.8	3.3	358.17
1997	8,318.4	4.4	136,927	2.1	1.7	456.54
1998	8,790.2	4.4	137,673	2.7	1.6	550.26
1999	9,299.2	4.2	139,368	4.2	2.7	619.16
2000	9,937.3*	3.6*	140,827*	5.3*	3.2*	645.5*

* Second quarter 2000.
† The New York Stock Exchange Composite Index includes all the stocks (more than 3,000) listed on the NYSE. December 31, 1965 = 100. It provides a broader gauge of the stock market than the Dow Jones average or the S&P but does not include many high-tech stocks traded on the NASDAQ or over the counter.

Source: Council of Economic Advisers, *Economic Report of the President, 2001* (Washington, DC: GPO, 2001).

election results of 1996 and public opinion polls revealed, the public retained great confidence in Clinton's handling of the economy.

Suggested Readings: Council of Economic Advisers, *Economic Report of the President, 2001* (Washington, DC: GPO, 2001); "Credit for Clintonomics," *Christian Science Monitor*, August 15, 2000, p. 10; http://www.access.gpo.gov/congress/ eibrowse/00julbro.html; http://www.whitehouse.gov/WH/Accomplishments/ econrecord.html; Richard Stevenson, "Roots of Prosperity Reach Past Clinton Years," *New York Times*, October 9, 2000, p. A14.

Related Entry: Domestic Policy.

EDUCATION. Particularly during his second term as president, Bill Clinton made enhancing education one of his top priorities. Most notably, the administration devised programs to help working- and middle-class families pay for college education. The **HOPE Scholarships** provided families up to $1,500 in tax credits per year for students to attend the first two years of college. Educational individual retirement accounts

(IRAs) allowed families and individuals to withdraw money from retirement accounts tax free to pay for higher education. Early during his presidency, Clinton fought for the expansion of Pell Grants (a federally funded program to help pay for college) and work-study programs. As a result, by the year 2000, four million students were eligible to receive $3,300 in federal aid. The administration established a direct loan program for students, instead of indirect federally guaranteed loans. In the areas of primary and secondary education, President Clinton called for federal programs that would help reduce class size and link all schools to the Internet. While the Republican-controlled Congress did not enact all of these programs, it did appropriate over $750 million for an education technology fund in fiscal year 2000, up from $23 million in 1993. The Clinton administration had less trouble convincing Congress to support **Head Start**, which saw its funding grow 90 percent between 1993 and 2000.

Even before Clinton ran for office, numerous Americans called for raising standards in the schools. In 1993, the Clinton administration backed these calls by prodding states and educators in the United States to adopt "Goals 2000," a comprehensive plan for education reform. Congress passed "Goals 2000: Educate America" in 1994, but it watered down the president's original proposal to make sure that the national government could not compel state and local governments to comply with federal standards. To help resuscitate failing schools in poor school districts, Clinton supported public charter schools, which grew in number from 1 in 1993 to 1,200 in 1998. Charter schools were individual public schools that were granted relative autonomy from larger bureaucracies and rules. Not usually attached to a single school district, they provided a degree of choice to students. At the same time, Clinton remained an opponent of school vouchers, an approach favored by many conservatives to improve schools. Like other opponents of school vouchers, Clinton worried that vouchers would hurt students left in the public schools and not provide enough accountability by the institutions that received funds through voucher programs. Clinton also continued to support taking race into consideration as a factor in admission to colleges and universities, in other words, **affirmative action**, in spite of several prominent efforts to make affirmative action illegal.

As a governor, Clinton gained a reputation as an educational reformer, and as president, he placed education toward the top of the political agenda. During the 2000 presidential campaign, both Vice President **Al Gore** and Texas governor **George W. Bush** pledged to improve education if elected. On one level, Bush's focus on education displayed the degree to which Clinton had helped transform the political scene, making federal initiatives to make college more affordable and improve education for students in elementary, middle, and high schools a position that both parties championed. On another level, the amount of attention paid to education suggested an implicit critique of the achievements of Clinton in the field of education on the one hand, and on the other, that he had not accomplished as much as he would have liked because of Republican opposition in Congress. Put somewhat differently, while Clinton hinted at times that he would like to be remembered as the educational president, he departed office with education at the top of the political agenda but with many still seeing much room for improvement in the schools.

Suggested Readings: Jeffrey Brainard, Stephen Burd, and Ben Gore, "The Clinton Legacy in Higher Education," *Chronicle of Higher Education*, December 15, 2000, p. A27; "A Nation Transformed: Education," http://clinton3.nara.gov/WH/ Accomplishments/education.html; "National Educational Goals Set," *Congressional Quarterly Almanac*, 1994, p. 397; "Statement by Gerald N. Tirozzi on Charter Schools," April 9, 1997, http://www.ed.gov/Speeches/04-1997/970409.html.

ELDERS, JOYCELYN. (August 13, 1933, Schaal, Arkansas– .) Surgeon General of the United States, 1993–1994.

Joycelyn Elders was the first **African American** woman to serve as surgeon general of the United States. She was forced to resign fifteen months after taking office because of controversial statements she made regarding sex education. Following her firing, the United States went without a surgeon general for several years.

Elders was born, raised, and educated in Arkansas. She received her B.A. in biology from Philander Smith College and her M.D. from the University of Arkansas Medical School in 1960. In between, she worked briefly as a nurse and then as a physical therapist for the U.S. Army. She became a well-known pediatrician and educator. An expert on childhood sexual development, Elders was promoted to full professor at the University of Arkansas Medical Center in 1976.

In 1987, Governor Bill Clinton appointed Elders director of the Arkansas Department of Health. In 1993, she became the surgeon general of the United States. She supported the administration's **health care reform** plan. Conservatives often criticized Elders for her controversial views, especially her forthright advocacy of sex education in the schools, aimed, in part, at decreasing teenage pregnancy and AIDS. At a World

AIDS Day conference in New York City, Elders was asked about the like-lihood of a more "explicit discussion and promotion of masturbation." Elders responded that she favored early comprehensive health or sex education. She added that insofar as masturbation was "something that is part of human sexuality . . . perhaps [it] should be taught." Conservatives jumped on the remark, claiming that Elders favored teaching children how to masturbate. Upon hearing reports of the controversy, Clinton demanded Elders's resignation. Even though Elders explained that she did not mean to advocate that students be taught how to masturbate, she agreed to step down because of the damage she was doing to the Clinton administration and the health care plan. Numerous African Americans and medical professionals came to Elders's defense, but President Clinton was unwilling to risk political capital to keep her as surgeon general.

Suggested Readings: "Clinton Fires Elders after Latest Gaffe," *St. Louis Post-Dispatch*, December 10, 1994, p. 1A; http://www.osophs.dhhs.gov/library/history/bioelders.htm.

ELECTION OF 1992. The campaign for the presidency in 1992 was one of the strangest in modern history. Following the Persian Gulf War, **George Bush**'s public approval ratings reached new highs, leading most political pundits to predict that he would easily win reelection in 1992. Bush's chances seemed so good that many Democrats who were expected to seek the presidency, from New York governor Mario Cuomo to New Jersey senator Bill Bradley, chose not to run. By the summer of 1992, as the recession lingered and public anger grew over political gridlock in Washington, D.C., however, Bush's public approval rating fell and the chances of his contenders rose.

By the summer of 1992, Bill Clinton, the youngest governor in Arkansas history, had sewn up the Democratic nomination. Steering a middle course, Clinton outmaneuvered his rivals in the primaries, most notably former Massachusetts senator **Paul Tsongas** and former California governor Jerry Brown. Just as important, Clinton secured the Democratic Party's nomination without antagonizing many of its traditional constituencies. As a result, Clinton encountered a united party at the Democratic convention. In contrast, the Republican Party took on characteristics generally associated with the Democrats. Bush had to beat back a primary challenge from the pugnacious Pat Buchanan. To counter Buchanan's courtship of the right wing of the party, Bush endorsed extremely con-

Democratic presidential candidate Clinton and Hillary acknowledge victory of the party's presidential nomination, 1992. AP/Wide World Photos.

servative platform pledges on abortion and other social issues. Unlike Ronald Reagan's carefully orchestrated and upbeat campaigns of the 1980s, Bush's campaign was shrill and disorganized.

However, it was not simply Democratic unity and Republican infighting that made 1992 so unusual. Rather, it was **H. Ross Perot**'s independent or third-party campaign that made the race for the presidency so different. A billionaire from Texas with a homespun look and populist message, Perot attracted voters from both parties who were disillusioned with politics as usual. He also energized Americans who usually did not take an active interest in politics. His popularity soared in the spring and summer of 1992, but he shocked even many of his closest supporters by withdrawing from the race following Clinton's nomination in July. Unpredictable and irascible to the end, Perot rejoined the race in early October, mounting a furious campaign filled with lengthy "infomercials" paid for with his own funds. Perot gained further exposure during a series of presidential debates with both Bush and Clinton. Performing

Table 8
Election Results of 1992

Candidate and Party	Popular Vote	Percentage	Electoral College
Bill Clinton (Dem.)	44,909,326	43.0	370
George Bush (Rep.)	39,103,882	37.4	168
Ross Perot (Ind.)	19,741,657	18.9	
Other	670,149	0.7	

Source: America Votes 20: 1992 (Chevy Chase, MD: Election Research Center, 1993), pp. 6–9.

admirably, he regained much of the support he had held earlier in the summer.

In the end, however, Perot's third-party candidacy, like others before it, failed. While he garnered nearly 19 percent of the popular vote, he did not win a single vote in the electoral college. Clinton, who maintained his focus and drive until the final day of the campaign, easily gained a majority of the electoral college vote, even though he won only 43 percent of the popular vote. Throughout the summer, Clinton had charmed voters with his charisma and oratorical skills, especially at the Democratic convention and during the presidential debates. Bush won just 38 percent of the popular vote, one of the worst showings by an incumbent or a Republican presidential candidate ever (Table 8). At the same time, the Democrats maintained control of both houses of Congress, leading many to argue that the public had turned against the policies of the Reagan-Bush years. Clinton's relatively small proportion of the popular vote and Perot's popularity, however, suggested that this view was insufficiently supported by evidence.

In addition, the campaign revealed a theme that would characterize the Clinton presidency. On the eve of the first presidential primary in New Hampshire, **Gennifer Flowers**, a former television reporter, nightclub singer, and Arkansas state employee, alleged that she had had a long-term sexual affair with Bill Clinton. Flowers's story, which she sold to the *Star*, a supermarket tabloid, threatened to end Clinton's campaign even before it really got started. To save his run for the White House, Bill and **Hillary Clinton** appeared on the television news show *60 Minutes*, where they admitted that their marriage had encountered its tests. Viewers could read between the lines on that. Nonetheless, Hillary vouched for their marriage, and the public, seemingly reassured, did not turn on him. Nonetheless, the seeds of viewing Clinton as a flawed character were planted and would not disappear over the course of the next eight years.

Suggested Readings: *America Votes 20: 1992* (Chevy Chase, MD: Election Research Center, 1993), pp. 6–9; Jack W. Germond and Jules Witcover, *Mad as Hell: Revolt at the Ballot Box, 1992* (New York: Warner Books, 1993); John F. Hale, "The Making of the New Democrats," *Political Science Quarterly* 110:2 (Summer 1995), p. 207; Mary Matalin and James Carville, *All's Fair: Love, War, and Running for President* (New York: Random House, 1994); Gerald M. Pomper, Walter D. Burnham, et al., *The Election of 1992* (New York: Seven Bridges Press, 1993).

ELECTION OF 1994. The election of 1994 was one of the most significant off-year elections of modern times. Prior to the election, 300 Republican candidates for Congress, some of them incumbents and some challengers, endorsed the **"Contract with America,"** a document developed by Republican congressman **Newt Gingrich** of Georgia. The contract listed ten specific promises that the signees pledged to promote if elected. In general, the contract represented a sharp criticism of the Clinton administration and an endorsement of an assortment of New Right views. For instance, the contract promised to repeal the tax hikes that had been part of President Clinton's **budget**-reduction package, as well as **gun-control** measures passed in Clinton's first two years in office. Republican Party candidates also tapped into the anti-Washington, anti-big-government sentiment that had been growing for some time and had become particularly pronounced in the wake of the defeat of President Clinton's national **health care reform** plan.

On election day, the Republicans pulled an amazing upset, taking control of both houses of Congress for the first time since 1946. The swing in the **House of Representatives** was especially large, as the Republican Party picked up fifty-four seats. Moreover, whereas Republicans held on to the majority they won in the election of 1952 for only two years, this time they remained in control of both houses of Congress for the rest of the decade. Long- and short-term factors accounted for the Republican sweep of both houses of Congress. For years, the Republican Party had been making steady gains in the South, once a bastion of the Democratic Party. In 1994, the Republican Party coupled its gains in the South with a backlash against Clinton among moderate suburban voters in the North. Low voter turnout among many traditional Democratic Party voters also helped the Republicans.

After the election, Newt Gingrich became the Speaker of the House and **Robert Dole** the majority leader of the **U.S. Senate**. Not only did the Democratic Party lose control of Congress, several of its better-known members were defeated at the polls. Most notably, Thomas Foley, the Speaker of the House, lost to George Nethercutt, becoming the first incumbent Speaker to lose in a bid to be reelected since 1862. On the Senate side, Harris Wofford, who had won a special election in 1991 and had helped usher in the cry for health care reform, lost to Rick Santorum, a young, conservative Republican who in many ways epitomized the class of 1994, the name given to the young rebels who swept into office in the election. About the only solace the Democrats could draw from the election was that Virginia's incumbent senator, Charles Robb, managed to beat back a challenge by Oliver North, a Reagan aide who had become a hero to ultraconservatives during and after the Iran-contra affair. So complete was the Democrats' defeat that some called Clinton irrelevant and predicted his imminent defeat in 1996.

Suggested Readings: "Rare Combination of Forces Make '94 Vote Historic," *Congressional Quarterly Almanac*, 1994, p. 561; Lee Edwards, *The Conservative Revolution* (New York: Free Press, 1999).

ELECTION OF 1996. In the wake of the off-year **election of 1994**, in which the Republican Party won control of both houses of Congress, many political pundits predicted that Bill Clinton, like **George Bush** and Jimmy Carter, would be a one-term president. Instead, in November 1996, Bill Clinton became the first Democrat to seek and win a second term as president since Franklin D. Roosevelt. He stood alongside Woodrow Wilson and Franklin D. Roosevelt as the only Democrats to be elected to the presidency in two consecutive elections since Andrew Jackson. Clinton not only was reelected, he won convincingly. In 1992, only 43 percent of the electorate voted for Clinton. If it had not been for **H. Ross Perot**, who won nearly 19 percent of the vote, George Bush might have narrowly defeated Clinton. In contrast, in 1996, with Perot in the race once again, Clinton won 49 percent of the popular vote and crushed his Republican opponent, **Robert Dole**, in the electoral college count, 379 to 159 (Table 9). Perot failed to win any electoral college votes in either 1992 or 1996.

Clinton's victory, which reinforced his reputation as the "comeback kid," rested on several developments. The conservative wing of the Republican Party, led by **Newt Gingrich**, overestimated its popularity. While its victory in 1994 suggested that voters had grown tired of liberalism,

Table 9
Election Results of 1996

Candidate and Party	Popular Vote	Percentage	Electoral College Vote
Bill Clinton (Dem.)	47,402,357	49.2	379
Robert Dole (Rep.)	39,198,755	40.7	159
H. Ross Perot (Reform)	8,085,402	8.4	0

Source: Richard M. Scammon, Alice V. McGillivry, Richard Cook, *American Votes 22, 1996* (Washington, D.C.: Congressional Quarterly, Inc., 1998), pp. 8–9.

the Republicans also owed their success in 1994 to the failure of the Democratic Party to get its base to the polls on election day. Only 36.6 percent of eligible voters cast ballots in the 1994 congressional elections. By galvanizing his political base, Clinton enhanced his ability to win re-election in 1996. The first sign that Clinton could do this came in late 1995 and early 1996 when battles over the **budget** produced two **government shutdowns**. By convincing the American public that conservatives in Congress, especially Gingrich, were responsible for the shutdowns, Clinton reestablished momentum in the ongoing battle for the backing of the electorate.

At about the same time, Clinton adopted an election strategy known as "triangulation." Largely the brainchild of **Dick Morris**, a prominent political consultant who had helped save Clinton's career in 1982, triangulation called for Clinton to co-opt certain traditional Republican wedge issues while at the same time standing firm against other, less popular Republican measures. Hence Clinton supported **welfare reform** and anticrime legislation while simultaneously defending Medicare, the **environment**, and an assortment of programs aimed at helping disadvantaged children from alleged Republican attacks. This strategy enhanced Clinton's appeal to the broad political middle, particularly suburban **women**, without sacrificing the allegiance of the Democratic Party's traditional base.

Clinton also owed his reelection to the growth of the **economy** and the decline of the federal budget deficit. Early in his first term, he had made a decision to focus on these issues at the expense of tax cuts that he had promised on the campaign trail. During the 1996 campaign, he pointed out that in the areas of job creation and deficit reduction, his administration had surpassed its lofty goals. The reduction of the deficit, in particular, allowed Clinton to win the support of many who had voted for H. Ross Perot in 1992. When Bob Dole sought to galvanize voters by promising a substantial tax cut, Clinton countered that cutting taxes would jeopardize the economy's recovery, which depended on deficit reduction and low **inflation** and interest rates. Unable to increase his appeal via his promise to cut taxes, in the waning weeks of the campaign Dole returned to the theme of morality, long one of Clinton's weaknesses. Revelations about possible campaign finance violations on the part of the Democratic Party, coupled with the ongoing **Whitewater** investigation, allowed Dole to slightly improve his showing in the public opinion polls, but by the last weeks of the campaign, he was simply too far back to overcome Clinton's lead.

On one hand, Clinton's victory was quite impressive and suggested that he had remade the Democratic Party into a winner, following a string of defeats in presidential elections stretching back to 1968. (Jimmy Carter won in 1976 largely due to Watergate.) A glance at the electoral college map displayed Clinton's achievement. By winning eight of the ten largest states, including California by a wide margin, Clinton established a recipe for keeping the White House out of Republican hands. At the same time, Clinton made important inroads in the South, winning Florida, Arkansas, Tennessee, and Louisiana. On the other hand, while Clinton won the White House, Republicans remained the majority party in both houses of Congress, leaving many to wonder if Clinton's own skills as a politician actually helped or hindered his party.

Suggested Readings: Jonathan Alter, "Thinking of Family Values," *Newsweek*, December 30, 1996, p. 30; R. W. Apple, Jr., "The 1996 Elections: The Presidency— The Outlook," *New York Times*, November 7, 1996, p. B6; Evan Thomas, *Back from the Dead: How Clinton Survived the Republican Revolution* (New York: Atlantic Monthly Press, 1997); C. Wilcox, "The Election of 1996: Reports and Interpretations," *Public Opinion Quarterly* 63:2 (Summer 1999), p. 285.

ELECTION OF 2000. The 2000 presidential election was one of the most memorable in history. Although it started in a fairly predictable fashion, with the two front-runners beating back challengers without a great degree of difficulty, it ended in a manner not seen since the election of 1876. (In 1876, Tilden appeared the winner over Hayes on election night. But when the electoral college votes from five states not originally included in the total were added to Hayes's total, Hayes was declared the victor.) When election night came to an end, the vote was too close to determine a winner. For over a month, the two main candidates, **Al Gore**

and **George W. Bush**, engaged in a heated battle over the right to lay claim to Florida's 25 electoral college votes. Even though Gore won the popular vote nationwide by about 500,000, Florida's electoral college votes were the difference between winning the presidency for both Bush and Gore (Tables 10 and 11). Not until December 13, after the U.S. **Supreme Court** halted a recount of the vote in Florida, which the Florida Supreme Court had approved in response to a suit by the Gore campaign, did Gore concede and Bush deliver his victory address.

The 2000 election was memorable for several other reasons. The Republican Party narrowly held on to its majority in the **U.S. House of Representatives**, but the **U.S. Senate**, for one of the few times in its history, ended up in a tie. Technically, since the vice president, who would be a Republican, would cast the tie-breaking vote, the Republicans maintained control of the Senate, but the equal division of senators between the two major parties was unusual, nonetheless. Just as notably,

Table 10
2000 Presidential Election: National Results

Candidate (and Party)	Popular Votes	Percentage	Electoral College
Al Gore (Democrat)	50,996,064	48.39	266
George Bush (Republican)	50,456,167	47.88	271
Ralph Nader (Green)	2,864,810	2.72	
Pat Buchanan (Reform)	448,750	0.43	
Harry Brown (Libertarian)	386,024	0.37	

Source: Washington Post, December 21, 2000.

Table 11
2000 Presidential Election: Florida Results*

Candidate	Popular Votes	Percentage	Electoral College
George Bush	2,912,790	49	25
Al Gore	2,912,488	49	
Ralph Nader	97,488	2	
Pat Buchanan	17,484	0	

Source: Washington Post, December 21, 2000.

* These were the vote counts when the recount was ordered stopped by the U.S. Supreme Court. Subsequent recounts by the *Miami Herald* and others showed Bush or Gore winning, depending on the standard used to recount the ballots.

one of the newly elected members of the Senate was First Lady **Hillary Clinton**. She won a closely watched race to represent the state of New York, becoming the first first lady to be elected to public office in U.S. history. What the election meant in terms of Bill Clinton's legacy remained unclear.

Even before the first presidential primary in New Hampshire, Texas governor George W. Bush, the son of former president **George Bush**, established himself as the clear front-runner for the Republican nomination. Amassing an enormous campaign treasury, building on his father's political connections, and positioning himself as a centrist within the Republican Party, Bush established a significant lead in the public opinion polls. Other contenders for the Republican nomination, former vice president Dan Quayle, millionaire Steve Forbes, conservative spokesman Gary Bauer, and Elizabeth Dole, a former cabinet member and the wife of **Robert Dole**, the Republican nominee in 1996, either dropped out before the first primary or shortly afterwards. This left only Arizona senator John McCain, a **Vietnam** War hero and champion of **campaign finance reform**, and conservative radio host Alan Keyes to challenge Bush, who cast himself as the inevitable nominee and the best man to run against Al Gore, the presumed candidate of the Democratic Party. McCain scored an upset over Bush in the New Hampshire primary and for a brief moment appeared poised to unravel Bush's aura as the inevitable nominee, but Bush rallied the conservative base of the Republican Party in the days leading up to the South Carolina primary and effectively utilized his resources to turn back McCain's challenge and cruise into the Republican convention as the party's nominee. Al Gore faced a somewhat similar situation. As the standing vice-president, he was the clear favorite to capture the Democratic nomination. He faced a brief but somewhat poignant challenge from former New Jersey senator Bill Bradley, a one-time Rhodes scholar and NBA basketball player. While Gore avoided an upset, Bradley raised questions about Gore's credibility that never fully disappeared.

George W. Bush selected Dick Cheney, who had served as his father's secretary of defense, to be his running mate. The two effectively used the Republican convention to bounce into a sizeable lead in the public opinion polls. The party's nominees homed in on several key issues or weaknesses on Gore's part. Not surprisingly, they sought to link Gore to Clinton's poor character reputation. A bit more surprisingly, Bush and Cheney criticized the Clinton-Gore administration for not reforming

Social Security and for its failure to provide leadership on an assortment of other social issues. Bush also pledged sweeping tax cuts, arguing that the public deserved to get most of the federal **budget** surplus back.

The Democratic convention began with Bill Clinton delivering a vintage address in which he forcefully summarized the accomplishments of the Clinton-Gore administration. Afterward, however, Gore and his running mate, Connecticut senator Joe Lieberman, did their best to distance themselves from the president and to establish that Clinton's personal reputation had nothing to do with Gore's own character. By adding Lieberman to the ticket, Gore also hoped to emphasize the Democratic Party's diversity and historical links to immigrants and the downtrodden. (Lieberman was the first Jewish person to be nominated as vice president.) Gore also broke with the centrist strategy Clinton had employed in 1996 to defeat Bob Dole. Instead, Gore cast himself as a family man and promised to "fight" for America's working men and women, which was a traditional Democratic approach. More specifically, Gore opposed Bush's tax plan and pledged to use the predicted federal budget surplus to save Social Security, establish a prescription drug plan, and increase federal spending for **education**.

The Democratic convention gave Gore a big boost. Yet Bush recovered, in part by performing much better than expected in the three presidential debates the two held. Bush also did an effective job of rallying conservative Republican activists around his candidacy, something his father had failed to do in 1992. At the same time, Bush reached out to moderate voters by promising to improve education, develop a prescription-drug plan of his own, and reform (not end) Social Security. Indeed, about two weeks before the election, Bush appeared to have built a comfortable lead. A last-minute revelation that Bush had once been arrested for drunk driving may have cost him some votes. In addition, the Democratic Party was extremely effective at getting out the vote in key regions of the country on election day. Hence, as the early returns rolled in, Gore appeared victorious. The major television networks declared Gore the winner in several key battleground states, of which the most important were Florida, Pennsylvania, Michigan, Missouri, Minnesota, and Wisconsin.

Then, however, the television stations withdrew their prediction that Gore had upset Bush in Florida. With Florida's 25 electoral college votes, Gore's election appeared inevitable. Without them, Bush began to surmount Gore's lead by sweeping the Plains states and the South. When the networks put Florida's electoral college votes in Bush's column, Gore conceded over the telephone to Bush, but while he was preparing to deliver his concession speech, he was alerted by a campaign aide that Florida was still too close to call. Thus he called Bush back and withdrew his concession, and the month-long battle to claim Florida's vote began. The fight for Florida's votes was complicated by the fact that Jeb Bush, George's brother, was the governor of Florida, and that Florida's secretary of state, who was responsible for certifying the vote, had played a key role in Bush's campaign.

Entire books will be written about the battle for Florida's 25 electoral college votes. It suffices to say that the Gore campaign challenged the results and convinced the Florida Supreme Court to order a recount of the vote. Many presumed that a hand recount would result in a Gore victory in the state. The Bush team, in contrast, argued in federal court that such a hand recount violated federal law, since the different countries that were conducting hand counts did not hold to a single standard, especially when it came to counting punch-card ballots used in some counties. The ending itself, a dramatic U.S. Supreme Court split decision to halt the recount, which many saw as politically motivated, left many wondering whether the nation could overcome the electoral conflict. Remarkably, there was some evidence that the post-election-day dispute strengthened the nation. The tightness of the race was a lesson in the importance of voting. The ability of the nation to resolve the crisis peacefully, even if many were disappointed, cemented the reputation of the United States as a nation that has faith in the electoral process and does not resort to extralegal means to choose its leaders.

Without a doubt, the full meaning and impact of the election was still to be determined. While many Democrats felt cheated by the Supreme Court's decision (first to stay the recount in Florida and then to halt it), several other factors contributed to Gore's defeat. Even though he won the plurality of the popular vote, Gore lost his home state of Tennessee. If he had won Tennessee, he would not have needed to win in Florida. Gore was also hurt by third-party candidate Ralph Nader. Nader appealed to a core of disaffected liberals who felt that Clinton and Gore had deserted the ideals of the Democratic Party. In Florida, for example, Nader won nearly 100,000 votes. If Gore had won these votes, he easily would have defeated George W. Bush. In contrast, the Republican Party, which had lost some of its core voters to **H. Ross Perot** in 1992 and 1996, convinced disaffected members of its base to stay home rather than desert to the Reform Party candidate, Pat Buchanan.

Suggested Readings: http://washingtonpost.com/wp-dyn/politics/elections/; Gerald M. Pomper, ed., *The Election of 2000: Reports and Interpretations* (New York: Seven Bridges Press, LLC, 2001).

EMANUEL, RAHM. (1959, Chicago–   .) Presidential adviser, 1993–1999.

Known for his abrasive style and centrist politics, Rahm Emanuel often butted heads with better-known advisers of Bill Clinton. Yet he outlasted many of them and over the course of Clinton's tenure became one of the president's closest and must trusted advisers. Emanuel helped shape the president's reelection strategy in 1996 and his reaction to the **impeachment** scandal. The successful outcome of both battles contributed to Emanuel's reputation as a powerful and pragmatic Washington insider.

The son of a Palestine-born Jew who secretly aided Menachem Begin's underground movement to establish the state of Israel, Rahm Emanuel was born in Chicago in 1959. As a child he traveled to Israel every summer, trained as a ballet dancer, and debated politics at the dinner table. (In 1991, during the Persian Gulf War, he briefly served on an Israeli army base.) Emanuel graduated from Sarah Lawrence College in 1981, where he got his first direct experience in politics, working for congressional candidate David Robinson. After earning an M.A. in speech and communications from Northwestern University in 1985, Emanuel worked for the Democratic Congressional Campaign Committee and established his own political consulting firm. He joined the Clinton campaign team in late 1991, focusing much of his time on fund-raising. After the election, Emanuel was put in charge of organizing the inaugural celebrations and then became the president's political director.

Partly due to clashes he had with **Susan Thomases**, a close aide to **Hillary Clinton**, Emanuel's clout within the White House declined, and some suggested that he should go to work for the Democratic Party. Instead, Emanuel persevered. After a stint as director of special projects, which included winning passage of **NAFTA** and the **Brady bill**, Emanuel moved to the communications office. In 1997, he assumed **George Stephanopoulos**'s post as senior adviser to the president. He was one of the last members of the so-called war room (a political strategy group) to be still part of the Clinton team. In 1999, Emanuel left the White House to work on Wall Street as an investment banker. While some criticized him for "cashing in" on his Washington connections—he had no experience as an investment banker—Emanuel's reputation was otherwise unscathed. Unlike many other administration members, he was not associated with any of the major scandals that plagued Clinton's presidency.

Suggested Readings: *Current Biography Yearbook*, 1998, pp. 180–83; *New York Times Magazine*, June 15, 1997, p. 23; John Harris, "Fond Farewell to an Original Clinton Warrior," *Washington Post*, October 16, 1998, p. A6.

Related Entries: Domestic Policy; Election of 1992.

EMPOWERMENT ZONES. In his first year in office, President Bill Clinton won substantial federal funding, $3.5 billion over five years, to help rebuild selected impoverished urban and rural zones or regions. Specifically, the **House** and **Senate** passed measures, which Clinton signed into law, that offered $2.5 billion in tax incentives and $1 billion in block grants to nine communities. An additional ninety-five communities were eligible for lesser benefits. The urban and rural zones that received the bulk of the funds, $100 million per zone, did so based on the soundness of the strategic plans they submitted to the government. The city of Baltimore, for example, was awarded a $100-million urban revitalization grant. Baltimore's strategic plan called for aiding three specific neighborhoods. In south Baltimore, government grants were to be used to create an "eco-industrial park," in which the "wastes of one company would be used as the raw materials of another" on the site of a former public housing project. The other cities to receive block grants were Atlanta, Chicago, Detroit, New York, and Philadelphia-Camden. In addition to the block grants, businesses were eligible for sizable tax credits if they employed people who lived in the zones.

Empowerment zones had their origins in the enterprise zones that were created in 1987 during the Reagan administration. Discussed as a possible means for sparking urban revitalization since 1982, these enterprise zones offered tax and regulatory relief to business that invested in the inner city or depressed rural communities. **Jack Kemp**, the secretary of housing and urban development under President **George Bush**, championed expanding the program, but in 1992, President Bush vetoed a bill that would have done this. Meanwhile, several states followed the federal lead, offering a variety of incentives to help revitalize U.S. cities. As a candidate for the presidency, Bill Clinton promised to do more.

In 1999, Congress approved a second round of funding, $3.8 billion, for an additional twenty empowerment zones. Cities that received block grants under this round of funding included Boston, Cincinnati, Miami, and St. Louis. The second round of funding authorized communities to issue $130 million in tax-exempt bonds over ten years and provide tax incentives to clean up contaminated industrial sites, retrain workers, and purchase new machinery. The funding also allowed state and local governments to issue bonds to enable schools to meet curricular and physical needs.

The creation of new empowerment zones in 1999 indicated a general agreement that the Clinton administration's approach to revitalizing distressed urban and rural areas was sound. Studies of the communities that won funding in 1993–1994 revealed gains, such as an increase in home-ownership rates and the retention of small business. However, these studies also showed that the empowerment zones failed to live up to some of the specific goals outlined in the strategic plans, not to mention the hyperbole that tended to greet the announcements of the initial awards. For instance, Baltimore abandoned the goal of creating an eco-industrial park.

Suggested Readings: Renee Berger, "People, Power, Politics," *Planning* 63:2 (February 1997), p. 4; "Congress Votes to Create Enterprise Zones," *Congressional Quarterly Almanac*, 1993, p. 422; "Renewal Efforts Move at a Slow Pace," *Baltimore Sun*, January 1, 2000, p. 1; "Vice President Gore Announces 10 New Empowerment Zones," January 13, 1999, http://rurdev.usda.gov/rd/newsroom/ezec.htm.

ENVIRONMENT. Many environmental groups saw the environmental record of the Ronald Reagan and **George Bush** administrations as a disaster. Beginning with James Watts, Reagan's secretary of the interior, the Republicans had demonstrated that they would favor business interests over environmental concerns. During the 1992 presidential campaign, George Bush argued that Bill Clinton's environmental position would cost Americans jobs, particularly in the Northwest, where battles between loggers and environmentalists had been taking place for years. In spite of the economic recession of the early 1990s, Clinton pledged to enforce the Endangered Species Act, which limited logging in the West. Clinton's selection of **Al Gore** as his running mate solidified the support the Democrats received from environmental groups because Gore had a strong record on environmentalism as a senator.

By nominating **Bruce Babbitt** of Arizona to serve as his secretary of the interior, President Clinton signaled his commitment to reversing the environmental neglect of the Reagan-Bush years. Babbitt, who grew up in rural Arizona, had a reputation as an environmental activist. During his first term as president, Clinton took several actions that further displayed his commitment to protecting and preserving America's natural resources. For instance, through an executive order he created the Grand Staircase-Escalante National Monument in Utah, which set aside 1.7 million acres of canyon land for recreation and limited commercial use. The Clinton administration secured funds to expand existing national parks, most importantly the Florida Everglades, and to help preserve Yellowstone National Park from pollution produced outside the park's boundary. In 1996, the administration prodded Congress to enhance and reauthorize the **Safe Drinking Water Act**. In addition, throughout Clinton's tenure, the Environmental Protection Agency (EPA), under the direction of **Carol M. Browner**, sped up the cleanup of toxic-waste sites, issued strict clean-air rules, and enacted new food-safety laws. Indeed, many conservatives complained vehemently that the EPA's regulations were issued without concern for their costs or impact on the **economy**.

Even though the sustained economic expansion of the 1990s tempered conservative complaints about the environmental actions of the Clinton administration, the president's tendency to compromise and avoid major initiatives on several key environmental concerns paved the way for a degree of dissatisfaction among environmental activists. While the administration issued stricter auto-emissions and air-pollution regulations than had existed under previous administrations, the regulations fell short of the demands of many environmentalists. In addition, sports utility vehicles (SUVs) and small trucks, which boomed in popularity during the 1990s, were largely exempt from federal auto regulations aimed at increasing fuel efficiency. This made it difficult to decrease the overall use of gasoline, one of the leading causes of air pollution. Similarly, while the Clinton administration participated in the international summit on global warning in Kyoto, Japan, in 1997 and pledged to reduce U.S. emissions of gases by 7 percent by the year 2012, it did not win congressional or international support for more dramatic measures aimed at addressing the problem of global warming. Perhaps even more ominously from the perspective of some on the left, the international trade agreements pursued by the Clinton administration encouraged U.S.-based corporations to relocate their factories in developing countries where fundamental environmental regulations either did not exist or were rarely enforced. In the long run, this spelled disaster for the effort to reduce global warming and protect the environment.

In some ways, Clinton was caught in a paradox. Record corporate profits and employment levels undermined conservative complaints that environmental regulations hurt businesses and American workers, but at the same time, cheap oil prices, which contributed to the economic boom of the 1990s, made it easier for more Americans to purchase larger and less efficient automobiles and homes well outside city centers, in exurbia as well as the suburbs. By the end of the 1990s, Americans were more addicted to fossil fuels and the suburban lifestyle than ever before. To a degree, this paradox fueled protests against the World Trade Organization in Seattle, Washington, and the presidential candidacy of Ralph Nader, the famous consumer advocate, who ran as the Green Party candidate in 2000. Even though Nader ultimately won less than 3 percent of the national vote, he won enough votes in select states to deny Gore the presidency. Many of his supporters argued that there was little difference between the two candidates.

In the waning days of his presidency, Bill Clinton issued a slew of new regulations that extended federal protection of the environment. Most important, the administration set aside nearly sixty million acres of forest land in thirty-nine states, the largest set-aside of public lands since Theodore Roosevelt was president in the early 1900s. Environmental groups hailed the action; President-elect **George W. Bush** pledged a thorough review of Clinton's executive orders.

Suggested Readings: "Drinking Water Act Wins Broad Support," *Congressional Quarterly Almanac*, 1996, p. 4-4; John J. Fialka, "Clinton Is Likely to Leave the Presidency with Record of Having Protected Lands," *Wall Street Journal*, Eastern edition, December 29, 2000, p. A18; http://www.epa.gov/globalwarming/home. htm; "A Vision of the 21st Century—Environment Accomplishments," http:// clinton3.nara.gov/CEQ/Accomp.htm.

ESPY, MIKE. (November 30, 1953, Yazoo City, Mississippi–   .) Secretary of Agriculture, 1993–1994.

Mike Espy's nomination and confirmation as secretary of agriculture in 1993 demonstrated the strides southern **African Americans** had made in the latter half of the twentieth century. Reared in the Mississippi Delta during the waning days of Jim Crow, Espy rose to a position of political prominence. His resignation in 1994 in the face of an investigation by the independent counsel's office symbolized the degree to which political controversy and scandals racked the Clinton administration.

Espy was born in the Mississippi Delta, the son of one of the most prominent black families in the region. His father graduated from Tuskegee Institute and established a prosperous funeral-home chain. Unlike most blacks, Espy attended the local Roman Catholic elementary school, which was not segregated, before becoming the first black person to enroll at Yazoo City High School, where he had to defend himself from white attackers. In his senior year, as other blacks enrolled, he was elected the black senior-class president, a post he held in conjunction with the white senior-class president. He earned his B.A. from Howard University in 1975 and a law degree from the University of Santa Clara in 1978. After graduating from law school, he became the first black assistant secretary of agriculture in Mississippi's history. He held a variety of other state government posts over the course of the next few years. In 1985, he was sworn in as the first black assistant state attorney general.

In 1986, in a hard-fought election, Espy defeated Paul Johnson, the grandson of a former Mississippi governor, and Hiram Eastland, the son of archsegregationist Senator James Eastland, to win the Democratic nomination to Congress. Upon defeating his Republican opponent, Espy became the first black to represent Mississippi in Congress since Reconstruction. In spite of attempts to characterize him as a radical leftist, Espy easily won reelection three times. Ironically, he also angered liberal Democrats by opposing **gun-control** legislation and touting his membership in the National Rifle Association. Seeking to meet the needs of his rural constituents, Espy gained a seat on the House Agriculture Committee.

In 1992, Espy was one of the first black elected officials to endorse Bill Clinton for president. His nomination to the post of secretary of agriculture surprised few. Facing tight budgets, Espy ushered in a series of reforms aimed at streamlining the department. As secretary, he fought for stricter food inspection, an expansion of the school-lunch program, and the sale of American food products abroad. In 1994, however, stories appeared in the press claiming that Espy had illegally accepted gifts from a variety of large food-product corporations. An independent counsel was appointed to investigate the charges, and even though he claimed that he was innocent, Espy resigned his post.

In 1998, Espy was acquitted of all thirty charges against him. Not long afterwards, he lambasted independent counsel Donald Smaltz for pursuing the case and wasting taxpayers' money. Smaltz spent an estimated $17 million pursuing the charges. Espy's acquittal lent some weight to those who claimed that charges against numerous Clinton associates had been politically motivated all along.

Suggested Readings: *Current Biography Yearbook*, 1993, pp. 183–86; "Mike Espy Testifies before House Subcommittee on Faults of Independent Counsel Statute," *Jet*, October 18, 1999, p. 22; Bill Miller, "A Harsh Verdict for Espy's Prosecutor," *Washington Post*, December 5, 1998, p. A1.

F

FAMILY AND MEDICAL LEAVE ACT. One of the first bills that President Bill Clinton signed into law (February 5, 1993) was the Family and Medical Leave Act. This measure, which Clinton pledged to support during the 1992 presidential race, provided that employees who had worked for a U.S. employer for a total of twelve months were entitled to take twelve workweeks of unpaid leave during a twelve-month period to care for their natural or adopted child or to care for an immediate family member with a serious health condition. In addition, the Family and Medical Leave Act insured that an employee could take twelve months' unpaid leave due to her or his own serious health condition. In all cases, the employer was required to rehire the employee. Employers were not allowed to penalize workers for taking this leave. All public employers and all private employers with fifty or more employees were covered by the act.

Clinton touted the Family and Medical Leave Act as evidence of his support for family values, one of the primary political issues of the late 1980s and 1990s. Even though both men and **women** were eligible to take family and medical leave, he especially championed the measure among women's rights groups. In addition, Clinton dismissed conservative complaints that the measure constituted one more cumbersome impediment to the profitability of the private sector. Four years after it went into effect, the Department of Labor estimated that about sixty-seven million employees were covered by the measure. Toward the end of his term, Clinton claimed that more than ten million families had taken advantage of the leave to care for a child or loved one. Most studies suggested that the bill did not hamper businesses. At the same time, many employees did not take advantage of the law because they could not afford to take an unpaid leave. To overcome this, President Clinton proposed studying ways for states to provide paid leave for working parents, but no uniform paid-leave program was established during his presidency.

Suggested Readings: "Clinton Wants Funds to Study Paid Leave for Parents," *New York Times*, February 13, 2000, p. 26; Robert B. Hudson and Judith G. Gonyea, "Time Not Yet Money: The Politics and Promise of the Family Medical Leave Act," *Journal of Aging and Social Policy* 11:2/3 (2000), p. 12; U.S. Department of Labor, "Press Release: Labor Department Celebrates FMLA Anniversary," http://www.dol.gov/dol/opa/public/media/press/opa/opa97041.htm; "Clinton Signs Family Leave Act," *Congressional Quarterly Almanac*, 1993, (Washington, D.C.: Congressional Quarterly Almanac, Inc., 1994), p. 389.

FEDERAL BUDGET. *See* **Budget, Federal**.

FEDERAL BUREAU OF INVESTIGATION (FBI). *See* **Filegate; Freeh, Louis J**.

FEDERAL RESERVE BOARD. *See* **Greenspan, Alan**.

FILEGATE. In the early summer of 1996, reports of a scandal erupted. It was termed "filegate" because it involved the alleged misuse of hundreds of FBI files by White House officials. Investigative reporters revealed that in 1993 and 1994, White House aides to President Bill Clinton received nearly three hundred confidential FBI files without proper authorization. Since many of the files involved White House employees who had been appointed by Presidents Ronald Reagan or **George Bush**, critics of the Clinton administration jumped on the stories as further proof of the unethical character of Clinton's presidency. FBI Director **Louis Freeh** apologized for the security breach, and Attorney General **Janet Reno** gave independent counsel **Kenneth Starr** jurisdiction over the "filegate" incident. Congressional committees investigated the matter as well. Even friends of the administration, such as the *New York Times*, opined that the mere investigation of the charges cast a dark shadow on the White House.

Ultimately, however, only two low-level aides were implicated in the scandal, Craig Livingston, the personal security chief at the White House, and Antony Marceca, Livingston's assistant. In March 2000, Starr's successor, **Robert Ray**, concluded that the independent counsel's office had uncovered no evidence of criminal wrongdoing by other White House officials. Ray added that at the time, the public had leapt "to some understandable but ultimately unsupportable conclusions." The files ended up in the White House, Ray contended, not because of some deep-laid plan to uncover dirt on Republican workers but rather due to a bureaucratic snafu. The "filegate" scandal did not figure directly in the **impeachment** charges against President Clinton, although it did affect the political climate out of which the drive to impeach Clinton grew.

Suggested Readings: "'Filegate' Departs Stage," http://www.Reporter-News.com, August 4, 2000; Robert L. Jackson, "Counsel Says No 'Filegate' Prosecution Called For," *Seattle Times*, March 17, 2000; Jeffrey Toobin, *A Vast Conspiracy* (New York: Random House, 1999), pp. 92–93.

Related Entries: Chinagate; Travelgate; Whitewater.

FISKE, ROBERT B., JR. Independent Counsel, 1994.

Robert Fiske, Jr., a onetime U.S. attorney for the Southern District of New York during Ronald Reagan's presidency and a partner at the prominent Wall Street law firm of Davis, Polk, and Wardwell, served as the independent counsel or special prosecutor in 1994. He was responsible for investigating the **Whitewater** matter.

Fiske grew up in Darien, Connecticut, the son of a lawyer who served as Dwight Eisenhower's assistant secretary general of **NATO**. He graduated from Yale University in 1952 and from Michigan University Law School three years later. As U.S. attorney for the Southern District of New York, Fiske presided over several high-profile cases. A low-key individual, he won praise from nearly all who knew him. Nonetheless, in 1989, his nomination by President **George Bush** to succeed U.S. Attorney General Richard Thornburgh was blocked by conservatives in the **Senate**, partly because he headed an American Bar Association committee on the federal judiciary that often gave high ratings to liberal judicial nominees.

While conservatives initially did not complain about Fiske's nomination as independent counsel, in August 1994 he was forced to step down when a three-judge panel of the Special Division of the U.S. Court of Appeals refused to reappoint him under the new **independent counsel law** to avoid the appearance of impropriety. Fiske was initially appointed by **Janet Reno**, at a point when the independent counsel law had lapsed. It was subsequently renewed. The appeals court appointed **Kenneth Starr**, a more conservative Republican with no prosecutorial experience, in his place. While the appeals court's decision did not stem directly from conservative displeasure with Fiske, some Republicans had recently expressed their concerns over the direction of Fiske's investigation. Fiske had concluded that **Vincent Foster** had committed suicide in 1993 and had yet to find any legal wrongdoing on the part of either Bill or **Hillary Clinton** in the Whitewater scandal.

Suggested Readings: Kim Masters, "Poised over Whitewater," *Washington Post*, April 4, 1994, p. B1; Susan Schmidt, "Judges Replace Fiske as Whitewater Counsel," *Washington Post*, August 6, 1994, p. A1.

FLOWERS, GENNIFER. Alleged mistress of Bill Clinton.

In the early stages of the 1992 presidential campaign, Gennifer Flowers, a former television reporter, nightclub singer, and Arkansas state employee, claimed that she had had a twelve-year sexual affair with Bill Clinton. The supermarket tabloid the *Star* paid Flowers approximately $150,000 for the rights to tell her story. Subsequently, Flowers allowed *Penthouse* magazine to publish nude photographs of her for an additional $250,000. Flowers also appeared on the television show *A Current Affair* for $15,000, where she reiterated her allegations. In a momentous appearance on *60 Minutes*, Bill Clinton and **Hillary Clinton** vouched for the solidity of their marriage without specifically denying Flowers's allegations. The Clintons' appearance quieted the story and helped save his campaign.

In January 1998, **Paula Jones**'s attorneys asked Clinton to testify about his relationship to Gennifer Flowers. Flowers had repeated her claims that she had had a twelve-year affair with him. This time, in his deposition Clinton admitted to having had intercourse with Gennifer Flowers, although he continued to deny that they had had a long-term affair. The **House of Representatives** did not charge Clinton with perjury in this matter. Between 1992 and 1998, Flowers marketed tapes of four telephone conversations she had had with Clinton in 1990–1991, which Flowers claimed supported her allegations. While the tapes included conversations of Clinton and Flowers discussing ways for her to deflect press inquiries about his alleged marital infidelity, they contained little else of value, leaving unclear whether he was advising her how to deal with their actual affair or only rumors of one. While talk-show hosts and Republicans continued to suggest that Clinton lacked the moral character to be president, Flowers's tapes did little to convince the public that he should not be reelected.

Suggested Readings: John Goldman, "Clinton Lied in Denying Affair, Woman Insists," *Los Angeles Times*, January 28, 1992, p. A10; "Key Player: Gennifer Flowers," http://www.washingtonpost.com/wp-srv/politics/special/clinton/players/flowers. htm; William C. Rempel, "Flowers to Market Tapes of Conversations with Clinton," *Los Angeles Times*, May 24, 1994, p. A18; David Stout, "Testing of a President," *New York Times*, March 21, 1998, p. A10.

Related Entry: Election of 1992.

FOOD QUALITY PROTECTION ACT. President Clinton signed the Food Quality Protection Act into law on August 3, 1996. The measure, which Clinton had first proposed in 1993, amended existing food regulations. Specifically, it regulated the amount and type of pesticides that could be used on foods and required that consumers be provided with greater information regarding the amount and type of pesticides that growers had used in producing the product. The bill gained bipartisan support in both houses of Congress and in many ways displayed the desire of both Democrats and Republicans to overcome the gridlock that had characterized much of 1995. After it was enacted, however, the Environmental Protection Agency (EPA) ran into numerous roadblocks in its attempts to fully enforce the law. Chemical manufacturers challenged EPA studies of certain pesticides. Within the health community, disagreements arose over whether to use human subjects to study the effects of pesticides before banning or limiting their use.

Suggested Readings: Tony Reichhardt, "Tight Deadlines and Data Gaps Fan Fight on Pesticide Safety," *Nature*, November 19, 1998, p. 207; "Remarks by the President in Radio Address to the Nation," August 3, 1996, http://www.whitehouse.gov/CEQ/Record/080396speech.htm.

Related Entries: Deregulation; Environment.

FOREIGN POLICY. Bill Clinton came to Washington, D.C., with little background in foreign policy and at least an implied pledge to devote himself, first and foremost, to **domestic policy**. Both Clinton's personal background and the historical situation dictated this approach. With the cold war over and the military supremacy of the United States demonstrated by the Persian Gulf War, the American public was more interested in addressing problems at home than it was in adventures abroad. While Clinton criticized some of President **George Bush**'s foreign policies, particularly the administration's tepid response to the crackdown on democratic insurgents in **China**, the governor from Arkansas made it clear that he considered that Bush's biggest flaws lay in the realm of domestic affairs.

Clinton's foreign policy team, headed by Secretary of State **Warren Christopher**, National Security Adviser **Anthony Lake**, and, to a lesser extent, Secretary of Defense **Les Aspin**, brought with them from the Jimmy Carter presidency a tendency to favor using American foreign policy to pursue humanitarian ends. At the same time, many of Clinton's advisers and the president himself were shaped by the **Vietnam** War, which nearly all of them saw as mistaken. How this combination of idealism, drawn from Carter, and pragmatism, learned from the failure in Vietnam, would play itself out remained to be seen.

Early in his presidency, Clinton had to grapple with the situation in **Somalia**. In one of his last acts as president, George Bush sent thousands of U.S. troops to Somalia to insure that humanitarian supplies reached its starving people. A bitter civil war tended to prevent UN aid from reaching its intended recipients. The American public supported this military effort and expected little trouble—American marines were met onshore by television cameras and media representatives. Under Clinton, however, the U.S. mission in Somalia drifted. In the words of Clinton's critics, Clinton's policy, or lack thereof, suffered from "mission creep." When UN forces proved incapable of settling long-standing disputes in the region, U.S. troops turned from protecting UN aid workers to "nation building," meaning attempting to help friends of democracy rise in power. The risks involved with this "mission creep" became evident on October 3, 1993, when eighteen American soldiers were killed and eighty more were wounded in a gun battle with soldiers allegiant to Somalian warlord Mohammed Aidid. The public reacted angrily to this attack, yet at the same time demonstrated its desire to see its boys return home safely and quickly. With his approval rating declining, Clinton temporarily increased the number of troops in Somalia while simultaneously pledging to end the military's involvement in the region.

Clinton's handling of the mission in Somalia confirmed that he lacked experience and perhaps needed to pay more attention to foreign policy. In response to Clinton's actions there and his general neglect of foreign affairs elsewhere, some experts argued that Clinton lacked a clear foreign policy vision. Clinton's foreign policy in the Balkans and Asia appeared particularly rudderless. While he had suggested that President Bush had responded too slowly and meekly to the war in **Bosnia and Herzegovina**, Clinton did not intervene in the region in response to continued

Bosnian Serb atrocities. Indeed, some suggested that Clinton's tough rhetoric or threats, which were not followed up by action, worsened the situation. In Asia, relations with China and Japan, which was locked in a battle with the United States over trade disputes, were tense and seemed to be growing more so.

Of course, Clinton was not the first president to stumble in the realm of foreign affairs early in his presidency. Clearly, Clinton gave greater priority to domestic affairs than he did to foreign policy. But although he might not have been driven by a clear philosophy of America's role in the world, in one area, Clinton exhibited a clear policy, namely, the link he saw between the strength of the **cconomy** at home and the role of the United States abroad. By the end of his presidency, one of his trademarks became an intense pursuit of free trade. Whereas independent presidential candidate **H. Ross Perot** warned that **NAFTA** would produce a great "whooshing" sound (the disappearance of jobs), Clinton embraced the lowering of tariff barriers with Mexico and Canada. Likewise, while organized **labor** and environmentalists, two of the prime constituencies of the Democratic Party, opposed NAFTA, and subsequently other free-trade initiatives, Clinton gained congressional support for this agreement by reaching out to Republicans. He forged a similar coalition to gain **Senate** support for **GATT** and the normalization of trade relations with China. Paradoxically, some of the same conservatives who chided Clinton for not having a clear philosophy and for being driven by the polls also criticized him for his pursuit of the ideal of free trade. When the administration helped U.S. aerospace industries sell their goods to China, some conservative Republicans claimed that Clinton was undermining national security in exchange for campaign funds. Yet closer analysis suggests that Clinton was motivated by his underlying faith in the marketplace as an engine of democracy, not by a desire for campaign funds, in his dealings with China. Similarly, Clinton's support of a financial bailout for Mexico and aid to the nations in the Pacific Rim region stemmed from his view that a sound economy and a sound foreign policy went hand in hand.

Particularly after **Madeleine Albright** and **Sandy Berger** were promoted to secretary of state and national security adviser, respectively, and following his defeat of **Robert Dole** in the 1996 presidential election, Clinton spent more time and energy on foreign policy, and the administration took on a clearer vision of America's role in the world. With the Dayton Agreement, which resolved the conflict in Bosnia and Herzegovina, through his aggressive pursuit of peace in **Northern Ireland** and the **Middle East** (between Israel and Jordan and Israel and the Palestinians), and via the **Kosovo** war, Clinton displayed a desire to intervene abroad to resolve long-standing conflicts. (Clinton's decision to support an invasion of **Haiti** to restore Jean-Bertrand Aristide prefigured his more aggressive actions of his second term.) Clinton also displayed a willingness to commit U.S. troops and resources to these ends. In fact, the prime criticism of Clinton's foreign policy by the time he left office was that he had overcommitted U.S. forces in pursuit of dubious peaces that would not last.

Clinton's critics also tended to overlook the basic facts of the standing of the United States in the world at the end of his presidency. Clinton built on progress Reagan and Bush had made in nuclear disarmament, including the deactivation of nearly 5,000 nuclear warheads in the former Soviet Union and the ratification of START II. In spite of the collapse of communism in the Soviet Union, **NATO** grew in size and displayed remarkable unity during the Kosovo war. Moreover, in relative terms, the United States was stronger militarily in 2000 than any other nation in world history. Obviously, dangers still existed, from the threat of nuclear **terrorism** to the possibility of renewed warfare in the Middle East. Yet as the twenty-first century began, it was easy to forget how preoccupied Americans had been with preserving their own security through much of the twentieth century.

Like much else of Clinton's legacy, only time will tell whether he was a great, good, or poor leader in the area of foreign policy. If the Protestants and Catholics of Northern Ireland end their century-old dispute, if the peace between Israel and Jordan and the process of building peace between Israel and the Palestinians holds, if tensions subside in the Balkans, and if democracy grows in Haiti, Vietnam, North **Korea**, and China, then Bill Clinton may well be looked upon as one of the most effective presidents in the area of foreign policy. If none of these developments come to fruition, then he will receive lower marks.

Suggested Readings: "The Clinton-Gore Administration: A Record of Progress," http://clinton4.nara.gov/WH/Accomplishments/foreign.html; William G. Hyland, *Clinton's World* (Westport, CT: Praeger, 1999); Moises Naim, "Clinton's Foreign Policy: A Victim of Globalization?" *Foreign Policy*, Winter 1997, p. 34; David Sanger, "Economic Engine for Foreign Policy," *New York Times*, December 28, 2000, p. 1.

Related Entries: Defense, Military; Iraq; South Africa.

FOSTER, VINCENT. (1945, Hope, Arkansas–July 20, 1993, Fort Mercy Park, Virginia.) Deputy White House Counsel, 1993.

On July 20, 1993, Deputy White House Counsel Vincent Foster, a long-time friend of the Clintons and a former law partner of **Hillary Rodham Clinton**, was found dead, apparently from a self-inflicted gunshot wound, in Fort Mercy Park in suburban Virginia. While the press and Clinton's aides claimed that Foster had committed suicide, almost immediately, rumors began to spread suggesting more sinister causes of Foster's death. Among the rumors were that Foster had been killed because he knew too much about **travelgate**, **Whitewater**, and/or other scandals involving the Clintons since he dealt extensively with Hillary Clinton's legal records. In addition, White House aides apparently removed some of Foster's papers from his office shortly after his death. Independent counsel **Robert Fiske** investigated these rumors and after finding none of them valid ruled Foster's death a suicide. **House** and **Senate** committees conducted their own investigations and came to the same conclusion, that Foster had killed himself. Independent counsel **Kenneth Starr**'s office spent nearly three years examining Foster's death, getting into a number of battles with the administration over missing documents. On October 10, 1997, Starr too concluded that Foster had killed himself. In spite of five separate investigations by the two independent counsels, both houses of Congress, and the U.S. Park Service police, rumors still abounded on the World Wide Web, on conservative talk-radio shows, and in the right-wing press about Foster's untimely death.

Born in Hope, Arkansas, Foster was a childhood friend of Bill Clinton. Like Clinton, he earned a law degree at the University of Arkansas Law School. After earning his degree, Foster went to work for the Rose Law Firm in Little Rock, Arkansas, the same firm where Hillary Clinton became a partner. A longtime supporter of Bill Clinton's political career, Foster moved to Washington in 1993 to serve as deputy White House counsel under **Bernard Nussbaum**. Foster's early days were rough. He was responsible for moving Clinton's **cabinet** nominees through the confirmation process. Foster took much of the blame for the troubles that grew out of the unsuccessful nominations of **Zoë Baird**, **Kimba Wood**, and **Lani Guinier**. The travelgate scandal also stained Foster's reputation. While the press described Foster as one of the Clintons' longtime confidants and suggested that he, like a number of other young newcomers to Washington, was not up to the job, few noticed that the pressure of serving as deputy White House counsel had left Foster deeply depressed. Starr's report later documented Foster's depression.

Regardless of the cause of Foster's death, the controversy over it exemplified the degree to which the media were willing to publish unsubstantiated innuendoes. Clinton's harshest critics refused to believe that Foster had committed suicide. Even after Starr gave a detailed explanation of Foster's suicide, stories of conspiracies to kill Foster continued to abound.

Suggested Readings: Gerald S. Greenberg, ed., *Historical Encyclopedia of U.S. Independent Counsel Investigations* (Westport, CT: Greenwood Press, 2000); Ronald J. Ostrow and Robert L. Jackson, "Foster Committed Suicide, Report Issued by Starr Says," *Los Angeles Times*, October 11, 1997, p. A15; Christopher Ruddy, *The Strange Death of Vincent Foster* (New York: Free Press, 1997); David Shaw, "Story of Foster's Suicide Is a Casebook of Problems," *Los Angeles Times*, September 16, 1993, p. A23.

FREEH, LOUIS J. (January 6, 1950, Jersey City, New Jersey–   .) Director, Federal Bureau of Investigation, 1993–2001.

A veteran FBI agent with a distinguished record, Louis Freeh received broad bipartisan support when President Bill Clinton nominated him to become the director of the FBI in 1993. In spite of a good deal of criticism from both conservatives and liberals due to his handling of numerous controversies, Freeh refused to step down from the office.

Freeh was born and raised in Jersey City, New Jersey. He earned his B.A. and law degree from Rutgers University in 1971 and 1974, respectively. He also was awarded an LL.M. in criminal law from New York University Law School in 1984. From 1975 to 1981, Freeh worked as an FBI special agent in New York City and Washington, D.C. In 1981, he went to work for the U.S. Attorney's Office in New York City, heading one of the largest organized-crime investigations and trials in history. After a fourteen-month trial, he won convictions of sixteen of seventeen codefendants. In 1991, President **George Bush** nominated him to be a federal district-court judge. Two years later, President Clinton nominated Freeh to head the FBI. At the time, the agency was reeling from the disaster in **Waco**, Texas, where a fifty-one-day standoff between federal agents and members of the Branch Davidians had resulted in the death by fire of almost all of the Davidians.

Freeh worked hard to restore the reputation of the FBI as the top **crime**-fighting unit in the nation. However, conservatives accused Freeh of protecting the president, first by leaking the personal files of several of Clinton's opponents to the press (**filegate**) and then by trying to cover up the leak. Later, some conservatives accused Freeh of withholding information regarding the president's knowledge about **Chinagate** and covering up the FBI's mishandling of the Waco incident. Ironically, many of Clinton's top aides felt that Freeh betrayed the president by supporting calls for an independent counsel to investigate the Chinagate scandal, in spite of Attorney General **Janet Reno**'s findings that none was necessary. The agency's inability to capture a suspect in a bombing incident at the 1996 Olympics in Atlanta as well as mistakes by the FBI's crime laboratory drew fire as well.

Nonetheless, the dramatic decline in crime in the United States, as well as the relative openness of the agency, especially compared to the FBI under previous longtime director J. Edgar Hoover, prompted others to credit Freeh with being an excellent director who was forced by circumstances to grapple with several extremely difficult developments. He did so, they added, in a very professional manner, consistent with his outstanding reputation within the criminal-justice community.

Suggested Readings: Ronald J. Ostrow, "Freeh Reign," *Los Angeles Times Magazine*, February 5, 1995, p. 20; David Johnston, "Smooth Start Turns Rocky for F.B.I. Director," *New York Times*, May 11, 1997, p. 1.

Related Entries: Drugs; Sessions, William Steele; Terrorism.

FREEMEN. On June 13, 1996, an eighty-one-day showdown between FBI agents and the Freemen in eastern Montana came to an end with the peaceful surrender and arrest of sixteen members of this white-supremacist, antigovernment organization. The Freemen was one of the better-known militia groups that had gained increasing public attention following the deadly bombing of a federal office building in **Oklahoma City** in 1995. Three years earlier, FBI agents had shot and killed the wife and child of Randy Weaver, a white supremacist associated with the Freemen, outside of Weaver's heavily fortified home in Ruby Ridge, Idaho. This killing, along with the tragic conclusion of the standoff in **Waco**, Texas, in 1993, prompted the FBI to adopt a less confrontational approach to arresting the members of the Freemen at their remote complex of ranches. The Freemen had been indicted in 1995 on fifty-one counts of bank and mail fraud, weapons' violations, and threatening public officials. Comprised largely of disaffected farmers and ranchers, the Freemen refused to pay taxes and declared that they had established their own government that did not recognize the laws of the United States. On March 25, 1996, FBI agents arrested two of the Freemen's leaders and surrounded their "headquarters." Negotiating through intermediaries, the

FBI gained the surrender of most of the Freemen. While still negotiating, law-enforcement officials also cut off the electricity of the Freemen's complex. This helped convince the remaining members to give up.

Almost all of the Freemen who were arrested were subsequently tried and convicted in federal court. On March 17, 1999, LeRoy Schweitzer, one of the Freemen's leaders, and six other defendants were convicted of seeking to "undermine the banking system of this country." Upon handing down Schweitzer's twenty-two-and-one-half-year sentence, U.S. District Court Judge John Coughenour declared that he intended to send "a loud and clear message to those who pass this hatred and ugliness around." Nine other Freemen had already been convicted the previous year.

Suggested Readings: "FBI Director on the Surrender of the Freemen," *Historic Documents*, 1996, p. 362; Mike Tharp, "Not All Montana Freemen Hang Together," *U.S. News & World Report*, June 8, 1998, p. 4.

FROM, AL. (May 31, 1943, South Bend, Indiana– .) President of Democratic Leadership Council. 1985–.

Al From helped found the **Democratic Leadership Council** (DLC) in 1985, an important political group that aimed at rejuvenating the Democratic Party by moving it to the center. From championed the creation of a "New Democrat movement," one dedicated to a "third way," distinct from the liberalism of the traditional Democratic Party and the conservatism of the Republican Party. Among the prominent politicians From attracted to the DLC were Arkansas governor Bill Clinton and Tennessee senator **Al Gore**. Indeed, in 1992, Clinton campaigned as a "New Democrat," espousing numerous policies fleshed out by the DLC. For example, unlike the two previous Democratic presidential candidates, Clinton supported **welfare reform** and the death penalty.

From, the DLC, and its think tank, the Progressive Policy Institute, continued to sponsor conferences and publish policy papers after Clinton's election. Most notably, in April 1999, the DLC hosted a conference entitled "The Third Way: Progressive Governance for the 21st Century," which attracted numerous worldwide leaders, including Bill Clinton, British prime minister Tony Blair, and German chancellor Gerhard Schröder. (The latter two had defeated conservative incumbents by adopting the DLC's vision to their own circumstances.)

Born in South Bend, Indiana, From earned an M.A. in journalism from Northwestern University, where he was the editor of the *Daily North-*

western. Through most of the 1970s, he worked for the U.S. Senate Subcommittee on Intergovernmental Relations. After serving in the Jimmy Carter administration for two years as the deputy adviser on **inflation**, he returned to Congress as the executive director of the House Democratic Caucus. Through contacts he made in Washington, D.C., he attracted numerous moderate Democrats, especially several prominent southern politicians, to join the DLC. Among the nonsoutherners who joined the DLC was Connecticut senator Joe Lieberman, Al Gore's running mate in 2000. In addition to directing the DLC, From wrote a regular syndicated column and served as the publisher of *Blueprint: Ideas for a New Century*, the DLC's policy journal, and *The New Democrat*, the DLC's bimonthly magazine.

Suggested Readings: Michael Duffy, "A Public Policy Entrepreneur," *Time*, December 14, 1992, p. 51; Jacob Heilbrunn, "The New New Democrats," *New Republic*, November 17, 1997, p. 20.

G

GATT (GENERAL AGREEMENT ON TARIFFS AND TRADE). One of Bill Clinton's main goals and achievements as president was the expansion of free trade. Early in his presidency, he prompted Congress to ratify the North American Free Trade Agreement (**NAFTA**). In late 1994, he enjoyed a second, perhaps more important victory when the **U.S. House of Representatives** and the **U.S. Senate** approved the General Agreement on Tariffs and Trade (GATT). Ironically, passage of this free-trade agreement depended on Republican votes in the House and Senate. To insure its enactment, Clinton made a deal with **Robert Dole**, the Republican leader in the Senate and Clinton's opponent for the presidency in 1996. Together with Dole, Clinton overcome objections that GATT would cost Americans jobs and jeopardize the nation's sovereignty.

GATT originated in trade agreements made in the wake of World War II. In 1986, new rounds of negotiations aimed at expanding global trade began under President Ronald Reagan. They were continued under his successor **George Bush**. These negotiations culminated with the signing of a new agreement on April 15, 1994, by the United States and 116 other nations in Marrakesh, Morocco. President Clinton touted GATT as "the largest world trade agreement in history" and contended that "it would provide a global tax cut of $740 billion dollars." Significantly for the United States, the new GATT protected intellectual property rights, such as computer software and films, opened doors for business services, such as accounting and construction, and opened markets for farmers. The new GATT also established the World Trade Organization (WTO), which was authorized to enforce trade agreements. Opponents of GATT complained that the creation of the WTO jeopardized American sovereignty, since the United States would have to abide by its rulings. Clinton assuaged these concerns by agreeing to a deal proposed by Senator Dole whereby a U.S. commission consisting of U.S. federal judges would have the right to review WTO rulings against the United States. If the commission found that the WTO had issued three unfair rulings in a period of five years, Congress could move to nullify U.S. participation in the trade agreement.

During Clinton's second term, political activists staged protests against the WTO and other symbols of global trade, particularly the World Bank and the International Monetary Fund. Most notably, environmental activists and trade unionists staged large demonstrations against the WTO in Seattle, Washington, in late November and early December 1999. These activists complained that GATT and other global trade agreements jeopardized environmental and labor regulations and threatened to exacerbate the divisions between rich and poor nations. Supporters of GATT countered that the pact actually promoted economic growth in developing nations. To a degree, Ralph Nader's run for the presidency in 2000, as the candidate for the Green Party, grew out of these protests. Whether this movement would grow or dwindle remained to be seen.

Suggested Readings: "Clinton's Remarks on GATT," *Historic Documents*, 1994, p. 555; "GATT Enacted in Lame-Duck Session," *Congressional Quarterly Almanac*, 1994, p. 123; Thomas W. Zeiler, *Free Trade, Free World: The Advent of GATT* (Chapel Hill: University of North Carolina Press, 1999).

GAYS IN THE MILITARY. While Bill Clinton was running for the presidency in 1992, he pledged to overturn the ban against gay men and lesbian women serving in the military. Still, many people were surprised when on January 29, 1993, at his first press conference, he announced his intention to fulfill this pledge. Some who did not disagree with overturning the ban worried that the new president was expending limited political capital on an issue that was not central to the administration's main mission of righting the **economy** and reducing the federal **budget** deficit. Others simply opposed ending the ban, including General Colin Powell, the chairman of the Joint Chiefs of Staff, and Sam Nunn, a prominent Democratic senator from Georgia who chaired the Senate Armed Services Committee, not to mention most conservative Republicans in Congress. Indeed, a political firestorm greeted Clinton's announcement that he felt that the ban against gays in the military should be lifted.

Partly to diminish such criticism, the president made some concessions to his opponents. He announced that gays who were already in the military could be removed, based on existing bans against gays and lesbians from serving in the military, until the government developed a permanent policy, a period of six months. At the same time, Clinton ordered the military to cease asking recruits if they were homosexuals and to stop investigating the sexual orientation of men and women in the armed services unless evidence of misconduct existed. This policy became known as "don't ask, don't tell." On July 19, 1993, Clinton announced that the "don't ask, don't tell" policy would become the permanent policy of the armed services.

For many conservatives, the issue of gays in the military was a symbolic issue that shed light on the nature of Bill Clinton and his administration. While Strom Thurmond, the ninety-year-old senator from South Carolina, praised gay servicemen for their years of exemplary service, most conservatives, on the contrary, believed that homosexuality was wrong in general and was particularly dangerous within the military. They felt that the military was a poor venue for social experimentation and became convinced that Clinton's willingness to overturn the ban on gays represented his unfitness to command the armed services and the nation at large. In contrast, many liberals saw conservative attacks on Clinton as emblematic of the depth of the New Right's intolerance and resistance to change. Some also noted that the same arguments that were being made against gays serving in the military had been used against **African Americans** during the late 1940s and early 1950s when the military first desegregated. Ironically, while gay advocates and many civil libertarians rallied behind Clinton for his willingness to buck popular opinion on this issue, they also expressed disappointment with his willingness to compromise. They found his incremental approach frustrating. Nonetheless, fearing the conservative alternative, most continued to support him. Since the "don't ask, don't tell" policy kept gays from openly declaring their sexual preference, it is difficult to assess the impact on their experience and on the military itself.

Suggested Readings: "Clinton Plan to Remove Military Homosexual Ban," *Historic Documents*, 1993, p. 153; "Interview with Chris Bull of the Advocate," *Weekly Compilation of Presidential Documents*, October 30, 2000, p. 2572; "New President Faces Gay-Soldiers Conflict," *Congressional Quarterly Almanac*, 1993, p. 454.

Related Entry: Defense of Marriage Act.

GENERAL AGREEMENT ON TARIFFS AND TRADE. *See* **GATT.**

GEPHARDT, RICHARD. (January 31, 1941, St. Louis, Missouri–   .) House Minority Leader, 1995–2001.

Through most of President Clinton's term, Richard Gephardt was the most powerful Democrat in the **U.S. House of Representatives**. Gephardt was the House majority leader, one step below Speaker of the House Thomas Foley, during Clinton's first two years in office. In 1995, following Foley's defeat and the Republican capture of the majority of seats in Congress, Gephardt became House minority leader. Deep partisan divisions between the Republicans and the Democrats, particularly during **Newt Gingrich**'s tenure as Speaker of the House, diminished Gephardt's role. Having little say in shaping legislation, he struggled to keep the Democrats united and their morale up in the wake of the Republicans' victory. A representative of the liberal wing of the party, with strong ties to organized labor, Gephardt opposed President Clinton on **NAFTA** but championed his **health care reform** plan. He criticized much of the Republican Party's **"Contract with America,"** arguing that conservatives sought to gut **Social Security** and other key aspects of the safety net. During the **impeachment** scandal, Gephardt rallied Democrats in support of the president with the hope that this would allow them to recapture Congress in the **election of 2000**. While the Democrats gained a few more seats in 2000, they remained in the minority in the House of Representatives, and Gephardt retained his post as minority leader.

Gephardt was born and raised in St. Louis, Missouri. He earned his B.A. from Northwestern University in 1962 and his law degree from the University of Michigan in 1965. He served in the Missouri Air National Guard from 1965 through 1971 and practiced law for nearly a dozen years. After six years as an alderman in St. Louis, he successfully ran for a seat in the U.S. Congress in 1976. In 1988, he unsuccessfully sought the Democratic nomination for the presidency. While he presented himself as a populist, a voice for the working American class, Gephardt mastered the insider game of politics in Washington, D.C., and quickly ascended the ladder in Congress. He gained a seat on the powerful Ways and Means Committee during his first term, served as chairman of the House Democratic Caucus, the party's fourth-highest post, and won the race for House majority leader in 1989.

Suggested Readings: Associated Press Candidate Bios, 1998; Richard L. Berke, "Richard A. Gephardt," *New York Times*, December 26, 1994, p. 15; Adam Clymer, "Democrats Pick Gephardt As House Minority Leader," *New York Times*, December 1, 1994, p. A28; *CQ's Politics in America: The 106th Congress* (Washington, D.C., Congressional Quarterly, Inc., 2000), p. 781.

GERGEN, DAVID. (May 9, 1942, Durham, North Carolina–   .) Special Adviser to the President, 1993–1994.

In May 1993, with the Clinton administration suffering from a series of public relations disasters, President Bill Clinton brought David Gergen to the White House to serve as his special adviser. The move surprised many because Gergen had spent much of his life advising conservative Republicans, including a stint as communications director for President Ronald Reagan. Clinton offered Gergen a post because he thought that Gergen could help him overcome some of the inexperience of many of his closest advisers. Gergen accepted the invitation. In the summer of 1994, Gergen moved from the White House to the State Department, which at the time was suffering from its own public relations difficulties. In November 1994, Gergen resigned to return to the private sector. Given the Republicans' resounding success in the midterm **election of 1994**, Gergen's impact was problematic, and in the post-1994 period Clinton turned instead to several consultants with whom he had much longer relations, most notably **Dick Morris**.

Gergen was born in Durham, North Carolina, in 1942. He earned his B.A. from Yale in 1963, where he served as the managing editor of the student newspaper. He worked briefly for North Carolina's Democratic governor, Terry Sanford, before enrolling at Harvard Law School, from which he graduated in 1967. After serving in the navy, Gergen was hired by Ray Price, President Richard Nixon's chief speech writer. For the following two decades, Gergen worked in various capacities in the Nixon, Gerald Ford, and Reagan administrations, at the American Enterprise Institute, and at *U.S. News & World Report*, where he rose to the post of managing editor in 1985. Gergen also appeared as a political commentator on *The MacNeil/Lehrer News Hour*.

As Clinton's special adviser, Gergen worked hard to cultivate the support of the mass media, which tended to feel unwelcomed by the Clinton administration during the early months of his presidency. In addition to shaping Clinton's public image, Gergen hoped to have an impact on Clinton's policies. From early on, he announced his intention to serve for only about one year. Upon his departure, Gergen announced that he would teach a course in political science at Duke University. He also continued to write columns and appear on televised news programs.

Suggested Readings: *Current Biography Yearbook*, 1994, pp. 204–8; Steven Greenhouse, "Gergen Has Given White House Formal Resignation, Aides Say," *New York Times*, November 4, 1994, p. A16.

Newt Gingrich (right), President Bill Clinton (middle), and Robert Dole (left). Library of Congress.

Related Entries: McClarty, Thomas "Mack"; Myers, Dee Dee; Stephanopoulos, George.

GINGRICH, NEWTON (NEWT) LEROY. (June 17, 1943, Harrisburg, Pennsylvania– .) House Minority Whip, 1989–1994; Speaker of the House, 1995–1998.

For ten years, Newt Gingrich, a congressman from Georgia, was one of the most powerful men in the United States. A leader of the New Right, Gingrich helped orchestrate the Republican Party's takeover of Congress in the **election of 1994**. Afterwards, as Speaker of the House, he promised to live up to the **"Contract with America,"** a list of ten specific items that over three hundred Republicans pledged to support. With some calling President Clinton "irrelevant" and predicting that Gingrich would become the next president, the **U.S. House of Representatives** passed nine of the ten items contained in the contract. At the end of 1995, *Time* magazine recognized Gingrich as its "Man of the Year."

Yet at about the same time, things began to unravel for Gingrich. The House Ethics Committee reprimanded him for a book deal he had signed with news mogul Rupert Murdoch. Gingrich's domineering personality, which initially helped unite Republicans in opposition to Clinton, hurt Republicans with swing voters, who tended to blame Gingrich for the **government shutdown**. Questions about GOPAC, the conservative political action committee Gingrich headed, cast further aspersions on him. Clinton's reelection in 1996 swung momentum away from Gingrich. In 1997, the House Ethics Committee fined Gingrich $300,000 for violating House rules by using a tax-exempt foundation for political purposes. The Democratic Party's near recapture of the House of Representatives in 1998 further hurt Gingrich. Both moderates, who had never particularly liked him, and conservatives, who felt that he was no longer helping their cause, questioned his ability to continue to lead the Republican Party. To make matters worse, Gingrich was forced to admit that he had had a sexual affair with his congressional aide, twenty-three years his junior. As a result of all of these troubles, Gingrich announced that he would not seek reelection for the position of Speaker of the House and would retire from his seat in Congress. While Gingrich continued to speak out after leaving government, claiming that Clinton deserved to be impeached, he soon found himself overshadowed by other Republican figures, such as **Trent Lott** and **George W. Bush**.

Gingrich was born in Harrisburg, Pennsylvania, and grew up around the world on numerous military bases. He earned his B.A. from Emory University (1965) and M.A. (1968) and Ph.D. (1971) in political science from Tulane University. For six years, he taught at West Georgia College. Twice, in 1974 and 1976, he ran unsuccessfully for Congress. The third time, however, proved a charm as he defeated Virginia Sharp. From the start, Gingrich distinguished himself through his brashness and unwillingness to abide by many traditional congressional customs. In 1987, he charged Speaker of the House Jim Wright with unethical conduct. Wright subsequently resigned. In 1989, when Dick Cheney left Congress to become **George Bush**'s secretary of defense, Gingrich became the House minority whip. His election to this post symbolized the rise of the so-called Young Turks over the traditional or established Republican elite. Gingrich remained the unofficial head of these insurgent Republicans throughout the early 1990s. When he resigned, several of Gingrich's former allies vied to replace him. **Robert Livingston**, another conservative Republican from the South, was slated to take over as the new Speaker of the House but withdrew his name after admitting that he too had had a sexual affair. Ultimately, **Dennis Hastert**, a centrist Republican from Illinois, took over as the Speaker, operating in a way that contrasted sharply with Gingrich's confrontational style.

Suggested Readings: *Current Biography Yearbook*, 1989, p. 256; Frontline, "The Long March of Newt Gingrich," http://www.pbs.org/wgbh/pages/frontline/newt/; Newt Gingrich, *Lessons Learned the Hard Way* (New York: HarperCollins, 1998); Robert Scheer, "Gingrich: Do As I Say, Not As I Do," *Los Angeles Times*, August 17, 1999, p. 7; Katherine Seelye, "Gingrich's Life," *New York Times Biographical Service*, November 1994, p. 1900.

Related Entry: Impeachment.

GINSBURG, RUTH BADER. (May 15, 1933, Brooklyn, New York–   .) Associate Justice of the Supreme Court, 1993–   .

Ruth Bader Ginsburg was Bill Clinton's first nominee to the **Supreme Court** and the second woman to join the court. She replaced Justice Byron White, becoming the first person to be appointed by a Democrat in a quarter of a century. Ginsburg had a moderate-liberal reputation as a judge before joining the Supreme Court, especially as a defender of equal rights and a consensus builder.

Born in Brooklyn, New York, the descendant of Eastern European Jewish immigrants, Ginsburg attended public school in Brooklyn, excelling academically. With the help of a scholarship, she enrolled at Cornell University, graduating in 1954. She married Martin D. Ginsburg and moved with him to Oklahoma when he was drafted into the army. After she gave birth to their first daughter, Jane, the Ginsburgs moved to Cambridge, Massachusetts, where both of them attended Harvard Law School—she was one of only nine **women** out of a class of more than five hundred. Ruth Bader Ginsburg distinguished herself, serving as editor of the *Harvard Law Review*. However, when her husband obtained a job in a New York City law firm, she transferred to Columbia University Law School in 1958. Although she graduated first in her class at Columbia, she had difficulty finding work in New York City because most private firms did

Ruth Bader Ginsburg.
Supreme Court Historical
Society.

not hire women. Similarly, several prominent federal judges, including
Supreme Court Justice Felix Frankfurter, refused to interview her because
they did not hire female clerks. Nonetheless, she landed a clerkship with
federal district-court judge Edmund Palmieri and then secured appointments at Columbia and then at Rutgers University law schools. Subsequently, she became the first woman to secure tenure at Columbia Law
School.

Ginsburg served as an attorney for the American Civil Liberties Union during the 1970s. President Clinton, among others, referred to her as the "legal architect of the modern women's movement." She argued six cases before the U.S. Supreme Court, winning five of them. Ironically, even though she supports a woman's right to have an abortion, she criticized the legal premise on which *Roe* v. *Wade* rests. In 1980, President Jimmy Carter nominated Ginsburg to the U.S. Court of Appeals in Washington, D.C. Her support of equal treatment for all led her to vote with the majority of the court that the Virginia Military Institute had to enroll women and that a Colorado constitutional amendment that prohibited the state government from protecting homosexuals from discrimination was unconstitutional. She usually voted with Justice **Stephen Breyer** and against the conservative bloc of the Supreme Court, William Rehnquist, Clarence Thomas, and Antonin Scalia. In *Bush* v. *Gore*, she sharply criticized the reasoning of the majority of the Court, which halted the vote recount in Florida and handed the presidency to **George W. Bush**.

To many Americans, Ruth Bader Ginsburg is a living legend, a woman who overcame long odds to become a justice of the Supreme Court. Her distinguished career as a teacher, attorney, and judge won her praise from a broad array of legal figures, including those who represented different political viewpoints. The American Bar Association gave Ginsburg its highest ranking, and in contrast to many other recent nominees, she won confirmation to the Supreme Court by a very wide margin, 96 to 3.

Suggested Readings: Linda N. Bayer, *Ruth Bader Ginsburg* (Philadelphia: Chelsea House, 2000); *Current Biography Yearbook*, 1994, pp. 213–16.

GINSBURG, WILLIAM. (Philadelphia, PA, March 25, 1943– .) Attorney for Monica Lewinsky.

William Ginsburg, a prominent medical-malpractice attorney from California and a family friend of the Lewinskys, served as **Monica Lewinsky**'s legal counsel from the time that stories first broke about her alleged affair with President Bill Clinton until June 1, 1998, when she replaced him with Plato Cacheris and **Jacob Stein**, two high-powered criminal defense attorneys from Washington, D.C. Ginsburg's flamboyant style and proclivity for appearing on interviews on television gained him great notoriety, but his lack of criminal defense experience may have hurt his client.

Born in Philadelphia, Ginsburg earned his B.A. from the University of California at Berkeley in 1964 and his law degree from the University of Southern California Law School in 1967. After opening a Los Angeles office of a large Houston-based medical-malpractice and product-liability firm, he built his own boutique firm in Beverly Hills. He represented several prominent clients, earning a reputation as a very skilled litigator. Yet he had little experience as a criminal defense attorney and thus could offer Lewinsky less advice on how to respond to the requests and questions of independent counsel **Kenneth Starr**. At the time that Lewinsky hired Cacheris and Stein to replace him, Ginsburg had failed to secure an agreement that provided her with immunity from prosecution, Ginsburg's stated goal. To the press, Ginsburg insisted that such a deal had been made, but Judge **Norma Holloway Johnson** ruled that no immunity agreement existed.

Suggested Readings: Larry Margasak, "Lewinsky Replaces Ginsburg with Two Veteran Washington Lawyers," Associated Press, June 2, 1998; Nicholas Riccardi and John M. Glionna, "Los Angeles Lawyer Is in Spotlight," *Los Angeles Times*, January 26, 1998, p. A1.

Related Entries: Impeachment; Tripp, Linda.

GLICKMAN, DANIEL ROBERT. (November 24, 1944, Wichita, Kansas–   .) Secretary of Agriculture, 1995–2001.

Dan Glickman served as President Bill Clinton's secretary of agriculture for nearly six years. Under his direction, the U.S. Department of Agriculture cut its work force by more than 13,000. In the area of policy, Glickman sought to enhance food safety, expand the opportunities for the export of agricultural goods, create rural **empowerment zones** to help impoverished regions, and improve efforts to feed the hungry. At the same time, Glickman oversaw both a boom and a bust in commodity prices, the latter of which hurt many small farmers during an otherwise-prosperous time. While the USDA provided relief where possible to farmers who faced hard times, dramatic reforms in the agricultural policies of the United States, more specifically a move toward a free market and away from government subsidies, limited the impact of the government's efforts.

Glickman grew up in Wichita, Kansas. He earned his B.A. from the University of Michigan and his law degree from George Washington University. After working in the private sector, Glickman successfully ran for Congress in 1976. He represented Kansas's Fourth Congressional District for eighteen years. In Congress, Glickman served on the House Agriculture Committee, including six years as its chairman. He helped author legislation that demanded a major reorganization of the USDA. As secretary, he had the responsibility of enacting this reform. One controversy Glickman faced while secretary regarded the use and expansion of biotechnology to genetically alter food. While the USDA supported such innovations, several European nations sought to ban the importation of foods that had been modified. Insisting that all genetically altered products that were being sold abroad had been scientifically tested and deemed safe, the Clinton administration pressured foreign governments to remove any and all barriers to the sale of such goods.

Suggested Readings: Douglas Jehl, "Daniel Robert Glickman," *New York Times*, December 28, 1994, p. A10; Ruth Marcus, "Dan Glickman," *Washington Post*, December 29, 1994, p. A4.

Related Entries: Cabinet; GATT.

GOLDBERG, LUCIANNE. (1952, Boston, Massachusetts– .) Literary Agent.

Lucianne Goldberg, a literary agent, was one of the key players in the **impeachment** of President Bill Clinton. Goldberg and **Linda Tripp**, a onetime White House employee and confidante of **Monica Lewinsky**, initially became acquainted when Tripp considered writing a book on various White House scandals, stemming in particular from **Vincent Foster**'s death. Ironically, Goldberg and Tripp had a falling out in 1996 after Tripp decided that she did not want to write a book after all. But in 1997, when Fox News talk-show host Tony Snow, who had first introduced the two, informed Goldberg that Tripp wanted to talk again, this time about Clinton's alleged sexual liaison with Lewinsky, Goldberg agreed to meet Tripp. According to Tripp, Goldberg encouraged her to tape her conversations with Monica Lewinsky. Indeed, Goldberg may have inaccurately informed Tripp that it was legal for her to tape the conversations without Lewinsky's knowledge. In addition to prodding Tripp to delve deeper into Lewinsky's relationship with the president, Goldberg helped bring allegations of Lewinsky's affair to the attention of Michael Isikoff, a *Newsweek* reporter who had already written about **Paula Jones**. Goldberg also helped alert Jones's lawyers to Clinton's relationship to Lewinsky, which in turn led to their decision to ask him questions about Lewinsky in his deposition in the Paula Jones sexual harassment suit. Rather than deny her role, Goldberg, who admitted that she disliked Clinton, took credit for the part she played in bringing to light Clinton's wrongdoings. "I'm a hero if this thing comes out the way my, quote, agenda would like to see it come out" (Toobin, *A Vast Conspiracy*), Goldberg declared in response to an attack upon her credibility. As far as Goldberg was concerned, her open dislike for the president did not affect the real issue, which was Clinton's behavior.

Goldberg was born in Boston and raised in Alexandria, Virginia. After dropping out of high school at sixteen, she married William Cummings. When their marriage ended in divorce, she moved back to Washington, where she worked briefly for the *Washington Post* as an aide to the copy editor. She held a variety of political jobs in the 1960s, including a position in Lyndon Johnson's presidential campaign. In the early 1970s, Murray Chotiner, Richard Nixon's longtime adviser, hired her at $1,000 a week to work as a spy inside the George McGovern campaign. She sought to dig up dirt on McGovern and his associates for Chotiner. Even before she met Tripp, Goldberg was involved in projects that sought to besmirch Clinton's reputation. She represented an Arkansas state trooper who wanted to write about Clinton's alleged womanizing. Dolly Kyle Browning, who sought a publisher for her fictionalized account of her alleged affair with the president, also used Goldberg as her agent.

Suggested Readings: George Lardner, Jr., "The Presidential Scandal's Producer and Publicist," *Washington Post*, November 17, 1998, p. A1; David Streifeld and Howard Kuntz, "Literary Agent Was Behind Secret Tapes," *Washington Post*, January 24, 1998, p. A1; Jeffrey Toobin, *A Vast Conspiracy* (New York: Random House, 1999).

GONZALEZ, ELIAN. The saga of Elian Gonzalez gripped the nation through much of the first half of 2000 and galvanized conservative opposition to the Clinton administration, particularly in the Cuban community in Florida. The saga began on November 21, 1999, when fourteen Cubans boarded a seventeen-to-twenty-foot boat in Cuba and headed for the United States. The attempt to flee to the United States was organized by Lazaro Munero. Among those who took the journey were Elizbet Breton Rodriguez, twenty-eight, Munero's companion, and her five-year-old son, Elian Gonzalez. Three days after it departed from Cuban shores, the boat broke apart in the open seas. Most of the passengers drowned, including Munero and Elian's mother. Elian, however, was rescued at sea, three miles off Florida's shore, by a fisherman and was rushed to a hospital. The following day, the boy was released to the custody of Lazaro Gonzalez, his father's uncle, who lived with several other relatives, all

Elian Gonzalez approached by government official April 22, 2000, in Miami. AP/ Wide World Photos.

members of the large Cuban American community in Miami. Immediately, the Cuban government requested that the boy be returned to his father, Juan Miguel Gonzalez, who lived in Cuba. While the State Department declared that it would not intercede, leaving the decision to the Florida courts, immigration law seemed to be clear that the boy should be returned to the custody of his father.

Over the course of the next few months, the dispute over Elian grew into a cause célèbre. Cuban leader Fidel Castro demanded Elian's return before large crowds of protesters in Cuba. Equally large crowds of Cuban Americans insisted that Elian should not be forced to return to Castro's Cuba. Attorneys representing Elian's relatives in Miami filed for political asylum and custody. On January 10, 2000, Circuit Court Judge Rosa Rodriguez granted Lazaro Gonzalez emergency custody on the grounds that Elian would face imminent harm if he were returned to Cuba. Several days later, however, Attorney General **Janet Reno** announced that jurisdiction lay with the federal government. A series of suits and countersuits ensued. On March 21, the relatives' suit for political asylum was dismissed by a federal court judge. Meanwhile, conservative congressmen called for special legislation to allow Elian to remain in the United States, and Vice President **Al Gore** broke with the administration, suggesting that he sided with the Cuban community in the United States. In early April, Elian's father arrived in the United States requesting that he be reunited with his son. The Cuban American community in Miami remained defiant; the mayor of Miami suggested that he would not help federal agents enforce court decisions to remove the boy. Nonetheless, on April 22, in a predawn raid, federal agents secured the release of Elian and returned him to his father, who was residing outside of Washington, D.C., at the time. Even though no one was hurt during the raid, photographs of heavily armed federal agents demanding the release of the boy from the arms of the Cuban fisherman who had rescued him at sea allowed many to lambast the heavy-handed tactics of the Clinton administration. Tens of thousands of Cuban Americans demonstrated against the action in the streets of Miami. Yet Reno insisted that she had no other choice.

On June 1, a federal appeals court upheld a lower-court decision to deny Elian political asylum. On June 28, after the U.S. **Supreme Court** rejected another bid to keep Elian in the United States, the boy and his father returned to Cuba. The entire incident displayed the power of the Cuban American community in the United States and the inability of the Clinton administration to significantly shift American policies toward Cuba. Reno secured Elian's return to his father in Cuba, but even Vice President Gore refused to buck the political power of the Cuban American community and forthrightly declare that the law demanded his return and that new policies toward Castro needed to be developed. Ironically, Gore's support of the Cuban American community did not appear to win him much support in the **election of 2000**. As in the past, most Cuban Americans supported the Republican Party's candidate.

Suggested Readings: Joseph Contreras, "A Little Boy Goes Home," *Newsweek*, July 10, 2000, p. 28; Steve Dunleavy, "Clinton, Castro, Elian, Injustice," *Human Events*, June 16, 2000, p. 21; http://www.herald.cm/content/archive/news/rafters99/elian.htm.

GORE, ALBERT, JR. (March 31, 1948, Washington, D.C.– .) Vice President of the United States, 1993–2001.

Albert Gore, Jr., was sworn in as the forty-fifth vice president of the United States on January 20, 1993. In 1996, Gore and Bill Clinton were reelected to a second four-year term. In the year 2000, Gore beat back a challenge by former New Jersey senator Bill Bradley to capture the Dem-

Bill and Hillary Clinton and Al and Tipper Gore. Library of Congress.

ocratic nomination for the presidency. In November of the same year, he barely lost the presidency to **George W. Bush**, 271 to 266 electoral college votes.

The son of Albert Gore, Sr., a prominent congressman and senator from Tennessee, Al Gore, Jr., was born in Washington, D.C., and raised in Carthage, Tennessee, and the nation's capital. He earned his B.A. from Harvard University, the only school to which he applied, in 1969, and then, even though he had doubts about the **Vietnam** War, enlisted in the U.S. Army. He spent two years in Vietnam. Upon resuming civilian life, he went to work for the *Tennessean*, a leading newspaper in Nashville. He studied philosophy and law at Vanderbilt University Divinity School and Law School, respectively. In 1976, after he earned his law degree, Gore ran successfully for a seat in the **U.S. House of Representatives**, a post he held for four terms. In 1984, he was elected to the **U.S. Senate**. He was reelected in 1990. In Congress, Gore gained a reputation as a moderate Democrat with a particular interest in arms control and the **environment**. In 1988, he ran unsuccessfully for the Democratic presidential nomination. Many predicted that he would seek the nomination in 1992, but he chose not to run again.

Clinton's selection of Gore as his running mate in 1992 served several political purposes. Gore brought Washington expertise to the ticket while simultaneously enhancing the Democrats' appeal in the South, a region that the Republicans had dominated since 1972 in presidential elections. Clinton's selection of Gore also reinforced two of the central themes of the Clinton campaign, youth or vigor and economic pragmatism. Put differently, Clinton sought to appeal to white suburban voters by casting himself as a moderate rather than as a tax-and-spend liberal. Insofar as Gore was perceived as a moderate, he helped Clinton achieve this goal. During the campaign, Gore debated Vice President Dan Quayle and **H. Ross Perot**'s running mate, Admiral James Stockdale. Most pundits viewed Gore as the victor. Gore also toured the nation with Clinton via bus, attracting large and enthusiastic crowds.

Not long after being inaugurated, Gore experienced one of the high points of his vice presidency when he debated H. Ross Perot on **NAFTA**. Gore began the debate by presenting Perot with a photograph of Reed Smoot and Willis Hawley, the congressmen associated with the infamous depression-era protectionist tariff that economists judged one of the biggest policy mistakes of the century. It was uphill for Perot from that point on. Whereas in 1992 some actually predicted that Perot had a shot at becoming the first third-party candidate in U.S. history to be elected president, after the debate Perot's political clout went into rapid decline. Moreover, the Clinton administration enjoyed an important boost following several setbacks.

Gore played an active role throughout Clinton's tenure in office. He regularly advised the president and served on numerous **cabinet-** and subcabinet-level groups, including the National Security Council and the National Partnership for **Reinventing Government**. The vice president took the lead in promoting the administration's initiative on **education** technology. Gore also played a prominent role in shaping the administration's environmental policies, including efforts to stem global warming and promote smart growth. Yet Gore's closeness to the president also created problems for him. Most important, Gore's vigorous efforts to raise money for their reelection campaign in 1996 led to some questionable actions. In particular, Gore skated a thin line of legality in his attempts to raise money from the Asian American community. While Attorney General **Janet Reno** reported that the Vice president had not violated any law, Republicans continued to call for the creation of an independent counsel to more thoroughly investigate Gore's role in the so-called **Chinagate** incident. Gore's loyalty to the president also prevented him from condemning Clinton's affair with **Monica Lewinsky**.

Gore's campaign for the presidency in 2000 was one of the strangest in U.S. history. Down in the polls to George W. Bush until after the Democratic convention, Gore emerged in the early fall as the front-runner by distancing himself from President Clinton and running as a populist who would "fight" for working Americans. In contrast to his Republican opponent, who promised broad tax cuts, Gore pledged to use the predicted budget surplus to save **Social Security**, establish a prescription-drug plan for elders, and enhance federal spending for **education**. On election night, he first conceded and then withdrew his concession when he learned that the vote in Florida was still too close to call. (Bush needed to win Florida to win the election.) For over a month, Gore's campaign remained in full gear, demanding a recount of Florida's vote, particularly in three heavily Democratic counties. Not until December 13, the day after the **Supreme Court** ruled that the recount had to be halted, did Gore concede. Even though he won the popular vote by more than half a million votes, without Florida he lost the electoral college by a narrow margin. Ironically, if Gore had won his home state of Tennessee, the entire Florida vote would not have mattered because Gore would have won a majority of the electoral college vote.

Suggested Readings: "Biography of Al Gore," www.whitehouse.gov; *Current Biography Yearbook*, 1987, p. 211; Albert Gore, *Earth in the Balance: Ecology and the Human Spirit* (New York: Plume, 1993); http://www.cnn.com/2000/ALLPOLITICS/stories/12/13/got.here/index.html; David Maraniss, *The Prince of Tennessee: The Rise of Al Gore* (New York: Simon and Schuster, 2000).

GORE, MARY ELIZABETH [TIPPER] AITCHESON. (August 19, 1948, Washington, D.C.–   .) Wife of Vice President Albert Gore.

Tipper Gore, the wife of Vice President **Al Gore**, was raised in Arlington, Virginia. She met Al Gore at his high-school prom, and they soon began to date. A year after he went to Boston to attend Harvard University, she enrolled at Boston University, earning her B.A. in psychology in 1975. They were married in 1970. She was twenty-one at the time. Later she earned her M.A. in psychology from Vanderbilt University (1976) and worked as a photographer for the Nashville *Tennessean* newspaper. In 1976, the Gores moved to Washington, D.C., following his election to Congress.

Tipper gave birth to the first of four children, Karenna, in 1973. Three more followed, Kristen in 1977, Sarah in 1979, and Albert III in 1982. Unlike **Hillary Clinton**, who continued to pursue her career after the birth of her daughter, Tipper did not. Nonetheless, she remained active, serving on several task forces and volunteer organizations. Whereas Hillary's critics cast her as an opponent of traditional values, Tipper Gore garnered headlines for her crusade against sexually explicit lyrics in rock-and-roll music. In 1987, she wrote *Raising PG Kids in an X-rated Society*, which described her efforts to get the entertainment industry to act in a responsible fashion. She led an effort to prompt record companies to label their music just as movies are rated. Tipper's crusade helped counter the claim of **George Bush** and Dan Quayle that the Clinton-Gore ticket posed a threat to family values. In spite of their personal differences, she campaigned frequently with Hillary Clinton in 1992.

After Clinton was elected president, she spent much time promoting mental health. She even began discussing her own struggle with clinical depression, hoping to use her story as a means to raise public awareness about the need for better mental health care. As the **election of 2000** approached, stories began to appear that emphasized the Gores' strong and loving relationship, in obvious contrast to the tempestuous relationship of Hillary and Bill Clinton. As Al Gore stated in one interview, "We had a fight once 23 years ago" (*Washington Post*, June 14, 1999). Indeed, some pundits credited Al Gore's jump in the polls to his passionate embrace of Tipper at the Democratic convention.

Suggested Readings: Celia W. Dugger, "The Prime of Tipper Gore," *New York Times*, July 19, 1992, sec. 9, p. 1; Lloyd Grove, "In Love for Their Country," *Washington Post*, June 14, 1999, p. C1.

GOVERNMENT SHUTDOWN. The political fortunes of President Bill Clinton and conservative Republicans in Congress experienced a remarkable turnaround following two partial shutdowns of the federal government in the winter of 1995–1996. In the wake of their historic victory in the **election of 1994**, Republicans in Congress pledged to balance the federal **budget** in seven years, largely by cutting social programs (or decreasing the rate of increase) while at the same time delivering on their promise to repeal President Clinton's tax increases of 1993 and to cut other taxes. While President Clinton accepted the concept of balancing the budget, he remained adamantly opposed to many of the specifics contained in the Republicans' budget. In general, conflicts between presidents and Congress had resulted in some sort of compromise, but in the late fall of 1995, many Republicans were eager for a showdown with President Clinton, and he proved willing to give them one.

In mid-November 1995, Republicans passed a budget bill that included deep decreases in social spending. Clinton had previously declared such deep cuts unacceptable and had pledged to veto any bill that contained them, which he did. Since the Republican budget measure included funds to keep government departments whose appropriation bills had yet to be enacted operating, Clinton's veto resulted in a government shutdown. On November 14, 1995, 800,000 "nonessential" federal employees were told to stay home. For seven days, these employees remained home until Congress appropriated emergency funds to reemploy them. Perhaps President Clinton would have received more of the blame for the crisis if it were not for the actions of Speaker of the House **Newt Gingrich** during the shutdown. Gingrich admitted that he had precipitated the crisis in part because President Clinton had offended him by treating him as a persona non grata during a flight on Air Force One. Other conservatives fueled public resentment by suggesting that the shutdown was not so bad because it would demonstrate how unnecessary much of the government was in the process.

After the first shutdown, the president and Congress agreed upon overall budget targets. However, on December 6, 1995, President Clinton again vetoed a Republican budget measure (HR 2491) because it was virtually identical to the earlier budget that the Republican House had sent to him. Terming the proposal an "extreme approach" that "would hurt average Americans and help special interests" and emphasizing that it would result in dangerous cuts in Medicare, Medicaid, and other key programs while simultaneously lowering the taxes paid by the wealthy, Clinton returned the bill to Congress unsigned. On December 15, budget talks between the Clinton administration and Republican leaders broke down. The following day, the government shut down for a second time because temporary funding measures enacted in the wake of the first shutdown had expired. Over two weeks later, on January 5, 1996, with public opinion polls showing that the majority of Americans blamed Gingrich and Republicans for the shutdown, Congress enacted new resolutions allowing the government to reopen.

Congress and the president never came to an agreement on an overall budget package that winter. Congress avoided another shutdown, however, by sending separate appropriation bills to the president, which Clinton signed. Most pundits agree that the shutdown marked a turning point for the president politically. Yet at the same time, many conservatives grew increasingly resentful of the president for the tactics he employed during the crisis. They argued that the spending proposals that Clinton and his allies termed cuts were, in fact, only decreases in the rate of growth of certain programs. Clinton and his aides countered that this represented real cuts, especially in cases where the rate of increased spending did not keep up with increased costs of providing individual benefits, such as school meals or medical benefits. Regardless of whether or not the alleged cuts were cuts, the public tended to blame Republicans for the government shutdown, and congressional leaders determined to avoid a similar showdown with the president in the future.

Suggested Readings: "Clinton, Republicans on Budget Impasse," *Historic Documents*, 1995, p. 737; "No Winners in Budget Showdown," *Congressional Quarterly Almanac*, 1995, p. 2-44; "Pact Aims to Erase Deficit by 2002," *Congressional Quarterly Almanac*, 1997, p. 2-18.

Related Entries: Election of 1992; Election of 2000.

GREENBERG, STANLEY B. (May 10, 1945, Philadelphia, Pennsylvania–   .) Political consultant.

An expert pollster, Stanley Greenberg played a key role during Bill Clinton's campaign for the presidency in 1992. Greenberg advised Clinton to adopt a middle-of-the-road strategy that would bring disaffected Democrats, such as those of Macomb County, Michigan, who had voted for Ronald Reagan, back into the Democratic fold. While Greenberg was not alone in emphasizing the need for a "New Democrat," his extensive research gave rise to specific means for creating one. For example, Greenberg's polling showed that by attacking black **African American** female rap singer Sister Souljah, Clinton could score points with moderates.

Born in Philadelphia, Greenberg received his B.A. from Miami University of Ohio in 1967 and his M.A. and Ph.D. in government from Harvard University in 1968 and 1971, respectively. From 1970 to 1979, he taught political science. He founded the Greenberg-Lake research firm in 1980, which did a good deal of political work for Democratic candidates, including Vice President Walter Mondale and Connecticut senator Christopher Dodd. Greenberg first met Clinton in 1988 and helped him in his gubernatorial reelection bid in 1990.

While Greenberg was stylistically opposite to **James Carville**, the two worked well together to help craft Clinton's campaign message in 1992. After the election, Greenberg served as a special adviser to President Clinton, conducting polls that continued to support the popularity of a moderate course. At the same time, Greenberg identified **health care reform** as an issue of central concern to American voters. When Clinton's plan for health care reform derailed, however, damaging the president's standing in the process, Greenberg took a good deal of the blame.

In the mid-1990s, Greenberg, along with James Carville and Philip Gould, an adviser to Britain's prime minister Tony Blair, formed GGC-NOP, an international consulting firm. He appeared regularly on televised news shows and wrote several books, most notably *Middle Class Dreams: The Politics and Power of the New American Majority* (1995) and, along with Theda Skocpol, *The New Majority: Toward a Popular Progressive Politics* (1997).

During the presidential **election of 2000**, Greenberg served as one of **Al Gore**'s top campaign strategists. Defying the conventional wisdom, which suggested that Gore should pursue a centrist course, Greenberg advised the vice president to paint himself as a populist willing to fight for the working American. If Gore had won the election, Greenberg probably would have received much of the credit. Given that Gore won the plurality of the popular vote but lost the electoral college, Greenberg's strategy recommendations may have proven more apt than many other pundits were willing to acknowledge during the campaign itself—they tended to argue that Gore's populist approach was misdirected.

Suggested Readings: David Brooks, "The Revenge of the Liberals," *Newsweek*, October 30, 2000, p. 39; Gwen Ifill, "The 1992 Campaign: Campaign Profile," *New York Times*, October 27, 1992, p. A20.

Related Entries: Democratic Leadership Council; Election of 1992.

GREENSPAN, ALAN. (March 6, 1926, New York, New York– .) Chairman, Federal Reserve Board, 1987– .

By the end of Bill Clinton's presidency, Alan Greenspan was one of the most widely known Americans, credited by many with the economic expansion of the 1990s. Although Greenspan is a Republican, he worked well with the Clinton administration, and Clinton renominated him to serve a fourth term, beginning in June 2000. Ironically, by pursuing tight fiscal policies, Greenspan, who was originally nominated to chair the Federal Reserve Bound by Ronald Reagan in 1987, helped precipitate the recession of the early 1990s that contributed to Clinton's defeat of **George Bush** in 1992.

Raised in the Washington Heights section of New York City, Greenspan studied at the Juilliard School of Music before enrolling at New York

Chairman Greenspan at the White House, January 4, 2000, accepting fourth term as Fed chairman. AP/Wide World Photos.

University (NYU), where he received his B.A. and M.A. in 1948 and 1950, respectively. He began but did not complete his Ph.D. in economics at Columbia University. At Columbia, he befriended Arthur Burns, who later served as the chairman of the Federal Reserve Board from 1970 to 1978. Greenspan later earned his Ph.D. from NYU. Partly due to the influence of conservative philosopher Ayn Rand, Greenspan became involved in public affairs.

Greenspan served as chair of the Council of Economic Advisers under Richard Nixon and on numerous economic and domestic policy boards during Ronald Reagan's presidency. During the Jimmy Carter years, Greenspan returned to the private sector, where he had worked prior to 1974, heading his own economic consulting firm, Townsend-Greenspan and Company. After being confirmed by the Senate, Greenspan largely followed the tight-money policy initiated by Greenspan's predecessor, Paul Volcker. Even when the **stock market** crashed in 1987, Greenspan maintained that **inflation** remained the Fed's top priority. After the stock market recovered, Greenspan continued to voice his concern over the high deficits of the Reagan-Bush years. His views influenced the Clinton administration's decision to focus on trimming the federal **budget** rather than promoting a tax cut upon taking office.

Greenspan's genius was his ability to slow the **economy** during the mid-1990s, bringing it to a "soft landing" without precipitating a recession. Such manipulation of the business cycle had been the dream of monetarists for years. Under Greenspan's hand, the U.S. economy even averted a dropoff when Asian nations suffered one of the worst financial crises ever. Greenspan became such a powerful figure that the press and investors carefully monitored and deciphered his every remark, including those aimed at cooling the "bull" stock market of the 1990s.

In the year 2000, President Clinton renominated Greenspan as chair of the Federal Reserve Board, stating, "Clearly wise leadership from the Fed has played a very large role in our strong economy." Clinton added that Greenspan's leadership had been good "not just for . . . [the] mavens of finance on Wall Street. It has been good for ordinary Americans" (Goldman, "Fourth Term"). Two full-length biographies of Greenspan, both published in 2000, reaffirmed that he deserved a good deal of credit for the strength of the American economy.

In an era replete with bitter partisan disputes, Greenspan remained popular with leaders of both political parties. In addition to promoting stable economic growth, Greenspan advocated sweeping banking reform. Perhaps his most controversial stance came in regard to **Social Security** and the ways in which the government measured the cost-of-living hikes given to recipients of it and other federal programs. Greenspan suggested that economists had overestimated the rate of inflation over the past several decades by underestimating the impact of technology on the standard of living.

Suggested Readings: *Current Biography Yearbook*, 1989, p. 214; M. Corey Goldman, "Fourth Term for Greenspan," http://cnnfn.com/2000/01/04/markets/greenspan; Justin Martin, *Greenspan: The Man behind Money* (Cambridge, MA: Perseus, 2000); Linton Weeks and John M. Barry, "The Shy Wizard of Money," *Washington Post*, March 24, 1997, p. 1; Bob Woodward, *Maestro: Greenspan's Fed and the American Boom* (New York: Simon & Schuster, 2000).

GRUNWALD, MANDY. 1958, New York, New York–   .) Political consultant.

From 1992 through early 1995, Mandy Grunwald served as one of Bill Clinton's top political consultants. Perhaps her greatest moment came early in the Clinton campaign in 1992 when she provided key advice on how he should respond to charges that he had had an affair with **Gennifer Flowers** and had dodged the draft. Shortly before Clinton appeared on *Nightline*, the widely watched television news program hosted by Ted Koppel, she quipped, "You know the media are trying to make this election about a woman you have never slept with and a draft you never dodged." Clinton effectively used this line on the television show. As a result, afterwards, Bill and **Hillary Clinton** increasingly turned to her for advice.

Born in New York City, the daughter of Henry Grunwald, a Republican and an editor of *Time* (and later ambassador to Austria under President Ronald Reagan), and Beverly Grunwald, a Democrat and columnist for *Women's Wear Daily*, Grunwald was raised on the upper east side of New York City. In the city and during her summer vacations on Martha's Vineyard, she traveled in high-society circles, including that of television personalities Mike Wallace and Barbara Walters. She graduated from Harvard University in 1979. Grunwald worked for the Sawyer-Miller Group, a prominent political consulting firm in New York, quickly establishing a reputation for her political and media savvy. Among those she successfully advised were Kentucky senator Wendell Ford and New York senator Daniel Patrick Moynihan. During the 1992 campaign, she suggested that Clinton call shock-radio jock Don Imus to counter Imus's negative remarks about him. To enhance his image among young voters, Grunwald advised Clinton to appear on *The Arsenio Hall Show* and **MTV**—advice he followed.

In 1995, the president turned increasingly to **Dick Morris** for advice on how to counter the New Right's insurgency. At about the same time, Grunwald left the White House. For a brief period, many in the press hypothesized that she was the anonymous author of **Primary Colors**, the best-selling novel that chronicled the rise of Bill Clinton and his personal foibles. Ultimately, Joe Klein revealed that he was the author. Along with several other former advisers, she appeared regularly on televised news shows and remained active in politics. In 1999, she began working again for Hillary Clinton, providing advice for her race for the **U.S. Senate** seat in New York.

Suggested Readings: Elisabeth Bumiller, "A Top Adviser to a Much-advised First Lady," *New York Times*, July 20, 1999, p. B2; Howard Kurtz, "The Woman Who Put Clinton on 'Arsenio,'" *Washington Post*, August 10, 1992, p. B1.

GUINIER, LANI. (April 19, 1950, New York, New York–   .) Justice Department nominee.

Lani Guinier's nomination and the withdrawal of her nomination to serve as the head of the Civil Rights Division of the Justice Department was one of the defining moments of the early years of the Clinton administration. Guinier, a civil rights lawyer with the National Association for the Advancement of Colored People (NAACP) Legal Defense Fund and a onetime attorney with the Justice Department, was a widely recognized expert on voting rights. As an **African American** woman, she seemed doubly attractive to the Clinton administration, which aimed at nominating a diverse range of men and **women** to government posts. Guinier's experience with voting rights law prompted her to develop some unorthodox views. In particular, she questioned the principle of majority rule and explored favorably the idea of proportional representation. While she made these views clear to Clinton's top aides, he withdrew her nomination in the face of conservative attacks that she would be unable to enforce existing civil rights law. The way Clinton handled Guinier's nomination, coupled with his earlier backtracking on **Zoë Baird**'s nomination to serve as attorney general, highlighted the administration's inexperience and Clinton's penchant for minimizing risk. The incident also suggested that bitter partisanship would be a main theme of the Clinton years.

The daughter of Edward Guinier, a prominent black educator, Guinier grew up in New York City, graduated from Radcliffe College and Yale Law School, clerked for Judge Damon Keith of the U.S. District Court in Eastern Michigan, and then began a distinguished career as a civil rights lawyer. She met the Clintons at Yale and remained personal friends with them afterwards. In a law-review article, "The Limits of Majority Rule," Guinier spelled out several of her concerns about the way African Americans were misrepresented. In a piece in the *Wall Street Journal*, Clint Bolick, a friend of Supreme Court Justice Clarence Thomas, sharply criticized Guinier, dubbing her the "quota queen." Other members of the press picked up on Bolick's criticism, and Clinton withdrew her nomination even before she had a chance to defend her ideas before Congress. In the years after the incident, Guinier wrote, appeared widely on the lecture tour, and taught. In *Lift Every Voice*, published in 1998, she detailed her travails and expanded on her provocative theories on voting rights law. In 1999, she became the first tenured black female professor at Harvard Law School.

Suggested Readings: Clint Bolick, "The Legal Philosophy That Produced Lani Guinier," *Wall Street Journal*, June 2, 1993, p. A15; David Firestone, "Lani

Guinier: Back in Queens, Fervor Intact," *New York Times*, April 2, 1998, p. B2; Neil Lewis, "Guerrilla Fighter for Civil Rights," *New York Times*, May 5, 1993, p. A19; Paul Rosenberg, "Tale of Failed Nomination," *Christian Science Monitor*, June 4, 1998.

Related Entry: Affirmative Action.

GUN CONTROL. While assuring voters during the 1992 campaign that he supported the right of hunters and sportsmen to own guns (he even went hunting during the presidential campaign), President Bill Clinton aggressively pursued gun control during his eight years as president. In 1993, he signed the **Brady bill** into law, the first new federal gun-control measure since 1968. This bill instituted a five-day waiting period for the purchase of handguns. The waiting period would be phased out when a national "instant-check" system became operational. According to the administration, the Brady bill prevented over half a million felons, fugitives, and others who were not eligible to buy a gun from doing so. A year later, in 1994, President Clinton prompted Congress to ban the sale of assault weapons. In 1998, via an executive order, Clinton banned the importation of more than fifty nonrecreational, modified assault weapons. In the wake of the killings at Columbine High School, the Clinton administration called for strengthening existing gun-control legislation. In particular, it sought to close loopholes in the Brady bill, which, among other things, allowed individuals to purchase handguns at gun shows from unlicensed dealers. The **U.S. Senate** passed new gun-control legislation, but the bill failed to make it through the Republican-controlled **House of Representatives**. Finally, the administration pressured Smith and Wesson, one of the largest gun manufacturers, to agree to add safety locks to all guns so as to prevent accidental shootings by children.

Clinton's advocacy of gun control earned him the enmity of a significant segment of Americans who contended that virtually any form of gun control represented a threat to their liberty and to the Second Amendment right to bear arms. The National Rifle Association (NRA), which some considered the most powerful lobbying organization in Washington, deemed Clinton public enemy number one. In the **election of 1994**, the NRA and other gun-control opponents singled out Democrats who had supported the Brady bill and the assault-weapons ban for defeat. Many political pundits agreed that the gun-control debate was one of the issues that accounted for the Republicans taking control of Congress. Yet at the same time, Clinton's advocacy of gun control probably added to the support he enjoyed among **women** at the polls. In May 2000, he endorsed the Million Moms March, a large demonstration of women in Washington, D.C., which focussed on the need for more gun control. A much smaller anti-gun-control women's group held a counterdemonstration.

Suggested Readings: http://clinton3.nara.gov/WH/Accomplishments/crime.html; "President Signs 'Brady' Gun Control Law," *Congressional Quarterly Almanac*, 1993, p. 300; "Remarks at a Rally for Gun Control Legislation," *Weekly Compilation of Presidential Documents*, March 20, 2000, p. 550.

Related Entry: Crime.

H

HAITI. "Your time is up. Leave now, or we'll force you from power." So declared President Bill Clinton to Lt. Gen. Raoul Cédras, the military leader of Haiti, in a nationally televised address to the American people on September 15, 1994. Clinton's proclamation, which he backed by sending an armada of warships toward Haiti, marked one of Clinton's most decisive actions as president. Even though public opinion against military action in Haiti remained high, and even though Republicans in Congress had expressed their clear objections to sending troops to Haiti to topple the military junta that had ousted Jean-Bertrand Aristide, the first democratically elected president in Haitian history, Clinton determined that he would display his support for Aristide with action. Clinton justified sending troops on four grounds. First, he argued that the United States needed to stop the abuse of human rights in Haiti. Second, by restoring Aristide to power, the president contended, the United States would demonstrate its determination to spread democracy. Third, an invasion would end the stream of refugees who had sought asylum in the United States since the military had ousted Aristide from power in 1991. Last, by sending troops, the United States would gain credibility throughout the world.

At the same time as troops headed for Haiti, a contingent of prominent Americans, former President Jimmy Carter, General Colin Powell, and Senator Sam Nunn, rushed to the Caribbean island to negotiate a last-minute settlement to the dispute. On September 18, after U.S. warplanes had already begun their flight to invade Haiti, Carter announced that the military leaders had agreed to step aside. As a result, when U.S. troops arrived on September 19, they met throngs of cheering Haitians, who viewed them as liberators, rather than military resistance. On October 15, 1994, Jean-Bertrand Aristide returned to Haiti to resume his position as

U.S. troops on patrol in Haiti, circa 1995. Department of Defense.

president of Haiti. The U.S. troop presence in Haiti peaked at 22,000, but quickly dwindled to less than 2,500. Those who remained operated as UN peacekeepers. Fewer than 500 troops remained as of the spring of 1996.

The crisis in Haiti began in the fall of 1991 when a military coup overthrew Aristide. While the **George Bush** administration declared its opposition to the coup, President Bush made it clear that he had no intention of sending troops to Haiti to restore Aristide. Indeed, Bush ordered the Coast Guard to intercept boat people or refugees who set out for the United States from Haiti in search of asylum. Many liberals, particularly several prominent **African American** leaders, condemned Bush's policy, and Clinton suggested that he would reverse it if he were elected president. As president, Clinton continued to express his support of Aristide, but he avoided sending troops to Haiti until the fall of 1994. Earlier, in the spring of 1994, six prominent senators sponsored the Haitian Restoration Democracy Act, which demanded a complete embargo of Haiti. Many conservatives and moderates opposed this measure, not to mention more drastic military action, partially because they distrusted Aristide. Jesse Helms of North Carolina, the senior Republican on the **Senate** Foreign Relations Committee, for instance, suggested that Aristide had Communist sympathies and called him a "psychopath" (*CQ Almanac 1994*, p. 451). At about the same time, Clinton made it easier for Haitians to apply for asylum in the United States and appointed William H. Gray, a former congressman from Philadelphia, as a special envoy to Haiti. Seeking to prevent Clinton from taking further action, Republicans in the **House of Representatives**, joined by some moderate Democrats, passed a nonbinding amendment to a military appropriations bill that expressed the House's opposition to the use of force. Senator **Robert Dole**, who was the Senate minority leader at the time, expressed his opposition to an invasion as well. Nonetheless, Clinton determined that he had to use force.

Whether Clinton attained his specific objective in Haiti is debatable. Haitian boat people quit streaming toward the United States. Yet democracy remained tenuous, with human rights abuses continuing to take place under Aristide, although they were not as widespread as under Cédras. Furthermore, Haiti proved unable to overcome its terrible economic woes—it was one of the poorest nations in the world. Nonetheless, with Haiti, Clinton disproved the conservative canard that he had no principles and only acted for political reasons, since public opinion was against an invasion.

Suggested Readings: "Aristide's Return to Haiti," *Historic Documents*, 1994, p. 436; "Clinton's Haiti Gamble Pays Off," *Congressional Quarterly Almanac*, 1994, p. 449; George Fouriol, "A Look at the Record of Clinton's Protege in Haiti," *Wall Street Journal*, Eastern edition, November 3, 2000, p. A21; "Haiti Mission Ends," http://www/defenselink.mil:80/news/Mar1996/n03011996_9603013.html.

Related Entry: Foreign Policy.

HARRIMAN, PAMELA DIGBY. (March 20, 1920, Kent, England–February 5, 1997, Paris, France.) U.S. Ambassador to France.

Pamela Harriman, once described as the "greatest courtesan of the century," was an important backer of Bill Clinton and served as his ambassador to France. She was born Pamela Beryl Digby in England in 1920. Her father, Edward Kenelm Digby, became Lord Digby two months after her birth. Her mother was the daughter of the Second Lord Aberdare. Educated at the Downham School in Hertfordshire and in Paris, in 1939, following a three-week courtship, she married Randolph Churchill, the son of Winston Churchill. As their marriage quickly deteriorated, she attracted numerous prominent admirers, including William Paley, the president of CBS, broadcaster Edward R. Murrow, and Averell Harriman, the U.S. ambassador to the Soviet Union and heir to a large railroad fortune. She divorced Churchill in 1946 and moved to Paris. In 1962, she married Leland Hayward, the producer of the Broadway hit *The Sound of Music*. After he died in 1971, she renewed her friendship with Averell Harriman, then seventy-nine and one of the richest men in America, and they wedded. Averell Harriman was one of the chief benefactors of the Democratic Party. During the Ronald Reagan and **George Bush** years, she held numerous fund-raisers for the Democrats at their house in Georgetown. After Averell Harriman's death in 1986, Pamela Harriman carried on her husband's tradition of supporting the Democratic Party.

Delighted by Clinton's selection of **Al Gore** as his running mate—she had supported Gore for president in 1988—Harriman backed Clinton in 1992. After his election, he nominated her to serve as the U.S. ambassador to France. Confirmed by the **Senate**, she became the first female ambassador to France. As ambassador, she helped iron out trade differences between the two nations, paving the way for the completion of **GATT**. She died at the age of seventy-six in Paris.

Suggested Readings: David L. Marcus, "Pamela Harriman, Envoy and Socialite, Dies at 76 in Paris," *Boston Globe*, February 6, 1997, p. A2; "Obituary," *Daily Telegraph*, February 6, 1997, p. 25; Christopher Ogden, *Life of the Party: The Biog-*

raphy of Pamela Digby Churchill Hayward Harriman (New York: Warner Books, 1995).

HASTERT, J. DENNIS. (January 2, 1942, Aurora, Illinois– .) Speaker of the House, 1999– .

In the midst of the **impeachment** process and in the wake of the 1998 midterm elections, in which the Democrats nearly recaptured the **House of Representatives**, Dennis Hastert was elected Speaker of the House. Hastert was much less confrontational than his predecessor, **Newt Gingrich**. Some argued that Hastert's election signaled the end of the conservative revolution. Others, however, noting Hastert's close ties to Texas congressman Tom DeLay, one of Clinton's most vehement opponents, were not so sure if this was the case.

Hastert was born about forty-five miles outside of Chicago in a Republican stronghold, not far from Ronald Reagan's hometown. He attended Wheaton College, an evangelical Christian college near his hometown, earning his B.A. in 1964. He earned his M.A. from Northern Illinois University in 1967. He taught government and coached the wrestling team for sixteen years at Yorkville High School, served in the Illinois General Assembly for three terms, and was elected to the House of Representatives in 1986. In Congress, he developed a reputation for reaching across partisan lines and as a "nice guy." He served as the only Republican on **Hillary Clinton**'s Health Care Task Force and helped write the **health care reform** bill that Congress enacted in 1996, which expanded health care coverage for the uninsured. Unlike most of his predecessors, Republican and Democrat, Hastert had not held any top party posts before being elected Speaker. As one of his Republican colleagues put it: "Here is a guy who is a family man, who is humble, not flashy, who connects with real people. He's not a Gingrich figure, or a Ronald Reagan figure, but a good, solid person" (*New York Times*, January 7, 1999, p. A1). In his acceptance speech, Hastert made it clear that he favored developing bipartisan solutions to the nation's problems. In the two years after assuming the Speaker's role, Hastert clashed with President Clinton on some issues and found common ground with the administration on others.

Suggested Readings: "Biography of House Speaker J. Dennis Hastert," http://www.speaker.gov; Karen Foerstal, "Hastert and the Limits of Persuasion," *CQ Weekly*, September 30, 2000, p. 2252; Lizette Alvarez, "The 106th Congress: The Speaker—Humble Man at the Helm," *New York Times*, January 7, 1999, p. A1.

HATE CRIMES. Throughout much of his presidency, President Clinton pushed for hate-crime legislation. Such measures would make it a **crime** or add to the sentence for the commission of other crimes in cases where a crime was committed due to the victim's race, religion, ethnicity, gender, or sexual orientation. In 1994, President Clinton signed into law the Hate Crimes Enhancement Act, which allowed for longer sentences for racial hate crimes. In 1997, he convened a White House Conference on Hate Crimes to build support for additional hate-crime legislation. The brutal murders of James Byrd, a black man, in Texas in June 1998, and Matthew Shepard, a gay man, in Wyoming in October 1998, added to the cry for additional federal hate-crime legislation. Yet the successful prosecution of those who had committed these specific murders allowed conservatives, who tended to oppose federal hate-crime legislation, to counter that hate-crime laws were unnecessary or redundant. As **George W. Bush** put it in his second presidential debate with Vice President **Al Gore** in 2000, Byrd's murderers had already received the most severe penalty, the death penalty. What, by inference, would be gained by a hate-crime enhancement? Advocates of hate-crime legislation countered that hate-crime legislation was necessary in order to provide additional protection for minorities who had historically been the victims of crimes motivated by hate. Polls showed that a sharp division existed between blacks and whites over the need for hate-crime legislation. **African Americans** overwhelmingly favoring it and whites displaying a much more ambivalent attitude toward the need for such legislation.

Suggested Readings: Elizabeth Palmer, "Hate Crime Language Fails in Defense Bill," *CQ Weekly*, October 7, 2000, p. 2350; "President Clinton: Getting Tough on Hate Crimes," http://clinton3.nara.gov/Initiatives/OneAmerica/move.html; Jim Yardley, "Bush Stance on Bias Crimes Emerges as a Campaign Issue," *New York Times*, October 13, 2000, p. A25.

Related Entry: President's Initiative on Race.

HEAD START. Throughout the 1990s, Head Start, the federal program launched during the mid-1960s to help low-income children attain preschool education, continued to receive strong bipartisan support. In October 1998, on the eve of **impeachment** hearings in the **House of Representatives**, Congress passed the Human Service Reauthorization Act of 1998, which substantially increased funding for Head Start. Even before Congress approved this measure, funding for Head Start had risen 68 percent since Bill Clinton became president. Indeed, Clinton had regularly urged Congress to increase its appropriations to Head Start, to make more children eligible for the program, to expand its range, and to enhance the quality of existing Head Start programs. Overall, funding for Head Start more than doubled between 1992 and 2000, from $2.2 billion in fiscal year 1992 to nearly $5 billion in fiscal year 2000. Increased funding enabled an additional 200,000 low-income children to attend Head Start programs and allowed the government to expand Early Head Start. Early Head Start, which began in 1994, established educational programs for children under the age of three. The expansion of Head Start, Clinton contended, was necessary to enhance the educational opportunities available to low-income children. Put differently, in an era when many middle- and upper-income families sent their children to preschool, it was necessary to provide low-income children with similar opportunities lest the education gap between the rich and poor widen further. Conservative pundits were almost the only people who questioned the value of Head Start, and even then they usually did so on pragmatic rather than ideological grounds.

Suggested Readings: Jeanne Ellsworth and Lynda J. Ames, *Critical Perspectives on Project Head Start* (Albany: University of New York Press, 1998); http://www. acf.dhhs.gov/news/press/1998/wh1pghs.htm; Darcy Olsen, "It's Time to Stop Head Start," *Human Events*, September 1, 2000, p. 4.

HEALTH CARE REFORM. During the 1992 presidential campaign, Bill Clinton emphasized several issues. He promised that if he were elected, he would create new jobs, cut the **budget** deficit, reduce taxes, institute **welfare reform**, and initiate sweeping health care reform. In the first months of his presidency, he focussed on promoting his economic package. Once much, if not all, of this package was enacted, he turned his attention to health care. Even before health care became the administration's top priority, Clinton's political standing was shaky. By the time of the off-year **election of 1994**, to a large degree because of the negative reaction to Clinton's health care proposal, he stood in terrible shape. Over the next two years, Clinton rebounded from his political troubles, but he did so, in part, by distancing himself from the goal of national health care reform. Ironically, by the end of his presidency, part of his health care plan had been enacted, and both **Al Gore** and **George W. Bush** proposed expanding health care benefits for the elderly to include some sort of prescription-drug package.

The call for national health care did not originate with President Clinton. As far back as Franklin D. Roosevelt's first term in office, the committee that recommended creating **Social Security** had proposed establishing national health insurance. Liberal Democrats and President Harry Truman revived this call in the 1940s, but opposition by the American Medical Association and conservative Republicans killed the measure. The establishment of Medicare and Medicaid by President Lyndon Johnson in the mid-1960s signified a major step toward providing health care insurance for all Americans, but as health care costs escalated in the 1980s, the demand for further reform of the health care system resurfaced. The restructuring of the **economy**, which left many employees either without health insurance or having to sacrifice wages and benefits to maintain company plans, added to the demand for national health care reform.

In a special election for the **U.S. Senate** in Pennsylvania in 1990, Harris Wofford, a former aide of President John F. Kennedy, upset Republican incumbent and onetime Attorney General of the United States Richard Thornburgh by emphasizing the health care issue. Wofford's victory left many feeling that it would be a winning issue for Clinton. Indeed, one of Wofford's campaign advisers was **James Carville**, who helped convince Bill Clinton that he could effectively use the issue to defeat President **George Bush**. Clinton's victory convinced many others that the time was finally ripe for sweeping health care reform.

On September 22, 1993, Clinton presented the administration's plan for reforming health care in the nation. Prior to issuing his 1,364-page health care reform bill, Clinton's wife, **Hillary Clinton**, and longtime friend **Ira Magaziner** held numerous private hearings on health care. Afterwards, they testified before Congress and preached the gospel of health care reform to the press. In general, the president, his wife, Magaziner, and their allies in Congress emphasized that health care costs were rapidly escalating and that an alarming number of Americans lacked insurance. In addition, the administration noted that Medicare was endangered by many of the same maladies that plagued health care in general.

Clinton's particular plan, which was called managed care, called for creating approximately two hundred regional health care alliances. These alliances would cooperatively market insurance to large employers, who would be required to purchase insurance from the alliances and to pay 80 percent of the insurance costs of their employees. Taxes on tobacco and reductions in Medicare and Medicaid costs would help pay for health insurance for the nearly forty million Americans who were not covered by this plan. In addition, Clinton's proposal called for the creation of a National Health Board to regulate the insurance industry. Clinton's plan also included prescription-drug coverage for the elderly and contained prohibitions against denying insurance to high-risk, high-cost insurees.

Even before Clinton delivered his specific proposal to Congress, opposition to it began to develop. Conservatives portrayed health care reform as a prime example of big government of the type that had been rejected in the 1980s by the election of Ronald Reagan. Radio talk-show host **Rush Limbaugh**, for example, warned that Clinton's proposal entailed the takeover of up to one-fifth of the economy by the federal government. Clinton's proposal ran into difficulty for several reasons. Many liberals favored a more radical single-payer system, whereby the federal government would insure all citizens, akin to the type used in Canada. Not only was such a system easier to understand than Clinton's extremely complex and confusing plan, arguably it made more sense economically. By the spring of 1994, it became clear that Clinton's plan was not going to be enacted. Not only did Clinton's proposal not win approval in Congress, it was never even brought to a vote on the floor of either the **House** or the Senate because Democratic leaders recognized that it lacked widespread public support. Proposals for a single-payer system did not win passage either.

Nonetheless, as mentioned earlier, several aspects of the broad goal of health care reform did go into effect during Clinton's presidency. The 1997 Budget Bill included provisions to provide health care coverage to uninsured children via the **Children's Health Insurance Program (CHIP)** and to extend the life of Medicare. Congress passed and Clinton signed into law the **Health Insurance Portability and Accountability Act of 1996 (HIPAA)**, which made it more difficult to deny insurance to high-risk and/or high-cost insurees. Congress also debated a health care bill of rights and prescription-drug plans for the elderly. In sum, while Clinton did not deliver on his pledge to enact comprehensive health care reform, neither did Republicans permanently kill efforts to enlarge the federal government's role in insuring health care for all Americans.

Suggested Readings: "Big Medicare, Medicaid Changes Enacted in Budget Bills," *Congressional Quarterly Almanac*, 1997, p. 6-3; "The Clinton Health Care Plan," *Historical Documents*, 1993, p. 781; http://clinton3.naragov/WH/Accomplishments/ health.html; Francine Kiefer, "Health Care Reform May Be Coming, But in Little Pieces," *Christian Science Monitor*, February 9, 2000, p. 2.

Related Entry: Domestic Policy.

HEALTH INSURANCE PORTABILITY AND ACCOUNTABILITY ACT OF 1996 (HIPAA).

Even though the Clinton administration failed to achieve sweeping health care reform in 1993 and 1994, it prodded Congress to enact several lesser measures, including the Health Insurance Portability and Accountability Act (HIPAA), which Clinton signed into law on August 21, 1996. The measure, which Clinton championed in his 1996 State of the Union Address, was cosponsored by Senators Nancy Kassebaum, a Republican from Kansas, and Edward Kennedy, a Democrat from Massachusetts. It protected health insurance coverage for workers and their families when they changed or lost their jobs. Part of the bill required insurers to offer individual policies to individuals after their COBRA coverage. COBRA stands for the Consolidated Omnibus Reconciliation Act and allows for insurees to continue health insurance coverage, for up to eighteen months at the individual's own expense, when the insuree's employment is terminated. HIPAA also prohibited insurers from refusing to cover or renew coverage to individuals because of their health status. In addition, the law sought to make health insurance more affordable for the self-employed by making it easier for them to set up medical savings accounts and by increasing the deductions they could take from their taxes for health care costs. HIPAA also established tax incentives to encourage Americans to purchase long-term-care insurance. While the bill had little impact on many working poor, who lacked insurance, and did not affect the escalating costs of health care, along with the **Children's Health Insurance Program (CHIP)**, it expanded the federal government's commitment to insuring that all Americans had access to some form of health coverage.

Suggested Readings: "Bill Makes Health Insurance 'Portable,' " *Congressional Quarterly Almanac*, 1996, p. 6-28; http://www.hcfa.gov/HIPAA/HIPAAHM.htm.

HERMAN, ALEXIS M. (July 16, 1947, Mobile, Alabama– .) Assistant to the President and Director of White House Public Liaison, 1993–1997; Secretary of Labor, 1997–2001.

Alexis Herman served in the Clinton administration from start to finish, as an assistant to the president and director of White House public liaison during Bill Clinton's first term and as secretary of labor during his second term. She was the first **African American** woman to serve as secretary of labor and the highest-ranking black woman in the **cabinet**. She was extremely loyal to the president, and her tenure as secretary of labor was a turbulent one. In 1998, Attorney General **Janet Reno** appointed an independent counsel to investigate charges that she had accepted money in exchange for access to the White House. While she was cleared of all charges in April 2000 by independent counsel Robert Lancaster, Jr., the stain of the accusations remained.

Born in Mobile, Alabama, the daughter of a mortician and community activist who was almost killed before her eyes by the Ku Klux Klan, Herman began her involvement in politics at a young age. Raised as a Roman Catholic, she was suspended from her Catholic high school for questioning why black students were not allowed to participate fully in religious pageants. She earned her B.A. from Xavier University in 1969. While she was taking graduate courses at the University of South Alabama, she was employed by Catholic Charities as a social worker. Through most of the early 1970s, she was involved in various worker-training and minority-employment programs. In 1977, Secretary of Labor Ray Marshall, who was black, appointed Ernest Green, the first black person to graduate from Central High School in Little Rock, Arkansas, as his deputy secretary. Green appointed Herman to direct the Women's Bureau of the Labor Department. After Jimmy Carter lost the presidential election in 1980, Herman and Green formed a consulting firm that focused largely on compliance with various federal regulations. During the same period, Herman became involved in Democratic politics, befriending Andrew Young, Jimmy Carter's UN ambassador, Marion Barry, one-time mayor of Washington, D.C., **Ron Brown**, and other prominent black politicians. In 1989, Brown, who was the chairman of the Democratic National Committee, named Herman his chief of staff. After Clinton's election, she served as deputy director of the president-elect's transition team and then was appointed director of the Public Liaison Office.

When **Robert Reich**, Clinton's well-known secretary of labor, resigned following Clinton's reelection, Clinton nominated Herman to take his place. Even though organized labor favored Harris Wofford, a onetime aide of President John F. Kennedy and senator from Pennsylvania, over Herman, they rallied behind her when Republicans in Congress stalled her confirmation. Early in her tenure as head of the Department of Labor, a dramatic strike erupted setting the Teamsters Union against the United Parcel Service (UPS). The centrality of UPS to many businesses led to calls for the Clinton administration to intervene. The administration refused to do so. As a result, when UPS gave in to the Teamsters' demands, organized labor praised Herman for her faith in collective bargaining. In contrast, business spokespersons criticized the secretary for treating the Department of Labor as "the department of organized labor" (*New York*

Times, September 6, 1999, p. A12). Aside from the UPS strike, Herman focused much of her attention on devising training programs, particularly for **women** who were compelled to return to work by **welfare reform**, and getting Congress to enact a patients' or health care bill of rights. As with most of Clinton's other cabinet members and aides, Herman defended the president during the **impeachment** process. While she stated that she was "disappointed" by Clinton's behavior, Herman added that she was "raised in a faith and a tradition of a forgiving gospel."

Suggested Readings: John M. Broder, "Amid Political Cynicism, Standing Steadfast in Her Faith," *New York Times*, September 6, 1999, p. A12; *Current Biography Yearbook*, 1998, p. 287.

Related Entry: Minimum Wage.

HIGH TECHNOLOGY. In the 1980s, social commentators began to speak of a high-technology or postindustrial revolution that was taking place in America. Pointing to the rapid growth of personal computers and other electronic devices, they forecast a transformation in the economy and perhaps society itself. By the end of the Clinton administration, the pace of technological development and change had reached new proportions. Personal computers, cellular telephones, and the Internet, which was virtually unknown when Bill Clinton assumed office, were ubiquitous. Individuals and corporations identified with this technological revolution, such as Bill Gates, Michael Dell, and Lawrence Ellison, the heads of Microsoft, Dell Computer, and Oracle, respectively, earned enormous fortunes and fame, displacing both old industrial giants and several of the originators of the high-tech revolution, such as Apple Computer and IBM, in the process. By the year 2000, for instance, Bill Gates and Paul Allen, two of the cofounders of Microsoft, were worth close to $100 billion each. The *Forbes* list of the 400 Richest People in America was replete with the founders of numerous high-tech companies, ranging from Gordon Moore of Intel to Philip Anschutz of Qwest Communications. With the exception of the descendants of Sam Walton, the founder of Wal-Mart, virtually every name on the list was associated with the telecommunications and computer revolution that had burst upon the scene in the past ten to twenty years. The Clinton administration also was the first to go online; citizens could e-mail the White House, access **cabinet** and other government departments online, and even e-file their taxes.

This high-tech revolution had a profound impact on millions of Americans. Government statistics showed that by the end of the 1990s, well over 50 percent of the population used computers, up from about 33 percent in 1990 and less than 20 percent in 1985. At the same time, the Census Bureau reported that one in five Americans used the Internet at home, in school, or at work. Nearly fifty million Americans used e-mail, and the numbers who went online grew each day. As the decade came to a close, e-commerce became the new rage, and companies like Amazon.com and eBay became household names overnight. Instant messaging, a service provided by AOL, the largest Internet server, threatened to displace the telephone as the most common means of communication among teens, and MP3, the term used for the most commonly used format for digitally storing and sending music over the Internet, stood on the verge of displacing tapes and compact discs.

During the same time span, cellular phones, used by only a small percentage of the population at the end of the 1980s, grew into a mass phenomenon. In 1985, there were 203,600 cell-phone users. By the year 2000, there were over 1 million cell-phone subscribers. Many families began to own more than one cell phone. Moreover, as the new millennium dawned, new technological developments were bringing these various technologies together. Cell-phone users could send e-mail and receive information on their stocks, favorite sports teams, and news headlines. Computer devotees could download their data onto hand-held computers, such as the Palm Pilot. Even old-fashioned game makers, such as Parker Brothers, enjoyed a rebound by manufacturing computer versions of their family favorites like Monopoly.

The Clinton administration played a central role in promoting this technological boom and addressing some of the problems associated with it. The administration's pursuit of free-trade agreements built upon the presumption that American high-tech firms would benefit from opening of new markets and enhanced protections against software piracy and copyright infringement. Likewise, the economic strategy of focussing on getting the **budget** deficit down first, rather than providing tax cuts, allowed for lower interest rates. In turn, this made it easier for entrepreneurs and new high-tech businesses to obtain loans and venture capital. Particularly during his second term in office, President Clinton prompted Congress to enact legislation specifically aimed at expanding the Internet and e-commerce. This included a three-year moratorium on taxes on e-commerce and updated copyright legislation to protect intellectual property in cyberspace. Along the same lines, President Clinton signed a comprehensive telecommunications reform bill in 1997 that provided for

greater competition in the rapidly changing telecommunications industry.

The greatest problem that the high-tech revolution produced that the
Clinton administration sought to address was the so-called digital divide.
Simply stated, personal computers, Internet service, and cellular phones,
although much cheaper than in the past, remained beyond the means of
many Americans. To overcome this divide, President Clinton and Vice
President **Al Gore** advocated connecting all classrooms and libraries to
the Internet and won approval of new programs that provided low-
interest loans to educational institutions to purchase computers. By 2000,
according to government calculations, 95 percent of all public schools
were connected to the Internet, up from 35 percent in 1994. Somewhat
similar measures made it easier for various disadvantaged groups, from
Native Americans to residents of public housing, to join the high-
technology revolution. Additional funding helped train teachers to use
the new technology. Each passing year, however, witnessed new innovations, making it quite difficult to conquer the digital divide. Thus it
remained unclear whether the high-technology revolution would transform society or reinforce existing trends of income inequality.

Suggested Readings: "Cellular Phone Use Skyrockets," *Baltimore Sun*, October 30,
2000, p. 2; Michael Mandel, "The Spoils of the New Economy Belong to High
Tech," *Business Week*, August 16, 1999, p. 37; "Richest Americans in History,"
Forbes, August 24, 1998, p. 32.

HOLBROOKE, RICHARD C. (April 24, 1941, New York, New York– .)
U.S. Ambassador to Germany, 1993–1994; Assistant Secretary of State,
1994–1995; U.S. Ambassador to the United Nations, 1998–2001.

One of the most important diplomats during the Clinton presidency,
Richard Holbrooke helped negotiate the Dayton Agreement or Accords
that brought an end to the war in **Bosnia and Herzegovina** in 1995. In
1998, he was nominated and confirmed as the U.S. ambassador to the
United Nations. Holbrooke's critics argued that he failed to achieve a
workable long-term solution to the turmoil in the Balkans, but others
credited Holbrooke with displaying remarkable diplomatic acumen in
achieving the Dayton Accords and as ambassador to the United Nations.

Born in New York City, the son of Jewish immigrants, Holbrooke was
raised in Scarsdale, New York. Among his close friends was Dean Rusk,
who served as secretary of state during the John F. Kennedy and Lyndon
Johnson administrations. Holbrooke earned his B.A. from Brown Univer-

sity in 1962 and then joined the foreign service. His first State Department assignment was in the U.S. Embassy in **Vietnam**, and he served on the U.S. delegation to the Vietnam peace talks in Paris in 1968 and 1969. After ten years of public service, he became managing editor of *Foreign Policy* and later a contributing editor to *Newsweek*. During Jimmy Carter's presidency, Holbrooke was the assistant secretary of state for East Asian and Pacific Affairs. Upon Ronald Reagan's election, Holbrooke returned to the private sector.

In 1993, Holbrooke became Clinton's ambassador to Germany. In the fall of 1994, he was named assistant secretary of state for European and Canadian affairs. His central concern during this period was the conflict in Bosnia and Herzegovina. During one trip to the region, three of his fellow diplomats were killed when the armored personnel carrier they were driving crashed off the side of a mountain. In response to a Bosnian Serb attack on Sarajevo, Holbrooke recommended that **NATO** launch air strikes against Serb positions. Not long after this, Holbrooke pushed through a cease-fire, culminating with the signing of the Dayton Agreement.

Holbrooke returned to the private sector in 1996, although he continued to consult for the White House on **foreign policy** matters. He succeeded **Bill Richardson** as ambassador to the United Nations, a **cabinet**-level post, in 1998. While NATO, not the United Nations, conducted the war against Yugoslavia in defense of **Kosovo**, Holbrooke worked hard behind the scenes to maintain international support for the combined European and U.S. air attack. As U.S. ambassador, Holbrooke also sought to smooth tensions between the United Nations and the United States. Indeed, as the Clinton presidency came to a close, some credited Holbrooke with mediating a seeming solution to the longstanding dispute between the Republican-controlled Congress and the president over U.S. support for the United Nations. The United Nations reduced the dues to be paid by the United States, and Congress seemed to accept this solution. Some suggested that if **Al Gore** had been elected president in 2000, he would have named Holbrooke as his secretary of state.

Suggested Readings: *Current Biography Yearbook*, 1998, p. 297; Elaine Sciolino, "Richard C. Holbrooke," *New York Times*, June 19, 1998, p. A4; James Traub, "Holbrooke's Campaign," *New York Times Magazine*, March 26, 2000, p. 41.

HOPE SCHOLARSHIPS. Among provisions of the Taxpayer Relief Act of 1997, which President Clinton signed into law on August 5, 1997, were ones that established tax credits and incentives to help pay for higher **education**. Clinton termed these tax benefits HOPE Scholarships. The scholarships were modeled after similar programs enacted first by the state of Georgia and then by other states. The name of the program invoked one of the themes of Clinton's run for the presidency, namely, that he was born in a town called Hope, Arkansas.

The HOPE Scholarships allowed students in the first two years of college or other eligible postsecondary institutions to take a tax credit of up to $1,500 per year to pay for tuition and fees. Since the poor did not pay taxes, the tax credits did not affect them. Only single filers or joint filers who made less than $50,000 or $100,00, respectively, were eligible for the credits. In addition to the HOPE Scholarships, the Taxpayer Relief Act of 1997 allowed families to establish education savings accounts or educational individual retirement accounts (IRAs) of up to $500 per year per child under the age of eighteen. Money put into these accounts could be withdrawn tax free to pay for college education. As with the HOPE Scholarships, educational IRAs were phased out for upper-income individuals and families. Other provisions of the tax bill made it easier to withdraw funds from traditional IRAs to pay for higher education.

While the Republican Party favored granting across-the-board tax cuts, enough Republicans proved willing to support these measures in the wake of Clinton's reelection to win congressional approval. Clinton opposed sweeping tax cuts in favor of targeted tax benefits limited to the poor and middle classes. In addition to education, the president proposed and won passage of tax benefits for health care and urban development. He argued that these measures met the nation's most pressing needs while at the same time maintaining fiscal discipline. During the 2000 campaign for the presidency, **Al Gore** followed Clinton's lead, calling for additional targeted tax benefits and opposing **George W. Bush**'s proposal for much more sweeping and unrestricted tax cuts.

Suggested Readings: David Dervarics, "Hope Scholarships: A Closer Look," *Black Issues in Higher Education*, September 4, 1997, p. 7; William Greider, "Professor Feelgood," *Rolling Stone*, April 17, 1997, p. 51; http://ed.gov/offices/OPE/PPI/HOPE/index.html.

HOUSE IMPEACHMENT MANAGERS. Thirteen Republican congressmen, all members of the House Judiciary Committee that drew up the original **impeachment** charges against President Bill Clinton, served as the House impeachment managers during the trial stage of the impeachment process before the entire **U.S. Senate**. All thirteen were lawyers, and the majority of them had experience as prosecutors. A number of them were members of the "class of 1994," which referred to the Republicans who swept into office in 1994 when the Republicans took control of both houses of Congress for the first time in decades. The House managers were responsible for presenting the case for removing the president from office. Since only one other president, Andrew Johnson in 1868, had ever been tried in U.S. history, the managers had few guidelines to follow. **Supreme Court** Chief Justice **William Rehnquist** presided over the trial, but yet he too lacked a clear set of procedures to follow. A brief biography of each of the managers and his particular role follows.

Bob Barr, age fifty, from Georgia, a former CIA analyst, was elected to Congress in 1994. The author of an anti-Clinton book, Barr was one of the first Republicans to call for the impeachment of the president. Barr had the task of outlining how the president's actions added up to obstruction of justice and perjury.

Ed Bryant, age fifty, from Tennessee, had served in the Army Judge Advocate General Corps and had taught law at West Point. He too was elected to Congress in 1994. Much less vocal than Barr and several other members of the Judiciary Committee, he outlined the factual case for convicting the president.

Steve Buyer, age forty, from Indiana, served as a legal counsel in the army during the Persian Gulf War and became a congressman in 1992. He focussed on how the president's actions constituted an impeachable offense.

Charles Canady, age forty-four, from Florida, held a law degree from Yale University and chaired the House Judiciary Subcommittee on the Constitution. He was elected to Congress in 1992. Like Buyer, Canady showed how Clinton's actions met the constitutional test for impeachment.

Christopher Cannon, age forty-eight, from Utah, was elected to Congress in 1996. A former member of the Reagan administration and an advocate of tax reform, Cannon described how Clinton had obstructed justice and committed perjury.

Steve Chabot, age forty-five, from Ohio, was elected to Congress in 1994. Like Cannon, he outlined the relationship between Clinton's actions and obstruction of justice and perjury.

George Gekas, age sixty-eight, from Pennsylvania, was elected to Congress in 1982. In the late 1980s, Gekas had taken part in hearings that led to the impeachment but not the conviction of federal judge Alcee Hasting, a Democrat. He played a role similar to that of Cannon and Chabot during President Clinton's trial in the U.S. Senate.

Lindsey Graham, age forty-three, from South Carolina, was elected to Congress in 1994. An archconservative, Graham had taken part in an effort to oust **Newt Gingrich** as Speaker of the House in 1998. He focussed on the constitutional merits of the impeachment charges.

Asa Hutchinson, age forty-eight, from Arkansas, was elected to Congress in 1996. As a federal prosecutor, Hutchinson had prosecuted Roger Clinton, Bill's brother, on **drug** charges. He outlined the factual case against Clinton.

Henry Hyde, age seventy-four, from Illinois, was elected to Congress in 1974. The chairman of the Judiciary Committee, Hyde had a reputation as a fair and principled leader. However, in the midst of the impeachment process, he admitted to having had an extramarital affair. His name was synonymous with the Hyde amendment that barred federal funding of abortions. He presented the opening and closing statements in the trial before the Senate.

Bill McCollum, age fifty-four, from Florida, was elected to Congress in 1980. As chairman of the House Judiciary Subcommittee on Crime, McCollum had a reputation as a tough law-and-order politician. From very early on, McCollum condemned the president's conduct. He summarized the factual case against Clinton. He ran for the U.S. Senate and lost in 2000.

James Rogan, age forty-one, from California, was elected to Congress in 1996. Prior to this, he had served as the deputy district attorney in Los Angeles County and as a judge. He focused on the charges that the president had obstructed justice and delivered closing remarks. He was defeated in his bid for reelection in 2000.

James Sensenbrenner, age fifty-five, from Wisconsin, was elected to Congress in 1978. After winning 91 percent of the vote for reelection in 1998, Sensenbrenner introduced the case against Clinton.

Suggested Readings: Frank Bruni, "The Impeachment Trial Managers," *New York Times*, December 26, 1998, p. A25; Frank Bruni, "The President's Trial: The Maverick," *New York Times*, January 17, 1999, p. 27; Melinda Henneberger, "The Georgia Republican Who Uses the I-Word," *New York Times*, May 9, 1998, p. A6; Kevin Merida, "The Judiciary Chairman's Trying Times," *Washington Post*, December 11, 1998, p. A1.

Related Entry: White House Defense Team.

HOUSE OF REPRESENTATIVES, U.S. One of the most significant developments of the Bill Clinton years was the Republican Party's takeover of both houses of Congress, especially the House of Representatives. Led by House Speaker **Newt Gingrich**, the Republican Party united around the **"Contract with America"** to sweep to victory in the **election of 1994** in both the House and the **Senate**. Not since the election of 1952 had the Republicans won a majority of seats in the lower house (the Democrats regained control of the House of Representatives in the election of 1954), and not since 1946 had the Republicans controlled both houses of Congress. Indeed, for a while, the Republican momentum seemed so great that some deemed Gingrich, who was elected Speaker of the House in 1995, a more important public figure than Clinton. True, the Democratic Party cut into the Republicans' control of the House of Representatives in 1996 and 1998. Nonetheless, Clinton's presidency and legacy were deeply shaped by the fact that he faced Republican majorities in both houses of Congress during six of his eight years in office, and he left office with the Republicans controlling both houses of Congress and the White House, something they had not done since 1932 when Herbert Hoover was president.

Clinton began his presidency with the Democratic Party in the majority in both the U.S. Senate and House of Representatives, but the Democratic margin was not great enough to allow him to achieve all of his goals. For instance, in 1993, Republicans blocked his economic stimulus package. A series of missteps by the administration and the backlash against liberalism engendered by Clinton's ill-fated **health care reform** proposal provided the opportunity Republicans needed to capture Congress. But few pundits expected the Republican victory to be as wide as it was (see Table 12). The disenchantment of a segment of the Democratic Party's base with some of Clinton's more conservative actions, most notably his support of **NAFTA**, contributed to the size of the Republican victory, as turnout in traditionally Democratic areas fell. The defeat of Tom Foley, the Democratic Party's Speaker of the House, by George Nethercutt, symbolized the extent of the Democratic Party's defeat. Foley was the first sitting Speaker of the House to lose a bid for reelection since 1862.

Not only did Republicans win a majority of seats in Congress, conservatives became more prominent within the party. Once they were in the majority, Republicans in the House set about enacting many of the promises they had made in the "Contract with America." Rather than oppose all of these measures, however, Clinton adeptly positioned himself in the political center, supporting some proposals, such as **welfare reform** and

Table 12
Party Makeup and Leaders of the House of Representatives, 1993–2001

Congress and Year	Democrats	Republicans	Other	Speaker of the House	Minority Leader
103rd 1993–1995	258	176	1	Tom Foley	Robert Mitchell
104th 1995–1997	204	230	1	Newt Gingrich	Richard Gephardt
105th 1997–1999	206	228	1	Newt Gingrich	Richard Gephardt
106th 1999–2001	211	222	2	Dennis Hastert	Richard Gephardt
107th 2001–2003	211	221	2 (+ 1 vacancy)	Dennis Hastert	Richard Gephardt

Source: Congressional Quarterly Almanac; http://clerkweb.house.gov/histrecs/househis/lead.htm

a cut in the capital-gains tax, while casting other Republican aims as extremist. This process of "triangulation" culminated with the **government shutdown** of the winter of 1995–1996. Gingrich and his allies argued that Clinton, not they, deserved the blame for the shutdown, yet public opinion polls suggested that the Speaker of the House and other conservatives got most of the blame.

While Clinton convincingly defeated **Robert Dole** in the 1996 presidential election, Republicans maintained control of both houses of Congress, showing that their 1994 victory was not a fluke. After the **Monica Lewinsky** scandal broke in 1998, Republicans in the House displayed their political muscle, uniting in support of **impeachment** hearings and ultimately voting for two articles of impeachment along party lines. Prior to these votes, however, Democrats made Gingrich's leadership and the extremely partisan tone of politics a major issue. Even though Republicans maintained control of both houses of Congress, inroads made by the Democrats in the 1998 election left Gingrich and many conservatives on the defensive. When Gingrich's personal transgressions were made public, particularly his sexual affair, disenchanted Republicans compelled him to resign his position as Speaker of the House. He was ultimately succeeded by Illinois congressman **Dennis Hastert**, who adopted a much less confrontational style than Gingrich.

As the **election of 2000** approached, Democrats and Republicans vied for who deserved credit for the economic prosperity of the 1990s. Emphasizing that not a single Republican had voted for Clinton's 1993 deficit-reduction package, the president and Democrats emphasized that they deserved credit for the eradication of the **budget** deficit. Republicans countered that the deficit disappeared because of their concerted efforts to shrink government spending, which the administration repeatedly resisted. Republicans also claimed that policies passed by President Ronald Reagan, not those enacted by Clinton, produced the prosperity of the 1990s. Hence the election of 2000 could be viewed as a referendum on these competing claims. Yet other factors obviously contributed to the final results, ranging from the personalities and skills of particular candidates in key races to the "character" issue that arose out of Clinton's affair with Monica Lewinsky. Moreover, by the time of the election, the Republican Party appeared far less conservative than in 1994. While they proposed tax cuts and a ban on partial birth **abortion**, many Republicans emphasized their records of constituent service and promised to enhance **education** and medical care for the elderly, both traditionally liberal Democratic issues.

One issue that largely disappeared between 1994 and 2000 was **term limits**. The "Contract with America" included a pledge to bring term limits for congressmen and senators to a vote, and many Republican newcomers had tapped into public displeasure with Washington, D.C., to gain office in the first place in 1994. As public disenchantment lessened and as the freshman class of 1994 accrued power, however, the idea of term limits grew less attractive, especially to incumbents. George Nethercutt, for example, who in 1994 had emphasized that Speaker of the House Tom Foley had been around for too long and pledged to serve for only six years, ran again in 2000. He justified his bid for a fourth consecutive term on the grounds that much still needed to be done. To some, this demonstrated that even though the Republican maintained control of the House, the Republican "revolution" of 1994 had passed.

Suggested Readings: "Democratic Stronghold Ends along with 103rd Congress," *Congressional Quarterly Almanac*, 1994, p. 3; Elizabeth Drew, *Showdown: The Struggle between the Gingrich Congress and the Clinton White House* (New York: Simon & Schuster, 1996); "104th Congress Ushers in New Era of GOP Rule," *Congressional Quarterly Almanac*, 1995, p. 1-3; "Shakeup in the House: Disaffected Republicans Force Gingrich Out," *Congressional Quarterly Almanac*, 1998, p. 7-4.

HUANG, JOHN. *See* **Chinagate**.

HUBBELL, WEBSTER L. (1948, Arkansas–   .) Associate Attorney General, 1993–1994; Whitewater defendant.

A longtime friend and associate of Bill and **Hillary Clinton**, Webster Hubbell was appointed associate attorney general, the third-highest post in the Justice Department, shortly after Clinton took office. Barely a year later, Hubbell resigned in the face of allegations that he had defrauded his partners at the Rose Law Firm in Arkansas. As independent counsel, **Kenneth Starr** pursued these charges. In June 1995, he was fined and sentenced to 21 months and agreed to cooperate with Starr's investigation, which was ultimately aimed at the president and the first lady. Yet when Hubbell refused to accuse the president of wrongdoing, Starr brought further charges against him. In the summer of 1999, Hubbell pled guilty to charges that he had misled federal regulators about work he had performed with Hillary Clinton. With the plea, Hubbell avoided additional prison time, and the Clintons were assured that they would not have to testify in court regarding Hubbell's misconduct and their knowledge, or lack thereof, of it.

Hubbell had been a starting tackle on the University of Arkansas football team that won the Sugar Bowl in 1969. A former mayor of Little Rock and chief justice of the Arkansas Supreme Court, Hubbell and the Clintons met in the 1970s. He was one of Hillary's partners at the Rose Law Firm and Bill's golfing buddy. They remained close professionally and personally. In the mid-1980s, Hubbell and Hillary worked together on a real-estate deal that contributed to the failure of Madison Guaranty Savings and Loan, owned by **James B. McDougal**. McDougal and the Clintons jointly invested in the **Whitewater** land deal. In the late 1980s, the federal government contracted with the Rose Law Firm to sue the accountants of Madison Guaranty. Independent counsel Starr alleged that Hubbell and Hillary Clinton failed to disclose their possible conflict of interest in the case. Hearings held by the **House of Representatives** lent weight to Starr's charges. Yet neither Starr nor Republicans in the House uncovered hard evidence that Hillary had broken the law or that either Clinton had paid Hubbell to cover up their involvement. Indeed, many interpreted the leniency of the final plea agreement as proof that Starr was unable to develop a case against the Clintons.

Suggested Readings: Frank Ahrens, "Webb Hubbell's Sorry Story," *Washington Post*, November 24, 1997, p. B1; Roberto Suro and Bill Miller, "Hubbell to Plead Guilty As Starr Wraps Up," *Washington Post*, June 29, 1999, p. A1.

Related Entries: Fiske, Robert B., Jr.; Foster, Vincent; Impeachment.

HUSSEIN, SADDAM. *See* **Iraq**.

I

ICKES, HAROLD, JR. (September 4, 1939, Baltimore, Maryland—   .) Special Assistant to the President, 1993–1994; Deputy Chief of Staff, 1994–1997.

Harold Ickes, Jr., the son of Harold L. Ickes, Sr., Franklin D. Roosevelt's secretary of the interior, served as Bill Clinton's assistant and as deputy chief of staff until he was forced to resign following the **election of 1996** amid charges that he had traded access to the president for campaign funds. In testimony before the **Senate** Governmental Affairs Committee, Ickes displayed a selective memory of the role he had played in these matters, leading to calls for the creation of another independent counsel, but Attorney General **Janet Reno** refused to appoint one. Ickes' voluminous private records of White House meetings provided senators grist for their investigations into Clinton's alleged campaign finance irregularities, but produced no hard evidence of any illegal actions on the president's or Ickes' part.

Ickes' father had a legendary reputation as a principled New Dealer who championed the causes of minorities and the poor. For instance, in 1939 after the Daughters of the American Revolution barred Marian Anderson from singing at its hall because she was black, he allowed her to perform in front of the Lincoln Memorial. Ickes, Jr., developed close ties to civil rights forces as well. In 1964, he volunteered to work for the Freedom Movement in Mississippi and was nearly shot to death by some white night riders in Louisiana in 1965 for attempting to register blacks to vote. He earned his B.A. from Stanford University in 1964 and his law degree from Columbia University in 1971. One of the persons he befriended at Columbia Law School was **Susan Thomases**, a close friend of Bill and **Hillary Clinton**. Ickes and Thomases worked on Eugene McCarthy's 1968 campaign for the Democratic nomination for the presidency. Through Thomases, Ickes met Bill Clinton in the early 1970s. Ickes ran Bill Clinton's 1992 presidential campaign in the state of New York and served as Clinton's convention manager in the same year. In Joe Klein's fictional account of the early Clinton years, *Primary Colors*, Ickes is represented by the fictitious character Howard Ferguson, 3rd, who appears in the opening scene of the novel and the film based on it.

After playing a prominent role on Clinton's transition team, Ickes accepted a post as special assistant of the president. He was promoted to deputy chief of staff in 1994. One of Ickes' responsibilities was dealing with the **Whitewater** scandal. Ickes earned a reputation as a "hard-edged operator, a cynical realist" (Lewis p. 58). Like Clinton, he was a politician, first and foremost, who understood that one had to win to achieve anything. Ironically, during the 1996 campaign, Ickes often battled **Dick Morris**, the calculating campaign adviser Clinton turned to following the 1994 Democratic debacle.

Like his father, who wrote one of the most famous diaries of the Franklin Roosevelt years, Ickes kept his own record of the inner workings of the Clinton administration. Altogether, Ickes accumulated about fifty boxes of notes, newspaper clippings, private memos, and other documents. Upon his departure from the White House, Ickes carted the boxes out of the White House to his home in Georgetown. Although he considered the notes to be his private papers, he complied with Republican request to see them as part of congressional investigations into campaign finance irregularities. His notes included records of meetings with **John Huang**, a Commerce Department official who had helped funnel donations of Chinese businessmen into the Clinton campaign. Newspapers ran stories claiming that Ickes turned over the documents to get even with the president, who had forced him to resign upon the request of the new chief of staff, **Erskine Bowles**, but Ickes and Clinton were too close personally and politically to allow the rumor mills to drive them apart. In testimony before Tennessee senator Fred Thompson's Governmental Affairs Committee, Ickes made clear his allegiance to the president. Not surprisingly, when Hillary Clinton chose to run for a seat in the U.S. Senate from the state of New York, she turned to Ickes to serve as one of her campaign advisers.

Suggested Readings: Francis X. Clines, "Harold Ickes Returns: A Happy Warrior for Mrs. Clinton," *New York Times*, June 14, 1999, p. A16; Michael Lewis, "Bill Clinton's Garbage Man," *New York Times*, September 21, 1997, sec. 6, p. 58.

Related Entries: Chinagate; Election of 1992.

"I DID NOT HAVE SEX WITH THAT WOMAN." *See* **Lewinsky, Monica.**

IMPEACHMENT. On December 19, 1998, the **U.S. House of Representatives** impeached President Bill Clinton. Only one other time in American history had a U.S. president, Andrew Johnson in 1868, been impeached. The House of Representatives voted in favor of two of four articles of impeachment recommended by the House Judiciary Committee. The vote, which split along partisan lines, was as follows: Article I, 228–206; Article II, 205–229; Article III, 212–212; and Article IV, 148–285. The articles that were adopted were Article I, which charged the president with lying to a grand jury about his affair with his intern **Monica Lewinsky** and Article II, which charged him with obstructing justice in the **Paula Jones** sexual harassment case. The articles that were rejected were Article III, which charged the president with lying during his grand-jury testimony in the Paula Jones case and Article IV, which charged him with abusing his power by providing false and misleading responses to written questions posed to him by the Judiciary Committee.

After impeaching the president, the House adopted Resolution 614, which formally notified the **U.S. Senate** of its decision. The resolution appointed a team of **House impeachment managers** to prosecute the case. Headed by Henry Hyde, the chairman of the House Judiciary Committee, the team presented its arguments for convicting the president beginning on January 7, 1999. President Clinton's own team of lawyers, the **White House defense team**, responded with their own trial memorandum. Both sides disagreed over the facts of the case and more importantly over whether Clinton's actions constituted an impeachable offense. With Chief Justice **William Rehnquist** of the **Supreme Court** presiding, the full Senate reviewed the arguments and counterarguments and viewed videotapes of several key witnesses. Throughout the trial, it did not appear that the Republican leadership would be able to muster enough votes to convict the president. Nonetheless, Republican leaders insisted on completing the process rather than working out a deal that would lead to the censure of President Clinton and an end to the ordeal. On February 12, 1999, the Senate voted not guilty on both charges against the president. The votes fell far short of the two-thirds majority necessary for conviction on both charges. In contrast, the Senate fell only one vote short of removing Andrew Johnson from office in 1868. Not even all Republicans voted for convicting President Clinton. The votes

Senate Impeachment Trial of President Bill Clinton, 1998. U.S. Senate Photograph.

were as follows: Article I, lying to the grand jury, 45–55; Article II, obstructing justice in the Paula Jones case, 50–50.

President Clinton's impeachment had multiple origins. In August 1994, **Kenneth Starr** was appointed independent counsel to investigate the **Whitewater** affair. In fact, Starr replaced **Robert Fiske**, who had found no evidence of wrongdoing on the president's part in his own investigation of the Whitewater matter. (Fiske was replaced when the independent counsel was officially renamed.) For three years, Starr aggressively pursed a variety of leads. His office and Republicans in the House and Senate, who conducted their own hearings on Whitewater and other matters, often complained of the Clinton administration's stonewalling and legal maneuvering, particularly its inability to locate key documents in a timely fashion and lack of memory when queried about specific matters. As of the fall of 1997, Starr's Whitewater investigation appeared stalled. Charges had been filed against a couple of the president's associates, most prominently **Webster Hubbell**, but, as the independent counsel subsequently revealed, there was not enough evidence to charge or convict either Bill or **Hillary Clinton** of any crime.

However, in early 1998, Starr's investigation took an unexpected turn. On January 12, 1998, **Linda Tripp**, a former White House employee, provided Starr's office with tapes she had made of telephone conversations with Monica Lewinsky, a former White House intern, that suggested that Lewinsky had had a sexual affair with the president. Lewinsky's affair in itself did not constitute an impeachable offense, but it became the key to the impeachment of Clinton because of testimony that the president made in a deposition in the Paula Jones sexual harassment case on January 17, 1998. In his deposition, President Clinton denied having had sexual relations with Lewinsky. Prior to this testimony, Lewinsky had filed an affidavit in which she denied having had an affair with the president. In addition, Tripp's tapes suggested that Clinton and his close friend **Vernon Jordan** had prodded Lewinsky to lie about her affair. The tapes also suggested that Jordan would help Lewinsky obtain a new job. Based upon these actions and this evidence, Starr requested and received permission to expand his investigation to include the Lewinsky matter. Four days after Clinton testified in the Jones case, the *Washington Post* broke the story of the Clinton-Lewinsky affair. Nearly simultaneously the media revealed that Starr had expanded his investigation. Shortly thereafter, President Clinton flatly denied having had "sexual relations with that woman" or having lied.

For the following nine months, the public watched the story of the

Clinton affair with Lewinsky unfold. Ironically, on April 1, 1998, Judge **Susan Webber Wright** agreed with arguments put forth by the president's lawyers in their summary-judgment brief that Jones's case lacked merit. Hence she dismissed Jones's suit, the reason for Clinton's testimony in the first place. Wright noted that even if Clinton had propositioned Jones, his alleged actions did not meet the standard of sexual harassment. Clinton and Jones subsequently reached a settlement whereby Clinton agreed to pay Jones $850,000, and she agreed to drop her appeal of Wright's decision. About a month after Wright dismissed Jones's suit, a grand jury in Little Rock, Arkansas, that had been investigating the Whitewater affair disbanded without having indicted the president. Nonetheless, Starr's investigation of Clinton's actions in the Lewinsky affair continued, with the independent counsel's office winning several key court rulings regarding who could and could not be compelled to testify. After much wrangling with Monica Lewinsky's attorneys, Starr's office convinced the former White House intern to cooperate with its investigations. On August 17, 1998, the president submitted to questioning via closed-circuit television before the grand jury. Subsequently, in an address to the nation, the president acknowledged having had an "improper relationship" with Lewinsky and stated that he was sorry for having "misled people."

On September 9, 1998, Starr issued a report on his investigation to the House of Representatives. The report listed eleven possible grounds for impeachment and was accompanied by thirty-six boxes of documents. A little less than two weeks later, the House Judiciary Committee voted in favor of releasing Clinton's videotaped grand-jury testimony and 2,800 pages of printed material. The former was broadcast by the major television networks, and the latter material was posted on the Internet. In early October, the House Judiciary Committee initiated a formal impeachment inquiry. Before it held public hearings, congressional elections were held. While the Republicans maintained a majority of seats in the House of Representatives, many perceived the gains that Democrats made—they picked up five seats—as a repudiation of the House leadership. Indeed, following the election, Speaker of the House **Newt Gingrich** resigned, partly due to allegations that he too had had an affair. Subsequently, **Robert Livingston**, a conservative Republican congressman from Louisiana and Gingrich's presumed successor, resigned as well after admitting a sexual affair. In his resignation speech, Livingston called on Clinton to resign to save the nation from having to go through the ordeal of an impeachment. Clinton refused to follow Livingston's suggestions.

For nearly a month, the House Judiciary Committee's impeachment hearings gripped the nation's attention. Kenneth Starr delivered lengthy testimony. Little of what he said was new; most of it supported the call for impeachment. The president's defense team testified that Clinton had not technically committee perjury and that even if the committee determined that he had lied in his deposition, this crime did not constitute an impeachable offense. When Robert Livingston requested that the president follow his example, Jerrold Nadler, a Democratic congressman from New York, responded that to do so would be to "surrender to sexual McCarthyism. . . . We are losing sight of the distinction between sins, which ought to be between a person and his God, and crimes, which are the concern of the state and of society as a whole" (*CQ Almanac*, 1998). House Judiciary Committee chair Henry Hyde rejected these and other defenses of the president, arguing that the principle at stake was "equal justice under the law." On December 11 and 12, the House Judiciary Committee approved four articles of impeachment against the president, voting strictly along partisan lines. The twenty-one Republicans on the committee supported the impeachment charges; the sixteen Democrats voted against them. The split vote reflected the partisan division that plagued the committee throughout its proceedings and indicated the difficulties that Republicans would face in convicting the president of the charges. Public opinion polls, as well, suggested that the majority of Americans opposed impeaching the president or removing him from office.

Prior to voting on the articles, the full House held one day of public debate on the charges. Many Republicans and Democrats made passionate speeches in support of or in opposition to impeaching the president. Given the final vote, there is little evidence that the speeches changed many minds. Nor did they produce a groundswell of public support for impeachment or dropping the charges in favor of a vote of censure. Five Republicans broke with their party and voted against impeachment. One of them, Peter King, of New York explained, "I strongly believe that for a president of the United States to be impeached . . . for an election to be undone, there must be a direct abuse of power. . . . How many of our former president would we have lost?" Similarly, only five Democrats voted in favor of impeachment. Ralph Hall of Texas declared, "You just have to vote your conscience, and I did that." The vast majority of representatives, however, chose to follow their party leaders, siding with or against the president depending on their party affiliation. The same was true in the Senate, although in the upper house there was even less support for removing the president from office. Exactly why two of the original articles of impeachment received a majority of votes but the other two did not remains a bit unclear. By and large, the vote ran along party lines. Once one article had been passed, it became less imperative to pass the other articles and a few Republicans switched sides.

Determining the historical significance of Clinton's impeachment is an extremely difficult task. Most simply, as many observed, since only one other president has ever been impeached (President Richard Nixon resigned from office before the House voted on articles of impeachment), it will remain a lasting mark on Clinton's presidency. Whether it should stand as the defining aspect of his presidency, however, is problematic. Unlike Andrew Johnson, Clinton was a two-term president who enjoyed relatively high **approval ratings** through much of his presidency, including ratings in the wake of the impeachment vote that were higher than those of many of his predecessors. Moreover, the impeachment was the byproduct of a long-drawn-out investigation into a matter, Whitewater, that produced no criminal charges, and of Paula Jones's sexual harassment suit that Judge Susan Webber Wright dismissed. When Hillary Clinton charged that the attacks on her husband were part of a "vast conspiracy," she may have exaggerated. Yet throughout his presidency, Clinton's foes took extraordinary measures to tarnish his reputation. This said, the specific source of Clinton's impeachment, his testimony in the Paula Jones case regarding his relationship with Monica Lewinsky, even if it was not an impeachable offense, speaks volumes about Clinton, the person. Even if a cabal existed to topple the president, Clinton, of his own volition, chose to have a sexual relationship with Lewinsky, and he chose to deny this relationship in his deposition and in a special televised address to the American people. These actions, which he ultimately admitted, stained his presidency and diverted attention from his many other accomplishments.

Suggested Readings: All quotes from "House of Representatives Casts Historic Vote to Impeach Clinton," *Congressional Quarterly Almanac*, 1998, pp. 12-3–12-48; Charles J. Cooper, "A Perjurer in the White House? The Constitutional Case for Perjury and Obstruction of Justice as High Crimes and Misdemeanors," *Harvard Journal of Law and Public Policy* 22:2 (Spring 1999), p. 619; *Historic Documents*, 1998, p. 564; http://www.washingtonpost.com/wp-srv/politics/special/clinton/clinton.htm; Bruce Miroff, "The Contemporary Presidency: Moral Character in the White House: From Republican to Democratic" *Presidential Studies Quarterly* 29:3 (1999), p. 708; Richard A. Posner, *An Affair of State* (Cambridge, MA: Harvard University Press, 1999).

INDEPENDENT COUNSEL LAW. First enacted in 1978 in the wake of the Watergate scandal (the attempted burglary of the Democratic Party's headquarters that led to Richard Nixon's resignation) the independent counsel law was reauthorized by the U.S. **House of Representatives** and the U.S. **Senate** in mid-1994 and was subsequently signed into law by President Bill Clinton on June 24, 1994. Ironically, after the first law expired in 1992, the Democratic Party, more than the Republicans, pushed for its reauthorization. Many Republicans had soured on the independent counsel law due to the long and costly Iran-Contra investigation headed by Lawrence Walsh. However, as the **Whitewater** scandal gained attention, an increasing number of Republicans clamored for the law's renewal. Even before it was reauthorized, **Robert Fiske** had been appointed as a special prosecutor to investigate the Whitewater affair. When the law was officially reauthorized, a special court that oversaw the appointment of special prosecutors removed Fiske and replaced him with **Kenneth Starr** to avoid the appearance of a conflict of interest.

Four years later, following the expansion of Starr's investigation into the **Monica Lewinsky** affair and the **impeachment** of President Clinton, the independent counsel law came under increasing fire. Just as Republicans had complained that Lawrence Walsh had overzealously pursued the Iran-Contra affair, Democrats criticized Starr for spending over $50 million to investigate Clinton. Other independent counsels, critics observed, similarly spent what the critics considered to be exorbitant sums in pursuit of the other members of Clinton's administration. To make matters worse, quite often, as in the case of independent counsel Donald Smaltz's investigation of Secretary of Agriculture **Mike Espy**, which cost about $17 million, an acquittal rather than a conviction was the final outcome of the investigation. In December 1998, the National Commission on the Separation of Powers, headquartered at the University of Virginia, termed the independent counsel law "seriously flawed" and called for allowing it to expire in 1999. After holding hearings on the independent counsel's office, Congress agreed to just that. While independent counsel offices that had already been established were allowed to continue their investigations and complete their reports, Congress chose not to renew the independent counsel law in 1999.

Suggested Readings: "Commission on the Role of the Independent Counsel," *Historic Documents*, 1998, p. 905; "Independent Counsel Law Renewed," *Congressional Quarterly Almanac*, 1994, p. 295.

Related Entries: Brown, Ronald; Cisneros, Henry G.; Herman, Alexis; Ray, Robert.

INFLATION. During the 1992 presidential campaign, some Republicans sought to call up the nation's memory of the last years of Jimmy Carter's presidency. Bill Clinton, like Carter, they suggested, favored big government and big spending, and his election would result in the return of double-digit inflation. (Consumer prices rose 11.3 and 13.5 percent in 1979 and 1980, respectively.) Contrary to these dire predictions, inflation remained very low throughout Clinton's presidency, averaging about 2.5 percent, less than the 4.2 percent average annual rate of increase during the Ronald Reagan and **George Bush** years (see Table 13). Indeed, stable prices lay at the foundation of the economic expansion of the Clinton years, allowing the United States to overcome years of stagflation and economic instability.

Inflation remained low for numerous reasons. Over a decade before Clinton was elected president, Federal Reserve Board Chairman Paul Volcker undertook a tight-money policy aimed at breaking the upward spiral of prices that peaked during the late 1970s and early 1980s. His successor, **Alan Greenspan**, maintained the Federal Reserve Board's hawkish stance toward inflation, raising interest rates whenever prices showed signs of increasing. Yet inflation did not remain low during the 1990s because of Chairman Greenspan alone. The globalization of the **economy** created a downward pressure on prices. Most simply, firms that had to compete globally had to become more efficient and competitive to survive. Simultaneously, increases in productivity allowed U.S. employers to pay higher wages without increasing the costs of their goods. The economic crisis in Asia, in 1998, which limited demand for key commodities, most notably oil, exerted a downward pressure on prices as well. Finally, the Clinton administration's decision to focus on cutting the **budget** deficit rather than stimulating the economy or cutting taxes, combined with Secretary of the Treasury **Robert Rubin**'s adept leadership, contributed to the low inflation of the era. Ironically, toward the end of Clinton's term, oil prices began to rise precipitously, threatening to set off a new round of overall price hikes or the end of the economic expansion, or both.

Suggested Readings: http://www.census.gov/statab/freq/99s0776.txt; Robert Pollin, "Anatomy of Clintonomics," *New Left Review*, May/June 2000, p. 17; *Statistical Abstract of the United States, 2000* (Washington, DC: GPO, 2000).

Related Entry: Economy.

Figure 9
Inflation Rate

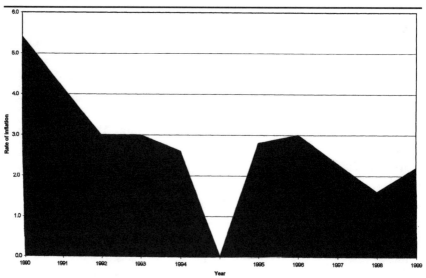

Source: Economic Report of the President, 2000.

Table 13
Inflation: Consumer Prices

Year	Rate of Increase
1990	5.4
1991	4.2
1992	3.0
1993	3.0
1994	2.6
1995	2.8
1996	3.0
1997	2.3
1998	1.6
1999	2.2
2000	(est.) 3.2

Source: Statistical Abstract of the United States 2000.

INTERNAL REVENUE SERVICE OVERHAUL ACT OF 1998. In 1998, Congress passed and President Bill Clinton signed into law the Internal Revenue Service Overhaul Act. The measure was aimed at providing taxpayers with greater protections in their dealings with the Internal Revenue Service (IRS). Most important, it shifted the burden of proof in many tax cases from the defendant to the federal agency. The law also restricted the right of the IRS to seize property, charge interest, and assess penalties and made it easier for citizens to sue the agency. Momentum for the bill grew out of several forces, ranging from long-standing cries for tax cuts and simplification to antigovernment fervor. In the fall of 1997, the **Senate** Finance Committee held hearings on the IRS, during which a parade of witnesses detailed stories of IRS abuse and malfeasance. Shortly after these hearings, the **House of Representatives** passed a bill to overhaul the IRS, but a similar measure did not reach the Senate floor until it had adjourned, because, according to some, the Republican Party sought to turn animosity against the IRS into a campaign issue in 1998. President Clinton's endorsement of the measure, along with support it received from Democrats in the House and Senate, however, compelled the leadership of the Republican Party to put the bill to a vote long before the election of 1998. Clinton signed the Act into law on July 22, 1998.

Suggested Readings: "Clinton Signs into Law IRS Overhaul Bill," *Congressional Quarterly Almanac*, 1998, p. 21-3; "IRS Overhaul Sails through House," *Congressional Quarterly Almanac*, 1997, p. 2-71.

INTERNET POLICY. *See* **High Technology; Magaziner, Ira C**.

IRAQ. President Bill Clinton inherited from the **George Bush** administration tenuous relations with the nation of Iraq. These relations remained strained throughout the Clinton presidency, producing several crises. The one constant throughout was **Saddam Hussein**'s ability to maintain his power in Iraq in spite of economic sanctions, military restrictions, and occasional U.S. attacks.

While the Bush administration effectively repulsed Iraq's invasion of Kuwait and threat to Saudi Arabia during the Persian Gulf War, President George Bush decided not to risk an all-out invasion of Iraq aimed at overthrowing Hussein. Instead, the United States established "no-fly zones" over sections of southern and northern Iraq, which prevented Hussein from attacking Kurdish rebels or menacing forces allied with the United States in the South. In addition, the Bush administration imposed strict economic sanctions on Iraq and insisted that they would remain in effect until Iraq destroyed all of its weapons of mass destruction and allowed United Nations weapons inspectors to conduct unfettered inspections of Iraq. The Clinton administration maintained these no-fly zones and economic sanctions. (Toward the end of the Clinton presidency, the sanctions were modified to allow Iraq to import more food and medicine for humanitarian needs.)

On several occasions, the Clinton administration authorized air strikes against Iraq to enforce these restraints and/or to punish other transgressions. In 1993, the United States twice attacked Iraq, once in retaliation for an alleged attempt on the life of former president George Bush. In the fall of 1996, the United States intervened again when Saddam Hussein sought to bolster a faction of Kurds that opposed the main faction of Kurdish rebels. Some Republicans criticized this action on the grounds that it was ineffective and allowed Hussein to win sympathy from Arab nations. Conservatives issued more serious charges against the president after he ordered a more massive bombing of Iraq in late 1998. The president insisted that he had ordered this attack, which lasted four days, to compel Hussein to allow UN weapons inspectors to complete their work within Iraq. In early 1999, the U.S. and British air forces conducted additional raids. Some Republicans questioned the timing of these bombings, suggesting that they were aimed at diverting the public's attention away from the **impeachment** scandal.

The disputes between UN inspectors and Hussein were ongoing. In late 1997, **Russia** brokered an agreement allowing UN experts to conduct their investigations, but in mid-January 1998, Iraq once again stopped the inspectors from checking eight presidential palaces. Throughout the spring of 1998, Hussein played cat and mouse with inspectors, agreeing to cooperate and then prohibiting UN experts from doing their job. The resignation of William Scott Ridder, Jr., a U.S. citizen who worked with the UN team, due to what he perceived as the U.S. refusal to compel Hussein to live up to his agreement, exacerbated the situation.

By ordering the bombing of Iraq, Clinton sought to punish Hussein for his intransigence, but at the same time, the bombing insured that Hussein would not allow inspections to resume in the near future. While Republican presidential candidate **George W. Bush** criticized the inability of the Clinton administration to end Hussein's rule, Vice President **Al Gore** defended the administration's record, arguing that long-term sanctions had worked in the past and could work again. Moreover, few in Washington or elsewhere offered specific alternatives to the policy begun at the end of the Persian Gulf War, and until or unless Hussein committed another major transgression, U.S. leaders were unlikely to win support, either at home or abroad, for a more sustained and dangerous armed intervention in the region.

Suggested Readings: Justin Brown, "Clinton Rethinks Iraq Policy As UN Sanctions Falter," *Christian Science Monitor*, March 1, 2000, p. 2; "CIA Director on Situation in Iraq," *Historic Documents*, 1996, p. 680; "Clinton on Air Strikes against Iraq," *Historic Documents*, 1998, p. 935; F. Gregory Gause III, "Getting It Backward on Iraq," *Foreign Affairs* 78:3 (May/June, 1999), p. 54.

Related Entries: Foreign Policy; Middle East.

ISRAEL. *See* **Middle East.**

"IT'S THE ECONOMY, STUPID." If Bill Clinton's campaign for the presidency in 1992 had one single message, it was "It's the **economy**, stupid." Coined as a slogan and adopted as a strategy for defeating **George Bush** by **James Carville**, the phrase emphasized what the Clinton team saw as Bush's primary fault and Clinton's key promise. Bush was considered a shoo-in for reelection following the Persian Gulf War, but his popularity fell precipitously as the economy sank into recession in 1991. Even though Bush argued that the recession had ended, Carville and others believed that if Clinton could keep the public focussed on the economy, Bush would lose. The Bush campaign did its best to focus the public's attention on issues of character and Clinton's lack of **foreign policy** experience, but the Clinton camp, in arguing why Americans should vote for the governor of Arkansas, continually emphasized, "It's the economy, stupid." In 2000, when Carville was asked whom **Al Gore** should nominate as his running mate, he suggested former Secretary of the Treasury **Robert Rubin** because, Carville argued, Rubin's nomination would capture the essential accomplishment of the Clinton presidency, which was "the economy, stupid."

Suggested Reading: Mary Matalin and James Carville, *All's Fair: Love, War, and Running for President*, (New York: Raven House, 1994); Gerald M. Pomper, Walter D. Burnham, et al., *The Election of 1992* (New York: Seven Bridges Press, 1993).

Related Entry: Election of 1992.

J

JOHNSON, NORMA HOLLOWAY. (1933, Lake Charles, Louisiana–   .)
U.S. District-Court Judge.

Judge Norma Holloway Johnson was a key player in the **impeachment**
process. As the chief U.S. district-court judge in the District of Columbia,
she supervised the proceedings of the grand jury that investigated President Bill Clinton's relationship to **Monica Lewinsky**. On numerous occasions, she issued rulings on motions filed by independent counsel
Kenneth Starr and/or the attorneys of other figures involved in the ongoing investigation into President Clinton's conduct. Perhaps most important, Judge Johnson determined that President Clinton could not
invoke executive privilege to avoid turning over documents requested by
the office of the independent counsel. On another occasion, she ruled
that Monica Lewinsky had not secured a grant of immunity from the
independent prosecutor, Lewinsky's lawyer **William Ginsburg**'s conten-
tions notwithstanding. In still another instance, Judge Johnson censured
Starr's office for violating grand-jury secrecy rules. Although Judge Johnson is a registered Democrat and a Jimmy Carter appointee, Republicans
had few complaints about Johnson's oversight of the case.

Johnson was raised in Lake Charles, Louisiana, a black girl in the segregated South. For years she taught school, and she put herself through
Georgetown Law School. As a judge, she gained a reputation for her
toughness and generally favorable relationship with prosecutors. Appointed a district-court judge in 1980, she oversaw several high-profile
cases involving government figures. In 1984, she sentenced Rita M. Lav-
elle, a Reagan appointee to the Environmental Protection Agency, to six
months in prison for lying to Congress. Similarly, she handed down a
seventeen-month prison term to Congressman Dan Rostenkowski, a
prominent Democrat from Chicago, for mail fraud. Johnson guarded her

own privacy, however, and turned down the media's requests to attend grand-jury proceedings and for access to written records. (Grand-jury proceedings are supposed to be secret or closed.) Her rulings in these instances were upheld by appellate courts.

Suggested Readings: Melinda Henneberger, "Testing of a President: The Judge," *New York Times*, May 7, 1998, p. A20; Ruth Marcus, "Lawyers and Erring Officials Feel Wrath of Chief Judge Johnson," *Washington Post*, March 20, 1998, p. A20.

Related Entries: Jones, Paula; Whitewater.

JONES, PAULA. (1966–   .) Plaintiff in sexual harassment suit *Jones v. Clinton.*

In May 1994, Paula Corbin Jones filed a lawsuit against President Bill Clinton alleging that in May 1991, while he was still governor of Arkansas, he had exposed himself and propositioned her at the Excelsior Hotel in Little Rock, Arkansas. Clinton denied Jones's claim. A state employee at the time, Jones claimed that Clinton's unsolicited advance constituted sexual harassment. In January 1998, Jones's attorneys asked Clinton about his relationship with **Monica Lewinsky** because they sought to establish a pattern of deception on the president's part. Clinton denied that he had had sex with Monica Lewinsky. Independent counsel **Kenneth Starr**'s investigation into Monica Lewinsky and the **impeachment** charges leveled against the president stemmed from Jones's suit. Clinton allegedly perjured himself in a deposition he gave in the Paula Jones case and in grand-jury proceedings.

Ironically, if it had not been not for an article that appeared in the January edition of the *American Spectator*, a conservative magazine, in which David Brock named Jones as one of the **women** with whom the president had had an affair, Jones probably would not have brought the suit. In addition, Jones nearly settled the suit out of court in exchange for about $700,000 prior to Clinton's deposition. The reasons they did not settle at that time are heavily debated by those who have examined the history of the case. Some claim that Clinton's unwillingness to apologize to Jones prompted her to reject the settlement. Others argue that archconservatives convinced Jones to dismiss her lawyers, who favored the settlement. In addition, Bill and **Hillary Clinton** were reluctant to settle because they felt that it would encourage more frivolous suits— they felt that Jones's suit was politically motivated from the start.

Paula Corbin grew up in Lonoke, Arkansas, a poor farming community

Paula Jones meets reporters in Washington, February 11, 1994. AP/Wide World Photos.

roughly thirty miles from Little Rock. After dropping out of high school, she held a variety of jobs, ultimately landing a position with the Arkansas Industrial Development Commission (AIDC), a state job. Clinton's contact with Jones stemmed from an AIDC conference held in 1991. Those who challenged the veracity of Jones's allegations emphasized that she did not file a complaint in 1991 or inform anyone about the proposition. Clinton's attorneys added that she could not prove that she suffered any retribution or penalties for rebuffing Clinton's alleged advance. After the alleged meeting, Corbin married, bore two sons, and relocated to California. Only after the *American Spectator* article did she seek legal advice. When her lawyer, Danny Traylor, failed to get the magazine to retract its statement that a woman named "Paula" had had an affair with Clinton, Jones hired two new lawyers, Joseph Cammarata and Gilbert Davis, to pursue her complaint further. Throughout the mid-1990s, she was prodded by a number of archconservatives who had long sought to damage Clinton's reputation, including Cliff Jackson, an Arkansas-based anti-Clinton activist, and Susan Carpenter-McMillan, an antiabortion activist who befriended Jones after she moved to California.

Jones experienced both victories and defeats in the courts. In 1994, a district court granted President Clinton temporary immunity from Jones's sexual harassment suit. Two years later, the Eighth Circuit Court of Appeals reversed this decision, and on May 27, 1997, the **Supreme Court** unanimously upheld the circuit court's decision. Writing for the Court, Justice John Paul Stevens reasoned that it was "highly unlikely" that Jones's suit would "occupy any substantial amount of [Clinton's] time." In fact, the Jones case and controversies stemming from it became the central focus of the Clinton administration and the nation through much of 1998. Less than a year later, U.S. District Judge **Susan Webber Wright** dismissed Jones's lawsuit, ruling that even if Jones proved that the president had propositioned her, she had no evidence of sexual harassment. However, before Wright issued her ruling, Jones's attorneys had deposed Clinton. Since they knew that they had little chance of establishing that Jones had suffered economic harm because of Clinton (technically, a sexual harassment suit is an employment-discrimination suit), they focussed on Clinton's sex life, particularly his relationship with Monica Lewinsky. They had been tipped off about Clinton's affair with Lewinsky by **Lucianne Goldberg**, **Linda Tripp**'s book agent. Following revelations of Clinton's testimony about Monica Lewinsky, in which he denied having had an affair with her, Clinton settled with Jones. She received $850,000, far less than her attorney's bills; Clinton neither apologized to her nor admitted any guilt. In April 1999, after the **Senate** acquitted President Clinton of impeachment charges brought by the **House of Representatives**, Judge Wright held Clinton in civil contempt for having testified falsely in his deposition in the Jones case. Independent counsel **Robert Ray** still had to determine whether to pursue criminal perjury charges against Bill Clinton. Already, Clinton had lost his license to practice law in the state of Arkansas as a result of his false testimony in the deposition.

On January 19, 2001, Clinton struck a deal with Ray in which he admitted having testified falsely during his deposition in the Jones case. In exchange for this admission, Ray agreed to not pursue the case against Clinton any further.

Chronology

May 8, 1991	According to Paula Corbin (Jones), she and Bill Clinton meet at the Excelsior Hotel in Little Rock, Arkansas.
Dec. 18, 1993 (Jan. 1994 edition)	David Brock's article "His Cheatin' Heart" appears in *American Spectator*, identifying Jones as one of the women in Clinton's life.
Feb. 11, 1994	Jones accuses Clinton of sexual harassment; she meets Michael Isikoff (then of the *Washington Post*), who was planning to write a book on Clinton's sex life.
May 6, 1994	Jones's lawyers file sexual harassment lawsuit against Clinton.
May 27, 1997	Supreme Court upholds circuit-court decision, 9–0, that Jones's suit may proceed.
Jan. 17, 1998	Clinton denies having had sex with Monica Lewinsky in deposition in the Jones case.
April 1, 1998	Judge Susan Webber Wright dismisses Jones's sexual harassment suit.
Nov. 19, 1998	Clinton settles case with Jones, paying her $850,000. He does not apologize or admit guilt.
July 30, 1999	Judge Susan Webber Wright finds President Clinton in civil contempt for falsely testifying in the Jones case about Monica Lewinsky.
Jan. 19, 2001	President Clinton admits that he testified falsely in his deposition in the Paula Jones case. Independent counsel Robert Ray agrees to drop all charges against the president.

Suggested Readings: Melinda Henneberger, "Testing of a President: The Accuser," *New York Times*, March 12, 1998, p. A1; Michael Isikoff and Stuart Taylor, Jr., "The Paula Problem," *Newsweek*, January 26, 1998, p. 24; Neil A. Lewis, "Clinton Settles Jones Lawsuit with a Check of $850,000," *New York Times*, January 13, 1999, p. A14; Lois Romano, "Exiting Center Stage, Jones Weighs Appeal," *Washington Post*, April 12, 1998, p. A1; Jeffrey Toobin, *A Vast Conspiracy: The Real Story of the Sex Scandal That Nearly Brought Down a President* (New York: Random House, 1999).

Related Entries: Bennett, Robert; Broaddrick, Juanita; Flowers, Gennifer; Whitewater; Willey, Kathleen.

President Clinton with friend and golfing partner, Vernon Jordan, Oak Bluffs, Massachusetts, August 26, 1997. AP/Wide World Photos.

JORDAN, VERNON EULION, JR. (August 15, 1935, Atlanta, Georgia– .) Adviser to President Clinton.

One of President Clinton's closest friends and advisers, Vernon Jordan became a key figure during the **impeachment** process when questions arose as to the role Jordan had played in getting **Monica Lewinsky** a job in the private sector and advising her and the president on how they should testify. Independent counsel **Kenneth Starr** accused President Clinton of perjuring himself in testimony about a conversation he had

had with Jordan regarding Lewinsky. Jordan denied urging Lewinsky to lie under oath or attempting to buy her silence by securing her employment. In his report to Congress, Starr did not officially challenge Jordan's testimony by accusing him of perjury.

The grandson of a sharecropper, Jordan was born in Atlanta, Georgia, in 1935. He received his B.A. from DePauw University in 1957 and his law degree from Howard University in 1960. For two decades, Jordan was a prominent civil rights activist, working for the National Association for the Advancement of Colored People (NAACP), the Voter Education Project of the Southern Regional Council, and the United Negro College Fund. From 1972 through 1981, he served as the director of the National Urban League. On May 29, 1980, he was shot in the back by a white supremacist in Fort Wayne, Indiana. After recovering, he remained director of the Urban League for another year. Throughout the 1980s and 1990s, Jordan practiced law, becoming a partner in a prominent Washington, D.C., firm. During this period, Jordan earned a reputation as a power broker and fixer. He also served on the corporate boards of some of the largest companies in the world.

Jordan and Clinton first met during the 1970s while Jordan was still working for the National Urban League. They became friends, bonding in part around their joint interest in civil rights. The two golfed and vacationed together and communicated regularly. During Clinton's presidency, they continued to vacation together on Martha's Vineyard and exchange Christmas presents. In 1991, Jordan and Clinton traveled together in Germany, where Jordan exposed Clinton to prominent foreign businessmen and political leaders. After the **election of 1992**, Jordan cochaired Clinton's transition team. Although Jordan had no official role or title, Washington insiders recognized their close relationship. Clinton often turned to Jordan for advice on important appointments to top-level posts. When **Vincent Foster** committed suicide, Clinton turned to Jordan for solace. Thus it was not surprising that Clinton directed Monica Lewinsky Jordan's way when she requested help finding a job. Given Jordan's unyielding loyalty to Clinton, it is unlikely whether the exact advice he gave to Lewinsky and precisely what she told him will ever be known— her testimony made it seem that she thought that he knew that she had had an affair with the president, but she did not detail the extent of her relationship with Clinton.

Suggested Readings: Marc Fisher, "First Friend," *Washington Post*, January 27, 1998, p. E1; Jeff Gerth, "The First Friend," *New York Times*, July 14, 1996, p. 1; Charles D. Lowery and John F. Marszalek, eds., *Encyclopedia of African-American Civil Rights* (Westport, CT: Greenwood Press, 1992), p. 290.

K

KANTOR, MICKEY. (August 7, 1939, Nashville, Tennessee– .) U.S. Trade Representative, 1993–1996; Secretary of Commerce, 1996–1997; Counsel to President Clinton, 1998–1999.

Mickey Kantor played various roles during Bill Clinton's presidency. After serving as Clinton's campaign chairman in 1992, he was appointed U.S. trade representative. In 1996, following the death of **Ron Brown**, Kantor became the secretary of commerce. Afterwards, he was a member of the legal team that advised President Clinton during the **impeachment** process. He often acted as an administration spokesperson on national news shows. Because he had helped Clinton survive the **Gennifer Flowers** scandal in 1992, the president often trusted Kantor to provide him with sound political advice.

Kantor was born in Nashville, Tennessee, and graduated from Vanderbilt University in 1961. After spending four years in the navy, he earned his law degree at Georgetown University. In 1972, he served as the staff coordinator for Sargent Shriver, George McGovern's running mate. In the following years he worked for several other Democratic candidates, including California senator Alan Cranston, California governor Jerry Brown, and Minnesota senator and vice president Walter Mondale. A good friend of **Hillary Rodham Clinton** from the time of their work together on the Legal Services Corporation, Kantor joined Clinton's campaign team in 1992, heading daily operations in New Hampshire and New York. After the election, Kantor organized an economic conference or summit that reinforced the message that Clinton intended to focus on the **economy** after assuming office.

As U.S. trade representative, Kantor oversaw the final rounds of negotiations of **GATT** and lobbied for passage of **NAFTA**. While the **trade deficit** grew steadily prior to and after Clinton took office, Kantor argued in favor of expanded trade as a key to sustained economic growth. In negotiations with the European Community, Kantor pushed hard to break down barriers to American goods and services, especially those that gave European companies advantages in the entertainment and software industries. He also demanded a reduction of subsidies to several highly protected European industries, such as wine. As secretary of commerce, Kantor continued to promote international trade and international agreements that opened markets to American goods.

At times Kantor was criticized for capitalizing on his position. During his confirmation hearing for secretary of commerce, some wondered about potential conflicts of interest stemming from work he had done for the law firm of Manatt, Phelps, Phillips and Kantor, which represented numerous foreign clients and large U.S. corporations. Other questions were raised regarding the role he had played in helping **Whitewater** defendant **Webster Hubbell** obtain business after he was forced to resign as associate attorney general. However, no formal charges were ever filed against Kantor. After he left the Clinton administration, Kantor went to work as a consultant in the business world. His clients included United Parcel Service, which sought to increase its trade with China.

Suggested Readings: *Current Biography Yearbook*, 1994, p. 289; "Poor Judgment But No Smoking Gun," *U.S. News & World Report*, April 14, 1997, p. 38; Richard W. Stevenson, "President Triple-Teams His Lewinsky Problem," *New York Times*, August 5, 1998, p. A20.

Related Entries: Barshefsky, Charlene; Cabinet; Election of 1992.

KEMP, JACK FRENCH. (July 13, 1935, Los Angeles, California–   .) Vice presidential candidate, 1996.

In 1996, Jack Kemp was Senator **Robert Dole**'s running mate against Bill Clinton and **Al Gore**. Dole hoped that Kemp would offer a nice balance to the Republican ticket. Dole represented the World War II generation; Kemp came of age after the war and held on to some of the elan of the Kennedy years. Dole hailed from the Plains states; Kemp was from Buffalo, New York. Dole had a reputation as a moderate; Kemp had coauthored the Kemp-Roth or Reagan tax cut, one of the cornerstones of the "Reagan revolution." Last, while Dole was often criticized for being dull and unimaginative, Kemp was full of energy and innovative.

Yet Kemp's nomination failed to give the Republican ticket the boost it needed to defeat Clinton and Gore. Although many thought that the vibrant Kemp would thrash Gore in their one-on-one debate, Kemp's explanation of Dole's proposed tax cut fell flat, and Gore was deemed the winner by most observers. Kemp's unwillingness to demand a constitutional amendment to ban abortion and to end **affirmative action** hurt him with the conservative base of the Republican Party. Indeed, insofar as Dole selected Kemp because he hoped that the onetime football star and congressman from New York would help the Republican Party win a sizeable segment of the **African American** vote, Kemp proved the wrong selection, because the vast majority of blacks remained loyal to Clinton and Gore. Nor did Kemp enable Dole to win back the so-called Reagan Democrats who had deserted the Republican Party in 1992.

Kemp served in Congress from 1971 to 1989 and as **George Bush**'s secretary of housing and urban development during 1989–1992. In this latter post, he earned notoriety for rushing off to Los Angeles in the immediate aftermath of the Los Angeles riots that followed the acquittal of four Los Angeles policemen on charges of beating Rodney King, a black man. This action, motivated by Kemp's long-standing interest in the concerns of the urban poor, embarrassed President Bush and hurt Kemp with many Republican stalwarts. Some expected him to pursue the Republican presidential nomination in 1996, but he chose not to for a variety of reasons, ranging from Dole's commanding lead to his own problems with social conservatives in the party who distrusted him because of his lukewarm endorsement of many of their top priorities. After the 1996 election, Kemp appeared on television news shows and lectured.

Suggested Readings: *Current Biography Yearbook*, 1980, p. 181; Jack Kemp, *An American Renaissance: A Strategy for the 1980s* (Falls Church, VA: Conservative Press, 1979); Tom Raum, "Back to the Campaign Trail," *Associated Press*, October 10, 1996; David Rosenbaum, "A Passion for Ideas," *New York Times*, August 11, 1996, p. 1.

Related Entry: Election of 1996.

KENDALL, DAVID. (May 2, 1944, Camp Atterbury, Indiana– .) Counsel to President Clinton, 1993–   .

David Kendall served as President Bill Clinton's private attorney through much of Clinton's presidency. A partner at Williams and Connolly, a prominent Washington, D.C., law firm, Kendall began working for Clinton in 1993, developing a legal strategy for dealing with the **Whitewater** scandal. When the Whitewater probe broadened into an investigation of Clinton's sexual relationship with **Monica Lewinsky** and his alleged perjury in the **Paula Jones** lawsuit, Kendall remained part of the president's defense team. During the **impeachment** hearings before the **House** Judiciary Committee, Kendall continued to play a leading role. Although numerous commentators criticized Kendall, arguing that he should have settled the case with Jones much earlier or prompted Clinton to tell the truth about his relationship with Lewinsky, others contended that his strategy guaranteed Clinton an acquittal in the **Senate** and protected him from criminal charges. Others added that given the drive of some of Clinton's adversaries to remove him from office, any accommodation or admission of guilt would have only whetted their appetite.

Born in Indiana, Kendall earned his B.A. from Wabash College in 1966. Afterwards, he studied at Oxford University on a Rhodes scholarship. Like Clinton, Kendall earned his law degree from Yale Law School (1971). After clerking for U.S. **Supreme Court** Justice Byron White, Kendall went to work for Williams and Connolly. Kendall knew Clinton from their days together in England and at Yale Law School.

Suggested Reading: Francine Kiefer, "All the President's Men (and One Woman)," *Christian Science Monitor*, January 22, 1999, p. 2.

Related Entries: Bennett, Robert; White House Defense Team.

KOREA. Once considered one of the weakest aspects of President Clinton's **foreign policy**, Korea may turn out to be his administration's greatest achievement. In the spring of 1994, a letter from Assistant Secretary of State Winston Lord to Secretary of State **Warren Christopher** that was sharply critical of the drift of American foreign policy in Asia was leaked to the press. As foreign policy expert William Hyland observed, Lord criticized the administration's policy of confronting **China** over most-favored-nation status and North Korea over its nuclear weapons program. Other foreign policy experts argued that the Clinton administration had demonstrated "little evidence that they understand the dynamics of Asia" (Hyland, *Clinton's World*), adding that the problem was due to the president's lack of interest in foreign policy. Put somewhat differently, various pundits contended that the administration lacked a long-term strategy in Asia and largely adopted a crisis-management approach to the region.

In 1994, Clinton nearly ordered the bombing of North Korea because of suspicions that it was developing nuclear weapons. Long considered one of the most isolated nations in the world, North Korea, many feared, might use its nuclear weapons for numerous reasons, none of them good.

Rather than ordering an air strike of potential nuclear facilities, however, the administration negotiated a compromise with North Korea. Former President Jimmy Carter traveled to North Korea to work out the details of the agreement. In exchange for North Korea's agreement to suspend its nuclear weapons program, the United States pledged to lift economic sanctions against it, to provide oil, and to help North Korea construct nuclear reactors that could be used to generate electricity but not weapons. The agreement represented one of the first thaws in relations between the West and North Korea since the end of the Korean War in 1953.

In 1998, however, tensions between the two nations developed again when North Korea launched a rocket over the Sea of Japan, a seeming violation of the 1994 agreement. Over the course of the following year, U.S. and North Korean diplomats negotiated a settlement to this dispute. The United States agreed to continue to lift economic sanctions, and North Korea pledged to suspend testing of long-range missiles. Moreover, North Korean leaders displayed an interest in normalizing relations with the West and reunifying with South Korea. Leaders from the two Koreas met at a summit in June 1999, paving the way for numerous other steps toward rapprochement. While nearly 40,000 U.S. troops remained in South Korea, committed to defending it from an invasion, U.S. diplomats welcomed North Korea's growing engagement with nations in Europe and Asia, including Australia and Japan. Other important symbolic steps toward reunification took place in 2000. For instance, North and South Korean athletes marched together in Olympic ceremonies in Sydney, Australia. In the wake of the Olympics, rumors spread that Clinton might even travel to North Korea. While he did not, Secretary of State **Madeleine Albright** met with North Korean leader Kim Jong Il in Pyongyang, North Korea. Their meeting was another first. While many barriers to the peaceful reunification of the Korean peninsula remained, the Clinton administration felt that important steps toward resolving one of the potentially most dangerous disputes in the world took place under its watch.

Suggested Readings: Bruce Cumings, "Toward a Comprehensive Settlement of the Korea Problem," *Current History*, 98, December 1999, p. 403; John Feffer, "In Focus: A New Era for the Korean Peninsula," 5:18 (June 2000), http://www.foreignpolicy-infocus.org/briefs/vol5/v5n18korea.html; Michael Hirsh, "Just Getting to Know You," *Newsweek*, November 6, 2000, p. 48; William G. Hyland, *Clinton's World*, (Westport, CT: Praeger, 1999), pp. 132–33.

KOSOVO. On March 24, 1999, U.S. military forces in concert with its **NATO** allies began air attacks on Serbian forces and military targets in

F-16 Fighting Falcon during the war in Kosovo. Department of Defense.

the former Yugoslavia. The United States and NATO commenced these attacks in order to compel Serbian forces to withdraw from Kosovo, one of the provinces of Yugoslavia. Yugoslavian troops had launched attacks on ethnic Albanians who constituted the majority of the population in the province of Kosovo. Many were forced to flee into Albania itself by the Yugoslavian and U.S./NATO attacks. Critics of Bill Clinton claimed that the U.S. attack prompted Yugoslavian forces to drive deeper into Kosovo, leading to a mass exodus of Albanian ethnics out of their homeland. The Clinton administration argued that masses of Serbian (Yugoslavian) troops had readied themselves for an invasion of Kosovo and that Serb forces and paramilitary groups had already commenced the "ethnic cleansing" of Kosovo prior to the first air raids.

Regardless of the exact sequence of events, the immediate impact of the air attacks appeared to backfire. Instead of withdrawing from Kosovo, Serb forces drove further into the province, and the wave of refugees fleeing for protection in Albania and elsewhere grew rapidly. In spite of much criticism of his actions, President Clinton held firm. At the same time, the president insisted that he would not need to introduce ground troops, which nearly all experts agreed would lead to a long and dangerous period of fighting. Congressional support of the president was weak at best, particularly among Republicans. Some conservatives argued that the war in Kosovo would turn into another **Vietnam**, trapping the military in another quagmire. In Kosovo, as in Vietnam, they contended, the United States lacked a clear objective and exit strategy. Others asserted that the Clinton administration unfairly singled out Serbs for criticism without acknowledging the complicity of ethnic Albanian radicals in the deterioration of the rule of law in Kosovo. Nonetheless, the president maintained that Yugoslavia, led by indicted war criminal **Slobodan Milosevic**, deserved the blame for the flood of refugees and insisted that air strikes alone would achieve the military objective of driving Serb forces out of Kosovo.

On June 10, 1999, Operation Allied Force, as the air war was officially known, came to an end. In the face of endless air strikes against his nation, Milosevic agreed to the cease-fire terms set out by the United States and NATO. Serb forces were completely withdrawn from Kosovo, and a process was established to resettle refugees in their homeland. An international peace force of 48,000, including 7,000 Americans, known as KFOR, entered the region. By the time the Clinton presidency came to a close, the total number of forces in Kosovo had shrunk considerably. The administration hoped to avoid permanently partitioning Kosovo into separate provinces or ethnic enclaves. Whether it could achieve this goal remained unclear, although the overthrow of Milosevic by a prodemocracy movement in Yugoslavia in the fall of 2000 offered a greater degree of hope for peace in the region than had existed in years.

One of the most significant aspects of the war in Kosovo was the power displayed by the U.S. military. For 78 days, U.S. and NATO warplanes bombed Yugoslavia with impunity. All told, the Pentagon reported that alliance aircraft flew 34,000 sorties. Throughout, U.S. and NATO forces suffered not a single casualty, and only two of its planes were lost. The Pentagon claimed that out of 23,000 bombs and missiles used, only 20 went astray and caused "collateral damage." Even if these claims were exaggerated, the main lesson of the war was that the U.S. Air Force had reached unparalleled power and efficiency. Simply stated, its planes had the ability to fly out of harm's way and to compel a determined foe to surrender. Predictions that the United States would have to send in ground forces to achieve its objectives proved wrong, as did warnings that Kosovo would end in another quagmire like that in Vietnam. As General **Henry Shelton**, the chairman of the Joint Chiefs of Staff, put it, "I do not believe Milosevic ever understood the level of damage that an expertly executed air campaign could achieve" (http://defenselink.mil/ news/June1999/n06111999_9906113.html). The same could be said for many of the Clinton administration's friends and foes, none of whom had ever witnessed such an imposing display of air power.

Suggested Readings: "The Balkans Keeping the Kosovo: The Costs of Liberal Imperialism," *National Review*, September 27, 1999, p. 22; David Callahan, "The

Lessons of Kosovo," *Washington Monthly*, July 1999, p. 34; Ivo Daalder and Michael O'Hanlon, "Unlearning the Lessons of Kosovo," *Foreign Policy* (September 22, 1999), p. 13; http://www.defenselink.mil/news/Jun1999/n06211999_9906212. html; "Kosovo's Darkening Skies," *Economist*, August 8, 1998, p. 42; James Steinberg, "A Perfect Polemic," *Foreign Affairs* 78:6 (November/December 1999), p. 128.

Related Entry: Bosnia and Herzegovina.

L

LABOR, ORGANIZED. Organized labor stood as one of President Bill Clinton's most faithful allies throughout his presidency. Even though Clinton supported several measures, most prominently **NAFTA, welfare reform**, and most-favored-nation status for **China**, that trade unions opposed, labor remained one of Clinton's most important backers. It did so because it saw him as a much better alternative to a conservative Republican president working with a conservative Republican Congress.

Organized labor's support for Clinton was rooted first and foremost in the labor policies of the Ronald Reagan and **George Bush** administrations and the reverses that trade unions experienced during the 1980s. Trade unions lost millions of members during the 1980s, largely because of deindustrialization but also due to the antilabor tone set by President Reagan. Reagan fired striking air traffic controllers early in his presidency, appointed foes of labor unions to the National Labor Relations Board, and cast organized labor as a special interest. Many of the Republican Party's leaders, even though they presented themselves as friends of average working Americans, had very poor records on issues that mattered the most to labor's leaders, such as right-to-work laws. Hence, even before Clinton won the Democratic presidential nomination in 1992, the AFL-CIO's leadership had committed itself to going all out for the Democratic candidate in the national election.

Clinton cemented his relationship with labor by appointing persons to administration positions who had good relations with organized labor. **Robert Reich**, his first secretary of labor, although he was a supporter of free trade, was a fervid advocate of job training and other government programs aimed at helping displaced workers. Repeatedly, the Clinton administration supported raising the **minimum wage** and defended Medicare from proposed cuts. (Organized labor was a firm supporter of

Medicare and raising the minimum wage.) Clinton won labor's support, like that of other Americans, through his charisma. Unlike Reagan and Bush, Clinton made labor leaders feel welcome. In addition, on several key occasions the Clinton administration either took prolabor actions or chose not to take antilabor actions. Most notably, during the United Parcel Service (UPS) strike in Summer 1997, many politicians called on Clinton to intervene because, they argued, the striking workers were jeopardizing the health and welfare of too many Americans. Clinton resisted doing so, instead offering to mediate the strike, which ultimately the Teamsters won.

Labor's support for Clinton was also rooted in several broader macroeconomic developments. In 1998, the Labor Department revealed that labor-union membership rose for the first time in years. Government workers, in particular, were joining union ranks, thanks in part to the support they got from Democratic administrations. Overall economic growth benefited many union members. From the mid-1990s onward, real wages increased at a rate of over 3 percent per year, the fastest real-wage growth in twenty years. Construction jobs, in which unions traditionally had a stronghold, grew at a record-setting pace. Even manufacturing jobs grew, although usually in nonunion plants. Record profits in the automobile industry bolstered Clinton's standing with the United Automobile Workers, traditionally one of the strongest labor unions. Finally, the Clinton administration opposed Republican efforts to limit the ability of unions to contribute funds to political campaigns.

Of course, potential rifts between the Democratic Party and organized labor existed. As a percentage of the labor force, trade unions remained much smaller than they had during their heyday. The administration's pro-free-trade policies prodded some trade unionists to join hands with anti–World Trade Organization protesters in Seattle and to a lesser extent anti–World Bank activists in Washington, D.C., in 1999 and 2000, respectively. The economic boom of the 1990s tended to benefit the well-off the most, widening rather than closing the wealth gap in America. But labor's fervid support for **Al Gore** in the **election of 2000** indicated that labor remained solidly behind the Clinton-Gore team.

Suggested Readings: Aaron Bernstein, "Labor's Last Laugh," *Business Week*, June 2, 1997, p. 36; Kevin Sack, "The Democrats and the Unions: Differences Aside, Labor Embraces the Democrats," *New York Times*, August 26, 1996, p. A9; "Union Membership Edges Up," *Monthly Labor Review*, January 22, 1999, p. 2.

LAKE, ANTHONY. (April 2, 1939, New York, New York– .) National Security Adviser, 1993–1997.

Anthony Lake, a longtime **foreign policy** expert, served as President Clinton's national security adviser from 1993 until 1997. In 1997, Clinton nominated Lake to become the director of the embattled Central Intelligence Agency (CIA). Lake withdrew his name from nomination in the face of Republican questions about his role in the loss of military secrets to **China**.

Lake was born in New York City in 1939. His grandfather, William Hard, had once edited the *New Republic*; his mother was an editor with *Reader's Digest*. Lake earned a B.A. from Harvard University in 1961 and did postgraduate work at Cambridge University. In part inspired by President John F. Kennedy, he entered the foreign service. His first post was in **Vietnam**, where, over the course of the decade, he expressed his growing concerns about the war. In 1969, Lake became the special assistant to Henry Kissinger, President Richard Nixon's national security adviser. He resigned his position in protest against the invasion of Cambodia. He then went to work as an adviser to Senator Edmund Muskie of Maine and as a project director for the Carnegie Endowment for Peace, simultaneously earning his Ph.D. from Princeton University. When Jimmy Carter was elected president in 1976, Lake returned to government work, serving as director of policy planning under Secretary of State Cyrus Vance. During the Ronald Reagan and **George Bush** years, Lake taught at Amherst and Mount Holyoke colleges.

Along with **Strobe Talbott** and **Madeleine Albright**, Lake was one of the main shapers of Clinton's foreign policy. Lake's views were shaped by the Vietnam War, which he saw as a catastrophe, and by Jimmy Carter. The war led Lake to advocate a limited use of power. Carter prompted him to see a necessary linkage between American foreign policy and American ideals. Some described Lake as a "pragmatic neo-Wilsonian." In the fall of 1993, at Johns Hopkins University, Lake spelled out his views, declaring that America should use its power to "preserve, protect and promote democracies" (Hyland, *Clinton's World*). The extent to which Lake's views became the administration's views, however, were limited by Clinton's own pragmatic approach to both foreign policy and **domestic policy** and by the more hawkish views of foreign policy held by Madeleine Albright.

Lake played an active role in bringing to an end the conflict in **Bosnia and Herzegovina**, shuttling between America, Europe, and **Russia** to nurture support for American intervention. He advocated the expansion of **NATO** to include former members of the Warsaw Pact. Lake also played a key role in convincing President Clinton to intervene in **Haiti**. While Republicans in Congress unanimously opposed using armed force in Haiti, Lake, reared on Carter's human rights view of foreign policy, argued otherwise. While democracy did not develop in Haiti following American intervention, the fact that the United States managed to restore Jean-Bertrand Aristide, Haiti's exiled president, to power without having to fire a shot enhanced Lake's position within the State Department and among liberals.

After the **election of 1996**, Clinton changed his foreign policy team. **Sandy Berger**, Lake's deputy, took his post, and Lake was nominated to become the new director of the CIA. Convinced that they could make political capital by using Lake's nomination to raise questions about possible Chinese espionage and procurement of favors from the Clinton administration in exchange for campaign contributions, in other words, trading secrets for campaign funds, the Senate Intelligence Committee, dominated by Republicans, vigorously questioned Lake about his role in the affair. While neither these questions nor subsequent investigations into the so-called **Chinagate** scandal uncovered any wrongdoing on Lake's part, he withdrew his name from consideration for the CIA post, another casualty of the partisan divisions that dominated the nation's capital during much of the 1990s. In 1997, he joined the faculty at Georgetown University.

Suggested Readings: *Current Biography Yearbook*, 1994, p. 316; William G. Hyland, *Clinton's World: Remaking American Foreign Policy* (Westport, CT: Praeger, 1999).

Related Entries: Christopher, Warren; Defense, Military.

LATIN AMERICA. The Clinton administration inherited a situation in Latin America that was much better than the situation faced by previous administrations. Armed conflicts in Central America, one of the dominant factors of life in the 1970s and 1980s, had come to an end, and democracy had taken hold in many South American nations, which had been ruled by military dictators for decades. Human rights abuses were down, and economic growth had recommenced following the debt crises of the 1980s. The Clinton administration pledged to build on these positive trends, placing free trade in the region as the centerpiece of its **foreign**

policy. Yet by the end of Clinton's presidency, not only had the drive toward free trade stalled, but some experts wondered if it was it the key toward overcoming the most serious problems in the region.

One of the administration's first priorities and achievements was gaining passage of the North American Free Trade Agreement (**NAFTA**). The administration contended that NAFTA would help both Mexico and the United States economically and curtail the steady influx of Mexican immigrants into the United States. However, in the short run, NAFTA did not produce the economic windfall many of its advocates predicted it would. In 1994, a financial crisis erupted in Mexico as nervous investors withdrew their money from Mexican financial institutions. The Clinton administration convinced a reluctant Congress to approve a financial bailout package for Mexico, but not before millions had lost their jobs in Mexico. (The crisis began in December 1994 and did not subside until the summer of 1995, when the full amount of the loan to Mexico was paid.) Moreover, the financial crisis in Mexico made it more difficult for the Clinton administration to gain congressional support for developing free-trade agreements with the rest of Latin America. Many Democrats closely tied to the **labor** and environmental movements opposed NAFTA; the financial crisis in Mexico, as well as reports of human rights abuses against indigenous peasants in the Chiapas region, reinforced their commitment to blocking additional free-trade agreements. In 1997 and 1998, Congress rebuffed Clinton's efforts to win "fast-track" authority to negotiate a Western Hemisphere free-trade pact.

With the goal of hemispheric free trade in limbo, the Clinton administration tended to focus instead on a series of crises. In 1998, Hurricane Mitch, which some estimated was the worst storm to strike in two hundred years, devastated much of Central America. The Clinton administration prodded Congress to pass a $1-billion relief package for the region. This funding helped the people of Central America recover, but it also reminded others that American aid to Latin America had fallen 50 percent since 1988, largely due to opposition to foreign aid by Republican leaders in Congress, most prominently Senator Jesse Helms of North Carolina. While foreign aid to the region fell, military aid to fight the **drug** trade in Colombia skyrocketed. This development highlighted the degree to which U.S. policy toward Latin America was driven by domestic politics. As one Latin American specialist wrote: "The vast majority of U.S. politicians perceive that they have little to gain by questioning the U.S. 'war on drugs' in Latin America. As a result," they regularly favor "pouring more taxpayer dollars into costly eradication and interdiction efforts abroad, despite the fact that to date these programs have failed, by any measure, to diminish the flow of illicit drugs into the United States" (Youngers, "U.S. Policy").

U.S. policy toward Cuba continued to be driven by domestic political considerations. Simply stated, the anti-Castro lobby in the United States stood ready to punish politicians who favored normalization of relations with Cuba in spite of the fact that it no longer represented a strategic threat to the United States. In the mid-1990s, the Clinton administration began to relax some restrictions on Cuba. In response, Congress passed the Helms-Burton bill, which tightened the U.S. embargo on Cuba. The downing of two private U.S. planes piloted by Cuban refugees convinced President Clinton to sign the bill. During the last years of his presidency, Clinton took some steps to ease restrictions on travel to and trade with Cuba. He was prodded to do so in part by Pope John Paul II, who visited Cuba in 1998. Yet fundamentally U.S. policy toward Cuba remained unchanged in spite of European complaints that the Helms-Burton bill violated the World Trade Agreement. The **Elian Gonzalez** affair further revealed the degree to which domestic politics drove U.S. policy toward Cuba, as both major-party presidential candidates in the **election of 2000** criticized the administration's decision to return the young boy to the custody of his father in Cuba.

Haiti was the only other nation in the hemisphere to receive significant attention from the Clinton administration. In spite of Republican opposition, Clinton threatened to invade the island if its military leaders did not step aside and allow Jean-Bertrand Aristide, Haiti's exiled president to return to power. While Clinton and his surrogates defended the decision to intervene, nearly all agreed that Aristide's return did not usher in an era of genuine democracy.

In Haiti and in much of Latin America, the greatest problem remained **poverty**. While the proportion of people living in poverty declined slightly during the 1990s, the total number of poor people increased because of the high rate of population growth and the persistence of economic inequality in the region. Whether the further relaxation of trade restrictions will ameliorate the situation remains unclear. The fact that the drive to create a hemispheric free-trade pact fell out of public view, however, displayed the degree to which Latin America did not remain a top priority for the Clinton administration, which looked to other regions of the world to cement its reputation as a world leader.

Suggested Readings: Michael Shifter, "United States–Latin American Relations: Shunted to Slow Track," *Current History* 97:6 (February 1998), p. 49; Coletta

President Clinton and Monica Lewinsky at a White House Christmas party, December 16, 1996. AP/Wide World Photos.

Youngers, "U.S. Policy in Latin America: Problems, Opportunities, Recommendations," http://www.irc-online.org/bulletin/bull53/index.html.

LEWINSKY, MONICA. (July 23, 1973, San Francisco, California–   .) White House intern.

When 1998 began, Monica Lewinsky was known primarily by her family, friends, and coworkers. Within one month, she had become a household name, as famous as any celebrity in the world. During this period, the media broadcast lurid stories about her alleged sexual affair with President Bill Clinton, and independent counsel **Kenneth Starr** initiated an investigation into these allegations. Over the next several months, reporters followed her everywhere, and the world wondered what she would tell Starr. Initially, in both his deposition in the **Paula Jones** case and in an address to the nation, President Clinton denied having had a sexual or improper relationship with Lewinsky. On January 26, 1998, in a live televised address, President Clinton declared, "I want you to listen to me. I did not have sexual relations with that woman, Monica Lewinsky" (Kettle, "Crisis in the White House"). On August 17, 1998, however, after Lewinsky signed an immunity agreement with Starr and agreed to cooperate with the independent counsel's office, Clinton admitted that he had had an improper relationship with Lewinsky. At the same time, he insisted that he had not perjured himself during his deposition in the Paula Jones case. Lewinsky signed an affidavit in which she denied having had a sexual relationship with Clinton. Subsequently, when questioned by Kenneth Starr, she admitted to having had sex with the president. In turn, Kenneth Starr issued a detailed report on Lewinsky's relationship with Clinton, the **U.S. House of Representatives** impeached the president on charges of perjury and obstruction of justice, and the **U.S. Senate** acquitted him on all charges.

Lewinsky remained a prominent public figure in the aftermath of the **impeachment**. In interviews with the press and in her biography, *Monica's Story*, released in April 1999, Andrew Morton portrayed Lewinsky as a victim of "political enemies and faithless allies who trampled her privacy and emotional well-being to promote their own agenda." Among those she lambasted was **Linda Tripp**, her confidante at the Pentagon to whom she had revealed her affair with President Clinton. (Tripp, in turn, spread word of the affair.) Lewinsky related how the scandal left her so distraught that she contemplated suicide. By the end of Clinton's term, the public appeared to have lost interest in her, turning its attention to other media-hyped developments.

Born in San Francisco in 1973, the daughter of a prominent Los Angeles physician, Bernard Lewinsky, and Marcia Lewis, a freelance writer, Lewinsky grew up in Beverly Hills. Her parents divorced when she was a teen. In the summer of 1995, after graduating from Lewis and Clark College, Lewis applied for and was accepted as an unpaid intern at the White House. She was twenty-one at the time. Although her job was mundane, she had an occasional opportunity to flirt with the president. On November 15, having gained full-time, paid employment at the White House, she had a chance encounter with the president in the West Wing of the White House. (Technically, since the paperwork was not completed, she was still an intern.) Because of the **government shutdown**, interns were working beyond their regular hours, and there were not as many regular staff members at the White House as usual. According to

her testimony to the Starr investigation, later that night, Clinton and Lewinsky engaged in the first of ten sexual encounters, which would take
place with decreasing frequency over the next sixteen months although
they never had intercourse. She did, however, keep the blue dress she
was wearing during a sexual encounter in which the President ejaculated,
leaving a stain on the dress.

In April 1996, Lewinsky was transferred to a job at the Defense Department by Clinton's deputy chief of staff, Evelyn Lieberman. While Clinton and Lewinsky saw or spoke to each other less frequently after her
departure from the White House, they did not terminate their relationship. In March 1997, they had their last sexual encounter. Months later,
in mid-December 1997, he informed her, in a phone conversation, that
her name was on a list of individuals whom Paula Jones's attorneys might
depose as part of the discovery phase of their sexual harassment lawsuit
against him. Over the course of the next several weeks, Lewinsky, Clinton,
Clinton's close friend **Vernon Jordan**, and the president's personal secretary, **Betty Currie**, had several interactions. The nature of the discussions they had on these occasions constituted the basis of the charges of
obstruction of justice leveled by the House of Representatives against the
president. While Clinton denied telling Lewinsky to lie in her deposition
in the Paula Jones case, on December 28, 1997, Betty Currie went to
Lewinsky's apartment and took a box from her that contained a variety
of gifts the president had given her.

Even without this evidence, however, Starr had other information that
corroborated the charge that Lewinsky and Clinton had had an affair and
had lied about it in testimony to Jones's lawyers. On the suggestion of
Lucianne Goldberg, a self-admitted hater of Clinton, Linda Tripp, another onetime White House employee and a friend of Lewinsky, began
to tape her phone conversations with Lewinsky, which Tripp offered to
Starr. These tapes provided Starr with the basis for broadening his **Whitewater** inquiry to investigate the sexual conduct of the president and
served as the basis for the stories that made Lewinsky a household name
in the first place. The fact that Tripp taped these conversations without
Lewinsky's knowledge produced another titillating theme to the saga.
Tripp claimed that she did so for her protection; Clinton's supporters
accused Tripp of being part of a right-wing conspiracy; Lewinsky and
others wondered what type of person taped phone conversations with
their friends.

Years from now, Lewinsky's name will probably be fodder for trivia
games and for history buffs. Yet for a brief moment in time she was

synonymous with one of the greatest scandals in American history and only the second impeachment of a president.

Suggested Readings: Alan M. Dershowitz, *Sexual McCarthyism: Clinton, Starr, and the Emerging Constitutional Crisis* (New York: Basic Books, 1998); Amy Goldstein and David Straitfield, "Lewinsky Is Scornful of Many," *Washington Post*, March 4, 1999, p. A1; Amy Goldstein and Lorraine Adams, "Self-Conscious and Intense, Lewinsky Never Quite Fit In," *Washington Post*, May 3, 1998, p. A1; Martin Kettle, "Crisis in the White House," *The Guardian*, January 27, 1998, p. 1; Andrew Morton, *Monica's Story* (New York: St. Martin's Press, 2001); Richard Posner, *An Affair of State* (Cambridge, MA: Harvard University Press, 1999); Jeffrey Toobin, *A Vast Conspiracy* (New York: Random House, 1999).

LIMBAUGH, RUSH. (January 1951, Cape Girardeau, Missouri–   .) Conservative radio talk-show host.

One of President Bill Clinton's most persistent adversaries was conservative radio talk-show host Rush Limbaugh. Limbaugh first gained national prominence in the late 1980s. His syndicated talk show, which focused on politics, quickly gained a wide audience among those who either agreed with him or found Limbaugh's lambasting of liberal groups and causes entertaining, or both. Introducing each show with the boast of "talent on loan from God," Limbaugh grew even more popular and powerful after Bill Clinton became president. By the mid-1990s, Limbaugh's five-days-a-week midday radio show reached about twenty million listeners; his late-evening television show was outrated only by those starring Jay Leno and David Letterman; and his two books, *The Way Things Ought to Be* (1992) and *See, I Told You So* (1993), stood at the top of the best-seller list. While the mainstream press caricatured Limbaugh as a simpleton, pointing to his oft-repeated attacks on "environmental wackos" and "feminazis," as proof of his demagogic style, Limbaugh was just as important for his ability to mobilize opposition to Clinton's **health care reform** plans and in favor of the **"Contract with America."** While Clinton's reelection in 1996 suggested that Limbaugh's power had begun to wane, he retained a very large audience throughout the latter part of the 1990s, articulating his desire and allowing others to voice their desire to see Clinton ousted from office. Just as important, Limbaugh represented a much larger phenomenon, the growth of a conservative alternative media, which included talk radio, the Internet—such as the "Drudge Report," which initially broke the **Monica Lewinsky** story—and an assortment of magazines and newspapers, such as the

Washington Times. Limbaugh and other representatives of these new media reached a much larger and younger audience than older conservative venues such as the *National Review* by blending traditional conservative views with a more up-to-date or hip approach to presenting these views.

Limbaugh grew up in Cape Girardeau, Missouri, the son of a prominent attorney. He attended Southeast Missouri State University before embarking on a career as a disc jockey. This included a brief stint working for the Kansas City Royals baseball team. In 1984, he started his own show in Sacramento, California, before moving to New York. He was married three times and divorced twice; thus his espousal of traditional values at times conflicted with his own life story. Nonetheless, he enjoyed millions of faithful listeners, who identified themselves as "dittoheads," and a wide assortment of powerful friends. Whether he would continue to work as a radio talk-show host after the Clinton presidency remained to be seen. Some media experts even rumored that he would join Al Michaels and serve as the color man on ABC's popular *Monday Night Football*.

Suggested Readings: David C. Barker, "Rush to Action: Political Talk Radio and Health Care (Un)Reform," *Political Communication* 15:1 (January–March 1998), p. 83; David C. Barker, "Rushed Decisions: Political Talk Radio and Vote Choice, 1994–1996," *Journal of Politics* 61:2 (May 1999), p. 527; *Current Biography Yearbook*, 1993, p. 345.

LINDSEY, BRUCE R. (1951, Little Rock, Arkansas– .) Deputy White House Counsel, 1992–2001.

Bruce Lindsey, an Arkansas lawyer and longtime friend and confidant of President Bill Clinton, was one of Clinton's most important and controversial advisers. Some considered Lindsey the president's most trusted aide. Others stated that only **Hillary Clinton** had more influence on the president than Lindsey. When independent counsel **Kenneth Starr** subpoenaed Lindsey to testify before the grand jury, the White House invoked executive privilege to prevent him from doing so. When the court ruled that Lindsey was not protected by executive privilege, Clinton's top aide invoked attorney-client privilege to avoid testifying. This led to a further legal fight with the independent counsel's office. In part because he was not the president's private counsel, but rather an aide paid with public funds, the courts compelled Lindsey to testify.

Officially Lindsey held the position of deputy White House counsel, but nearly all agreed that this title did not do justice to his importance.

Like Clinton, Lindsey hailed from Arkansas and displayed an interest in politics throughout his adult life. After earning his B.A. from Rhodes College in Memphis, Tennessee, and his law degree from Georgetown University, Lindsey returned to Arkansas. The son of a prominent Arkansas lawyer, Lindsey became active in local politics even before he completed law school. He became friends with Clinton in the mid-1980s and worked tirelessly for the Clinton presidential campaign in 1992.

In addition to providing legal and political advice, Lindsey headed the personnel office at the White House and advised the president on **Supreme Court** nominees. The former duty meant that he was officially responsible for firing the workers in the White House travel office, an incident that became known as **travelgate**. Independent counsel Kenneth Starr named him as an unindicted coconspirator in a case against two bankers accused of concealing bank withdrawals to help Clinton run for governor in 1990. Even though the bankers, and thus Lindsey, were acquitted on these charges, Lindsey retained a reputation as a shady behind-the-scenes character. While other advisers left the White House to pursue their own interests (and/or because of their disillusionment with the administration), Lindsey remained loyal to his boss.

Suggested Readings: Sharon LaFraniere, "The Man at Portal of the President's Past," *Washington Post*, July 7, 1994, p. A1; Adam Nagourney, "Testing of a President," *New York Times*, February 9, 1998, p. A15; David Von Drehle, "Little-known Arkansas Lawyer Plays Big Role in Clinton Decisions," *Washington Post*, January 17, 1993, p. A18.

Related Entries: Whitewater; White House Defense Team.

LINE-ITEM VETO. For years, the Republican Party had endorsed the line-item veto as an important means to allow the president to restrain the spending power of Congress, which the Democrats had controlled for decades. A line-item veto would allow the president to veto or cross out a single line or item of an appropriation measure, rather than vetoing (or signing) the entire bill. In 1994, the Republican Party made enacting the line-item veto one of its top priorities, including it in its **"Contract with America."** However, since Bill Clinton, a Democrat, was the president, many Republicans had second thoughts about passing the measure when they actually became the majority party in Congress. As a result, not until 1996 did both houses of Congress pass a line-item veto, and even then they delayed the date President Clinton could use it until 1997, that is, until after the election. Technically, the law was not a line-item veto like ones enjoyed by many state governors. Rather, the law allowed the president to "cancel" some tax provisions and entitlement spending. Savings from these cancellations were to be used to cut the federal **budget** deficit.

While Democrats traditionally opposed the concept of a line-item veto, partly because they saw it as a threat to their power in the **U.S. House of Representatives**, Clinton supported the measure. In 1997, he used the line-item veto eleven times. He crossed out items on nine of thirteen appropriation measures and on two budget-reconciliation bills. Altogether, however, his vetoes did not amount to much in real dollar terms. Over a five-year period in which the government was budgeted to spend $9 trillion, he cut or vetoed only $1.9 billion in spending, or about 0.5 percent of total spending. Thus the line-item veto, which for years had been touted (or opposed) as a revolutionary shift in power away from Congress to the president, proved a paper tiger.

Nonetheless, no sooner had the line-item veto become law than a group of Democratic and Republican senators and congressmen, led by West Virginia senator Robert Byrd, a longtime champion of the **Senate**, challenged it in court as unconstitutional. On April 10, 1997, U.S. District Court Judge Thomas P. Jackson found in favor of the plaintiffs and struck down the line-item veto. Byrd and his cohorts celebrated, with Byrd declaring, "It was a great day for the Constitution and the American people because it was their [Congress's] power—not mine—their power of the purse that was preserved" (*CQ Almanac*, 1997). However, on May 27, 1997, the **Supreme Court** overturned Judge Jackson's ruling, largely on the technical grounds that Byrd and his cohorts lacked standing. This still provided the opponents of the line-item veto with an opening to overturn the law. In June 1998, the Supreme Court issued another ruling on another challenge to the line-item veto. This time the Court ruled in favor of the plaintiffs, declaring that the line-item veto was a violation of the Constitution. This particular case involved a group of hospitals from New York and potato farmers from Idaho who had lost funding due to Clinton's exercise of the veto. Justice John Paul Stevens, who wrote the majority decision in the 6–3 case, observed that Congress could propose a constitutional amendment to provide the president with the line-item veto, but otherwise it lacked the power to grant the president such power. Supporters of the line-item veto acknowledged that they lacked the votes to pass a constitutional amendment. Moreover, much of the original zeal for the measure had disappeared since it was now a Democrat who was cutting Republican-enacted measures. As the budget deficit turned into a budget surplus, talk of passing such a constitutional amendment virtually disappeared.

Suggested Readings: Helen Dewar and Joan Biskupic, "Line Item Veto Struck Down," *Washington Post*, June 26, 1998, p. 1; "Line-Item Veto Makes Rocky Debut," *Congressional Quarterly Almanac*, 1997, p. 2-63.

LIVINGSTON, ROBERT L., JR. (April 30, 1943, Colorado Springs, Colorado– .) Congressman from Louisiana.

In the midst of the **impeachment** hearings and vote in the **U.S. House of Representatives**, Robert Livingston, who had been selected to succeed **Newt Gingrich** as the Speaker of the House following Gingrich's resignation, stepped down as Speaker-elect after admitting that he too had a sexual affair. "I was prepared to lead our narrow majority as Speaker and I believe I had it in me to do a fine job," Livingston declared. "But I cannot do that job or be that kind of leader that I would like to be under the current circumstances. So I must set the example that I hope Clinton will follow" (Seelye, "Impeachment," p. 1). While Livingston and the Republican Party hoped to embarrass Clinton into resigning, which would have allowed the House to avoid an impeachment vote, the president did not. Democrats responded to Livingston's action by describing him as a good person and decrying the sexual "McCarthyism" that was consuming the city. Instead of Livingston, **Dennis Hastert**, a more moderate Republican from Illinois, took Gingrich's place as Speaker of the House.

Born in Colorado and reared in New Orleans, Livingston attended Tulane, dropped out after a year, and joined the navy. After four years of service, he married and returned to Tulane, where he earned his B.A. and law degree. He practiced briefly in the private sector and then worked as an assistant U.S. attorney. In 1977, he was elected to the U.S. Congress, becoming one of the first Republicans to represent the Deep South since Reconstruction. For over twenty years, he earned a reputation as a fierce fiscal conservative. Following the Republican sweep of both houses of Congress in the **election of 1994**, he was elected to chair the powerful House Appropriations Committee. Even before Gingrich announced his resignation, Livingston had expressed his interest in becoming Speaker. Like Gingrich, Livingston supported the showdown with the president that produced the **government shutdown** in 1995. However, as Republican fortunes waned, Livingston presented himself as a more stable and decisive leader than Gingrich. The poor showing of the Republican Party in the congressional election of 1998 proved the last straw for Gingrich and provided Livingston with the opportunity to become Speaker. However, shortly thereafter, reports surfaced that Livingston had had a sexual affair, and Livingston stepped down even before he assumed the post.

Suggested Readings: Katherine Q. Seelye, "Early Out of the Blocks in the Race for Speaker," *New York Times*, May 26, 1998, p. A18; Katherine Q. Seelye, "Impeachment: the Fallout: Livingston Urges Clinton to Follow Suit," *New York Times*, December 20, 1998, p. 1.

LOTT, TRENT. (October 9, 1941, Grenada, Mississippi–   .) U.S. Senate Majority Leader, 1996–   .

Trent Lott, a Republican from Mississippi, was elected majority leader of the **U.S. Senate** in 1996. Less flamboyant and more pragmatic than **Newt Gingrich**, the conservative Speaker of the House who orchestrated the Republican Party's rise to power in both houses of Congress in the **election of 1994**, Lott initially received less notoriety than Gingrich, but Lott outlasted the Speaker and the **impeachment** process and remained one of the most powerful politicians in the United States throughout Bill Clinton's presidency.

Born in Grenada, Mississippi, the son of a shipyard worker, Lott first displayed his political acumen while attending the University of Mississippi in the early 1960s. Even though he failed in his bid to become student-body president, Lott was elected head cheerleader and headed the college's alumni office after graduation. He received his B.A. and law degree from Ole Miss in 1963 and 1967, respectively. Shortly after completing law school, he became an aide to Congressman William Colmer. In 1972, upon Colmer's retirement, Lott successfully ran for his seat, although as a Republican, not a Democrat. (Colmer, like almost all politicians in the Deep South during the age of Jim Crow, was a Democrat.)

Lott moved up the political ladder in the **U.S. House of Representatives**, becoming the House minority whip in 1980. He was the first southern Republican to hold this post in U.S. history. In 1988, Lott ran successfully for the U.S. Senate and quickly rose to a position of power. He became Senate majority whip in 1995 and rose to majority leader following **Robert Dole**'s resignation from the Senate in 1996. While Lott was philosophically conservative, he proved willing to find common ground with the president on numerous issues. For instance, he supported free trade and **welfare reform**.

Perhaps Lott's greatest challenge came during the impeachment process. As Republicans in the House pressed forward with their plans to impeach the president, Lott sought to maintain a judicious and fair posture. Knowing that the votes in the Senate to convict the president on the impeachment charges did not exist, he worked to streamline the trial stage so as to prevent paralyzing the government. At the same time, he voted in favor of convicting the president. After the Senate voted to acquit the president, Lott emphasized that the body needed to return to the everyday business of government. While some sought to paint Lott as an old-fashioned white supremacist, a symbol of the old South in new clothing, more sophisticated analysts observed that Lott represented a new breed of southern politician who could achieve and maintain power without invoking cries of racial prejudice.

Suggested Readings: *Current Biography Yearbook*, 1996, p. 325; Kevin Merida, "3 Consonants and a Disavowal," *Washington Post*, March 29, 1999, p. C1.

M

MAGAZINER, IRA C. (November 8, 1947, Queens, New York– .) Adviser to President Bill Clinton, 1993–1998.

Ira Magaziner, who first met Bill Clinton when they were both Rhodes scholars in England during the 1960s, served as his special adviser, first on **health care reform** and later on federal Internet policy. His attempt to devise sweeping health care reform proved disastrous, but he won much higher marks for his work on the Internet, especially electronic commerce.

Born in Queens, New York, Magaziner began his involvement in liberal political causes during his childhood. At age sixteen, he participated in the March on Washington, the famous civil rights demonstration in 1963. As a student at Brown University, he developed a plan to radically liberalize the curriculum, much of which was enacted. After earning his B.A., he enrolled at Oxford University as a Rhodes scholar. In England, he befriended Bill Clinton, who was also a Rhodes scholar. Upon his return to the United States, Magaziner turned to social activism, promoting urban renewal in Brockton, Massachusetts, an old industrial community near Boston. In 1973, he entered the private sector as a management consultant for the Boston Consulting Group. Five years later, he founded his own firm, Telesis. At both companies he earned a reputation as an innovative businessman. Based on his work, he wrote several well-received books, including *Japanese Industrial Policy* (1980), with Thomas M. Hout, and, with **Robert Reich**, *Minding America's Business* (1982).

In the early 1990s, Magaziner began working for Bill Clinton, who was in the early stages of his presidential campaign. After the **election of 1992**, he was given the official post of senior White House policy adviser. Along with **Hillary Clinton**, Magaziner headed the health care task force that sought to devise a new national health care system. Comprised of thirty-four subgroups, each of which examined a particular aspect of the health care question, the task force worked diligently to study ways to control health care costs. In September 1993, it released a 1,364-page report that spelled out the administration's proposed health care plan.

In many ways, however, the plan was dead on arrival. Some on the left objected to the plan because they wanted to nationalize health care or at least move toward a single-payer health insurance plan, whereby all would pay into and receive health insurance from the federal government. Others on the right opposed any move toward nationalization. Magaziner's efforts to allow the task force to work in secrecy, without public meetings, may have made sense from a scientific or policy point of view but hurt the plan politically. One group even filed a suit against Hillary Clinton claiming that such private meetings violated federal sunshine laws, which demanded open, not closed, hearings. Even though the court ruled that Magaziner and Hillary Clinton had not violated the law, the secret meetings left the impression that Magaziner and Hillary Clinton were not open to public input. To make matters worse, many in Congress viewed Magaziner as arrogant. Still others opposed the plan because of their dislike for Hillary Clinton. Magaziner's efforts were further hindered by Clinton's stipulation that managed care was the only acceptable option.

After the health care plan was defeated—the administration did win passage of some piecemeal reforms—Magaziner turned his attention to a different concern, **high technology**. For most of 1996 and 1997, he served as the president's chief Internet adviser, devising federal policies toward e-commerce. Most simply, Magaziner favored private-sector development of the Internet and limited restrictions or regulations. This included not taxing e-commerce transactions. Upon resigning from this post in 1998, Magaziner reaped praise from many in the computer industry. He returned to the private sector, becoming a member of the board of directors at several health care and high-technology firms.

Suggested Readings: *Current Biography Yearbook*, 1995, p. 383; Elizabeth Drew, *On the Edge: The Clinton Presidency* (New York: Simon & Schuster, 1994); David Wighton, "Government Set to Appoint First Digital Envoy," *Financial Times*, June 28, 1999, p. 8.

Related Entry: Domestic Policy.

McCAFFREY, BARRY R. (November 17, 1942, Taunton, Massachusetts–   .) Director of the White House Office of National Drug Control Policy (Drug Czar), 1996–2001.

President Bill Clinton's nomination of General Barry R. McCaffrey as the drug czar was aimed at emphasizing the administration's commitment to the war on **drugs**. The youngest person to become a four-star general, McCaffrey had a distinguished military record. After graduating from the U.S. Military Academy at West Point, McCaffrey rapidly moved up the military ranks. His posts included commander in chief of the U.S. Armed Forces Southern Command, which lent him experience and connections in one of the key parts of the world where the United States was conducting its war against drugs. McCaffrey had also been decorated for his leadership of the 24th Infantry Division during Operation Desert Storm and had served as the assistant to Joint Chiefs of Staff Chairman Colin Powell. His nomination as "drug czar," a post created during the Reagan presidency with **cabinet** status, was confirmed unanimously by the **U.S. Senate**.

While McCaffrey's appointment suggested that military expertise was crucial to the administration's attempt to decrease drug use in the United States, McCaffrey tried to make it clear that he supported Clinton's emphasis on drug treatment as well as interdiction at the border and reducing the production of drugs in foreign countries, especially Colombia. During McCaffrey's tenure, expenditures on the drug war remained very high, over $17 billion a year, not counting federal or state expenditures on prosecuting criminals and maintaining hundreds of thousands of prison cells. The impact of this war was problematic. While the usage of drugs decreased, as did drug-related crimes, drug use and the smuggling of drugs remained very high by historical standards. The lack of alternative crops for peasant farmers of the developing world, combined with relatively high demand and profits to be made from the drug trade, bodes poorly for any hope of a quick victory in the war against drugs. Nonetheless, neither McCaffrey, the Clinton administration, nor the Republican-led Congress proposed any drastic shift in strategy.

Suggested Readings: www.ondcp.gov; Christopher Wren, "Gen. Barry McCaffrey: A Drug Warrior Who Would Rather Treat Then Fight," *New York Times*, January 8, 2001, p. A12; Christopher Wren, "General Urges Combination of Solutions in Drug Abuse," *New York Times*, February 28, 1996, p. A13.

Related Entry: Crime.

McCURRY, MICHAEL D. (October 27, 1954, Charleston, South Carolina– .) White House Press Secretary, 1995–1998.

In January 1995, following the Republican takeover of both houses of

Congress, Bill Clinton replaced **Dee Dee Myers** with Michael McCurry as his press secretary. McCurry, who had worked as the spokesperson for the State Department, had a reputation as an experienced political spokesperson who had a good relationship with the Washington press corps. McCurry left the White House in the fall of 1998 as the **Monica Lewinsky** scandal reached a climax. Much of the press praised McCurry for his work. Clinton declared that his press secretary had "set the standard by which future White House press secretaries will be judged." However, conservatives accused McCurry of obfuscation and doublespeak and claimed that the Clinton administration mistook spin for truth.

Born in Charleston, South Carolina, McCurry spent most of his youth in the San Francisco Bay area. He received his A.B. from Princeton University in 1976 and got his first job as a press secretary for New Jersey senator Harrison Williams. After Williams was compelled to resign in 1981 in the face of bribery charges, McCurry went to work for Senator Daniel Patrick Moynihan of New York. Over the course of the next ten years, he worked on several unsuccessful presidential campaigns, including Robert Kerry's bid in 1992. During this time, McCurry also served as the director of communications for the Democratic National Committee and earned an M.A. from Georgetown University (1985).

Following Clinton's election, McCurry went to work as a spokesperson for the State Department. McCurry became Clinton's press secretary following a broader shake-up at the White House. He inherited a number of crises, including **Vincent Foster**'s suicide and the burgeoning **Whitewater** scandal. Furthermore, McCurry had to deal with an energized Republican Party that hoped to make Clinton a one-term president. He often used humor to counter barbs aimed at hurting the president. McCurry earned a favorable rating from much of the White House press corps, although some complained about his combative style.

When McCurry resigned in the summer of 1998 amid the Monica Lewinsky scandal, he denied knowing any of the details about Clinton's relationship with the former White House intern. McCurry's critics complained that McCurry intentionally did not seek out information about the affair after the story first broke because he did not want to know the details. Regardless of the cause, McCurry was not called to testify before the grand jury or accused of any wrongdoing by independent counsel **Kenneth Starr**.

Suggested Readings: Geraldine Baum, "The Smooth Operative," *Los Angeles Times*, December 22, 1994, p. E1; John Corry, "Fawning All over Themselves," *American*

Spectator 31:9 (September 1998), p. 52; *Current Biography Yearbook*, 1996, p. 348; http://www.washingtonpost.com/wp-srv/politics/daily/july98/mccurry24.htm.

Related Entry: Gergen, David.

McDOUGAL, JAMES (1941, Arkansas–March 8, 1998, Fort Worth, Texas) **AND SUSAN McDOUGAL.** (1955, Germany–   .) Whitewater defendants.

In 1978, James and Susan McDougal and Bill and **Hillary Clinton** purchased 230 acres of land in the Ozark Mountains in what became known as **Whitewater** Estates. The two McDougals owned a small financial institution, Madison Guaranty, into which, as federal authorities subsequently showed, the McDougals illegally dipped to help bankroll their Whitewater project and other schemes. In 1994, **Kenneth Starr** was appointed independent counsel to investigate the Whitewater land deal and to determine whether Bill Clinton had benefited from funds diverted from Madison Guaranty while he was governor of the state of Arkansas, and if so, if he had covered up his involvement. In 1996, both Jim and Susan McDougal, along with Arkansas governor **Jim Guy Tucker**, were convicted on fraud charges. During the trial, David Hale, a former municipal judge and banker, testified that Clinton had discussed an illegal $300,000 loan with himself and Jim McDougal. Clinton denied the charges. Threatened with a sentence of up to eighty-four years in prison and over $4 million in fines, Jim McDougal decided to cooperate with the office of the independent counsel. In exchange for agreeing to testify to the Whitewater grand jury, his sentence was reduced to three years, but Starr did not learn much new from him. Moreover, McDougal's death from a heart attack while he was in prison in March 1998 further reduced Starr's ability to prove that Clinton had broken the law.

Meanwhile, Susan McDougal, who was sentenced to three concurrent twenty-four-month prison terms, chose not to cooperate with Starr. When she refused to answer questions before the Whitewater grand jury, she was charged with contempt of court and sentenced by Judge **Susan Webber Wright** to eighteen months in prison. In still another trial, Susan McDougal was tried for obstruction of justice and again on contempt charges. In this trial, McDougal accused Starr of badgering her to try to get her to falsely testify against Clinton. Even though FBI agent Mike Patkus testified that a link existed between Clinton and McDougal, the jury acquitted her of obstruction of justice and deadlocked on the contempt charges. Starr chose not to retry McDougal on the contempt charges.

Jim McDougal, who grew up in a depressed farming community and became a real-estate developer, was close to many of the most prominent politicians in the state of Arkansas. He worked in the offices of Senators John McClellan and J. William Fulbright, roomed with Jim Guy Tucker before he became governor, and befriended Bill Clinton years before he rose to prominence. But in the mid-1980s, McDougal's financial empire began to crumble, as did his health. As of 1992, he was bankrupt and faced numerous legal problems, ironically, none of them stemming from his investment in Whitewater.

Jim McDougal met his wife, Susan Henly, at his alma matter, Ouachita Baptist College, in 1976 while he was teaching a course in political science. She was born in Germany and raised in Arkansas. They married in 1976 and formed a business partnership. In 1988, he and two of her brothers were charged with bank fraud. After he was acquitted, she moved to California and filed for divorce. In 1992, she was fired by her employer, Nancy Mehta, the wife of the famous conductor Zubin Mehta, who suspected her of embezzling close to $200,000. On November 23, 1998, a California court acquitted her on these embezzlement charges. In one of his last acts as president, Clinton pardoned Susan McDougal on January 20, 2001.

Suggested Readings: Paul Duggan, "Jury Acquits McDougal of Obstruction," *Washington Post*, April 13, 1999, p. A1; Jim McDougal and Curtis Wilkie, *Arkansas Mischief: The Birth of a National Scandal* (New York: Henry Holt, 1998); Howard Schneider, "Down the Whitewater Rapids," *Washington Post*, January 13, 1994, p. C1; "Whitewater Figure James McDougal Dies," *Newsday*, March 9, 1998, p. A4; Curtis Wilkie, "James McDougal Went Down Talking," *Boston Globe*, March 10, 1998, p. A13.

Related Entries: Fiske, Robert B., Jr.; Impeachment.

McLARTY, THOMAS (MACK). (1946, Hope, Arkansas– .) Chief of Staff, 1993–1994; Adviser and Special Envoy to the Americas, 1995–1998.

One of Bill Clinton's oldest friends, Thomas "Mack" McLarty served as Bill Clinton's first chief of staff. McLarty and Clinton first met in kindergarten. Both of them were born in Hope, Arkansas, and even though Clinton moved to Hot Springs, their paths crossed numerous times. Both were student leaders and represented Arkansas in Washington, D.C., as part of the Boys' Nation program. While Clinton went to Georgetown to college, McLarty stayed in his home state, earning a B.A. at the University of Arkansas. Both became successful politicians at a young age. McLarty was elected to the Arkansas House of Representatives at the age of twenty-three. When Clinton ran for governor, McLarty served as his campaign treasurer. He assumed the same post during Clinton's 1992 bid for the presidency. Even though many expected Clinton to select someone with experience in Washington as his chief of staff, Clinton instead named McLarty to the post.

McLarty remained Clinton's chief of staff until June 1994. Clinton replaced him with **Leon Panetta**, a onetime congressman who had much more experience in the nation's capital than McLarty. Throughout Mc-Larty's tenure, many political pundits wondered if he was up to the job. Often he got the blame, or part of it, for the shakiness of Clinton's first two years as president. Along with a number of other longtime friends of Clinton, he was considered by many pundits too inexperienced and unskilled for the task of managing Clinton's affairs. At the same time, he probably deserved some of the credit for the passage of **NAFTA** and the enactment of the 1993 deficit-reduction package. After being replaced by Panetta, he remained on the White House staff as an adviser on political and legislative matters. After Clinton's reelection in 1996, he served as special envoy to the Americans. In the mid-1990s, questions arose regarding McLarty's role in helping **Webster Hubbell** obtain business and his knowledge of certain campaign finance irregularities. However, Mc-Larty was not called to testify before Senator Fred Thompson's Governmental Affairs Committee, nor was he ever charged with any crime.

Suggested Readings David Marsaniss, *First in His Class* (New York: Simon & Schuster, 1994); "Poor Judgment But No Smoking Gun," *U.S. News & World Report*, April 14, 1997, p. 38.

Related Entries: Chinagate; Domestic Policy.

MIDDLE EAST. As Bill Clinton's presidency drew to a close, many experts suggested that he hoped to cement his legacy as a great president by securing a lasting peace in the Middle East. Even before the summer of 2000, the administration could point with pride to its achievements in the region. For instance, the White House bragged that it had helped broker agreements between Israel and its neighbors. Jordan and Israel had ended years of enmity; Yasir Arafat, the leader of the Palestine Liberation Organization (PLO), had shaken hands with Israeli prime minister

Agreement to the 1993 peace accord by Israeli Prime Minister Yitzhak Rabin, left, and PLO chairman Yasser Arafat, right. AP/Wide World Photos.

Yitzhak Rabin on the South Lawn of the White House. This historic hand-shake was followed by the negotiation of a series of agreements between the Palestinians and Israel, including the Wye River Memorandum on October 23, 1998, which sought to secure earlier agreements between the two. When disagreements between Palestinians and Israel threatened to derail the peace process, Clinton brought the leaders of the two sides together for another round of around-the-clock negotiations at Camp David, the locale of the historic treaty between Egypt and Israel in 1978. At Camp David, Israeli prime minister Ehud Barak, who had been elected in part on his promise to restart the peace initiative, displayed a willing-ness to make concessions on the sovereignty of part of Jerusalem, per-haps the most important sticking point between Israel and the Palestinians. To President Clinton's chagrin, Arafat rejected Barak's over-ture. More important, not long after the Camp David sessions, a new wave of violence erupted in the Middle East. This development threat-ened to undo years of negotiations between Israel and the Palestinians, ended talk of a possible accord between Syria and Israel, and diminished

President Bill Clinton and Hillary Clinton tour the Middle East. The White House.

Clinton's chances of securing his legacy as a peacemaker. Indeed, at the tail end of 2000 and in early 2001, the peace process collapsed.

Prior to this outbreak of violence, a new round of fighting erupted between Israelis and Palestinians. Areial Sharon, a long-time hawk, was elected prime minister and Arafat made little effort to quash protest within Palestinian-controlled lands. Several factors had opened the door for renewed efforts to end years of hostility in the Middle East. The Persian Gulf War against **Iraq** in 1991 brought together a coalition of moderate Arab states and the United States and tended to undermine the stature of radicals in the region who supported Saddam Hussein and opposed recognition of the state of Israel. Hussein unsuccessfully sought to unite Arab nations by attacking Israel during the war. The collapse of the Soviet Union left radicals without a power broker to support their ambitions. The emergence of Yitzhak Rabin, a long-time advocate of negotiations with the Palestinians, as prime minister of Israel in June 1992 displayed the desire of the Israeli people to achieve peace. The negotiation of the Oslo Agreement, which spelled out a process for further negotiations, symbolized the commitment that both Israelis and Palestinians were willing to make to end years of enmity. The agreement was signed in Washington on September 28, 1995. However, the Clinton administration understood that the drive for peace would not be an easy one and committed itself to the process in spite of numerous setbacks. The assassination of Yitzhak Rabin by a reactionary Israeli on November 4, 1995, was one such setback. Rabin was succeeded by the less popular Shimon Perez. In turn, Perez was defeated by Benjamin Netanyahu, whose commitment to the Rabin's peace process was tepid at best. Nonetheless, the Clinton administration endured Netanyahu's leadership.

Some pundits charged that the Clinton administration had always overestimated the chance to achieve peace in the region, but they offered few alternatives to endless conflict. Perhaps a more serious criticism of Clinton's policy in the Middle East was that by focussing so much on resolving the dispute between Israel and the Palestinians, it lost track of broader objectives in the region. Others countered that the long-term stability of the Middle East was so fundamentally tied to Israel's security that it deserved to get the attention it received.

Suggested Readings William Hyland, *Clinton's World* (Westport, CT: Praeger, 1999), ch. 12; Rashid Khalidi, "The United States and the Middle East at the End of the Cold War," *Diplomatic History* 23:3 (Summer 1999), p. 553; Scott Macleod et al., "A Bridge to Peace," *Time*, January 8, 2001, p. 42.

Related Entry: Foreign Policy.

MILOSEVIC, SLOBODAN. (1941, Pozarevac, Serbia—   .) President of the Republic of Serbia/Federal Republic of Yugoslavia, 1989–2000.

Throughout the Clinton presidency, one of the most important concerns was the ongoing turmoil and war in the Balkans, and at the center of this turmoil was Yugoslavia's president, Slobodan Milosevic. Educated in Belgrade as a lawyer, Milosevic rose within the ranks of the Communist Party, which controlled Yugoslavia, in the 1960s, 1970s, and 1980s. He was named the leader of the Communist Party in 1986. As the Communist bloc crumbled in Eastern Europe, nationalist sentiment threatened to tear apart the Republic of Yugoslavia, which longtime Yugoslavian leader Marshal Tito had largely held in check. In 1989, Milosevic became president of Serbia largely by stirring up nationalist feelings and animosities toward the Albanians. In December 1990, running as the candidate of the newly formed Socialist Party of Serbia, he was overwhelmingly elected president.

Within a year of his election, Milosevic commanded Serbian military forces to help Serbian minorities in **Bosnia and Herzegovina** put down independence movements led by non-Serbian forces. A protracted period of civil war resulted, with much of the international community blaming Milosevic for the atrocities that took place. In 1992, the United Nations enacted trade sanctions against Yugoslavia to try to stop the bloodshed. Finally, in 1995, Milosevic agreed to the Dayton Agreement, which ended the civil war in Bosnia and Herzegovina. Still, Yugoslavia remained in dire economic straits, and ethnic or nationalist rivalries threatened to erupt into bloodshed in other parts of the Serb Republic, especially **Kosovo**.

In 1998, with the backing of Milosevic, Serbian police in Kosovo began to round up and reportedly to kill Albanian ethnics. In response, the Clinton administration and **NATO** tightened economic sanctions against Yugoslavia. In turn, Milosevic assembled the Yugoslavian army along the Kosovoan border. Finally, on March 24, 1999, NATO commenced an air war against Serbia, whose military forces had already begun to rush into Kosovo. For nearly eleven weeks, U.S. and European air forces bombarded Yugoslavia, largely with impunity. Only after Milosevic agreed to withdraw did NATO agree to a cease-fire. In spite of heavy casualties and much economic loss, Milosevic maintained his power, partly because the international attack allowed him to rally nationalist sentiment and winnow out dissent within Serbia.

But by the end of 1999, support for Milosevic had dissipated. In September 2000, Yugoslavians went to the polls and apparently elected Milosevic's opponent, Vojislav Kostunica, as president. Milosevic, nonetheless, refused to step down, insisting on a recount or a runoff. Mass protests erupted in the nation's capital and elsewhere. To the surprise of many, Milosevic proved unable to squelch the protests. Finally, on October 6, 2000, Milosevic resigned. This action symbolized a major victory for the Clinton administration's **foreign policy** in the region. Many Republicans had opposed the war in Kosovo. In the end, not only did the war protect Albanian lives, it helped displace Milosevic, who was perceived as the source of much of the trouble in the region.

Suggested Readings: Steven Erlanger, "Showdown in Yugoslavia," *New York Times*, October 9, 2000, p. A1; http://www.defenselink.mil/news/June1999; William G. Hyland, *Clinton's World* (Westport, CT: Praeger, 1999); David Owen, *Balkan Odyssey* (New York: Harcourt Brace, 1995).

MINIMUM WAGE. On August 20, 1996, President Bill Clinton signed into law the first mandated hike in the minimum wage since 1989. The increase, from $4.25 to $5.15 an hour, brought to a close a lengthy battle between Democrats, who favored the hike, and Republicans, most of whom opposed it. To gain passage of the increase, Clinton and Democrats in Congress emphasized that the minimum wage stood at the lowest level in real terms in forty years. Republicans countered, as they had in earlier fights over the minimum wage, that a rise in the wage would actually cost some workers their jobs. While such an argument swayed a number of experts during the 1980s and early 1990s, the booming economy tended to dispute the claim that the former automatically led to the latter. Holding firm to their principles, Republicans had opposed President Clinton's call for a minimum-wage hike in 1995, but this time they did not.

In addition to helping low-income workers, the rise in the minimum wage signaled that a shift had taken place in Washington, D.C. Two years earlier, Republicans in Congress had united around the **"Contract with America."** In the contract and in their campaign rhetoric, they pledged to stage a conservative revolution. Their desire to drive home their agenda came to a climax with the **government shutdown** of the winter of 1995–1996. After the shutdown, however, Republicans faced declining poll numbers and a reenergized President Clinton. To decrease their risk of losing control of the **House of Representatives** and the **Senate**, Speaker of the House **Newt Gingrich** and the new Republican majority leader of the Senate, **Trent Lott**, adopted a more conciliatory policy than they had in 1995. The minimum wage was a prime example of this shift. While many conservative House leaders remained adamantly opposed to the minimum-wage hike in 1996, the decision of a cluster of moderate Republicans to side with Democrats on the bill put the leadership in a bind. Unable to stop the bill from passing, Gingrich convinced most Republicans to support the bill. As Gingrich declared, "Some of us swallowed more than we wanted to, yet it was clearly the American will" (*CQ Almanac*, 1996, p. 7-3).

As the **election of 2000** approached, Clinton and Democrats in Congress once again called for raising the minimum wage. With the economy still growing, they argued that such a hike was necessary to help those who had benefited the least from the economic expansion of the 1990s. Republicans in Congress, however, sought to trade their vote in favor of a minimum-wage hike for the president's pledge to support a Republican-sponsored tax cut. This the president refused to do, arguing that the tax cut threatened to squander the **budget** surplus that was necessary to save **Social Security**, bolster Medicare, improve **education**, and pay down the public debt. As a result, the minimum wage was not raised again.

Suggested Readings "Congress Clears Wage Increase with Tax Breaks for Business," *Congressional Quarterly Almanac*, 1996, p. 7-3; Juliet Eilperin, "House GOP Offers Deal on Tax Cuts," *Washington Post*, August 29, 2000, p. A2; Ellen Nakashima and Juliet Eilperin, "Clinton Pushes for Minimum Wage Hike," *Washington Post*, September 6, 2000, p. A4.

MITCHELL, GEORGE. (August 20, 1933, Waterville, Maine–   .) U.S. Senate Majority Leader, 1989–1994; Chair, Northern Ireland peace negotiations, 1997–1998.

In January 1995, after the Republicans won control of both houses of Congress, George Mitchell, a senator from Maine and the majority leader between 1989 and 1994, unexpectedly announced his retirement from the **U.S. Senate**. He turned down an appointment to the **Supreme Court**, and many thought that he would return to Maine for a quiet retirement. Instead, after Bill Clinton appointed him an economic adviser for **Northern Ireland**, Mitchell headed to his ancestral homeland to chair negotiations aimed at ending years of civil war in the region. On Easter weekend in 1998, Mitchell announced that an agreement had been reached, based on the so-called Mitchell Principles, that promised to bring an end to the bloodshed. The agreement, known as the Good Friday Accord, established that British direct rule would give way to a provincial assembly and that both Protestants and Catholics would demilitarize. Northern Irish voters ratified the agreement the following month. Even though many of the details awaited final resolution, Mitchell drew widespread praise for his efforts.

Born in Waterville, Maine, Mitchell earned his B.A. from Bowdoin College in 1954 and his law degree from Georgetown University in 1960. In between, he served in the U.S. Army. After completing law school, he went to work for Senator Edmund Muskie of Maine, who was Hubert Humphrey's running mate in 1968 and ran for the Democratic nomination for the presidency in 1972. Mitchell unsuccessfully ran for governor of Maine in 1974 but became a U.S. senator in 1980 to complete Muskie's term when Muskie became President Jimmy Carter's secretary of state. Mitchell quickly rose within the ranks of the Democratic Party, playing a prominent role in the Senate investigations into the Iran-contra affair. As Senate majority leader, he earned a reputation as a patient, and relatively bland politician. These characteristics, especially his patience, served him well as negotiator of the peace agreement.

Suggested Readings: Richard L. Berke, "Gray Eminence in U.S.," *New York Times*, May 6, 1998, p. A3; T. R. Reid, "Irish Peace Would Be Mitchell's Moment," *Washington Post*, April 5, 1998, p. A1.

Related Entry: Foreign Policy.

MORRIS, DICK. Political consultant.

For over twenty years, Dick Morris, a gifted political consultant whom *Time* magazine once called the most influential private citizen in America, enjoyed an on-again, off-again relationship with Bill Clinton. In 1978, Morris helped Clinton get elected governor in the state of Arkansas. After the election, Clinton fired Morris because of Morris's reputation as a hard-edged political consultant. In 1982, Clinton brought Morris back on board to help him win back the governorship, which he had lost in 1980. Once again, in 1995, following the Republican sweep of both houses of Congress, Clinton turned to Morris for political advice. Largely following Morris's strategy of "triangulation," which entailed co-opting traditional Republican issues like **welfare reform** and **crime**, and by promoting incremental rather than sweeping reforms aimed at satisfying the needs of middle-class suburban voters, Clinton was reelected in 1996. Prior to Clinton's victory, however, Morris and Clinton split one more time. While the Democrats were holding their national convention, Sherry Rowlands, a prostitute, revealed that she was having an affair with Morris, who was married at the time. In response, Clinton quickly broke his official ties with Morris, much to the satisfaction of many of his advisers, who distrusted Morris because of his Machiavellian demeanor and antiliberal views. Indeed, Morris advised **Trent Lott**, the conservative Republican senator from Mississippi, as well as Clinton.

When the **impeachment** scandal broke, Clinton secretly turned to Morris for advice. On January 21, 1998, the day the **Monica Lewinsky** story broke, Clinton asked Morris to take a poll to determine the impact of the news. Morris did so and reported back that the public would favor impeachment if Clinton lied under oath. Hence Morris suggested that Clinton should publicly admit his affair with Lewinsky. Not only did Clinton not take Morris's advice, on the contrary, he informed the nation in a televised address that he did not even know Lewinsky. Subsequently, after it became clear that Clinton had lied about his relationship with Lewinsky, Morris revealed to the press the conversation he had had with Clinton in January and the advice he had given the president.

Morris chronicled his relationship with Clinton and his own travails and philosophy in several books, most notably *Behind the Oval Office: Winning the Presidency in the Nineties* (1997) and *The New Prince: Machiavelli Updated for the Twenty-first Century* (1999). Morris was often given backhanded compliments by those who recognized his political genius but despised his lack of principles. Perhaps the one time Morris acted on his principles was when he advised President Clinton on whether the federal government and several state governments should sue the major tobacco companies, on the grounds that the tobacco companies had hidden internal studies that documented the hazards of smoking to one's health. Morris's poll data helped convince Clinton that the tobacco case was popular, but one other reason Morris favored going after the tobacco companies was that his own mother, a lifelong smoker, had died of lung cancer in 1993.

Suggested Readings: Howard Kurtz, "Dick Morris, Burning His Bridges," *Washington Post*, February 3, 1999, p. C1; Stephen Robinson, "Sex Scandal Fails to Dent Clinton's Lead," *Daily Telegraph*, September 1, 1996, p. 13; David Stout, "Testing of a President: The Adviser," *New York Times*, August 19, 1998, p. A22.

Related Entry: Election of 1996.

MOTOR VOTER BILL. During the 1992 campaign, Bill Clinton pledged to sign the motor voter bill that President **George Bush** had vetoed. The bill sought to make it easier for citizens to register to vote by requiring

President Clinton signs the motor voter bill, May 20, 1993. Library of Congress.

states to provide citizens the opportunity to register to vote when they applied for or renewed their driver's license. Democrats in the **U.S. House of Representatives** passed such a measure in 1990, only to have it die in the **U.S. Senate**. Again in 1991, Senate Republicans blocked motor voter legislation. In 1992, both houses passed the bill, but President Bush vetoed it on the grounds that it would lead to "fraud and corruption." After the **election of 1992**, the House and Senate quickly passed the measure again. President Clinton signed it into law on May 20, 1993. In addition to providing citizens with an opportunity to register when they obtained their driver's license, the law allowed for "mail-in" registration and made it easier to register at government agencies where public support was provided.

Ironically, while Republicans opposed the bill in part because they feared that more Democrats would register than Republicans, it is not clear that the bill had this impact. At the same time, neither did the law result in greater voter turnout. Nor was there evidence that the motor voter bill produced widespread corruption or fraud.

Suggested Readings: Peter Baker, "Motor Voter Apparently Didn't Drive Up Turnout," *Washington Post*, November 6, 1996, p. B7; "Motor Voter Bill Enacted After 5 years," *Congressional Quarterly Almanac*, 1993, p. 199.

MTV (MUSIC TELEVISION). Established in 1981, MTV quickly grew into the most important venue for selling popular music and introducing new rock and hip-hop performers to youths. To enhance his standing among young voters and to reinforce his image as an energetic and youthful leader, Bill Clinton agreed to appear on and be interviewed by MTV during the 1992 presidential campaign. Clinton's vice presidential running mate, **Al Gore**, appeared separately on MTV. The decision to interview Clinton and Gore grew, in part, out of MTV's desire to diversify and to add legitimacy to itself as a broadcasting entity. Around the same time, Clinton appeared on the Arsenio Hall late-night television show, where he played the saxophone to an exuberant audience that was unaccustomed to seeing a presidential candidate appear so hip. Clinton's appearances on these popular television programs, both of which were deemed political successes, were the first of their kind by a major candidate. Henceforth, politicians would not limit themselves to appearing on "news" shows. In 1996, Clinton and his opponent, **Robert Dole**, were interviewed by MTV. Before the **election of 2000**, both candidates, Al

Gore and **George W. Bush**, appeared on a wide range of talk shows, from the Oprah Winfrey program to the David Letterman show.

Suggested Readings: Joshua Hammer, "Not Just Hit Videos Anymore," *Newsweek*, November 2, 1992, p. 93; "Interview with Tabitha Soren of MTV," *Weekly Compilation of Presidential Documents*, September 9, 1996, p. 1596.

MYERS, DEE DEE. (September 1, 1961, Quonset Point, Rhode Island– .) White House Press Secretary, 1993–1994.

Dee Dee Myers was the first woman to serve as the White House press secretary. She had joined Clinton's campaign team early in 1992 and in spite of her youth—she was thirty-one in 1993—was named press secretary after his election. While Myers was generally well liked, largely because of the many snafus of the early months of the Clinton administration, many considered her ineffective, and she resigned at the end of 1994 following the Republican takeover of both houses of Congress in the **election of 1994**. In September 1994, White House Chief of Staff **Leon Panetta** had attempted to replace her with **Michael McCurry**, but by personally appealing to the president, Myers had temporarily thwarted Panetta's efforts.

Born Margaret Jane Myers, she was nicknamed Dee Dee by her younger sister, who could not pronounce her first name. She earned a B.A. from Santa Clara University in 1983 and went to work on Walter Mondale's presidential campaign in 1984. Even though Mondale lost, she gained important experience and connections. Her boss was **Mickey Kantor**, who served as Clinton's campaign chair. From 1985 to 1989, she worked as deputy press secretary for Los Angeles mayor Tom Bradley and on Michael Dukakis's unsuccessful presidential campaign in 1988. She also worked for Dianne Feinstein, who lost in her bid to become governor of California in 1990. In 1991, she served as press secretary for Frank Jordan, who overcame long odds to become mayor of San Francisco. Shortly thereafter, Kantor recruited her to Clinton's presidential campaign team.

In addition to her inexperience, Myers was hindered by the unusual relationship she had with **George Stephanopoulos**, whom Clinton named his director of communications. Officially they shared many of the responsibilities traditionally assumed by the press secretary, although he clearly had much greater access to the president. Nonetheless, she won the favor of many journalists, partly through her spunk and humor. After leaving the White House, she appeared regularly on various news programs. At one point she criticized Clinton for running a "white boys club" that made it hard for **women** to be heard, but overall she tended to present favorable commentary on the Clinton presidency.

Suggested Readings: Ian Brodie, "Former Aide Accuses Clinton of Operating Club for 'White Boys,'" *The Times of London*, April 10, 1996; *Current Biography Yearbook*, 1994, p. 392; Martin Fletcher, "Press Chief Myers Quits As Clinton Fightback Falters," *The Times of London*, December 17, 1994.

N

NAFTA (NORTH AMERICAN FREE TRADE AGREEMENT). One of the centerpieces of the Clinton administration's **domestic policy** and **foreign policy** was NAFTA. In spite of opposition to the plan to create a North American free-trade area by several of the key constituencies of the Democratic Party, including organized **labor**, Bill Clinton pledged to enact the treaty if he were elected president. Holding firm to this pledge, the administration lobbied hard for legislation that would allow the administration to implement the pact, which had been negotiated and signed by President **George Bush**. Many pundits felt that the turning point for NAFTA came with Vice President **Al Gore**'s debate with **H. Ross Perot**, a fierce opponent of the pact. The debate took place on the Larry King television show on November 9, 1993. Perot warned that NAFTA would lead to great job losses as American firms rushed to set up shop in Mexico. Gore countered by presenting Perot with a photograph of Willis Hawley and Reed Smoot, the cosponsors of protective legislation that had helped create the Great Depression of the 1930s. Gore also argued that the principle of free trade was supported by nearly all economists. Not only did the vast majority of viewers feel that Gore won the debate, the showdown was seen by many as a major political turning point for the Clinton administration. On November 17, 1993, by a vote of 234–200, the **U.S. House of Representatives** passed legislation that allowed the implementation of the treaty. Three days later, the **U.S. Senate** passed the same bill by a much wider margin of 61–38. In both cases, passage depended on forging a coalition with Republicans, who by and large supported the treaty, and clusters of conservative and moderate Democrats.

NAFTA created a free-trade pact between the United States, Mexico, and Canada. Implementation of the treaty began on January 1, 1994. The treaty removed many trade barriers immediately; others were to be phased out over a period of five to fifteen years. While American industries, particularly in the textile and other low-wage sectors, continued to set up plants south of the border, they did not flee the United States en masse, as critics of the treaty had predicted they would. The overall growth of the **economy** stabilized employment in the manufacturing sector. In fact, unemployment reached twenty-five- to thirty-year lows in the industrial Midwest. NAFTA's greatest impact was on the trade of agricultural goods. Between 1992 and 1998, U.S. farm exports to Mexico and Canada grew by 48 percent. During the same time period, imports of food crops from both of these nations grew. American consumers benefited from sustained low food prices, as did large agricultural exporters. The administration also argued that by promoting growth in Mexico, NAFTA stemmed the tide of Mexican immigrants into the United States, although the collapse of the peso in Mexico in 1994, which depressed the Mexican economy, probably offset many of the benefits that NAFTA produced.

Even though NAFTA did not unleash a rush of jobs south of the border, as Perot had predicted it would, the Clinton administration had difficulty building on the agreement to negotiate a similar pact for the rest of **Latin America**. Although Republicans in the House and Senate were supportive of free trade in principle, they sought to deny Clinton additional political victories that would have come if they had granted him "fast-track" privileges to negotiate such a pact. Such privileges had been granted to President Bush. At the same time, anti-free-trade sentiment among trade unionists and other liberal groups, particularly among radical environmentalists, made it difficult for Clinton to win support for liberalized free-trade agreements in the Western Hemisphere.

In the late 1990s, anti-free-trade sentiment showed its face via several protests, most notably against the World Trade Organization meeting in Seattle, Washington, in November 1999. In the **election of 2000**, consumer advocate and Green Party presidential candidate Ralph Nader, a foe of NAFTA and other free-trade agreements, tapped into this anti-free-trade sentiment. His candidacy arguably cost Al Gore the presidency.

Suggested Readings: Maxwell Cameron, *The Making of NAFTA* (Ithaca, NY: Cornell University Press, 2000); "Congress OKs North American Trade Pact," *Congressional Quarterly Almanac*, 1993, p. 171; "Clinton Remarks on House Passage of NAFTA, November 17, 1993," *Historic Documents*, 1993, p. 953; http://ffas. usda.gov/info/factsheets/nafta.html; Anne Krueger, "NAFTA: Effects: A Preliminary Assessment," *World Economy* 23:6 (June 2000).

NANNYGATE. *See* **Baird, Zoë; Wood, Kimba.**

NATIONAL ECONOMIC COUNCIL (NEC). President Bill Clinton created
the National Economic Council (NEC) following his inauguration as president in 1993. In many ways, the council was to operate as the domestic
equivalent of the National Security Council (NSC). The NSC brought together representatives of various agencies and departments so as to better
coordinate national security policy. Similarly, the NEC was created to
coordinate the domestic initiatives of the administration. The first director of the NEC was **Robert Rubin**, who went on to become secretary of
the Treasury. Rubin was succeeded by **Laura D'Andrea Tyson**, the chair
of the president's Council of Economic Advisers from 1993 to 1995. Upon
Tyson's retirement, **Gene Sperling**, a longtime adviser to the president
on economic matters, became the director of the NEC. President Clinton
credited the National Economic Council with playing a key role in developing and gaining passage of the administration's most important economic programs, including the 1993 **budget** deficit-reduction plan,
NAFTA, empowerment zones, and targeted tax cuts to help pay for college **education**. Some argued that the NEC created another unnecessary
level of bureaucracy, since the president already had a Council of Economic Advisers, secretaries of the Treasury, commerce, and the Interior,
and a director of the Office of Management and Budget to aid him in
setting economic policy. Yet Clinton emphasized the need to have a more
streamlined branch that was not responsible to other constituencies and
that combined economic expertise with political pragmatism. The Council of Economic Advisers, for example, was comprised of economists
whose political experience was often limited.

Suggested Readings: I. M. Destler, *The National Economic Council: A Work in
Progress* (Washington, DC: Institute for International Economics, 1996).

Related Entries: Domestic Policy; Economy.

NATO (NORTH ATLANTIC TREATY ORGANIZATION). In the wake of the
end of the cold war, the Clinton administration developed a modified
vision of the role of the North Atlantic Treaty Organization (NATO). For
years, NATO had existed as a buffer against the Soviet Union and as a foe
of the Communist Warsaw Pact. As communism collapsed in Eastern Europe and the Soviet Union, however, NATO had to determine whether it

was still necessary, and if so, whether it should shrink in size and mission or take on an expanded role, particularly in Europe. The Clinton administration sought to expand NATO's role. The president and the State Department argued in favor of admitting new members, in particular, former members of the Warsaw Pact, and using NATO to resolve crises in the region. At the same time, the Clinton administration sought to convince the leaders of **Russia** that the expansion of NATO did not signify a threat to its security or interests.

On April 30, 1998, by a vote of 80–19, the **U.S. Senate** formally ratified an amendment to the 1949 treaty that had established NATO. The amendment admitted Poland, Hungary, and the Czech Republic as members of NATO. Nearly two years earlier, on July 8, 1996, European and U.S. diplomats had announced their intention to expand NATO in the Madrid Declaration. While the idea to include these three Eastern European nations in NATO won the support of most Republicans and Democrats in the Senate, some fretted about antagonizing Russia through such a move. Others expressed their concern that opening the door to Poland, Hungary, and the Czech Republic would lead to the inclusion of other Eastern European nations, diluting the strength of the alliance and further antagonizing Russia. (President Jacques Chirac of France favored admitting Romania and Slovenia.) While the Clinton administration did not rule out the possible admission of other nations in the future, it sought to limit the number of new member nations to three at this time.

The new NATO, which the Clinton administration claimed would add to the stability of Europe, received its first real test when **Slobodan Milosevic** defied U.S. and European demands to cease the policy of ethnic cleansing of Albanians in **Kosovo**. In response to Serb aggression, NATO forces attacked Yugoslavia for over seventy-five days. Even though Russia and other non-NATO nations objected to these attacks, NATO remained united in its commitment to punish Milosevic for his defiance. On June 9, 1999, Milosevic finally agreed to withdraw Yugoslavian troops from Kosovo, and the air raids terminated. Subsequently, an international peace force of 48,000, known as KFOR, entered the region to maintain the peace. Some critics of NATO and the Clinton administration argued that stories of Serb atrocities in Kosovo had been exaggerated; they also expressed concern that the war unnecessarily antagonized Russia and threatened to splinter NATO itself. For example, during the war, large anti-NATO protests were staged in several European nations, most notably Greece and Italy. However, the ability of NATO to stick together, especially when the initial air attacks seemed ineffective, suggested that such worries were overstated. Milosevic's fall from power in 2000 further vindicated NATO's actions.

Suggested Readings: "Lawmakers Seek to Limit NATO Expansion to Three New Members," *Congressional Quarterly Almanac*, 1998, p. 8-21; "NATO Expansion Forges Ahead," *Congressional Quarterly Almanac*, 1997, p. 8-23. "NATO Summit Meeting Statement on Expansion, July 8, 1997," *Historic Documents*, 1997, p. 514; Martin A. Smith and Graham Timmins, *Building a Bigger Europe: EU and NATO Enlargement in Comparative Perspective* (Aldershot, VT: Ashgate, 2000).

Related Entry: Foreign Policy.

NETANYAHU, BENJAMIN. *See* **Middle East**.

NEW DEMOCRAT. *See* **Democratic Leadership Council**.

NORTH AMERICA FREE TRADE AGREEMENT. *See* **NAFTA**.

NORTHERN IRELAND. The Clinton administration considered its efforts to achieve peace in Northern Ireland one of its greatest accomplishments. Catholic and Protestant forces in Northern Ireland had been engaged in a bitter, violent fight for decades. This fight stemmed from seemingly irreconcilable differences between the two ethnic groups. Protestants, who constituted a slight majority of the population in Northern Ireland, wished to remain part of Great Britain. Most Catholics, however, wanted to unite Northern Ireland with the rest of Ireland, which had gained its independence from Britain in the 1920s. Nearly every attempt to overcome these differences had failed during the 1970s and 1980s.

The Clinton administration undertook several key steps to revive the peace process. In 1994, it issued a visa to Gerry Adams, the head of Sinn Fein, the political arm of the paramilitary Irish Republican Army (IRA). Clinton hoped to bolster Adams's standing within the IRA by doing so, reasoning that Adams would prove amenable to the peace process. A year later, President Clinton visited Northern Ireland, where he pledged U.S. support for peace. In 1996, **George Mitchell**, the former **Senate** majority leader, headed up peace talks in Ireland. For nearly a year, Mitchell's efforts led nowhere, but Tony Blair's election as prime minister of Great Britain in 1997 injected a new sense of possibility into the negotiations.

On April 10, 1998, Good Friday, Mitchell announced that an agreement had been made. According to the agreement, British direct rule of Northern Ireland would give way to a provincial assembly and both Protestants and Catholics would demilitarize. On May 22, 1998, more than 70 percent of voters in Northern Ireland ratified the agreement. A little over a month later, moderate forces won nearly as many seats as staunch antiunionists in parliamentary elections. The agreement did not end tensions in the region or mark a final solution to the disagreement over whether Northern Ireland would become part of Ireland or remain part of Great Britain. Nonetheless, it established a peaceful process for resolving this dispute. Furthermore, even though acts of violence and **terrorism** did not come to an end, the seemingly endless cycle of violence did. Following a bombing in Omagh, Northern Ireland, on August 15, 1998 which killed twenty-eight and wounded two hundred, President Clinton visited Northern Ireland for a second time. He was greeted by enthusiastic crowds who cheered his calls for reconciliation. Several months later, Tony Blair became the first British prime minister to speak to Ireland's parliament in Dublin, where he too won the applause of Ireland's representatives for his commitment toward "a new beginning." Whether the peace would hold, no one could tell for certain, but most granted the Clinton administration credit for moving the region in the right direction.

Suggested Readings: Bret Begun, "Goodbye Peace?" *Newsweek*, December 18, 2000, p. 6; "Northern Ireland Peace Agreement, April 10, 1998," *Historic Documents*, 1998 pp. 203–219; http://clinton4.nara.gov/WH/Accomplishments/foreign. html; "7 Days," *New Statesman*, September 4, 1998, p. 5.

Related Entry: Foreign Policy.

NORTH KOREA. *See* **Korea**.

NUCLEAR NONPROLIFERATION. Prior to Bill Clinton's election as president, the Ronald Reagan and **George Bush** administrations negotiated a series of agreements with the Soviet Union to decrease the number of nuclear weapons. Some of these treaties, most prominently START I, went into force during Clinton's presidency. The president remained committed to implementing these agreements and to promoting additional reductions in nuclear weapons. By the end of Clinton's term as president, all nuclear weapons had been removed from Ukraine, Belarus, and Kazakhstan. For a while there was concern that these three territories of the former Soviet Union would not comply with START I. START II, signed in January 1993, which aimed at reductions in strategic nuclear forces, particularly land-based ballistic missiles with multiple warheads, was ratified by the **U.S. Senate** in January 1996. At Helsinki, in March 1997, Presidents Clinton and Boris Yeltsin of **Russia** pledged to abide by START III by December 7, 2007. This agreement set a ceiling on strategic weapons for both the United States and Russia 80 percent below the number of strategic nuclear weapons that had been deployed by the two superpowers at the peak of the cold war. Altogether, in a twelve-year period, beginning in 1988, the United States dismantled over 13,000 nuclear warheads and decreased its warhead stockpile by 59 percent.

In addition, on September 24, 1996, President Clinton signed the Comprehensive Nuclear Test-Ban Treaty. The treaty aimed at banning all nuclear weapon test explosions. The United States had maintained a test moratorium since September 1992. In September 1997, President Clinton submitted the treaty for ratification to the U.S. Senate. The Senate, however, stalled going forward with ratification. Opponents noted that several nuclear nations, of which the most important were India, Pakistan, and North **Korea**, refused to ratify the treaty. Indeed, both India and Pakistan tested nuclear weapons after the treaty was negotiated. The United States and the other nations that had nuclear weapons, most notably China, Russia, France, and the United Kingdom, had stopped testing nuclear weapons via explosions on their own, without the treaty.

One potential stumbling block to the steady progress toward nuclear disarmament was the Strategic Defense Initiative (SDI), sometimes labeled "Star Wars." President Reagan had initiated calls for an antiballistic-missile **defense** system based in outer space. Even though the Soviet Union adamantly opposed SDI, Reagan insisted that he would go ahead with the development of such a system. Whether such a space-based system could even work remained a matter of much controversy. Research on SDI continued during George Bush's presidency. Even though many Democrats had opposed Star Wars, President Clinton continued to sign appropriation bills that allowed for its development. In the final months of his presidency, Clinton announced that he would leave the decision over whether or not to deploy a modified SDI to the next administration. One reason for concern was that Russia contended that a space-based missile defense system would violate the long-standing Antiballistic Missile (ABM) Treaty, which had been negotiated by the Richard Nixon administration. Critics of SDI warned that going ahead with deployment might jeopardize the commitment of the United States and Russia to decreasing the danger of nuclear war for a system that might not ever work.

Suggested Readings: Joseph Cirincone, "The Assault on Arms Control," *Bulletin of the Atomic Scientists* 56:1 (January/February 2000), p. 32; Jonathan Schell, "The Folly of Arms Control," *Foreign Affairs* 79:5 (September/October 2000), p. 22; "U.S. Commitment to the Treaty of the Non-Proliferation of Nuclear Weapons," May 3, 1999, Factsheet.

NUSSBAUM, BERNARD WILLIAM. (March 3, 1937, New York, New York– .) White House Counsel, 1993–1994.

Bernard Nussbaum served as Bill Clinton's first White House counsel. He resigned amid controversy regarding questions about his actions in relationship to several burgeoning controversies, particularly **Whitewater**, the death of **Vincent Foster**, and **filegate**. Although Nussbaum was accused of many misdeeds by conservative pundits, independent council **Robert Ray**, who took over from **Kenneth Starr**, cleared Nussbaum of any wrongdoing in the filegate affair. No other formal charges of wrongdoing were brought against Nussbaum.

The son of Jewish immigrants from Poland, Nussbaum was born on the lower east side of New York City. He earned a B.A. from Columbia University and his law degree from Harvard University. After law school, he worked as a lawyer for the House Judiciary Committee that called for the impeachment of President Richard Nixon. Among the junior attorneys he worked with was **Hillary Clinton**, then Hillary Rodham. At the time, she privately told him about the man she would soon marry and whom she predicted would one day become president, namely, Bill Clinton. By the time that Clinton was in fact elected president, Nussbaum had become a prominent corporate attorney in New York City.

Almost from the start, Nussbaum played a role in several of Clinton's more controversial decisions. As White House counsel, he helped select nominees to several top Justice Department post, including **Zoë Baird** and **Kimba Wood**, both of whose nominations were withdrawn. More notably, he had to defend the firing of employees of the White House travel office in the incident known as **travelgate**. Nussbaum faced even further criticism for his actions following Vincent Foster's suicide. Many argued that Nussbaum's experience as a corporate litigator ill suited him to the job of White House counsel, since the latter demanded as much political skill as it did legal savvy. For instance, after Foster's death, Nussbaum, with law-enforcement officers present, examined the papers in Foster's office to determine if there was anything relevant to his suicide. This led to charges that he was covering up something, perhaps even the cause of Foster's death. In the face of such accusations, Nussbaum resigned. In 1996, independent counsel Starr enlarged his Whitewater probe to determine whether Nussbaum had lied to Congress in testimony regarding the filegate scandal. As noted earlier, Starr's successor cleared Nussbaum of any charges.

Suggested Readings: Gwen Ifill, "Nussbaum Out As White House Counsel," *New York Times*, March 6, 1994, p. 1; Neil Lewis, "Man in the News: Bernard William Nussbaum," *New York Times*, February 5, 1994, p. 9.

O

OKLAHOMA CITY BOMBING. On April 19, 1995, a truck bomb exploded outside the Alfred P. Murrah Federal Building in Oklahoma City, Oklahoma, killing 168 people, including a number of children who were located in a day-care center on the second floor of the office structure. The bombing was the worst case of domestic **terrorism** in U.S. history. While some initially contended that Arab nationalists had committed the act, two American-born suspects, Timothy McVeigh and Terry Nichols, were quickly arrested and charged with committing the crime. In 1997, in separate trials, McVeigh was convicted of eleven counts of conspiracy and murder and was sentenced to death; Nichols, who had helped McVeigh obtain the materials out of which McVeigh constructed the bomb, was convicted of conspiracy and involuntary manslaughter. While neither McVeigh nor Nichols testified at their trials, prosecutors and news reporters contended that both of them were associated with right-wing groups that held extreme antigovernment views. The bombing of the federal building took place on the second anniversary of the federal raid on the Branch Davidians in **Waco**, Texas, which many conservatives viewed as somewhat of an Alamo for those outside of the liberal mainstream. At the trial, Michael Fourier, who had pled guilty to a lesser charge of withholding evidence in exchange for a light sentence, testified that McVeigh hoped to cause a "general uprising" against the federal government.

The national response to the bombing of the federal building was the exact opposite of that hoped for by McVeigh. Four days after the incident, thousands of people gathered in Oklahoma City to honor the dead. President Bill Clinton pledged to "do all we can to help you heal the injured, rebuild the city, and to bring to justice to those who did this evil" ("Remarks at Prayer Service"). In the wake of the bombing, national concern

The north side of the Alfred P. Murrah Federal Building in Oklahoma City, April 19, 1995. AP/Wide World Photos.

about the danger posed by right-wing groups, especially paramilitary groups, grew. Some liberals accused critics of the president, such as conservative radio talk-show host **Rush Limbaugh**, of fostering a dangerous climate of hate and antigovernment views. President Clinton requested passage of antiterrorism legislation. The **U.S. Senate** quickly passed a bill that gave the federal government increasing powers to fight domestic terrorism in spite of objections by civil libertarians who worried that the new law jeopardized individual privacy rights. Moreover, in the wake of the bombing, President Clinton received a bump in the polls and began to reverse the momentum gained by Republicans in the **election of 1994**. Perhaps the most significant reaction to the bombing came from local residents and travelers who left tokens of their respect for the dead at the bombing site. Thousands of items, ranging from wreaths to poems, were left in memory of the dead. On April 19, 2000, a memorial to those who had lost their lives in the bombing was dedicated in Oklahoma City. Hundreds of thousands of Americans visited the site within a year.

Suggested Readings: "Remarks at Prayer Service for Bombing Victims, April 23, 1995," *Historic Documents*, 1995, p. 176; "McVeigh on His Sentencing for Oklahoma City Bombing, August 14, 1997," *Historic Documents*, 1997, p. 623; David Hoffman, *The Oklahoma City Bombing and the Politics of Terror* (Venice, CA: Feral House, 1998); http://connections.oklahoman.net/memorial/; http://www. cnn.com/US/OKC/bombing.html; Richard Serrano, *One of Ours: Timothy McVeigh and the Oklahoma City Bombing* (New York: Norton, 1998).

O'LEARY, HAZEL R. (May 17, 1937, Newport News, Virginia–   .) Secretary of Energy, 1993–1997.

Hazel O'Leary, an **African American** woman, was one of President Bill Clinton's most surprising nominees to serve in his **cabinet**. O'Leary did not meet Clinton until December 18, 1992, three days before he announced his intention to nominate her as secretary of energy, and her relative lack of experience and/or prominence led few to think that she would be tapped for the post. Yet Clinton's desire to appoint more **women** and minorities gave her the edge over an assortment of other front-runners, including Senator Tim Wirth of Colorado, an expert on energy matters.

Born in Newport News, Virginia, the daughter of two physicians, O'Leary attended racially segregated schools until ninth grade, when she went to live with her aunt in Essex County, New Jersey. O'Leary earned her B.A. from Fisk University in 1959 and a law degree from Rutgers University in 1966. In the mid-1970s, she worked for the Federal Energy Administration, and when the Department of Energy was created, she was appointed its deputy administrator in charge of the Economic Regulatory Administration. During the Ronald Reagan and **George Bush** administrations, she worked in the private sector, first with her husband in an energy consulting firm and then for Northern State Power Company of Minneapolis, Minnesota. While many business groups praised her nomination, especially her support of the nuclear energy industry, many environmentalists expressed their concern over her lack of experience in the field of nuclear waste management; some in the scientific community similarly expressed their reservations about her knowledge of nuclear weapons research. Nonetheless, she won **Senate** confirmation fairly easily.

As secretary of energy, O'Leary championed several components of

President Clinton's economic stimulus and tax package. This included a proposed BTU tax, aimed at fostering research into alternative fuels and raising revenues. This tax proposal, however, failed to gain congressional support. Several other Energy Department initiatives, including a super-collider that the science community touted as a key to basic energy-related research, failed to win congressional approval as well. As secretary, she promoted research into global warming and the declassi-fication of hundreds of thousands of classified government documents left over from years of nuclear research during the cold war. Faced with increasing costs, particularly for nuclear waste cleanup, and decreasing revenues, O'Leary also sought to reorganize the department. Her relative success in doing so, however, tended to be obscured by several expensive trips she took at taxpayer expense. When reports of such trips appeared in the press, conservatives focused on them as an example of what was wrong with the Clinton administration, which critics charged was driven by the desire to be diverse rather than effective, while Vice President **Al Gore** and President Clinton defended O'Leary's journeys as beneficial to business and the economy. When Clinton won reelection, he announced that he would replace O'Leary with Transportation Secretary **Federico Peña**.

O'Leary left office under a cloud of suspicion, accused of using her position to raise funds for Clinton's reelection bid in 1996. More specif-ically, **Johnny Chung**, one of the figures associated with the campaign finance scandal of 1996, alleged that O'Leary prodded one of his clients to donate $25,000 to her favorite charity in exchange for an appointment with her. Even though U.S. Attorney General **Janet Reno** found no evi-dence of any illegal actions on O'Leary's part, the stigma of incompetence and unethical actions remained. Virtually only the black press continued to praise O'Leary, suggesting that conservative criticism of her was part of a broader pattern of attacks on black officials in the Clinton adminis-tration, including **Lani Guinier**, whose nomination to head the Civil Rights Division of the Department of Justice was withdrawn in the face of claims that she favored reverse discrimination, and Surgeon General **Joycelyn Elders**, who was forced to resign following a statement on mas-turbation and teen pregnancy.

Suggested Readings: Paul Akers, "O'Leary's in Clear, But Energy Isn't," *The Arizona Republic*, December 8, 1997, p. B7; "O'Leary, Patrick Exit Clinton Administration," *Jet*, December 2, 1996, p. 26.

P

PALESTINIANS. *See* **Middle East**.

PANETTA, LEON. (June 28, 1938, Monterey, California–   .) Director, Office of Management and Budget, 1993–1994; Chief of Staff, 1994–1997.

Leon Panetta, a prominent Democratic congressman from California, served as Bill Clinton's first director of the Office of Management and Budget (OMB) and as his second chief of staff. Clinton's nomination of Panetta as director of OMB demonstrated that one of the administration's top priorities would be balancing the federal **budget**. His selection of Panetta to succeed his lifelong friend **Thomas "Mack" McClarty** as chief of staff signaled the president's acknowledgment that he needed a savvy Washington insider to help him turn around his often-troubled presidency. The enactment of Clinton's economic plan in 1993, the drastic reduction of the federal budget deficit, and Clinton's reelection in 1996 suggested that Panetta played both roles well. As a *Washington Post* editorial put it, Panetta "made a career out of taking on some of the harder jobs in this city . . . and doing them with distinction" ("A Good Man").

Panetta grew up on the west coast of California, the son of Italian immigrants. He earned his B.A. and J.D. from the University of Santa Clara in 1960 and 1963, respectively. At the time, he was a supporter of Richard Nixon, the Republican nominee for president in 1960 and then governor of California. After serving in the U.S. Army for two years, he went to work for Thomas Kuchel, California's moderate Republican senator. After Kuchel was defeated in the Republican primary in 1968, Panetta went to work for Massachusetts Republican Edward Brooke, the only black person in the **U.S. Senate**, and then for the Nixon administration's Department of Health, Education, and Welfare as its chief civil rights officer. In

1970, Panetta resigned in protest against the increasingly conservative civil rights policies of the Nixon administration and the Republican Party. Afterwards he worked for New York City mayor John Lindsay, in the private sector as a lawyer, and as counsel for the National Association for the Advancement of Colored People (NAACP).

In 1976, as a Democrat, Panetta successfully defeated Republican incumbent Burt Talcott to gain a seat in the **U.S. House of Representatives**. He was reelected every two years until he joined the Clinton administration in 1992. While he was a sharp critic of President Reagan's defense and foreign policies, Panetta earned a reputation as a fiscal moderate. He played a key role in the writing of the Gramm-Rudman deficit-reduction act in 1985 and the 1990 budget agreement with President **George Bush**. His appointment as director of the Office of Management and Budget flowed from his years of experience on the House Budget Committee and his reputation for favoring deficit reduction. Along with his deputy, **Alice Rivlin**, and top Treasury Department officials, he lobbied hard for the Clinton deficit-reduction plan, which narrowly won congressional approval in spite of unanimous Republican opposition. Panetta's strong connections to Democrats in the House of Representatives were key to the bill's passage.

At the time Panetta became chief of staff, the Clinton administration was reeling from a series of missteps, from its early mishandling of several key nominations to the emergence of the **Whitewater** scandal. Panetta also had to overcome divisions that had arisen with the defeat of the **health care reform** package. Panetta moved to replace other initial Clinton appointees with more seasoned veterans. After leaving the White House, Panetta worked as a consultant and headed the Leon and Sylvia Panetta Institute for Public Policy in Monterey, California. He served on the boards of numerous corporations and nonprofit organizations and commented regularly on political developments.

Suggested Readings: *Current Biography Yearbook*, 1993, p. 441; Ann Devroy, "Another Miserable White House August," *Washington Post*, August 10, 1994, p. A17; "A Good Man Heads Home," *Washington Post*, November 10, 1996, p. C6; Douglas Jehl, "Hinting at More Changes, Panetta Takes the Reins," *New York Times*, June 29, 1994, p. A18.

Related Entries: Domestic Policy; Economy.

PARDONS. On his last full day in office, January 20, 2001, President Clinton issued 140 pardons and commuted the sentences of 36 individuals.

Among the most prominent individuals affected by the president's actions were **Henry Cisneros**, the former secretary of housing and urban development, who had pled guilty to charges that he lied to the FBI in regard to payments to his mistress, John Deutch, the former director of the CIA, who had pled guilty to charges that he had mishandled classified intelligence documents, **Susan McDougal**, one of the key figures in the **Whitewater** scandal, John Fife Symington III, a former governor of Arizona, Patty Hearst, the heir to the Hearst fortune, and Roger Clinton, the president's half brother, who had been convicted on **drug** charges. (Clinton had earlier pardoned Dan Rostenkowski, a longtime Democratic congressman from Chicago who had resigned from the **U.S. House of Representatives** in the face of fraud charges.)

While it was common for presidents to issue pardons and commute the sentences of individuals at the tail end of the their terms—**George Bush**, for example, had pardoned former Secretary of Defense Caspar Weinberger—the number of pardons and commutations issued by Clinton and the fact that he issued so many on the last day of his term were unusual. Moreover, in the weeks following Clinton's departure from office, his pardoning of several individuals developed into another major scandal of the type that had characterized his presidency. Nearly every political poll showed that the pardons damaged Clinton's reputation, reinforcing the public's image of him as lacking character. Ironically, some argued that he issued many of the pardons because of his own experience with overzealous prosecutors and his desire to help those whom he felt had faced similar persecution.

Somewhat surprisingly, the pardons that drew the greatest fire were not those of high-profile political figures, such as Cisneros, nor of individuals who had been convicted for crimes related to their political activism, such as Peter MacDonald, a former leader of the Navajo Nation who had been convicted in 1992 of a federal conspiracy charge for his role in a 1989 Window Rock riot that resulted in two deaths, or Linda Sue Evans, who had been sentenced to forty years in prison for her part in a plan to bomb the U.S. Capitol in 1983 to protest the invasion of Grenada. Rather, the pardons that drew the greatest fire were those of Marc Rich, a fugitive financier indicted on charges of tax evasion, Pincus Green, Rich's business partner, and Carlos Vignali and A. Glenn Braswell, who had been convicted on charges of drug smuggling, perjury, and mail fraud, respectively. Not only did a wide variety of Americans, ranging from members of Congress to political analysts, question why these felons merited pardons or commutations of their sentences, they raised serious questions about the reasons why President Clinton granted them. Both Congress and the U.S. attorney, Mary Jo White of the Southern District of New York, began investigations into whether Clinton had broken the law by accepting bribes in exchange for issuing pardons or granting clemency.

Even if investigators proved unable to uncover evidence of an actual quid pro quo, they quickly revealed information that seemed to display the power of political connections and money to the former president. Vignali and Braswell, for example, paid Hugh Rodham, **Hillary Clinton**'s brother, $400,000 to pursue their clemency applications. Marc Rich's former wife, Denise Rich, was a major contributor to the Democratic Party and to Clinton's presidential library. Rich was also represented by Jack Quinn, a former White House counsel and friend of the president. Quinn took the case for pardoning Rich directly to the president, bypassing normal channels that would have entailed a full review by the Justice Department. Congressional investigators and the press also raised questions about pardons issued to James Manning and Bob Fain, two Little Rock businessmen convicted on tax-evasion charges. The two were represented by William Cunningham III, a law partner of former White House official **Harold Ickes**. Not surprisingly, Hillary Clinton's involvement in some of the pardons drew fire as well. Besides Hugh Rodham's connections to two of the more controversial cases, reports surfaced that the U.S. attorney's office in New York was concerned about whether Bill Clinton commuted the sentences of four Hasidic Jews convicted of fraud in exchange for Hasidic votes for Hillary's run for the **U.S. Senate**.

As in the past, Clinton sought to deflect these charges. Most notably, in an op-ed article that appeared in the Sunday *New York Times*, on February 19, 2001, the former president countered charges that he had pardoned Marc Rich in exchange for campaign contributions. On the contrary, Clinton argued that he was influenced by the good work Rich had done for Israel and that Rich could still face stiff civil penalties. Likewise, Hillary Clinton denied that she knew that her brother had accepted payment in exchange for representing two of the individuals who were pardoned and stated that she had no memory of her brother's involvement in the affair. The fact that Republican congressman Dan Burton, a longtime foe of the Clintons, raised much of the ruckus about the pardons also allowed some to suggest that "pardongate," like the many scandals and investigations that preceded it, was politically motivated and, like Whitewater, would produce no hard evidence of wrongdoing.

Regardless of the outcome of the dispute over Clinton's pardons, the dispute itself reflected the degree to which the battle over Clinton's legacy would be a contentious one and the extent to which Clinton managed to dominate the news even after leaving office. The initial opinion of most political pundits was that the pardons would hurt the way history judged Clinton and would lessen his stature within the Democratic Party. Others, however, recalling how Clinton had come back from other scandals, were not so quick to make such conclusions.

Suggested Readings: "Clinton's Pardons and Commutations," http://www.msnbc.com/news/519073.asp; Weston Kosova "Backstage at the Finale," *Newsweek*, February 26, 2001, p. 30; "Pardoned Felons Allegedly Paid Hillary Clinton's Brother," http://www.msnbc.com/local/kshb/206701.asp.

PARTIAL BIRTH ABORTION. *See* **Abortion, Partial Birth**.

PASTER, HOWARD. (December 6, 1944, Brooklyn, New York–   .) Presidential aide, 1993.

During Bill Clinton's first year in office, Howard Paster served as one of the president's political aides, specifically as his chief lobbyist or liaison to Congress. Paster came to the White House with a reputation as one of the more powerful political lobbyists in Washington, D.C. First at Timmons and Company and then at Hill and Knowlton, Paster represented some of the largest corporations in America and the National Rifle Association, one of the administration's strongest critics. Paster's political experience made him a valuable member of the White House team, especially since many of Clinton's aides lacked inside-the-beltway connections. While Paster took much of the blame for the defeat of the administration's economic stimulus package, he also deserved much of the credit for forging the coalition that ratified **NAFTA** and passed several of the administration's other proposals, particularly Clinton's balanced-budget plan.

Born in the Flatbush section of Brooklyn, New York, Paster spent most of his childhood in Nassau County on Long Island, New York. After graduating from Alfred University in 1967, he earned his M.A. in journalism from Columbia University. Afterwards, he worked briefly as a journalist for the *Suffolk Sun* newspaper and then as an aide for Indiana senator Birch Bayh and congressman Lester Wolff. After leaving the public sector, he quickly earned a reputation as one of the keenest professional political lobbyists in Washington. Among those he represented were the United

Automobile Workers Union during its and Chrysler's successful effort to prod the federal government to bail out the ailing automaker in the late 1970s. Through Michael Berman, a prominent Democrat, and via his connections with several **House** and **Senate** leaders, Paster came to the attention of President Clinton, who named him his chief liaison to Congress. He took a large salary cut when he left Hill and Knowlton. Paster resigned at the end of 1993, citing political burnout and personal needs. He returned to Hill and Knowlton.

Suggested Readings: Lloyd Grove, "Clinton's Arm-Twister," *Washington Post*, August 6, 1993, p. D1; Gwen Ifill, "2 Clinton Aides Are Leaving on a Winning Streak," *New York Times*, November 24, 1993, p. A20.

Related Entry: Domestic Policy.

PEÑA, FEDERICO FABIAN. (March 15, 1947, Laredo, Texas–   .) Secretary of Transportation, 1993–1997; Secretary of Energy, 1997–1998.

Federico Peña was the U.S. secretary of transportation during President Clinton's first term as president. After Clinton was reelected, Clinton nominated him to replace **Hazel O'Leary** as secretary of energy. Peña was the highest-ranking Hispanic in the Clinton administration. He resigned in the spring of 1998, citing a desire to return to private life so he could spend more time with his family. While he earned a mixed record as secretary of energy, a field in which he had little experience, he gained higher marks for his years as head of the Transportation Department. As secretary of transportation, he helped negotiate agreements with forty nations to open markets to American airline carriers, enhanced safety in the aviation field, and streamlined the department's massive work force by 11,000. His confirmation as secretary of energy was delayed briefly to give the Justice Department time to investigate several possible wrongdoings; he was confirmed without much difficulty after he was cleared of any illegal actions. He left the Energy Department while trying to push through legislation that would ease the deregulation of the utility industry. He also left his successor, **William Richardson**, to deal with the final stages of a plan to clean up massive amounts of nuclear waste, a byproduct of the cold war.

Born in Laredo, Texas, Peña earned his B.A. and law degree from the University of Texas in 1969 and 1972, respectively. He worked in a Denver law firm for about five years and then ran successfully for a seat in the Colorado General Assembly. Between 1983 and 1991, Peña served as the mayor of Denver, overseeing the city's revival, including the landing of a professional baseball team and the construction of a new convention center and a massive new airport. While some criticized the modernistic airport as a waste of money, over time, its construction insured Denver's prominence as a transportation hub. His experience with the airport lent credibility to his nomination as Clinton's secretary of transportation. After resigning as secretary of energy, he returned to Denver and became a senior adviser at the investment banking firm of Vestar Capital Partners.

Suggested Readings: Tom Ichniowski, "Shuffling Begins to Replace Peña as Energy Secretary," *Engineering News-Record*, April 13, 1998, p. 11; Robert Stewart, "Clinton's Transportation Nominee Gets Mixed Grades," *Los Angeles Times*, December 25, 1992, p. A42; Matthew Wald, "Peña Resigns as Energy Secretary," *New York Times*, April 7, 1998, p. A22.

Related Entry: Cabinet.

PEROT, H. ROSS. (June 27, 1930, Texarkana, Arkansas–   .) Third-party candidate for President, 1992 and 1996.

H. Ross Perot, a multimillionaire businessman, shook up the political world with his independent candidacy for the presidency in 1992. During the campaign (one of the most bizarre in history, in which Perot first entered the race, then withdrew, and then reentered), the wealthy Texan, with a net worth estimated at approximately $2 billion, sought to portray himself as a populist who represented the little man and opposed Washington, D.C., and conventional politics. Although he failed to win a single electoral college vote, his 18.9 percent of the total popular vote established him as the most successful third-party candidate since Theodore Roosevelt in 1912. Moreover, by emphasizing the danger of persistent federal deficits and ever-increasing federal debt, Perot prodded the Clinton administration to focus on balancing the budget after the election. Perot also was a vociferous opponent of **NAFTA**, warning that it would lead to a massive job loss in the United States. To secure passage of this trade treaty, Vice President **Al Gore** agreed to debate Perot. To the surprise of many, Gore put Perot on the defensive from the beginning of the debate, and Perot never recovered. Subsequently, NAFTA won congressional approval, and Perot's popularity waned. Perot ran again for president in 1996, but with the deficit in decline and the **economy** on the rise, he won only 8 percent of the vote. Moreover, the Reform Party, which Perot had created in 1992, split into warring factions after 1996, further diminishing Perot's promise to transform politics.

Perot grew up in Texarkana, a town on the Texas-Arkansas border. He did not leave his hometown until he was nineteen, when he entered the U.S. Naval Academy in Annapolis. Perot did well in school and was elected senior-class president. However, in 1956, after only three years of active service, he left the navy and went to work for International Business Machines (IBM). Perot rose quickly through the ranks of "Big Blue," becoming one of its top salesmen. In 1962, he left IBM to establish his own company, Electronic Data Systems (EDS), which he built into a Fortune 500 company.

Throughout the 1970s and 1980s, Perot was active in politics. By personally trying to win the release of several hostages in Iran and by criticizing the stoic corporate culture at General Motors (GM)—he briefly served on GM's board of directors—Perot gained an image as an iconoclast and patriot. During the 1992 campaign, as antigovernment and anti-Washington fervor grew, he emphasized that he was a businessman, not a politician, and argued that he had the experience to make government work. Using plain charts and graphs and paying for half-hour infomercials, he emphasized that American wages were stagnating while the federal **budget** deficit kept rising. At the same time, he infused politics with an antiestablishment message that continued to resonate after the **election of 1992**. During the **impeachment** scandal, Perot called for Clinton's removal from office while simultaneously criticizing the Republicans for their partisanship. Jesse Ventura's election as the Reform Party candidate for governor of Minnesota on November 3, 1998, suggested that the third way initiated by Perot had grown in strength, but sharp ideological divisions between Pat Buchanan, a conservative columnist and one-time candidate for the Republican presidential nomination, Ventura, and Perot diminished the party's image, suggesting that it had never been much more than a one-man show. Buchanan won the party's nomination but received less than 2 percent of the national vote in the **election of 2000**.

Suggested Readings: *Current Biography Yearbook*, 1996, p. 428; Jack Germond and Jules Witcover, *Mad As Hell: Revolt at the Ballot Box, 1992* (New York: Warner Books, 1993); H. Ross Perot, *United We Stand* (New York: Hyperion, 1992).

Related Entries: Election of 1992; Election of 1996.

PERRY, WILLIAM J. (October 11, 1927, Vandergrift, Pennsylvania–   .) Secretary of Defense, 1994–1997.

Secretary of Defense William Perry with General Jack Nix. Department of Defense.

William Perry served as President Bill Clinton's second secretary of defense, succeeding **Les Aspin**, who faced much controversy during his tenure in office, and giving way to **William S. Cohen** following Clinton's reelection. While he was Clinton's second choice to replace Aspin—his first choice, Bobby Ray Inman, a retired admiral and deputy director of the Central Intelligence Agency, withdrew his name from consideration for the position because of heated partisan attacks that Inman argued would only escalate and result in an unwarranted destruction of his reputation if he did not withdraw his name from nomination—Perry enjoyed a relatively smooth tenure in office. Republicans complained about the decline in morale in the armed services, but neither the Republican-controlled Congress nor Republican presidential candidate **Robert Dole** was able to make a major issue out of Clinton's **defense** policy. As secretary of defense, Perry strongly supported the expansion of **NATO** and a defense budget that would allow the federal government to continue to cut the federal deficit. Perry's greatest challenge came with the crisis in **Bosnia and Herzegovina**, which he inherited from his predecessors. While he initially opposed U.S. military involvement in the region, he ultimately oversaw U.S. participation in United Nations air strikes against Serb forces. Perry also opposed calls for lifting the arms embargo on the Serbs, arguing that this would produce further violence. Following the Dayton Agreement or Accords, the United States sent troops to Bosnia to take part in a NATO-led peacekeeping force. At first, Perry stated that the troops would remain in Bosnia for no more than a year, but a sizeable number of American forces remained in the region throughout Clinton's presidency. Perry also inherited a crisis in **Haiti** revolving around the military junta's refusal to reinstate president Jean-Bertrand Aristide. In the face of the threat of a military invasion, the junta was compelled to give way to Aristide. As in Bosnia and Herzegovina, U.S. troops were stationed in Haiti as peacekeepers. The reinstallation of Aristide as president in February 1996 and the withdrawal of American troops allowed the Clinton administration to declare its strategy in Haiti successful, but continuing tensions in Haiti led some critics to question whether anything had really been achieved.

Born in Vandergrift, Pennsylvania, Perry received his B.S. (1949) and M.A. from Stanford University (1950) and his Ph.D. in mathematics from Pennsylvania State University in 1957. For nearly two decades, he worked in the private sector, first at the Electronic Defense Laboratories of Sylvania/GTE and then as president of his own electronics company, ESL, Inc. From 1977 to 1981, Perry served as under secretary of defense for research and development. During the Ronald Reagan and **George Bush** presidencies, Perry returned to the private sector and served on the faculty of Stanford University. In 1993, he became the deputy secretary of defense. He was confirmed as Aspin's successor without much difficulty. He was considered the first technocrat to hold the post since Harold Brown, President Jimmy Carter's secretary of defense, and was touted as a skilled manager with experience in the private sector. During confirmation hearings and in pronouncements to the press, Perry emphasized that the United States needed to retain a modern military force that could fight two major regional wars simultaneously, but the downsizing of the military that had begun with the end of the cold war, combined with the commitment of U.S. forces to various crises, in conjunction with the economic expansion, which made it more difficult to recruit and retain skilled service members, led some to wonder if the United States was meeting this goal. At the same time, the ability of the United States to use its military to reinstate Aristide in Haiti and reestablish peace in the Balkans, not to mention retaining a "no-fly" zone over **Iraq**, suggested that complaints that the U.S. military was overextended were exaggerated.

After Perry left office, he was awarded the Presidential Medal of Freedom and the Marshall Award. He returned to Stanford University, where he had taught prior to joining the Clinton administration.

Suggested Readings: http://www.defenselink.mil/specials/secdef_histories/bios/perry.htm; William Hyland, *Clinton's World* (Westport, CT: Praeger, 1999); "Inman Withdraws As Defense Nominee," *Historic Documents*, 1994, January 24, 1994, p. 22; Douglas Jehl, "Pentagon Deputy Is Clinton's Choice for Defense Chief," *New York Times*, January 25, 1994, p. A1.

PETS. The Clintons owned two pets while they were in the White House. Socks, the Clintons' cat, moved into the White House with the family in 1993. Socks was the first cat to live in the White House since Misty Malarky Ying during the Jimmy Carter administration. Buddy, a chocolate Labrador retriever, was the Clintons' second pet. Buddy became a member of the family in December 1997. Unnamed when he arrived at the White House, he was named after one of President Clinton's uncles, who had died earlier that year. Thousands of schoolchildren wrote the White House to suggest a name for the Clintons' puppy, but the president felt that "Buddy" was particularly appropriate since his uncle had raised dogs.

The White House home page contained information on Buddy, Socks, and other pets who had lived in the president's mansion. President Abraham Lincoln allowed his sons, Tad and Willie, to keep an assortment of pets, including rabbits, turkeys, horses, and goats. Theodore Roosevelt's family pets included a small bear, a pig, and a badger. Franklin D. Roosevelt's dog, Fala, was probably better known than his vice presidents. Caroline Kennedy's ponies, including Macaroni, who was given to her by Vice President Lyndon Johnson, often were photographed drawing the Kennedy children across the White House lawn. First Lady Barbara Bush wrote *Millie's Book* (1992), a dog's-eye view of the White House. Somewhat similarly, **Hillary Clinton** compiled hundreds of letters written by schoolchildren and published her compilation as *Dear Socks, Dear Buddy* (1998). When the Clintons left the White House, Buddy moved with them to their new home in New York. Socks, however, did not remain in the family. Instead, Socks went to live with **Betty Currie** in Virginia, because, according to the Clintons, she never got along with the dog.

Suggested Readings: Hillary Clinton, *Dear Socks, Dear Buddy* (New York: Simon & Schuster, 1998); http://clinton4.nara.gov/WH/kids/inside.html.spring99–3.html.

PODESTA, JOHN D. (January 8, 1949, Chicago, Illinois–   .) Chief of Staff, 1998–2001.

John Podesta became President Bill Clinton's fourth chief of staff on October 20, 1998. He immediately had to face the **U.S. House of Representatives** vote on **impeachment** and the **U.S. Senate** trial of Clinton. The grandson of Italian immigrants and the son of working-class parents, Podesta received his B.A. from Knox College in 1971 and a law degree from Georgetown University in 1976. A supporter of Eugene McCarthy's campaign for the presidency in 1968, Podesta worked briefly for the Justice Department after graduating from law school and then went to work for Vermont senator Patrick Leahy. After rising to the post of chief counsel of the Senate Agriculture Committee, Podesta left the public sector to form his own law and lobbying firm with his brother, Anthony. In 1988 and 1992, he worked on the Michael Dukakis and Clinton campaigns, respectively, helping the candidates prepare for their presidential debates and doing fund-raising. From 1993 to 1995, Podesta served as an assistant to the president and as staff secretary. He took one year off from the White House to teach law at Georgetown University before returning as the deputy chief of staff under **Erskine Bowles** in 1996. Prior to becoming the chief of staff, Podesta spent much of his time and energy on the **Whitewater** and **Monica Lewinsky** scandals.

In some ways, Podesta's appointment represented the maturation of the Clinton administration. Upon being elected, Clinton appointed his childhood friend **Thomas "Mack" McLarty** as his chief of staff. When McLarty left, Clinton turned to **Leon Panetta**, a prominent Democratic congressman from California. In contrast, Podesta had few personal ties to the president and was not well known outside of the beltway. In spite of, or perhaps because of, his lack of notoriety, Podesta may have been Clinton's most successful chief of staff. Among his skills that Washington insiders praised was his ability to manage ambitious people. While Republicans criticized Podesta as partisan, they too acknowledged his personal integrity and political skills. Once the impeachment process ended, Podesta focussed much of his time on securing President Clinton's legacy, trying to make sure that the administration got credit for the economic expansion of the 1990s and enhancing Clinton's reputation as a peacemaker.

Suggested Readings: Charles Babington, "For the President's 4th Chief of Staff, a Measure of Success," *Washington Post*, July 3, 2000, p. A4; John Harris, "President Chooses Podesta As Top Aide," *Washington Post*, October 21, 1998, p. A17; "Knox

College Graduate John Podesta Named White House Chief of Staff," http://
www.knox.edu/knoxweb/news/.

POPULAR OPINION. *See* **Approval Rating**.

POVERTY. Particularly during his last years in office, President Bill Clinton
touted the administration's record of lowering the poverty rate in the
United States. For nearly twenty years, administration spokespersons observed, the **economy** had slowed down. While overall GNP rose during
President Ronald Reagan's tenure in office, real wages for many Americans, particularly those on the bottom, either stagnated or fell. In 1993,
when Clinton took office, the poverty rate, defined as the percentage of
Americans living below the poverty line, stood at 15.1 percent. By the
end of 1999, the poverty rate had declined to 11.8 percent. All evidence
suggested that it would fall even further during Clinton's final year in
office. This represented the largest sustained decline in the poverty rate
in over a generation. In absolute numbers, seven million fewer people
lived in poverty in 1999 than had in 1993. The child poverty rate declined
from 25.6 percent in 1993 to 16.9 percent in 1999. All subgroups of the
population, including **African Americans**, Hispanics, and Caucasians, experienced a decline in child poverty rates.

Administration spokespersons took much credit for these declining
poverty rates. They argued that Clinton's macroeconomic policies, which
produced the longest sustained economic expansion in U.S. history, underlay the decrease in poverty. Declining unemployment rates, record job
creation, and low **inflation**, in particular, resulted in a "virtuous" cycle,
observed **Gene Sperling**, head of Clinton's **National Economic Council**. Clinton aides added that specific programs of the administration insured that the growing economy would not just benefit the well-off. In
particular, the administration touted its decision to expand the earned-
income tax credit in 1993, its support for raising the **minimum wage**,
and its creation of numerous **empowerment zones**.

Many liberals in the Democratic Party warned that **welfare reform**
would increase the poverty rolls. President Clinton responded that welfare reform would increase incentives to work and drive down the poverty rate. At the same time, Clinton pledged to expand health and child
care programs for the working poor to make it easier for those on welfare
to seek employment. While declining poverty rates tended to support

Figure 10
Poverty Rate

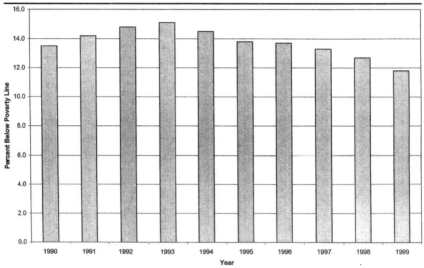

Source: *Economic Report of the President, 2000*.

Clinton's contention that welfare reform would not increase poverty, some longtime antipoverty activists warned that an economic downturn would quickly reverse the gains of the latter half of the 1990s and leave the poor in a worse situation than they had been in decades. In addition, some experts argued that it would become harder and harder to decrease the poverty rate, noting that macroeconomic policies failed to help those at the very bottom whose low educational and skill levels left them in a very vulnerable position in an increasingly global and **high-technology** world economy.

Suggested Readings: Steven A. Holmes, "A War on Poverty Subtly Linked to Race," *New York Times*, December 26, 2000, p. A1; Daniel Schorr, "Clinton's Poverty Plan," *New Leader*, July 12, 1999, p. 4; U.S. Census Bureau, *Poverty in the United States, 1999* (Washington, DC: GPO, 2000).

PRESIDENT'S INITIATIVE ON RACE. On June 14, 1997, President Bill Clinton announced a special effort to improve race relations in the United States, officially entitled "One America in the 21st Century: The President's Initiative on Race." The initiative grew out of Clinton's long-standing interest in civil rights and his post-reelection desire to cement a place in history that went beyond his record on the **economy**. The initiative involved the appointment of an advisory board consisting of seven notable persons who were charged with advising the president on ways to improve race relations. The board included John Hope Franklin, a noted black historian, Thomas Kean, the former Republican governor of New Jersey, and Linda Chavez-Thompson, an executive vice president of the AFL-CIO. The board held a series of town meetings on race and issued a report aimed at stimulating dialogue on race. The report, *One America in the 21st Century: Forging a New Future*, which the Clinton administration cast as a "blueprint for improving race relations in the 21st century," reaffirmed the administration's commitment to mending rather than ending **affirmative action**. At about the same time, the Council of Economic Advisers released *Changing America: Indicators of Social and Economic Well-Being by Race and Hispanic Origin*, a compilation of statistics that documented the improving yet continuing gaps between whites and minorities.

By the time that the advisory board issued its report, the Clinton administration was consumed with the **Monica Lewinsky** affair. As a result, the President's Initiative on Race's report was overshadowed by this story and the drive to impeach the president. Even before the Lewinsky scandal broke, conservatives had begun to question the value of the initiative. For instance, they argued that Clinton had stacked the advisory board with members who agreed with the administration's racial policies, particularly its views of affirmative action. As a result, conservatives noted, the initiative did not really produce genuine dialogue. However, many television stations, newspapers, magazines, and educational institutions participated in the broader dialogue on race. The precise impact of these discussions is difficult to measure.

Suggested Readings: "Feeling Findings: Advisory Board to President Clinton's Initiative on Race," *New Republic*, October 12, 1998, p. 8; "One America," http:// clinton4.nara.gov/Initiatives/OneAmerica/america_onrace.html.

PRIMARY COLORS. In January 1996, Random House published *Primary Colors*, a "fictional" account of President Bill Clinton's 1992 primary campaign. Written by "Anonymous," the novel provided a keen behind-the-scenes perspective on Clinton's rise to power. While neither Clinton's name nor those of any of his close aides appeared in the book, critics easily figured out the real identity of each of the key characters (see the list). Much of the novel, which quickly became a best-seller, focussed on the New Hampshire primary, particularly Clinton's and his team's efforts to overcome charges of marital infidelity and other character flaws. "Clinton-haters," wrote one reviewer, "will find plenty to keep them going [since] . . . some of the novel's sub-plots echo the most scurrilous right-wing gossip" (Elaine Showalter, *London Review of Books*). At the same time, the novel portrayed Clinton as an extremely complex character, a "colossus," to borrow the word of another reviewer (Murphey, *"Primary Colors"*). Much of the buzz about *Primary Colors* stemmed from the anonymity of the author. Harold Evans, the book's publisher, stated that even he did not know who wrote it. The nature of the novel suggested that it could have been written only by an insider. Political pundits, especially within the Washington Beltway, offered numerous guesses. Ultimately, *Newsweek* reporter Joe Klein was revealed to be the author. A movie based on the novel was made a couple of years after the novel was released. Starring John Travolta and Emma Thompson as Bill and **Hillary Clinton**, it faithfully followed the novel.

Character in Novel	Real Person
Jack Stanton	Bill Clinton
Susan Stanton	Hillary Clinton
Henry Burton	**George Stephanopoulos**
Richard Jemmons	**James Carville**
Daisy Green	**Mandy Grunwald**
Libby Holden	Betsy Wright
Norman Ashwer	David Garth
Fred Picker	**H. Ross Perot**
Senator Harris	**Paul Tsongas**
Lucille Kaufman	**Susan Thomases**
Howard Ferguson, 3rd	**Harold Ickes, Jr.**

Suggested Readings: Anonymous, *Primary Colors* (New York: Random House, 1996); Dwight D. Murphey, *"Primary Colors*: A Novel of Politics" [book review], *Journal of Social, Political, and Economic Studies* 22:2 (Summer 1997), p. 189; Elaine Showalter, *London Review of Books*.

Related Entry: Election of 1992.

Q

QUAYLE, DANFORTH (DAN) JAMES. (February 4, 1947, Indianapolis, Indiana–   .) Vice President of the United States, 1989–1993; Presidential candidate, 2000.

Dan Quayle, President **George Bush**'s vice president, was a consistent critic of Bill Clinton and **Al Gore**, first during the 1992 presidential campaign and again in his own brief effort to secure the Republican nomination in 1999–2000. Emphasizing the theme of "family values," Quayle sought to cast Clinton as a threat to American moral standards. During the 1992 campaign, he debated Al Gore, the vice presidential nominee of the Democratic Party, and Admiral James Stockdale, **H. Ross Perot**'s running mate. While he performed better than many expected, Quayle could not reverse the political decline of the Bush-Quayle administration.

In his bid for the 2000 presidential nomination, Quayle sought to portray himself as a true Reagan Republican who would cut taxes, maintain a strong military, and exude traditional values. However, he never gained much momentum, falling well short of **George W. Bush** in the crucial game of raising campaign funds and failing to distinguish himself among a crowded field of would-be nominees. Months before the New Hampshire primary, he announced his decision to disband his campaign.

The grandson of a multimillionaire, Quayle grew up in a very conservative and privileged milieu. His father belonged to the John Birch Society, an arch-conservative organization, and was a strong supporter of Barry Goldwater, the Republican nominee for president in 1964. Quayle earned his B.A. from DePauw University in 1969, joined the National Guard, and received his law degree from Indiana University in 1974. Afterwards, he joined his family business at the Huntington (Indiana) *Herald Press*. In 1976, he successfully ran for a seat in the **U.S. House of Representatives**. Four years later, he became the youngest senator from the state of Indiana in history. While he was relatively unknown to the public at large, George Bush selected him as his running mate in 1988. Often a target of liberals and the press, in part due to his gaffes and misstatements, Quayle strengthened Bush's ties to the conservative base of the Republican Party. However, by the year 2000, a whole new cast of conservatives, including John Kasich, Pat Buchanan, and Alan Keyes, tended to split the vote of the right wing of the party, while President Bush's son successfully portrayed himself as a winner and as someone who could represent both the conservative and moderate wings of the Republican Party.

Suggested Readings: *Current Biography Yearbook*, 1989, p. 448; Ron Fournier, "Former Vice President Dropping out of GOP Race," Associated Press, September 26, 1999; Dan Quayle, *Standing Firm* (1994), (Grand Rapids, MI: Zandervan Publishing House, 1994).

Related Entries: Election of 1992; Election of 1996.

R

RABIN, YITZHAK. *See* **Middle East**.

RACIAL ISSUES. *See* **African Americans; President's Initiative on Race**.

RAINES, FRANKLIN D. (January 14, 1949– .) Director, Office of Management and Budget, 1997–1998.

In 1997, Franklin D. Raines became the first **African American** appointed to the post of director of the Office of Management and Budget (OMB), one of the top economic posts in the federal government. Raines had the additional distinction of being the director of the OMB when the federal **budget** was balanced for the first time in decades. He left office with the administration and other economic agencies forecasting the largest federal budget surplus in the nation's history.

Raines earned his B.A. and law degree from Harvard University in 1971 and 1976, respectively. He also attended Magdalen College, Oxford University, as a Rhodes scholar. For several years, he served as the associate director for economics and government in the Office of Management and Budget and as the assistant director of the White House Domestic Policy Staff. In 1979, he accepted a job with Lazard Freres and Company, a prominent investment banking firm. Between 1991 and 1996, Raines was the vice chairman of the Federal National Mortgage Association, better known as Fanny Mae. He replaced **Alice Rivlin** as head of the Office of Management and Budget. After resigning as head of the Office of Management and Budget in 1998. Raines was named to the Board of Directors of America Online (AOL).

Suggested Reading: "General Powell and Franklin Raines Elected to AOL Board of Directors," *Business Wire*, September 28, 1998 [via Lexis-Nexis].

RAY, ROBERT. Independent Counsel, 1999–   .

In October 1999, **Kenneth Starr** resigned as the independent counsel after recommending that President Bill Clinton be impeached but before completing his investigation of **Whitewater** and other related matters. He was replaced by Robert Ray, a veteran of independent counsel Donald Smaltz's investigation of President Clinton's first secretary of agriculture, **Mike Espy**. Initially, many Democrats complained about Ray's appointment, noting that the investigation of Espy had cost millions of dollars but had resulted in the acquittal of the former secretary of agriculture. Over time, however, the White House tamed its response to Ray's appointment. In the summer of 2000, Ray officially cleared the president and First Lady **Hillary Clinton** of any criminal charges stemming from the **travelgate** scandal. Ray also did not find enough evidence to charge the president or the first lady with any crime stemming from Whitewater. As Clinton's term neared completion, Ray still had not issued his final report or determined whether to indict the president on perjury charges stemming from his deposition in the **Paula Jones** case. In a dramatic announcement on January 19, 2001, Clinton's last full day in office, an agreement between the president and the Office of the Independent Counsel was made public in which President Clinton admitted having testified falsely in his deposition in the Paula Jones case. In exchange for this admission, Ray announced that President Clinton would be immune from all charges stemming from his office's investigation of the **Monica Lewinsky** and Whitewater matters. In addition, Clinton agreed to pay a $25,000 fine to the Arkansas Bar Association and had his license to practice law in his home state suspended for five years. In May 2000, a disciplinary committee of the Arkansas Supreme Court had recommended that Clinton be disbarred. The agreement allowed President Clinton to leave office with his legal worries resolved. At the same time, the announcement once again displayed the degree to which scandal consumed much of his presidency.

Suggested Reading: Loraine Adams, "Starr to Resign," *Washington Post*, October 15, 1999, p. A6; Neil Lewis, "Exiting Job, Clinton Accepts Immunity Deal," *New York Times*, January 20, 2001, p. 1.

REED, BRUCE. Domestic policy adviser, 1993–2001.

When Bill Clinton began his presidency, Bruce Reed was one of many young, relatively inexperienced persons who went to work for him. By the end of Clinton's eight years in office, many of his better-known aides and associates, from **George Stephanopoulos** to **Robert Reich**, had departed, while Reed continued to work by the president's side, rising to the post of chief domestic policy adviser.

Raised in Coeur d'Alene, Idaho, Reed earned his B.A. from Princeton University in 1982 and then attended Oxford University as a Rhodes scholar. An avid baseball fan, he spent his honeymoon with his childhood sweetheart and wife, Bonnie LePard, attending six baseball games in a week and Willie Stargell's induction into the baseball Hall of Fame in Cooperstown, New York. From 1985 to 1989, Reed worked for then Senator **Al Gore**, for a time as his chief speech writer. He also worked for the **Democratic Leadership Council** and then on Bill Clinton's presidential campaign in 1992. After being elected president, Clinton appointed Reed one of his domestic policy advisers. Reed was responsible for framing policy initiatives and garnering public support for them. For example, early in Clinton's presidency, Reed helped launch what came to be known as the **Reinventing Government** campaign. Headed by Al Gore, this program aimed at cutting waste and bureaucracy in the federal government, one of the chief public concerns in the 1992 campaign. Along with **Gene Sperling**, he cochaired a task force on community empowerment that devised proposals for **empowerment zones** in depressed urban areas. He also helped develop **welfare reform** initiatives and, during Clinton's final years in office, **gun-control** and **education** reforms. Reed described his job as an easy one given President Clinton's keen interest and vast knowledge of **domestic policy**, but Reed clearly had a unique ability and personality to survive in Washington where other much more prominent members of the Clinton team did not.

Suggested Reading: Stephen Barr, "Linking Politics and Policy," *Washington Post*, May 17, 1993, p. A19.

REHNQUIST, WILLIAM HUBBS. (October 1, 1924, Milwaukee, Wisconsin–   .) Associate Justice, U.S. Supreme Court, 1972–1986; Chief Justice, U.S. Supreme Court, 1986–   .

William Rehnquist served as chief justice of the U.S. **Supreme Court** throughout President Clinton's tenure. Originally appointed as an associate justice by President Nixon in 1972 and then elevated to chief justice by Ronald Reagan in 1986, Rehnquist presided over a court that handed down numerous conservative decisions during the 1990s. For instance, on several occasions, he sided with the majority of the Court in striking down laws favored by President Clinton as a violation of states' rights. Rehnquist ruled with the majority in allowing **Paula Jones** to go ahead with her sexual harassment suit against the president, in spite of claims that this could lead to an undue disruption of the nation's business (which many legal scholars argue proved to be the case). However, perhaps the most memorable role Rehnquist played during Clinton's presidency was as the presiding judge in the trial phase of the **impeachment** process in the **U.S. Senate**. With humor and humility, he insisted on a dignified and fair proceeding and appeared relieved when he declared the president "acquitted of the charges" leveled against him by the **U.S. House of Representatives**. Rehnquist was only the second chief justice to have to assume this role. Remarkably, he had written a book on impeachments in the American past, *Grand Inquests* (1992), which had found no good reason for the only other presidential impeachment, that of Andrew Johnson in 1868.

Born in Milwaukee, Wisconsin, Rehnquist briefly attended Kenyon College before enlisting in the U.S. Army at the onset of World War II. After the war, he earned his B.A. and law degrees from Stanford University in 1948 and 1952, respectively. He graduated first in his law class; Sandra Day O'Connor, one of his fellow Supreme Court justices, graduated second. After clerking for U.S. Supreme Court Justice Robert Jackson, he went to work in Arizona and became active in politics. When Richard Nixon was elected president, he joined the Justice Department before being nominated as an associate Supreme Court justice in 1971.

In his nearly thirty years on the Court, Rehnquist earned a reputation as a staunch conservative who frowned on the judicial activism of the Warren and Burger courts. Along with Justices Antonin Scalia and Clarence Thomas, he consistently voted to interpret the Constitution in an extremely conservative or narrow manner. When Justices Anthony Kennedy, O'Connor, and sometimes David Souter ruled with him, he often wrote the majority opinion, but he was unable to convince the majority of the Court to overturn several of the most controversial rulings of the Warren and Burger courts, most notably *Roe* v. *Wade* on abortion. One final very controversial decision that Rehnquist made during Clinton's presidency involved the outcome of the 2000 presidential election. In *Bush* v. *Gore*, the Supreme Court ruled 5–4 that the recount in Florida, which had been ordered by the Florida Supreme Court, had to halt. As a result, **George W. Bush** was declared the winner. Ironically, Rehnquist and the four justices who voted to halt the recount did not defer to the state court in this case, nor did Rehnquist, Scalia, Thomas, Kennedy, and O'Connor appear to abhor judicial activism in this decision and in the steps they took to reach it. Whether this would sully the Rehnquist Court's reputation remained to be seen.

Suggested Readings: Donald Boles, *Mr. Justice Rehnquist, Judicial Activist* (Ames, Iowa: Iowa State University Press, 1987); "The Senate Verdict," *Los Angeles Times*, February 13, 1999, p. A25; Tinsley Yarbrough, *The Rehnquist Court and the Constitution* (New York: Oxford University Press, 2000).

Related Entry: Election of 2000.

REICH, ROBERT B. (June 24, 1946, Scranton, Pennsylvania–   .) Secretary of Labor, 1993–1997.

A close friend of Bill Clinton since their days together as Rhodes scholars at Oxford University, Robert Reich was one of the administration's more visible **cabinet** members during Clinton's first term as president. During the 1992 campaign and after, Reich criticized the economic policies of the Ronald Reagan and **George Bush** years and promoted a new national industrial policy in its place. Although he did not belong to a trade union, he won the support of organized **labor**, which applauded his liberal views. Several of his specific programs, including an economic stimulus plan, however, failed to win the support of Congress, and his influence within the administration waned.

Born in Scranton, Pennsylvania, Reich spent his childhood and youth in New York City. An outstanding student, valedictorian of his high-school class, he graduated from Dartmouth College in 1968 and attended Oxford University as a Rhodes scholar, where he befriended Bill Clinton. After being awarded an M.A. from Oxford, he earned his law degree from Yale Law School (1973). He clerked for the chief judge of the U.S. Court of Appeals in Boston and worked at the Justice Department and then for the Federal Trade Commission. During the 1980s, Reich taught at the John F. Kennedy School of Government at Harvard University, authoring *Minding America's Business* (1982) and coauthoring *The Next American Frontier* with Ira C. Magaziner (1983), both of which promoted a new industrial policy as opposed to supply-side economics as the solution to the stagnation of the U.S. **economy**. In several other books and articles that he wrote over the course of the 1980s, he emphasized the need for government, business, and labor cooperation to make the United States competitive in the global economy. In opposition to many within the labor movement, however, he favored expanding trade rather than protection.

Both during the 1992 campaign and after becoming secretary of labor, Reich advocated investing in American workers and technology. While Congress did not enact the administration's economic stimulus plan, it did pass several other measures fostered by Reich, including the **Family and Medical Leave Act** and the School-to-Work Opportunities Act, which aimed at enhancing the skills of American workers. Reich also promoted a consolidation of numerous employment-related government agencies so that workers could go to one source for information on careers, job training, employment opportunities, and unemployment insurance.

Perhaps Reich's greatest joy came with the steady decline of the unemployment rate and the remarkable creation of millions of new jobs. In addition, while the earnings of many workers did not increase much at first, over the course of the 1990s, real income rose, as did American productivity. Still, Reich continued to push for policies that narrowed the gap between the rich and the poor, which entailed a more activist government than Clinton was willing to promote in the wake of the defeat in the midterm **election of 1994**. After departing from government, Reich returned to academe, teaching at Brandeis University and appearing regularly on news talk shows. Reich also wrote a witty memoir of his years as secretary of labor, *Locked in the Cabinet* (1997), which described the challenges and frustrations of working in Washington, D.C., and many of the key personalities of the capital city.

Suggested Readings: *Current Biography Yearbook*, 1993, p. 481; http://www.dol. gov/dol/asp/public/programs/history/reich/reich.htm; David E. Sanger, "Parting Benediction by Lonely Liberal," *New York Times*, January 9, 1997, p. B8.

Related Entries: Americorps; Domestic Policy; Workforce Investment Act of 1998.

REINVENTING GOVERNMENT. Early in his administration, President Clinton announced his Reinventing Government initiative. Headed by Vice President **Al Gore**, the effort called for a panel of experts, officially called the National Performance Review Panel, to review the operations of the federal government and to make recommendations for reducing government waste and improving government services. In the fall of 1993, the panel released a 167-page report that listed 384 specific recommendations for streamlining the government. According to the report, the government could save billions of dollars and eliminate 252,000 jobs, a bit over one-tenth of the federal payroll, if it followed the panel's recommendations, and it could do so without reducing government services. Among the panel's recommendations was a call to decrease the number of field service officers employed by the Department of Agriculture. Based on the initiative, Congress enacted several reforms in 1994. A procurement-overhaul bill simplified the process whereby the federal government purchased many basic items, such as pens and notepads. To reduce the number of middle-level managers, Congress allowed federal agencies to offer cash buyout packages to federal employees who voluntarily resigned prior to their mandatory retirement age. The Agriculture Department was reorganized.

During the **election of 2000**, in particular, Vice President Gore highlighted his record of reducing the number of federal employees and saving taxpayers billions of dollars. According to Gore and the White House, the government saved over $130 billion because of recommendations made by the Reinventing Government initiative. Since Clinton's election, the number of federal workers had decreased by 377,000, nearly a 20 percent reduction, the administration claimed. The **George W. Bush** campaign, however, countered that most of the savings came from the Defense Department, jeopardizing military readiness and morale. In addition, Bush argued that Clinton and Gore really did not favor smaller government and that if it had not been for conservative opposition to national **health care reform**, the size and reach of the federal government would have grown dramatically during the 1990s. Much to Gore's chagrin, the Bush campaign supported this claim by citing a General Accounting Office report that concluded that the administration had overcounted the number of jobs that had been cut.

Suggested Readings: " 'Better Government' Plan Unveiled," *Congressional Quarterly Almanac*, 1993, p. 191; Sean Page, "New News Is Bad News for Al Gore," *Insight on the News*, September 13, 1999, p. 47; " 'Reinventing' Government Advances in Steps," *Congressional Quarterly Almanac*, 1994, p. 143; Lee Walczak and Susan B. Garland, "Getting Smaller with Al," *Business Week*, January 23, 1995, p. 38.

Related Entry: Budget, Federal.

RENAISSANCE WEEKEND. Each New Year, President Bill Clinton and First Lady **Hillary Clinton** traveled to Hilton Head Island, South Carolina, to attend a two-day retreat known as Renaissance Weekend. This get-together, which the Clintons began attending in the mid-1980s, brought together an assortment of VIPs, including Nobel Prize winners, justices of the **Supreme Court**, politicians, journalists, and business executives. Dignitaries ran the political gamut from the very liberal to the ultracon-servative, although the overriding atmosphere at the posh retreat was one of gentility. In addition to mingling with over a thousand guests, Clinton and his family went for walks on the beach, listened to and/or delivered speeches, attended musical spoofs, and wined and dined. As 1998 came to a close, many wondered whether Clinton would attend the Renais-sance Weekend. In spite of the fact that he was in the middle of defending himself from **impeachment** charges, Clinton maintained his tradition and attended the weekend's festivities. The picture of Clinton at a social gathering with political conservatives who had voted or called for his impeachment appeared incongruous to some, but with his **approval rat-ings** high, Clinton seemed assured of weathering the political storm.

In January 1996, in the midst of Clinton's showdown with Republicans over the federal **budget**, an assortment of conservatives convened their own version of Renaissance Weekend in Miami, Florida. They termed their gathering the Dark Ages Weekend, in reference to Clinton's control of the White House, and pledged to reconvene with even more members as long as Clinton held power. Perhaps symbolically, while Renaissance Weekend continued to flourish, the Dark Ages Weekend did not.

Suggested Readings: "Clinton Celebrates New Year with Like-minded 'Big-Thinkers,'" http://www4.nando.net/newsroom/ntn/politics/010196/politics132t. html; "Clinton Goes on New Year's Intellectual Retreat," *Corpus Christi Times*, December 31, 1998; Maureen Dowd, "Camp Can Do," *New York Times Maga-zine*, October 2, 1994, p. 28; Weston Kosova, "Schmoozing in the Sand," *New-sweek*, January 8, 1996, p. 42.

RENO, JANET. (July 21, 1938, Miami, Florida–   .) U.S. Attorney General, 1993–2001.

While Janet Reno was not President Bill Clinton's first choice as attor-ney general, she was the administration's most controversial and visible **cabinet** member. The first woman to head the Justice Department in U.S. history, Reno served through both terms of Clinton's presidency in spite of persistent calls for her resignation. From the fiasco in **Waco**, Texas, to the **Elian Gonzalez** affair, conservatives accused her of ineptitude and protecting the president. Even though she appointed several indepen-dent counsels to investigate various charges, Republicans argued that she

Janet Reno with President Bill Clinton. Library of Congress.

hindered and/or covered up numerous illegal activities. In the face of these attacks, Reno defended her actions and the president, emphasizing instead the significant reduction of **crime** that took place during Clinton's presidency. She also took great pride in the professionalism and growing diversity of the attorneys and other personnel who worked for the Justice Department.

Born in Miami, Florida, the daughter of two newspaper reporters, Reno earned her B.A. from Cornell University in chemistry in 1960 and her law degree from Harvard University in 1963. One of only sixteen women at Harvard out of a class of more than five hundred, she had difficulty finding employment in spite of her strong academic record. After becoming a partner at Lewis and Reno, she held several posts within the state legislature and state attorney's office. She returned briefly to the private sector before being appointed the top state attorney in Dade County in 1978, the largest such office in the state. While she was on the list of possible attorney general nominees at the time of Clinton's election in 1992, the nomination went first to **Zoë Baird** and then to **Kimba Wood**, both of whom withdrew in the wake of revelations that they had acted illegally or unethically by hiring day-care providers (nannies) who were illegal immigrants for their children. Committed to naming a woman to the post, Clinton nominated Reno, who, as an unmarried woman, had no similar liabilities.

At first, Reno was not part of Clinton's inner or closest circle of advisers and cabinet members. Unlike Secretary of Labor **Robert Reich**, she was not a "FOB," in other words, a longtime friend of Bill or **Hillary Clinton**. Lacking years of experience in Washington, she did not have the clout of several of his other top cabinet members, such as Treasury Secretary **Lloyd Bentsen** or Secretary of State **Warren Christopher**. Moreover, she was beset by a series of problems within the Justice Department, largely not of her making, from the start. The crisis in Waco, Texas, which ended with the death of eighty Branch Davidians, garnered her much animosity from conservatives in spite of her candor and willingness to take full responsibility for the raid. The **Whitewater** scandal, which led to the resignation of her deputy, **Webster Hubbell**, a former associate of Hillary Clinton, the suicide of **Vincent Foster**, and accusations of illegal conduct on the part of several other members of the Clinton administration, provided further ammunition for her critics. This criticism did not subside even though she appointed independent counsels to investigate Whitewater, Secretary of Agriculture **Mike Espy**, Secretary of Commerce **Ron Brown**, and Secretary of Housing and Urban Development **Henry Cisneros**. In fact, at Clinton's behest, one of her first actions was to ask Congress to extend the **independent counsel law**. Yet, following the president's reelection, Republicans once again demanded her resignation when she refused to appoint still another independent counsel to investigate possible campaign finance law violations by Clinton and or Vice President **Al Gore**. Conservatives lambasted Reno one last time when she insisted that Elian Gonzalez, the son of a Cuban woman who had died while trying to flee to America on a ramshackle boat, had to be returned to his Cuban father. Even though the federal courts upheld her position and that of the immigration bureau that legally Elian belonged with his father, conservatives decried her decision to order federal law-enforcement agents to forcibly take the boy away from his relatives in Miami, who sought to keep the boy in the United States.

Reno's defenders, and there were many of them, countered conservative attacks by arguing that the attorney general was simply enforcing the law rather than evading her responsibility in Waco and in the case of Elian Gonzalez. They also touted the larger picture, namely, the dramatic decrease in violent crime that took place under her tenure, as well as the more stringent enforcement of civil rights laws that took place in the 1990s than had taken place during Ronald Reagan's presidency. Although

Bill Richardson during press
conference at the U.S. Embassy in
Tokyo, February 13, 1998, re Iraq.
AP/Wide World Photos.

Clinton and Reno never became close friends, he developed a great respect for her as a cabinet member. Moreover, unlike many who knew
him more intimately, such as **George Stephanopoulos** and **Dick Morris**,
she remained loyal to him throughout his presidency.

Suggested Readings: *Current Biography Yearbook,* 1993, p. 485; Jeffrey Goldberg, "The Mystery of Janet Reno," *New York Times Magazine,* July 6, 1997, p. 16;
http://www.usdoj.gov/ag/jreno.html; "Janet Reno: Attorney General," http://
washingtonpost.com/wp-srv/politics/govt/admin/reno.htm.

RICHARDSON, WILLIAM (BILL) BLAINE. (November 15, 1947, Pasadena,
California–   .) U.S. Ambassador to the United Nations, 1997–1998; Secretary of Energy, 1998–2001.

One of the highest-ranking Hispanics in the Clinton administration, Bill
Richardson stood out for his energy and flair for the dramatic. He gained
national attention while he was still a congressman from New Mexico by
successfully negotiating the release of hostages, American servicemen,
and prisoners in North **Korea**, **Iraq**, Cuba, and **Sudan**. Although he held
two relatively lesser-known **cabinet** posts, Richardson was one of the
administration's more visible representatives. As U.S. ambassador to the
United Nations, he successfully pushed for an investigation of human
rights abuses in the Congo and grappled with Iraq's reluctance to allow
international arms inspectors to conduct their investigations in compli-

ance with resolutions passed by the United Nations at the end of the Persian Gulf War. As secretary of energy, he grappled with two headline-making developments, rising oil prices and revelations of espionage at the Los Alamos National Laboratory. Some even suggested that Richardson would make a strong vice presidential nominee for **Al Gore** in 2000.

Born in Pasadena, California, the son of Luisa Zubiran Richardson, a native of Mexico, and William Richardson, an American banker, Richardson spent much of his youth in Mexico City. A gifted athlete, he was drafted as a pitcher by the Oakland Athletics but decided to attend college instead. He earned his B.A. from Tufts University and his M.A. from the Fletcher School of Law and Diplomacy in 1970 and 1971, respectively. After graduation, he worked for the State Department and then for the **Senate** Foreign Relations Committee. After moving to New Mexico, he ran unsuccessfully for a seat in Congress against Republican incumbent Manuel Lujan, Jr., in 1980. Two years later, he won a seat representing a newly created congressional district in New Mexico. He was reelected seven times. He moved up the political ladder within the Democratic Party and gained notoriety in 1994 when he became the first outsider to be granted an audience with Burmese human rights activist Aung San Suu Kyi. While he was still a congressman, he trekked to **Haiti**, North Korea, Iraq, and Cuba as a special emissary of the United States.

Whereas Clinton had appointed **Hazel O'Leary** as his first secretary of energy, his nomination of Richardson to succeed **Federico Peña** displayed his desire to maintain a Hispanic as a member of the cabinet and to see if some of Richardson's magic could rub off on the somewhat tarnished Energy Department. Richardson quickly had to grapple with revelations of espionage at the Los Alamos laboratory and with rising oil prices. He appointed a committee headed by Howard Baker and Lee Hamilton, two veteran lawmakers, to investigate the security lapses. The investigators concluded that the problems went back to the Reagan presidency. In response, Richardson pledged to tighten security at Los Alamos and other sites overseen by the Department of Energy. Richardson and President Clinton pressured Saudi Arabia and other members of the Organization of Petroleum Exporting Countries (OPEC) to increase production to decrease gasoline prices. He also oversaw the continuing cleanup of large nuclear-material stockpiles and helped develop legislation that allowed for the **deregulation** of the utility industry.

Suggested Readings: *Current Biography Yearbook*, 1996, p. 458; Neil A. Lewis, "Man in the News: William Blaine Richardson," *New York Times*, June 19, 1998, p. A26.

Richard Riley. Department of Education.

RILEY, RICHARD W. (January 2, 1933, Greenville County, South Carolina– .) Secretary of Education, 1993–2001.

Janet Reno, Bruce Babbitt, Donna Shalala, and Richard Riley were the only four **cabinet** members to serve in the cabinet throughout Bill Clinton's presidency. Based on his reputation as an educational reformer, Riley was Clinton's first and obvious choice to serve as secretary of education. As secretary, he helped promote **education** as one of the main themes of political discourse. Perhaps because he avoided any allegations of wrongdoing and because of his generally amiable personality, he remained one of the least known members of the administration to the public at large.

Born in Greenville County, South Carolina, Riley attended segregated schools and graduated in 1954 from Furman University. After service in the U.S. Navy, he earned his law degree from the University of South Carolina in 1959. Between 1963 and 1977, Riley served in both houses of South Carolina's legislature and then was elected governor in 1978. He was so popular that the state amended its constitution to allow him to run for a second consecutive term, which he did successfully in 1982. As governor, he promoted educational reform in the state and befriended another southern governor and educational reformer, Bill Clinton.

Unlike his predecessor, William Bennett, who used his position as secretary of education as a bully pulpit to rally the public around the goal of reviving traditional values, Riley tended to avoid controversy and conflict. Never known for his flamboyance, Riley quietly pushed for numerous educational reforms, including increased federal funding and tax breaks for college students (and their parents) and enhanced technology in primary and secondary schools. At the same time, he thwarted conservative efforts to abolish the Department of Education by denying charges that he was the proxy of the teacher unions. Riley also worked with high-placed legislators, such as William Goodling, a Republican congressman from Pennsylvania who chaired the House Committee on Education and the Workforce.

Perhaps the greatest controversy of Riley's tenure erupted over proposed national standards in the field of history. Although the standards were initially suggested by a committee headed by Ronald Reagan and **George Bush** appointees, conservatives jumped on the history proposal, claiming that it promoted political correctness over traditional history. While Riley backed away from the history proposal, he continued to push for national standards in math and science and for reduced class size and improved teacher training. Riley also promoted the continued expansion of **Head Start** programs and other preschool programs, both of which tended to win support from the Republican-controlled Congress.

Ironically, in the waning months of the Clinton presidency, a general consensus developed that the federal government would need to become more involved in education than it had been during Riley's tenure. Texas governor **George W. Bush** contended that there was an education recession in the United States, and unlike conservative Republicans of the mid-1990s, who had called for abolishing the Department of Education, he pledged a concerted federal effort to improve the situation. Many of his goals, in fact, sounded like those of Richard Riley. Vice President **Al Gore** retorted that he would spend more than Governor Bush on education. Some might view this debate as a critique of Riley's leadership, but others credited Riley with raising public awareness of the issue and stemming the tide of those who would have taken the federal government out of the education business.

Suggested Readings: Michael Fletcher, "Putting Education Agenda to the Test," *Washington Post*, January 10, 2001, p. A17; Linda Perlstein, "Pursuing a Mild-mannered Passion for Education," *Washington Post*, December 15, 1998, p. A25; David Savage, "Riley Reforms Won Applause of Experts," *Los Angeles Times*, December 22, 1992, p. A26.

RIVLIN, ALICE. (March 4, 1931– .) Deputy Director, Office of Management and Budget (OMB), 1993–1994; Director, OMB, 1994–1996; Vice Chair, Federal Reserve Board, 1996–1999.

Alice Rivlin was one of President Bill Clinton's key economic advisers during his first term as president. First as deputy director of the White House Office of Management and Budget and then as director of the OMB—the first woman to hold this post—she promoted a conservative fiscal policy, consistent with the goal of balancing the budget so as to spur a decrease in interest rates and encourage long-term economic growth. Subsequently, as vice chairwoman of the Federal Reserve Board, she followed Chairman **Alan Greenspan**'s lead in keeping a tight leash on **inflation**. In many regards, she should be considered one of the chief architects of the sustained economic expansion of the 1990s.

Born Georgianna Alice Mitchell as the Great Depression took a turn for the worse, Rivlin excelled in school, earning a B.A. in Economics from Bryn Mawr College in 1952 and a Ph.D. from Harvard University in 1958. She married Lewis Rivlin, a lawyer, in 1955, bore three children, and went to work for the Brookings Institution. Following several years at the Department of Health, Education, and Welfare and another stint at the Brookings Institution, she was picked to serve as the first director of the Congressional Budget Office, a post she held for eight years (1975–1983). During most of the Ronald Reagan and **George Bush** presidencies, she returned to the Brookings Institution, earning a reputation as an expert on the federal **budget**. In 1993, **Leon Panetta**, Clinton's first director of the Office of Management and Budget, named her his deputy. When Panetta became Clinton's chief of staff in 1994, Rivlin was promoted to director of the OMB.

Throughout Clinton's first term, she consistently argued in favor of cutting the deficit over initiating new programs aimed at stimulating the

economy. This often put her at odds with several of the president's closer friends, including **Robert Reich**. Rivlin also headed the District of Columbia's control board, which was responsible for righting the finances of the nation's capital, left in disarray by the administration of Mayor Marion Barry. After leaving the administration, Rivlin focused much of her energy on the District of Columbia control board and spent more of her time with her family.

Suggested Readings: Paul Blustein, "Rivlin to Step Down as No. 2 at Fed," *Washington Post*, June 4, 1999, p. A1; Steven Greenhouse, "Shake-up at the White House: Budget Director," *New York Times*, June 28, 1994, p. A13.

Related Entry: Domestic Policy.

RUBIN, ROBERT EDWARD. (August 23, 1938, New York, New York–   .) Director, National Economic Council, 1993–1995; Secretary of the Treasury, 1995–1999.

Robert Rubin played a leading role in formulating and carrying out the Clinton's administration's economic policy, first as assistant to the president for economic policy, in which capacity he directed the newly created **National Economic Council**, and then as secretary of the Treasury. Upon his resignation on July 2, 1999, many credited him with the economic expansion of the 1990s, with some even predicting that his departure would end the **stock market**'s boom.

Rubin was born in New York City, the son and grandson (on his maternal side) of successful lawyers. At age nine, Rubin and his family moved to Miami Beach, Florida, where he worked at a variety of jobs in spite of his family's comfortable circumstances. He was awarded his B.A. in economics from Harvard University in 1960, studied at the London School of Economics, and then earned his law degree from Yale Law School in 1964. After two years of work for a Wall Street law firm, he accepted a position with Goldman Sachs and Company, one of the most famous investment banking firms in the nation. He rose to the rank of partner and eventually to co–senior partner, becoming one of the most influential financiers in the nation in the process. Throughout his career, Rubin played an active role in Democratic Party politics, including serving as a major supporter of Michael Dukakis, the Democratic Party's unsuccessful presidential nominee in 1988. Prior to and after the Democratic Party's 1992 convention, Rubin advised Bill Clinton on economic matters. After

Robert Rubin, right, talks with Lawrence Summer, undersecretary of the Treasury Department, before the House Banking Committee, January 30, 1998. AP/Wide World Photos.

being elected president, Clinton nominated Rubin to head the newly formed National Economic Council.

In 1993, Rubin helped formulate and gain passage of the Clinton administration's economic policy. While Clinton had pledged middle-class tax relief and an economic stimulus package during the campaign, after his election Rubin helped convince the president that shrinking the **budget** in order to earn the trust of the bond market had to take priority. This approach won Rubin few fans among either traditional liberals or conservatives. Nonetheless, the steady decline of interest rates, accompanied by the growth of the **economy** and the nearly miraculous disappearance of budget deficits, left Rubin vindicated and won him at least the grudging admiration of erstwhile adversaries.

As secretary of the Treasury, Rubin favored policies aimed at maintaining stable financial markets, which he felt underlay sustained economic growth. For example, he championed a controversial bailout of Mexico in early 1995. Later that same year, Rubin had to deal with a crisis caused by the impasse between the Republican-controlled Congress and President Clinton over the Republicans' proposed budget. The Republican Party's refusal to increase the debt ceiling unless Clinton agreed to its budget threatened to leave the Treasury Department in a situation where it would not have enough money to pay off its debts. Very creative financing by Rubin, however, allowed the government to avoid defaulting and enabled President Clinton to claim a political victory over the Republicans, who were blamed for the **government shutdown**. In 1997, along with Federal Reserve Board Chairman **Alan Greenspan**, Rubin traveled to Asia as part of a largely successful effort to stabilize another international economic crisis.

By the time he announced his decision to return to private life, Rubin had become one of President Clinton's closest advisers. He remained loyal to Clinton throughout the **Monica Lewinsky** scandal, waiting for the **impeachment** process to end before he announced his resignation. At the time, the stock market had risen to all-time highs, and unemployment had fallen to thirty-year lows. In the late fall of 1999, Rubin accepted a post on Wall Street as chairman of Citigroup, the nation's largest financial corporation, which was well positioned to take advantage of the new banking reforms that Rubin had helped pass.

Suggested Readings: Paul Blustein, "Rubin Resigns Treasury Post," *Washington Post*, May 13, 1999, p. A1; *Current Biography Yearbook*, 1997, pp. 470–74.

Related Entries: Domestic Policy; Government Shutdown.

RUSSIA. Bill Clinton was the first U.S. president to be elected after the end of the cold war. Partly because the United States did not have to focus as much attention on containing the Soviet Union, his **foreign policy** tended to be reactive and lacked a unifying theme. Certainly, Russia was less central to Clinton's foreign policy than it had been to his predecessors. However, U.S. relations with Russia received a good deal of attention during Clinton's presidency.

One of the Clinton administration's top priorities was to solidify arms-control agreements negotiated by the Ronald Reagan and **George Bush** administrations with the former Soviet Union and to negotiate further reductions with Russia. Ironically, the breakup of the Soviet Union complicated the arms-reduction process because several of the Soviet Union's former republics resisted destroying nuclear weapons as agreed to by the

Russian President Boris Yeltsin, left, and Bill Clinton at Kremlin reception, April 19, 1996. AP/Wide World Photos.

Soviet Union in START I. Not until after the Clinton administration convinced the Ukraine, the last holdout, to abide by START I was it able to convince the **U.S. Senate** to ratify START II, which had been signed by President Bush. In 1997, President Clinton and Russian leader Boris Yeltsin agreed in principle to negotiate START III, which would further reduce the number of nuclear warheads held by each nation to between 2,000 and 2,500.

Efforts to attain further nuclear arms reductions, however, were hampered by the Strategic Defense Initiative (SDI). This program to develop a space-based system capable of intercepting intercontinental ballistic missiles had been initiated by the Reagan administration. From the start, the Soviet Union objected to SDI. While the Clinton administration toned down the original SDI plan, its decision to go forward with the research and development of a missile defense system angered Russian leaders, who insisted that such a system violated the antiballistic-missile (ABM) treaty that had been signed in 1972. Ultimately, the Clinton administration left to its successor the decision of whether or not to deploy such a system and the thorny problem of how to do so without further antagonizing Russia.

The Clinton administration sought to work with Russia to limit the proliferation of nuclear weapons and weapons technology. In 1992, Russia announced that it would unilaterally stop the testing of nuclear weapons. The following year, Congress enacted legislation that called for a nine-month moratorium on nuclear testing and the end of all testing by 1996. In 1996, the Clinton administration signed the Comprehensive Nuclear Test-Ban Treaty, which aimed at enacting a ban on the testing of nuclear weapons by all nations. The U.S. Senate, however, refused to ratify the treaty because several nuclear nations, not including Russia, refused to sign the agreement. The administration abided by the treaty, nonetheless, in part because Russia was a party to it and worked with the United States to prevent more nations from obtaining nuclear weapons.

The other major thrust of U.S. policy toward Russia during Clinton's presidency was economic. For years, American foreign aid had been aimed at helping nations outside the Soviet orbit. With the end of the cold war, the role of foreign aid took an abrupt turn. Even after the fall of the Communist Party and the collapse of the Soviet Union, the Bush administration was reluctant to fulfill Russia's request for large sums of economic aid. On the campaign trail and as president, Bill Clinton pledged to do much more to help Russia and the other former Soviet republics. To this end, in 1993 and 1994, it requested large sums of unrestricted aid to Russia, supported the Nunn-Lugar plan, which allowed U.S. dollars to go to Russia to help it denuclearize, and pushed for the G-7 industrial nations (the seven largest noncommunist nations: United States, Germany, Japan, Great Britain, Italy, France, and Canada), World Bank, and the International Monetary Fund to loan money to Russia to help it modernize its economy. U.S. direct aid to Russia and the former Soviet republics peaked in 1993 and 1994, with Russia receiving more than $3 billion. With the exception of Israel and Egypt, no other nation received as much aid, and Russia received more money than all of Africa and nearly as much as all of Africa, Central America, and **Latin America** combined.

In the mid- and late 1990s, economic aid to Russia diminished for several reasons. The Republican-controlled Congress cut funds for foreign aid in general, making it more difficult for the Clinton administration to expand its aid to Russia and the former Soviet republics. Russia's ongoing war in Chechnya, which many perceived as an affront to human rights, weakened public support for extending economic aid to Russia. Even more important, reports of widespread corruption and misuse of funds in Russia, in many cases by top Russian officials, cut further into public support for foreign aid, in general, and aid to Russia, in particular. Likewise, Russia's ongoing economic difficulties raised doubts about the efficacy of loaning funds to Russia, particularly when these loans demanded free-market reforms and tight-money policies that, according to some experts, actually retarded Russia's economic growth.

In spite of these difficulties, one sign that the United States and Russia had entered a new phase in their relationship was the summits that Clinton and the president of Russia held on a regular basis. During much of the cold war, summits between the Soviet Union and the United States were rare and dramatic affairs. In contrast, President Clinton met with Russia's leader Boris Yeltsin seven times and with his successor, Vladimir Putin, once. U.S. and Russian leaders often used these summits as an opportunity to reaffirm their commitment to nuclear nonproliferation and arms reductions and to reiterate their general desire to cooperate in a wide range of endeavors. For instance, in the spring of 1994, Clinton and Yeltsin met in Vancouver, Canada, where they declared their commitment to a U.S.-Russian partnership that promoted international stability. At the same time, President Clinton assured President Yeltsin of America's desire to help Russia overcome its economic problems as it made its transition to a market economy.

Among the topics that Clinton and Yeltsin (and later Putin) discussed were the expansion of **NATO** to include several former Eastern-bloc nations and NATO's increasing involvement in the Balkans, first in **Bosnia and Herzegovina** and later in **Kosovo**. Russian officials persistently objected to both developments, particularly the war in Kosovo. However the summits served as a mechanism for the Clinton administration to reassure Russian leaders that the United States harbored no aggressive intentions toward Russia.

Suggested Readings: Stephen Cohen, *Failed Crusade: America and the Tragedy of Post-Communist Russia* (New York: Norton, 2000); Moises Naim, "Clinton's Foreign Policy: A Victim of Globalization?" *Foreign Policy* 109 (Winter 1997), p. 34; "US-Russia Summit Agreements & Joint Statements," http://www.ceip. org/files/projects/npp/resources/us-russiasummits.htm#topic; Steven M. Walt, "Two Cheers for Clinton's Foreign Policy," *Foreign Affairs* 79:2 (March 2000), p. 63.

Related Entries: Nuclear Nonproliferation; Talbott, Strobe.

RWANDA. In 1990, a civil war erupted in the African nation of Rwanda between rival ethnic groups, the majority Hutus and the minority Tutsis.

In April 1994, Rwandan president Juvénal Habyarimana's plane was shot down minutes before it was scheduled to land at the Kigali airport in Rwanda. The *New York Times* and other sources report that the plane was shot down by "unidentified attackers." Habyarimana was returning from peace talks in Uganda with Tutsi rebels. His assassination set off one of the worst waves of genocide in world history. Approximately 800,000 Tutsis and their allies were killed by Hutu forces. The genocide did not abate until Tutsi rebels defeated Hutu forces. The 1994 genocide in Rwanda was not the biggest in history, but it may have been the fastest. It happened in less than one hundred days. Fearing retaliation, about 2 million Hutus fled into neighboring countries, particularly Burundi.

Whereas the Clinton administration intervened in **Haiti** and ultimately in **Bosnia and Herzegovina** and **Kosovo**, it limited U.S. involvement in Rwanda. Chastened by his experience with **Somalia**, Clinton chose not to send U.S. troops to Rwanda in 1994 to try to stop the genocide. In 1996, however, he sent a small contingent of eight hundred troops to the region to participate in a UN-sponsored humanitarian mission, largely aimed at helping the hundreds of thousands of refugees who had been displaced by the war or had fled the nation in the wake of the genocide.

In March 1998, President Clinton made a brief stop in Rwanda during his tour of Africa. He limited his visit to the Kigali airport. While he met with Rwandan president Pasteur Bizimungu, Clinton did not visit a memorial to the Rwandan genocide because of security fears. At the airport, President Clinton asserted that the international community shared "responsibility for this tragedy" and urged it to take measures to prevent such a tragedy from occurring again. Yet it remained unclear exactly what type of measures either his administration or others would take. Indeed, in the 2000 presidential debates between **Al Gore** and **George W. Bush**, the latter appeared even less willing than Clinton or Gore to commit U.S. troops to intervene abroad for humanitarian reasons.

Suggested Readings: "CIA Factbook," http://www.odci.gov/cia/publications/factbook/geos/rw.html; "Clinton Meets Rwanda Genocide Survivors," http://www.cnn.com/WORLD/9803/25/rwanda.clinton/index.html; Gerard Prunier, *The Rwanda Crisis* (New York: Columbia University Press, 1997).

S

SAFE DRINKING WATER ACT. On August 6, 1996, President Bill Clinton signed the Safe Drinking Water Act. (Technically, he signed amendments to the 1974 Safe Drinking Water Act.) Clinton had proposed strengthening federal clean-water regulations in 1993, but Congress did not act on his request until the summer of 1996. The act that Clinton signed required all owners and operators of public water systems to comply with health-related standards established by the Environmental Protection Agency (EPA) and to provide their customers with regular reports on the quality of their drinking water. The act also established the EPA's Drinking Water State Revolving Fund, which allowed the EPA to provide grants to states to pay for water projects to help states comply with the Safe Drinking Water Act. The passage of the act was one of several examples of cooperation between the Republican-led Congress and the administration during the summer and fall of 1996.

Suggested Readings: http://www.epa.gov; http://www.whitehouse.gov/WH/Accomplishments/environment.html; "The New Public Health Laws," *Amicus Journal* 18:4 (Winter 1997), p. 11.

Related Entry: Environment.

SENATE, U.S. During Bill Clinton's first two years in office, he enjoyed a Democratic majority in both houses of Congress, but for the final six years of his presidency, he faced a Republican majority in the Senate and the U.S. House of Representatives (see Table 14). Even before they took control in 1995 following the election of 1994, Republicans in the Senate, led by Robert Dole, blocked several of Clinton's key initiatives or compelled the president to compromise. They did this by threatening to

Table 14
Party, Makeup and Leaders of the Senate, 1993–2003

Congress (Years)	Democrats	Republicans	Majority Leader	Minority Leader
103rd (1993–1995)	57	43	George Mitchell	Robert Dole
104th (1995–1997)	47	53	Robert Dole	Thomas Daschle
105th (1997–1999)	45	55	Trent Lott	Thomas Daschle
106th (1999–2001)	46	54	Trent Lott	Thomas Daschle
107th (2001–2003)	50	50	Trent Lott	Thomas Daschle

Source: Congressional Quarterly Almanac; http:www.senate.gov.

filibuster. Democrats lacked the votes to gain a cloture vote to end the filibusters. At the same time, Clinton worked with Republicans in the Senate, both before and after they became the majority in 1995, to pass **NAFTA**, **welfare reform**, and capital-gains tax reductions. On several occasions, particularly following his reelection in 1996, Clinton enjoyed the support of a coalition of Democrats and Republicans in the Senate, leading to the passage of several of his key initiatives, most notably expansion of **Head Start**, an increase in the **minimum wage**, and health care benefits for children, a plan known as the **Children's Health Insurance Program (CHIP)**.

Perhaps the most telling moment of Clinton's relationship with the Republican-controlled Congress came in early 1999, when the U.S. Senate voted against convicting him on **impeachment** charges. While the vote largely followed partisan lines, under the lead of Senate Majority Leader **Trent Lott** of Mississippi, the trial proceedings and debate were tame, especially compared with the rancorous proceedings in the House Judiciary Committee. Lott knew that he could not muster enough votes to convict the president. Hence he sought to conclude the trial rapidly and with the least amount of acrimony possible. At the same time, Lott refused to push through some sort of deal that would have allowed President Clinton to avoid the trial in exchange for a censure vote.

This is not to suggest that the relationship between the Republican-controlled Senate and the president was amicable. Clinton regularly complained about the Senate's refusal to confirm his nominees to federal posts, particularly in the judiciary. The administration also criticized key Republican senators, such as Jesse Helms of North Carolina, for blocking funding on key **foreign policy** initiatives. Even more, the administration and the Republican-controlled Senate seemed perpetually locked in battles over investigations into one matter after another, from **Whitewater** to alleged campaign finance irregularities. As his term drew to a close, the president enjoyed a degree of vindication. In the **election of 2000**, **Hillary Clinton** won a seat in the U.S. Senate, representing the state of New York, and the Senate ended up evenly split along party lines. Since the Republicans won the White House and since the vice president casts the tie-breaking vote in the Senate, Republicans remained de facto in control of the body.

Suggested Readings: http://www.senate.gov; Richard S. Conley, "Unified Government, the Two Presidencies Thesis, and Presidential Support in the Senate," *Presidential Studies Quarterly* 27 (Spring 1997), p. 229; Bill Frenzel, "Assessing the 104th Congress," *Brookings Review* 14 (Spring 1996), p. 40.

SESSIONS, WILLIAM STEELE. (May 27, 1930, Fort Smith, Arkansas– .) Director, Federal Bureau of Investigation, 1987–1993.

When Bill Clinton became president, William Sessions was the director of the Federal Bureau of Investigation (FBI). Sessions, who was appointed director by Ronald Reagan in 1987, did not officially have to depart, even though he was a Republican, because his term had yet to expire. However, even before the **election of 1992**, Sessions had encountered rough waters. A report issued by an investigative branch of the Justice Department revealed that Sessions had abused his office by taking free trips to visit friends and family, among other things. When Clinton assumed office, he and his attorney general, **Janet Reno**, hoped to convince Sessions to depart gracefully, but Sessions refused to resign. Lest they be accused of dismissing Sessions for political reasons, Clinton and Reno sought to convince him that it would be better for the agency if he did not serve out his full ten-year term, which would come to an end in 1997. The fiasco at **Waco**, Texas, which culminated with the death of eighty Branch Davidians, damaged Sessions's reputation further. Hence, on July 20, 1993, Clinton announced Sessions's dismissal.

Ironically, when Sessions took over as director of the FBI, he had a reputation for integrity that brought him praise from both Republicans and Democrats. Born in Fort Smith, Arkansas, the son of a minister who served as an army chaplin, Sessions enlisted in the U.S. Air Force at the outbreak of the Korean War. After four years of service, he enrolled at Baylor University, earning his B.A. and law degree in 1956 and 1958, respectively. During the 1960s, he practiced law in Waco, Texas, and, following Richard Nixon's election as president, joined the government operations section of the Justice Department. After serving for a brief period as U.S. attorney in western Texas, Sessions was nominated and confirmed as a U.S. district-court judge, a position he held until he became director of the FBI in 1987. Some suggested that Sessions's troubles stemmed from his wife, Alice, and Sarah Munford, two strong-willed women in the otherwise traditionally all-male world of the FBI. His wife complained that an inner circle of agents who came of age under J. Edgar Hoover opposed her husband from the start. Regardless of the sources of Sessions's problems, few rallied behind him when Clinton compelled him to leave the FBI.

Suggested Readings: *Current Biography Yearbook*, 1988, p. 518; David Johnston, "Change at the F.B.I." *New York Times*, July 21, 1993, p. A10; David Johnston, "Defiant F.B.I. Chief Removed from Job by the President," *New York Times*, July 20, 1993, p. A1.

SEX SCANDALS. *See* **Broaddrick, Juanita**; **Jones, Paula**; **Lewinsky, Monica**; **Tripp, Linda**; **Willey, Kathleen**.

SHALALA, DONNA E. (February 14, 1941, Cleveland, Ohio–   .) Secretary of Health and Human Services, 1993–2001.

One of the few **cabinet** members to serve through both of President Bill Clinton's terms, Donna Shalala directed the Department of Health and Human Services for longer than any other person in U.S. history. As secretary of the department, she managed a large budget (over one-third of a trillion dollars in fiscal year 2000), over 60,000 employees, and some of the most prominent social programs, including Medicare and most federal welfare programs. Ironically, in spite of the length of her service, she could not claim any major victories. Although **welfare reform** was signed into law by President Clinton, it was more of a Republican initiative than a Democratic one, and the Republican-controlled Congress rebuffed the president's attempts (and hers) to significantly expand Medicare, not to mention enact sweeping **health care reform**. Still, during her tenure, Shalala celebrated the considerable shrinking of the welfare rolls and the gradual expansion of health coverage via programs such as the **Children's Health Insurance Program (CHIP)**.

Born in Cleveland, Ohio, Shalala earned a B.A. from Western College for Women in 1962 (today part of Case Western Reserve University) and a Ph.D. in Urban Affairs from the Maxwell School of Citizenship and Pub-

Donna Shalala. Department of Health and Human Services.

lic Affairs of Syracuse University in 1970. She enjoyed a distinguished career in academe and government, including a term as assistant secretary in the Department of Housing and Urban Development under President Jimmy Carter, seven years as president of Hunter College, and nearly as many years as chancellor of the University of Wisconsin at Madison. (She was the first woman to head a Big Ten university.) Along with **Hillary Clinton**, Shalala also served on the board of directors of the Children's Defense Fund. Ironically, Marian Wright Edelman, the president of the Children's Defense Fund, decried welfare reform as a "moral blot" on the Clinton presidency. While several other liberals allied with Edelman resigned from the Clinton administration in protest against the president's support of the plan, Shalala did not, preferring instead to try to rid it of its most unfair parts, such as denying legal immigrants coverage, rather than quit.

At the time of her nomination, numerous conservatives complained about Shalala's liberal views. The top aide to Republican Senator **Trent Lott** described the speech code implemented by the University of Wisconsin as a terrible example of political correctness. Yet whereas the president refused to spend political capital to defend several other female nominees from conservative attacks, such as **Lani Guinier** and **Zoë Baird**, he never backed away from Shalala. Indeed, over the course of her eight years in Washington, Shalala remained loyal to the president and vice versa. Whatever differences they may have had remained private, and unlike several of his other appointees, Shalala steered clear of any serious allegations of wrongdoing.

Suggested Readings: Francis X. Clines, "Shalala Still Has Her Zest for Battle," *New York Times*, January 12, 1997, sec. 1, p. 12; http://www.hhs.gov/about/bios/dhhssec.html; Barbara Vobejda, "Shalala: A Lifetime Spent in the Center of Storms," *Washington Post*, January 14, 1993, p. A13.

SHALIKASHVILI, GENERAL JOHN MALCHASE DAVID. (June 27, 1936, Warsaw, Poland–   .) Chairman, Joint Chiefs of Staff, 1993–1997.

General John Shalikashvili chaired the Joint Chiefs of Staff (JCS) during most of President Bill Clinton's first term in office. He was responsible for providing military advice on numerous problems. He inherited U.S. troop presence in **Somalia**, oversight of **Iraqi**'s compliance with the United Nations' resolutions in the Persian Gulf, and a growing crisis in **Haiti**, not to mention long-standing U.S. commitments in Europe and Asia. While he was chair of the JCS, U.S. troops participated in a humanitarian mission in Zaire to help it deal with the refugee crisis created by the civil war in **Rwanda**. Shalikashvili also readied American forces for an invasion of Haiti, which the military junta in Haiti avoided at the last minute by agreeing to allow Jean-Bertrand Aristide to resume power. Through much of his tenure, Shalikashvili also provided military advice to the president on the situation in the Balkans, particularly the ongoing civil war in **Bosnia and Herzegovina**. In the summer of 1995, **NATO** initiated air strikes against Serbian targets that helped produce the Dayton Agreement. Subsequently, U.S. troops participated as peacekeepers in the region. Beyond these military engagements, Shalikashvili grappled with the need to downsize the military, close bases, and modernize American troops for the challenges of the post–cold-war world. Unlike General

Colin Powell, who was the chairman of the Joint Chiefs of Staff when Clinton assumed office and publicly voiced his opposition to the administration's policy toward **gays in the military**, Shalikashvili did not join other conservatives in criticizing the "don't ask, don't tell policy."

Shalikashvili was born in Warsaw, Poland, to a family with a long military tradition. While his father fought with German units, young John grew up in war-torn Poland. The family migrated to the United States in 1952; John went to high school in Peoria, Illinois. He earned his B.S. in mechanical engineering from Bradley University in 1958. He joined the Air Force ROTC while he was in college, but poor eyesight kept him from becoming a pilot. He was drafted into the army and became an artillery officer. He rose rapidly through the ranks while simultaneously earning an M.A. in international relations from George Washington University and studying at the Naval War College and the U.S. Army War College. He won accolades for his command of Operation Provide Comfort, a massive relief effort to help Kurdish refugees in the Iraqi-Turkish border region. Afterwards he served as Colin Powell's assistant while Powell was the chair of the JCS. From June 1992 until his appointment as chair of the JCS, he was the supreme allied commander of U.S. forces in Europe and of NATO. He was the first foreign-born chairman of the Joint Chiefs of Staff. He retired after completing his second two-year term in office, as had other chairmen of the JCS.

Suggested Readings: *Current Biography Yearbook*, 1995, p. 524; Claudia Dreifus, "Who's the Enemy Now?" *New York Times Magazine*, May 21, 1995, p. 34.

Related Entries: Defense, Military; Foreign Policy.

SHELTON, GENERAL HENRY H. (January 2, 1942, Tarboro, North Carolina–   .) Chairman, Joint Chiefs of Staff, 1997–2001.

The first chairman of the Joint Chiefs of Staff to come from a special-operations command, General Henry Shelton, who oversaw the bombardment of Yugoslavia, served as President Bill Clinton's chief military adviser for most of his second term as president. His initial appointment in October 1997 came after U.S. Air Force General John Ralston, Secretary of Defense **William Cohen**'s first choice, withdrew his name from consideration after revealing that he once had an extramarital affair. Shelton, in contrast, had an unassailable moral reputation.

Born in Tarboro, North Carolina, on a thousand-acre farm, Shelton earned his B.S. in textiles from North Carolina State University in 1963.

During college, he joined the ROTC, and after graduating, he served in the army for two years. After a brief period working at a textile mill, he rejoined the military. For the next twenty-four years, Shelton held various command positions in the army. He served two tours in **Vietnam**, including leading a Green Beret unit. During the Persian Gulf War, Shelton, then a brigadier general, was the assistant division commander for operations for the 101st Airborne Division. After the war, he was promoted to major general and then lieutenant general. He commanded the Joint Task Force that conducted Operation Uphold Democracy in Haiti in 1994. Shelton was decorated numerous times, including a Bronze Star and a Purple Heart, for his service in Vietnam. Aside from his B.S., he earned his M.S. in Political Science from Auburn University in 1973 and received further military education from the Air Command and Staff Colleges and the National War College. An extremely fit commander, Shelton personally led special-operations units on grueling runs while still in his fifties.

Some commentators felt that Shelton, whose background was with special-operations forces, fit the direction of the military in the post–cold-war world. He declared that one of his major goals was modernizing American forces, which many took to mean readying them to respond rapidly to crises all around the globe. He also faced the challenge of training U.S. soldiers to serve as peacekeepers in **Bosnia and Herzegovina** and other areas.

Suggested Readings: *Current Biography Yearbook*, 1998, p. 528, "General Henry H. Shelton," http://www.dtic.mil/jcs/core/chairman.html.

Related Entries: Defense, Military; Foreign Policy.

SLATER, RODNEY E. (February 23, 1955, Marianna, Arkansas–   .) Secretary of Transportation, 1997–2001.

Rodney Slater, an **African American** and native of Arkansas, was the secretary of transportation during Bill Clinton's second term as president. Prior to becoming secretary of transportation, Slater served as the administrator of the national highway system. While he was secretary of transportation, the Republican-controlled Congress passed massive increases in highway and transportation appropriations, 40 percent higher than appropriated in 1991 and more than the amount requested by the Clinton administration. The bill provided for the upgrading of thousands of miles of road and enhanced mass transit. Even though the president and

Slater complained that the bill included too much pork, Clinton signed it into law. Two of Slater's main goals were to attract young people to begin careers in the field of transportation and to insure that former welfare recipients had access to public transportation so that they could obtain and maintain employment.

Born in Marianna, Arkansas, one of the poorest communities in the nation, Slater earned his B.A. from Eastern Michigan University, where he was a star football player, and his law degree from the University of Arkansas. He was a member of the Arkansas State Highway Commission from 1987 to 1992 and held several other state government positions under then Governor Bill Clinton. At both the state and federal levels, he earned a reputation as an efficient administrator. For example, under his direction, the Federal Highway Administration increased investment in the national highway system by 20 percent while simultaneously decreasing its staff by 10 percent. One of only three Arkansas citizens to serve as a **cabinet** member, Slater was also recognized as one of the 100 Most Influential Black Americans by *Ebony* magazine.

Suggested Reading: Joyce Jones, "From the Inner Circle," *Black Enterprise* 30:3 (October 1999), p. 28.

SOCIAL SECURITY REFORM. In his acceptance speech at the Republican National Convention in Philadelphia, Pennsylvania, in 2000, Republican presidential nominee **George W. Bush** accused the Bill Clinton and **Al Gore** administration of having failed to provide leadership on one of the most pressing issues of the times, Social Security reform. Bush repeated these charges in the closing weeks of the campaign. In response, Vice President Gore contended that Bush's plan, which called for allowing younger workers to divert some of their Social Security savings into private investments, was fiscally unsound and would jeopardize the security of many seniors. Ironically, President Clinton had raised the issue of Social Security reform himself and had made saving Social Security the centerpiece of his 1999 State of the Union Address. However, many pundits observed that even though the Clinton administration extended the life of Social Security, it did not resolve the larger question of what would happen when the baby boomers began to retire en masse.

For nearly twenty years, Social Security reform was a prominent issue that cropped up again and again, only to be avoided because of the political dangers attached to it. In the early 1980s, the National Commission on Social Security Reform was created to raise awareness about the actuarial unsoundness of the Social Security system and to suggest means for fixing it. Several of its recommended reforms, namely, raising the retirement age from sixty-five to sixty-seven and partially taxing the benefits of upper-income retirees, were enacted by the Ronald Reagan and Clinton administrations, respectively. Clinton's economic plan of 1993, which was passed in spite of unanimous Republican opposition, raised taxes on Social Security benefits paid to upper-income retirees. Yet during most of the 1980s and early 1990s, both Republicans and Democrats avoided calling for more dramatic reforms because they feared invoking the wrath of elderly voters.

In the mid-1990s, however, momentum for reforming Social Security began to rebuild. Bipartisan groups such as the Concord Coalition pushed hard for Social Security reform. The coalition's leaders, such as **Paul Tsongas**, argued that the Social Security trust fund would run short of funds when the baby-boom generation reached retirement age if the Social Security system were not reformed immediately. A study issued by the trustees of the Social Security fund similarly showed that the Social Security trust fund would begin to run a deficit in 2012 if the system were not altered. Partly in reaction to these findings and to the expansion of the **economy**, which made Social Security reform more feasible, President Clinton appointed an advisory panel to investigate ways to save the system. Some even predicted that Social Security reform could become his greatest legacy.

In his 1999 State of the Union Address, Clinton went one step further. Even though he was still facing his trial in the **U.S. Senate** on **impeachment** charges, Clinton seized the moment to demand Social Security reform. In the address and afterwards, he suggested that the reform could include allowing part of the trust fund to be invested in the private sector. Many assumed that funds invested in the **stock market** would garner greater returns for future retirees than was being generated by savings sitting in the Social Security trust fund. In his last two years in office, however, Social Security reform got nowhere, partly because of related debates between Republicans and Democrats over what to do with the projected federal **budget** surplus, partly due to the battle over whether or not to cut taxes, and partly due to partisan posturing. Clinton, and even more so Al Gore, sought to dedicate a large part of the budget surplus toward paying down the national debt and thus extending the solvency of the Social Security trust fund. Republicans, in contrast, sought to use the surplus to provide substantial tax cuts. In addition, Social

Security reform stalled because most Republicans in Congress objected to some of the specifics of Clinton's proposals, particularly the idea of having the federal government invest part of the trust fund in the private sector. Republican presidential candidate George W. Bush favored giving individuals control over their retirement funds and allowing individuals, not the government, to determine what to do with at least part of their savings. Al Gore countered that Bush's plan was fiscally unsound, in particular because it did not explain how to free young workers to invest some of their savings while simultaneously meeting obligations to pay current retirees. Whether George W. Bush would be able to push through his plan remained to be seen.

Suggested Readings: http://concordcoaliton.org; http://socialsecurityreform.org; Sue Kirchoff, "Social Security: Next Salvo," *CQ Weekly Report*, October 30, 1999, p. 2579; Robert Samuelson, "Clinton's Squandered Legacy," *Washington Post*, November 4, 1999, p. A35; "White House Puts Social Security on Ice," *Congressional Daily/A.M.*, September 16, 1999.

Related Entries: Domestic Policy; Election of 2000.

SOMALIA. On December 9, 1992, in one of his last acts as president, **George Bush** sent thousands of U.S. troops to Somalia. Their mission, according to Bush, was to work with United Nations forces as peacekeepers to insure that humanitarian supplies reached starving Somalians who were devastated by years of civil war between rival forces in this East African nation. As Bush declared, "I can state with confidence we come to your country for one reason only: to enable the starving to be fed." President-elect Bill Clinton offered his support for the military initiative, as did many liberals in Congress. The American public seemed supportive of the effort, even if it was a bit bemused by the strangeness of the initial invasion—U.S. marines were met onshore by television cameras and media representatives.

By the fall of 1993, however, public support for U.S. involvement had declined considerably. Several factors led to this change in public opinion. To begin with, in the spring of 1993, U.S. forces in Somalia came under the direction of UN commanders. Conservatives, in particular, expressed their reservations about this and what they perceived as a shift in the mission of troops in the region, from delivering aid to "nation building." Former President Bush, for example, complained about "mission creep." As UN forces proved incapable of settling long-standing disputes in the region, other experts claimed that Clinton's lack of **foreign**

U.S. Army AH-1 Cobra attack helicopter providing air support in Mogadishu, Somalia. Department of Defense.

policy experience was beginning to show. To make matters worse, on October 3, 1993, Mohammed Farah Aidid's forces engaged in a heated battle with U.S. forces. During the battle, eighteen American soldiers were killed, eighty were wounded, and helicopter pilot Michael Durant was captured. Public opinion polls showed a strong desire to remove American troops, and Clinton's **approval rating** declined precipitously. Nonetheless, Senator Robert Byrd, a Democrat from West Virginia, thwarted conservative efforts to demand an immediate withdrawal of troops by sponsoring an amendment to a **defense** bill that required the president to report on troop deployment in the region and to request authorization for the mission. The **U.S. Senate** supported this measure by a vote of 90–7. The **U.S. House of Representatives** approved the bill on November 10, and Clinton signed it a day later. Clinton sent an additional 1,700 troops to Somalia and stationed even more marines nearby to insure the safety of U.S. forces already there.

By the summer of 1994, nearly all American forces had left Somalia. Foreign policy experts chided Clinton for allowing the mission to expand without a clear exit strategy, but at the same time, they acknowledged that Somalia did not represent an all-out disaster, as charged by some of the president's Republican critics. "The failure in Somalia," wrote William Hyland, "obviously hurt the cause of humanitarian intervention and may well have strengthened anti-UN sentiment" (Hyland, *Clinton's World*). However, Hyland added, Somalia was not a terrible failure. It saved thousands of lives and restored a semblance of order. Hyland could have added that compared to the foreign policy ordeal of another young and inexperienced president, namely, John F. Kennedy, whose authorization of the invasion of the Bay of Pigs represented one of the most embarrassing moments in the history of the United States, Clinton's missteps in Somalia were minuscule.

Suggested Readings: John R. Bolton, "Wrong Turn in Somalia," *Foreign Affairs*, January/February 1994, p. 56; *Congressional Quarterly Almanac*, 1993, p. 489; William Hyland, *Clinton's World* (Westport, CT: Praeger, 1999), chap. 4.

SOUTH AFRICA. The Clinton administration inherited a situation in South Africa that was vastly improving. During the late 1970s and particularly the early 1980s, relations between the United States and South Africa reached a low point, largely due to the latter's commitment to racial apartheid. Many Americans, particularly those allied with the liberal wing of the Democratic Party, called on U.S. companies to divest them-

President Clinton and South African President Nelson Mandela on tour of Robben Island, South Africa, March 27, 1998. AP/Wide World Photos.

selves of their business investments in South Africa. In general, the Ronald Reagan administration resisted such radical demands, although, toward the end of its tenure, it began to put substantial pressure on South Africa to reform itself. In the early 1990s, change came quickly to South Africa. In February 1990, South Africa's newly elected president, F. W. de Klerk, overturned the long-standing ban on the African National Congress, the most prominent antiapartheid group in South Africa. A couple of weeks later, Nelson Mandela, the foremost opponent of white supremacy, was released from prison. A year later, South Africa repealed legislation that restricted blacks in South Africa to specific "homelands." In December 1993, South Africa adopted a new constitution that granted blacks the vote for the first time. The following spring, Nelson Mandela was elected as South Africa's new president.

The Clinton administration welcomed all of these developments. In the fall of 1994, Mandela visited the United States. In a special radio address, President Bill Clinton heralded Mandela as a "man who has been a hero for people in every corner of the world" (Clinton, Radio Address, October 8, 1998). Clinton also pledged to help South Africa make a peaceful transition to democracy. After the visit, relations between the United States and South Africa remained good. The United States provided financial aid and sent Peace Corps volunteers to the region. In 1998, President Clinton made a historic visit to South Africa, where he reaffirmed the U.S. commitment to working with its people. In return, Mandela toasted Clinton and the American people for supporting the fight for independence in South Africa. When Nelson Mandela resigned five years after taking office, the administration lent its support to his successor, Thabo Mbeki. While Mbeki faced many problems, stemming largely from the tremendous economic disparities between the black majority and the white minority in South Africa, the Clinton administration remained committed to helping South Africa succeed in its experiment with democracy.

Suggested Readings: http://clinton6.nara.gov/1994/10/1994-10-08-radio-address-with-mandela-on-south-africa.html; Susan E. Rice, "Testimony before the House International Relations Committee, Subcommittee on Africa," October 14, 1999, http://www.state.gov; Kenneth Walsh, "A Hopeful Tour of a Troubled Land," *U.S. News & World Report*, April 6, 1998, p. 49.

Related Entries: Foreign Policy; Somalia.

SPACE PROGRAM. One of the greatest setbacks for space exploration occurred on January 28, 1986, when the space shuttle *Challenger* exploded seventy-three seconds after launch, killing all seven crew members. Following the tragedy, the shuttle program was grounded for over two years. In September 1988, the program resumed, and over the course of the next ten years, the National Aeronautics and Space Administration (NASA) safely launched sixty-five shuttle missions. Combined, the crews of *Atlantis, Columbia, Discovery*, and *Endeavor* conducted a wide variety of scientific and engineering experiments. Still, as the federal **budget** deficit grew, the space program remained one of the primary targets for those who sought to cut the budget. Among those who sought to drastically reduce NASA's budget were many Republican newcomers to Congress, members of the so-called class of 1994. Only by working with veteran Republican lawmakers did Bill Clinton resist their efforts to reduce NASA's budget.

Perhaps the highlight of the reborn shuttle program came when John Glenn, who had become the first American to circle the earth in a space ship in 1962, joined the crew of *Discovery* on a nine-day mission in the fall of 1998. Glenn, who had served in the **U.S. Senate**, 1975–1999, and had run for the Democratic nomination for president in 1984, was the oldest person ever to go into space. One of the main goals of NASA during the 1990s was the construction of a space station. To prepare for this mission, U.S. astronauts participated in a series of shuttle trips to the Russian space station *Mir*. As Clinton's second term came to an end, Russia announced plans to disassemble *Mir* and to commit itself to helping the United States construct its own, newer space station. NASA also continued to sponsor numerous unmanned missions into space. In December 1993, a team of astronauts performed a risky space walk to repair the Hubble Space Telescope, which had been launched into space three years earlier. While the Mars *Observer* spacecraft "disappeared" just before it was to go into orbit around Mars in 1993, other Mars probes enjoyed much more successful missions. The Mars *Pathfinder*, in particular, which landed on Mars on July 4, 1997, sent back startling photographs of the red planet.

Suggested Readings: Allan Freedman, "Space Station, Earth Mission Still Big Targets for Budget-Cutters," *CQ Weekly Report*, July 22, 1995, p. 2172; http://www. nasa.gov; Chuck McCutcheon, "Dismayed Members Ask Clinton for Direction on Space Station," *CQ Weekly Report*, June 27, 1998, p. 1768.

SPERLING, GENE B. (1958, Ann Arbor, Michigan–   .) Deputy Assistant to the President for Economic Policy, 1993–2001; Director, National Economic Council, 1996–2001.

One of Bill Clinton's longtime advisers, Gene Sperling was named director of the **National Economic Council** (NEC) in December 1996 following Clinton's reelection. Prior to this appointment, Sperling had served as the deputy director of the NEC under Directors **Robert Rubin** and **Laura D'Andrea Tyson**, respectively. After being elected in 1992, President Clinton created the NEC to coordinate the work of various economic agencies, much in the same way that the National Security Council oversaw security-related agencies. Sperling also held the title of deputy assistant to the president for economic policy. Prior to Clinton's election as president, Sperling advised the Clinton-Gore campaign on economic matters.

Born in Ann Arbor, Michigan, in 1958, Sperling received his B.A. from the University of Minnesota in 1981 and his law degree from Yale Law School in 1985. He also attended Wharton Business School. From 1990 to 1992, he worked as New York governor Mario Cuomo's economic adviser. While Sperling lacked the economic and business expertise of his former bosses—Rubin had been a senior partner at Goldman Sachs and Tyson an economics professor at the University of California at Berkeley—his political instincts were excellent. As director of the NEC, Sperling was responsible for responding to the Asian financial crisis in 1998 and promoting free-trade agreements and mechanisms. As the **economy** continued to expand, Sperling also had the task of helping the president determine what to do with the federal **budget** surplus. In contrast to the Republican Party, which proposed enacting tax cuts, the Clinton administration advocated allocating most of the surplus to bolstering **Social Security** and Medicare and enhancing **education**.

Throughout his tenure at the White House, colleagues praised Sperling for his ability to grasp complex and technical finance issues and to convey the administration's policy succinctly to the media and the public. In addition, Sperling had a reputation as a workaholic and a fierce loyalist. Ironically, his loyalty did not grow out of his lifelong friendship with Clinton but rather out of his faith in Clinton's policies and the good they were doing for the nation.

Suggested Readings: Gerard Baker, "Gene Sperling," *Financial Times*, October 2, 1998; Robin Toner, "A Clinton Whiz Kid Who's Still There and Still a Believer," *New York Times*, October 25, 1999, p. A18.

Related Entry: Domestic Policy.

STARR, KENNETH W. (July 21, 1946, Vernon, Texas–   .) Independent Counsel, 1994–1999.

Kenneth Starr began and ended his tenure as independent counsel in the **Whitewater** affair in controversy. Originally, Attorney General **Janet Reno** appointed **Robert B. Fiske, Jr.**, a former federal prosecutor under Ronald Reagan, to investigate the Whitewater scandal, but when conservative Republicans complained that Fiske was not conducting a broad- or tough-enough investigation, a federal appeals-court panel replaced him with Kenneth Starr. (Officially the reason for the removal of Fiske was the renewal of the expired **independent counsel law**. Fiske was appointed directly by Reno because the law had expired. When it was renewed, a panel of judges replaced Fiske to avoid an appearance of impropriety.) Immediately, many Democrats protested against Starr's selection because, as they noted, he had served as President **George Bush**'s solicitor general and had issued remarks critical of Clinton. Others observed that he had no prosecutorial experience. Starr had experience as a federal appeals-court judge. As Starr's investigation dragged on and the costs of his efforts escalated, claims that Starr was out to get the president mounted. In 1998, when Starr expanded his investigation to include a probe of President Clinton's alleged affair with **Monica Lewinsky**, which he learned of from **Linda Tripp** and other conservative sources, the criticism of Starr increased. Yet Starr persevered, supported by Republicans in Congress and driven by his conviction that he was conducting his investigation in an ethical and legal manner. He also believed that he was acting in a manner consistent with the mandate given to him by the legislation that had created the independent counsel's office in the first place.

On September 9, 1998, following months of legal wrangling and heightened media coverage, Starr issued a 453-page report to Congress replete with sexually graphic material. In it, Starr listed eleven possible grounds for **impeachment**, all revolving around President Clinton's testimony and his alleged attempt to cover up his affair with Lewinsky. Three days later, the House Judiciary Committee made the report available to the public via the Internet. Subsequently, following weeks of hearings, including testimony by Starr, the House Judiciary Committee voted in favor of impeaching the president, and the full **House of Representatives** concurred. Most of the evidence in support of impeachment derived from Starr's report.

Over a year after releasing his report and about nine months after the **U.S. Senate** voted to acquit the president on the impeachment charges brought by the House of Representatives, Starr resigned. He was succeeded by **Robert Ray**, who had joined Starr's office earlier in the year. At the time, Starr had still not completed his final report, and Ray was left having to determine whether President Clinton should face criminal indictments stemming from either the Lewinsky matter or the Whitewater affair. While Clinton's most fervid supporters continued to insist that Starr had acted improperly, several legal scholars disagreed. For instance, in *An Affair of State: The Investigation, Impeachment, and Trial of President Clinton* (1999), federal appeals-court judge Richard A. Posner contended that Starr engaged in overkill, "given the intrinsic triviality not only of the President's extramarital escapades but also of the **Paula Jones** litigation, the original scene of the President's criminal violations" (p. 7). Nonetheless, Posner found other parties, including the president and to an extent the U.S. Supreme Court (which had allowed Paula Jones to go forward with her suit) more to blame than Starr. Indeed, Posner countered Democratic assertions that Starr was out to get the president, writing: "There is no basis for the claim by Clinton's defenders . . . that the vigor with which Starr pursued the investigation into the affair was the consequence of his being a sex-obsessed puritan witch hunter . . . [there is] no basis either . . . for thinking him a fire-breathing right-wing prosecutorial pit bull" (p. 69). Jeffrey Toobin, author of *A Vast Conspiracy* (1999), came to a somewhat similar conclusion. While Toobin faulted Starr for running an office that was overly concerned with looking and acting tough, and questioned whether a normal prosecutor would have pursued a case of perjury in a civil suit that had questionable legal merit, he did not conclude that Starr was part of a right-wing conspiracy to get the president.

Born in Vernon, Texas, the son of a minister, Starr spent most of his youth in San Antonio. After attending Harding College in Searcy, Arkansas, for two years, he transferred to George Washington University, where he received his A.B. in 1968. After earning his master's degree in political science from Brown University in 1969, he completed law school at Duke University in 1973. Having graduated near the top of his class, Starr gained an appointment as a law clerk to Supreme Court Chief Justice Warren Burger. After completing the clerkship, he went to work for the Los Angeles law firm of Gibson, Dunn and Crutcher. When Ronald Reagan appointed one of the firm's senior partners, William French Smith, U.S. attorney general, Starr followed him to the Justice Department. Two years later, in 1983, he became a judge on the U.S. Court of Appeals for the District of Columbia. At thirty-seven, he was the youngest person ever to gain a lifetime appointment on such a prestigious court. While he generally handed down conservative rulings, he was considered less dogmatic than his colleagues Robert Bork and Antonin Scalia. In 1989, he resigned his judgeship to serve as President Bush's solicitor general. When Clinton defeated Bush, Starr returned to the private sector. During his first several years as independent counsel, Starr focussed on the Whitewater affair. His investigation led to the prosecution of several individuals associated with President Clinton and First Lady **Hillary Clinton**. However, as of January 1998, when he asked a federal court for the right to expand his investigation to include the president's alleged affair with Monica Lewinsky and possible perjury, he had not uncovered enough evidence to argue that the president had acted illegally in relation to the original Whitewater matter.

Ironically, when Starr was first appointed, he promised not to become another Lawrence Walsh. This meant that he intended to complete his investigation promptly and to avoid the prosecutorial excesses associated with Walsh's investigation of the Iran-contra affair during the Reagan administration. After two years as head of the Office of the Independent Counsel, he announced his intention to resign to become the dean of Pepperdine Law School. However, when conservatives vociferously protested against this move, he decided to stay on as independent counsel. His unending pursuit of Clinton renewed criticisms of the independent counsel law, and one of the byproducts of the Whitewater investigation was that the law under which Starr was appointed was not renewed.

Suggested Readings: Lorraine Adams, "Starr to Resign," *Washington Post*, October 15, 1999, p. A6; *Current Biography Yearbook*, 1998, p. 552; http://www. washingtonpost.com/wp-srv/politics/special/clinton/players/starr.htm; Richard A. Posner, *An Affair of State* (Cambridge, MA: Harvard University Press, 1999); Jeffrey Toobin, *A Vast Conspiracy* (New York: Random House, 1999).

Related entries: Foster, Vincent; Travelgate; Tripp, Linda; Willey, Kathleen.

START II. *See* **Nuclear Nonproliferation.**

STEELE, JULIA HIATT. Whitewater witness.

On January 7, 1999, Julia Hiatt Steele was indicted on charges of making false statements and obstructing justice in relation to independent counsel **Kenneth Starr**'s investigation of President Bill Clinton and the **Whitewater** and **Monica Lewinsky** matters. According to Starr, Steele had lied to investigators regarding President Clinton's alleged groping of **Kathleen Willey**. Rumors of the president's alleged sexual pass at Willey first appeared in the late summer of 1997. A *Newsweek* article observed that Steele first confirmed that Willey had told her that the president had groped her. The story went on to note that Steele later retracted this statement, claiming instead that Willey had asked her to lie about the incident. Subsequently, **Paula Jones**'s attorneys deposed both Willey and Steele. Willey testified that Clinton had made a pass at her, but Steele testified that Willey had asked her to falsely confirm the story. Believing Willey's story, Starr indicted Steele.

Many of Clinton's supporters saw the indictment of Steele as proof of Starr's heavy-handedness. Steele was the first person to face indictment stemming from Starr's expanded investigation (aside from those associated with the original Whitewater matter).

In the fall of 1999, after Steele's trial ended in a hung jury, Steele called for the appointment of an independent counsel to investigate Starr's prosecutorial misconduct. Like **Susan McDougal**, Steele alleged that Starr had pressured her to give false testimony against the president. Starr chose not to retry the case against Steele. An independent counsel to investigate Starr was not appointed.

Suggested Readings: Michael Isikoff, "A Twist in Jones v. Clinton," *Newsweek*, August 11, 1997, p. 30; Susan Schmidt, "Woman Who Disputed Willey Is Indicted," *Washington Post*, January 8, 1999, p. A7; "Steele Joins Complaint against Starr," AP State and Local Wire, October 6, 1999, on Lexis-Nexis.

Related Entry: Independent Counsel Law.

STEIN, JACOB A. (March 25, 1925–   .) Attorney for Monica Lewinsky.

Along with Plato Cacheris, Jacob Stein served as **Monica Lewinsky**'s attorney. Born in 1925, the son of a prominent Washington, D.C., lawyer, Stein graduated from George Washington Law School in 1948. He became a partner in his own firm and a prominent figure in Washington, D.C. Stein had a long list of prominent clients and positions. In the mid-1980s, he served as independent prosecutor, investigating possible wrongdoing by Ronald Reagan's attorney general and close friend Edwin Meese III. He represented Oregon senator Robert Packwood in his fight against sexual harassment charges and was involved on the defense side of the Watergate investigations. Cacheris had a similar record. The two took over from **William Ginsburg**, a family friend of Lewinsky's father, about five months after **Kenneth Starr**'s office first began investigating Lewinsky's relationship with President Clinton. According to many pundits, Ginsburg, who lacked Stein and Cacheris's experience as a criminal defense lawyer, had done a poor job of representing Lewinsky. Most notably, numerous pundits, including AP writer Larry Margasal, argued that Ginsburg had failed to gain an immunity agreement for his client. (Jeffrey Toobin argues that Ginsburg did an excellent job of protecting his client and that it was Starr's office that missed an opportunity to get her to testify shortly after the case first broke.) One of the first things that Stein and Cacheris did was to negotiate an immunity agreement with Starr's office. This paved the way for Lewinsky's testimony before a grand jury and Starr's recommendation that the **House of Representatives** impeach the president on perjury charges.

Suggested Readings: http://www.washingtonpost.com/wp-srv/politics/special/clinton/players/stein.htm; Stuart Taylor, Jr., "Unconventional Lawyer with a New

Task," *New York Times*, April 3, 1984, p. A20; Jeffrey Toobin, *A Vast Conspiracy* (New York: Random House, 1999).

Related Entry: Impeachment.

STEPHANOPOULOS, GEORGE. (February 10, 1961, Fall River, Massachusetts– .) Director of Communications, 1993; Senior Adviser to the President, 1993–1996.

A member of the so-called war room, the name given to Bill Clinton's closest political advisers during the 1992 campaign, George Stephanopoulos, who worked out of a small cubbyhole adjoining the Oval Office, was one of President Clinton's closest advisers during his first term in office. While Clinton passed Stephanopoulos over for the post of chief of staff, the young political savant still exerted a great deal of influence on the president. Often allied with **Hillary Clinton** and several of Clinton's other younger and more liberal aides, Stephanopoulos engaged in ongoing battles with political consultant **Dick Morris**, who sought to move Clinton toward the center following the Republican takeover of Congress in the **election of 1994**. After departing the White House and joining ABC as a political commentator, Stephanopoulos wrote *All Too Human: A Political Education* (1999), a memoir of his years on the Clinton campaign and in the White House. In it, Stephanopoulos described his personal journey from being a young idealist who joined the Clinton campaign to being a battle-toughened political veteran who had experienced the hardball reality of presidential politics. According to Stephanopoulos, the relentless political attacks and inside-the-beltway scheming took such a toll on him that he had to leave the White House.

Born in Fall River, Massachusetts, the descendant of Greek immigrants, George Stephanopoulos was reared in Rye, New York, and then in Orange Village, Ohio, a Cleveland suburb. He earned his B.A. from Columbia University in 1982, working briefly on **George Bush**'s unsuccessful 1980 bid for the Republican presidential nomination. After graduating at the top of his class, Stephanopoulos studied for two years at Oxford University on a Rhodes scholarship. In 1988, he worked as the director of communications for the Democratic presidential nominee, Michael Dukakis. Following a brief period with the New York City Public Library, he went to work for **Richard Gephardt**, the majority leader of the **U.S. House of Representatives**. Stephanopoulos joined Bill Clinton's presidential campaign team in its early stages. When stories of Clinton's alleged affair with **Gennifer Flowers** and his effort to avoid the draft emerged, he bunkered down with several of Clinton's other closest advisers in the so-called war room to devise responses to the attacks. Along with **James Carville** and **Paul Begala**, Stephanopoulos deflected these charges and kept the president focussed on the main theme of the campaign, the **economy**.

Originally appointed the director of communications in the White House, Stephanopoulos had his title and responsibilities changed in May 1993. To overcome a rough beginning, Clinton appointed **David Gergen**, a Reagan aide, to head the communications office and renamed Stephanopoulos senior adviser. Although some saw this as a demotion, Stephanopoulos continued to enjoy great access to the president and influence on the administration's course. After the Republican victory in the election of 1994, however, Clinton increasingly turned to Dick Morris, who did not hold an official position at the White House, for advice. Politically and personally the two did not get along, although Stephanopoulos worked hard for the president through the **election of 1996**. Upon resigning and in his memoir, Stephanopoulos expressed his overall admiration for Clinton. Yet, unlike James Carville, Paul Begala, and **Mandy Grunwald**, who, like Stephanopoulos had been members of the war room during the 1992 campaign, Stephanopoulos suggested that Clinton might deserve to be impeached for his refusal to come clean on the **Monica Lewinsky** affair. However, in grand-jury testimony, Stephanopoulos provided little new or damaging information to independent counsel **Kenneth Starr**.

Suggested Readings: *Current Biography Yearbook*, 1995, p. 547; George Stephanopoulos, *All Too Human: A Political Education* (Boston: Little, Brown, 1999); Thomas Vinciguerra, "Word for Word/Political Memoirs," *New York Times Book Review*, April 18, 1999, p. 9.

STOCK MARKET. The Clinton presidency coincided with one of the greatest bull markets in U.S. history. The Dow Jones industrial average, the most commonly used gauge of the stock market, nearly tripled during Clinton's eight years as president (the Dow Jones average peaked at 11,497 in 1999). Other indexes of stocks listed on the New York Stock Exchange rose as well (see Table 15). Just as important, the composite value of stocks on the NASDAQ skyrocketed. This included stocks in many **high-technology** companies such as Microsoft, whose values reached historical highs and created unprecedented fortunes. During the same time period, the number and percentage of Americans who owned shares of

Table 15
Stock Indexes, 1990–2000

Year	Dow Jones Industrial Average	NASDAQ Composite Index
1990	2,633.7	373.8
1995	5,117.1	1,052.1
1998	9,181	2,192
1999	10,464	3,728
2000	10,787	2,471

Source: Economic Report of the President, 2001; "Share Prices Finish Lower on Last Day of
a Tough Year," *New York Times,* December 30, 2000, p. B3.

Figure 11
Stock Market: Dow Jones and NASDAQ Averages

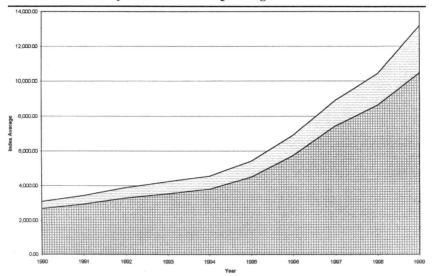

Source: Economic Report of the President, 2000.

stock, individually and via their pension or retirement plans, also reached
new highs. The volume of stocks traded rose astronomically. In 1992, the
average daily volume of stocks traded on the New York Stock Exchange
was roughly 200 million shares. By the end of the decade, it was not
uncommon for over 1 billion shares to be traded each day. President
Clinton often cited the stock market's rise as proof of the effectiveness
of his economic policy. He and his aides argued that the administration's
fiscal policies, in particular, which kept **inflation** and thus interest rates

low, encouraged investment in the stock market. Clinton also signed legislation in August 1997 that reduced the rate at which capital gains were taxed from 28 to 20 percent for investments held more than 18 months. In Clinton's final year in office, the stock market did not continue to boom. Some viewed this shift as a sign of an impending recession, while others argued that the overvaluation of stock prices combined with the Federal Reserve Board's decision to cool the **economy** produced the market's off year.

Suggested Readings: Council of Economic Advisers, *Economic Report of the President, 2001* (Washington, DC: GPO, 2001); http://www.census.gov/statab/freq/ 99s0840.txt; http://www.nyse.com.

SUDAN. On August 7, 1998, terrorist bombs exploded outside the U.S. embassies in Nairobi, Kenya, and Dar es Salaam, Tanzania. Less than two weeks later, on August 20, President Bill Clinton ordered U.S. armed forces to respond by bombing alleged terrorist targets in Afghanistan and Sudan. Clinton asserted that the sites that were bombed in Sudan were being used to produce materials for chemical weapons and that Sudan was implicated in the bombings of the U.S. embassies. Some of Clinton's critics, however, suggested that the president ordered the bombing to distract attention from the ongoing **Monica Lewinsky** scandal. In fact, President Clinton had just testified before the grand jury regarding his relationship with Lewinsky and had apologized about his affair in a speech to the American public. Furthermore, subsequent investigative reporting cast doubt on the administration's claim that the site that was bombed in Sudan was anything but a pharmaceutical factory producing legitimate products. Nonetheless, there was little outcry over the bombing of Sudan, in part because the United States and Sudan had had poor relations for years. During the Persian Gulf War, Sudan was one of the few Arab states to oppose U.S. troop presence on holy land. The State Department added Sudan to its list of nations that supported **terrorism** in 1993. Throughout the mid-1990s, relations between the United States and Sudan remained poor. Reports that Sudan tolerated the trafficking of slaves did nothing to enhance the relationship between the two nations. Last, the bombings of Sudan and Afghanistan appeared to send a message to terrorists to be more wary about attacking U.S. sites.

Suggested Readings: Richard Newman, "Our Target Was Terror," *U.S. News & World Report*, August 31, 1998, p. 38; Robert E. Precht, "Missile Attacks Send Wrong Message," *National Law Journal*, September 21, 1998, p. A26.

SUMMERS, LAWRENCE H. (1954, New Haven, Connecticut– .) Deputy Secretary of the Treasury, 1995–1999; Secretary of the Treasury, 1999–2001.

First as **Robert Rubin**'s deputy and then as secretary of the Treasury, Lawrence Summers presided over a healthy **economy** and federal treasury. Unlike most of his predecessors of the past quarter of a century, he had the luxury of grappling with what to do with a federal **budget** surplus and sustained economic growth as opposed to rising federal budget deficits and stagflation. In concert with the president, he devised no new dramatic proposals or departures, maintaining that the federal government should shore up **Social Security** and Medicare rather than committing the surplus to major tax cuts.

Born in New Haven, Connecticut, Summers earned his undergraduate degree from Massachusetts Institute of Technology (MIT) in 1975 and his Ph.D. in Economics from Harvard University in 1982. From 1979 through 1993, he taught economics at MIT and then at Harvard, serving as the Nathaniel Ropes Professor of Political Economy at Harvard from 1987 to 1993. He was the youngest tenured professor in the history of Harvard, authoring more than one hundred articles and winning numerous honors. In addition to teaching, Summers served as the chief economist for the World Bank from 1991 to 1993. Following the **election of 1992**, Summers came to work for the Clinton administration, initially as under secretary of the Treasury for international affairs and then as deputy secretary of the Treasury.

Summers clearly had big shoes to fill upon being named secretary of the Treasury. The economy and **stock market** were booming, and some were comparing Rubin to Alexander Hamilton, the first secretary of the Treasury. Summers was the first academic to serve as the secretary of the Treasury since George Shultz held the post during the Richard Nixon administration. Some expressed concerns that Summers lacked Rubin's clout and experience on Wall Street. Others worried that he lacked the political tact to deal with foreign leaders. Yet even though the stock market stumbled in 2000 and the economy slowed down at the tail end of the same year, Summers could take pride in the fact that he left a record budget surplus to Clinton's successors and the opportunity to retire much of the federal debt.

Suggested Readings: "Biographical Sketch of Lawrence H. Summers," http://www.ustreas.gov/opc/opc0080.html; "A Rough Diamond," *Financial Times*, May 13, 1999, p. 20.

Table 16
The Supreme Court during the Clinton Presidency

Name	Dates of Term	Appointed by
Byron White	April 16, 1962–August 10, 1993	Kennedy
Harry A. Blackmun	June 9, 1970–August 3, 1994	Nixon
William H. Rehnquist (Chief)*	January 7, 1972	Nixon
John Paul Stevens	December 19, 1975	Ford
Sandra Day O'Connor	September 25, 1981	Reagan
Antonin Scalia	September 26, 1986	Reagan
Anthony Kennedy	February 18, 1988	Reagan
David H. Souter	October 9, 1990	Bush
Clarence Thomas	October 23, 1991	Bush
Ruth Bader Ginsburg	August 10, 1993	Clinton
Stephen G. Breyer	August 3, 1994	Clinton

*Appointed Chief Justice by President Reagan on September 26, 1986.

SUPREME COURT. President Bill Clinton appointed two justices to the Supreme Court, **Ruth Bader Ginsburg** and **Stephen G. Breyer** (Table 16). Both arrived with moderate to liberal judicial records and maintained these records during Clinton's presidency. However, since the Supreme Court remained dominated by Republican nominees, it continued its conservative drift.

The most important development of the 1990s was the Court's increasing defense of states' rights. Chief Justice William Rehnquist had long believed that the federal government had overstepped its constitutional boundaries during the middle decades of the twentieth century, but it was not until the Clinton presidency that Rehnquist was able to carve a majority in favor of his position. In 1995, in the case of *United States* v. *Lopez*, the Court ruled 5–4 that a federal law that prohibited the possession of guns near a school was unconstitutional because the law did not fall under Congress's right to regulate interstate commerce. In 1997, the Court reaffirmed its commitment to narrowing the reach of Congress, striking down parts of the **Brady bill** and the Religious Freedom Restoration Act. Even more important, in 1999, in the case of *Alden* v. *Maine*, the Supreme Court ruled 5–4 that states could not be sued for violating a federal law. Sandra Day O'Connor, Antonin Scalia, Anthony Kennedy, Clarence Thomas, and William Rehnquist constituted the majority in all of these cases.

The Supreme Court also intervened in several high-profile cases that directly affected the **impeachment** of President Clinton. Most important,

The Supreme Court. Supreme Court Historical Society.

in 1997, the Court ruled that **Paula Jones**'s sexual harassment lawsuit against President Clinton could go forward, on the grounds that the suit was "unlikely to occupy any substantial amount of the petitioner's [Clinton's] time." If the Jones suit had been delayed until after Clinton completed his term, then his affair with **Monica Lewinsky** would not have mattered, as he would not have had to testify as to his relationship with his White House intern during his term in office. The Court also upheld the **independent counsel law**.

To the surprise of many, the Supreme Court also agreed to hear arguments in *Bush* v. *Gore*, which dealt with the results of the vote in Florida in the presidential **election of 2000**, which, in turn, would determine who became president. **Al Gore** successfully challenged the vote in Florida state court. Wanting to stop a recount, **George W. Bush** appealed a series of decisions in the federal courts. Simply stated, the Supreme Court first stayed the Florida Supreme Court's decision to demand a recount and then, by a vote of 5–4, halted the recount. The manner by which the Court reached the decision and the narrowness of the vote appalled many. (Officially, the case was remanded back to the Florida courts, but no further recount was allowed.) With Chief Justice William Rehnquist writing the majority decision, the majority ruled that the Florida Supreme Court had violated the equal protection clause of the Fourteenth Amendment. Justices Stevens, Ginsburg, and Breyer wrote stinging dissents in the case. Numerous legal experts questioned the Court's reasoning. At the same time, the public was provided a unique personal glimpse of the Court in action—the audio of the oral arguments was released almost immediately. In some ways, this unique glimpse enraptured the public, even those who disagreed with the Court's verdict.

While the Supreme Court continued to drift in a conservative direction during Clinton's presidency, it simultaneously did not overturn or reverse the most controversial cases of the Warren Court (1953–1969) and Burger Court (1969–1986). Most important, the Rehnquist Court did not overturn the *Roe* v. *Wade* decision on abortion. While Rehnquist, Thomas, and Scalia hinted that they would vote to overturn the decision, the majority of the Court continued to uphold the right to an abortion. Somewhat similarly, in the case of *Adarand Constructors* v. *Peña* (1995), the Court significantly narrowed the reach of federal **affirmative-action** programs, ruling that they had to meet the rule of "strict scrutiny" and deal with the "lingering effects of racial discrimination" to be deemed constitutional, but it upheld the concept of affirmative action nonetheless. Furthermore, much to the displeasure of many conservatives, the Court issued a series of liberal rulings in a variety of First Amendment cases. In *Reno* v. *ACLU* (1997), the court struck down by a 7–2 vote parts of the 1996 telecommunications law that sought to prohibit "indecent" sites on the Internet. Congress and Clinton claimed that the law protected children from pornography, but the Court argued that the law was so broad it could have a chilling impact on free speech. Likewise, in *Romer* v. *Evans* (1996), the court ruled that an amendment to the Colorado constitution that prohibited the state from enacting laws that protected gays and lesbians from discrimination was unconstitutional.

Two other important areas of law that drew the Supreme Court's interest were voting rights and sexual harassment. The Court handed down several rulings that made it more difficult to create congressional districts favorable to minority candidates. In the cases of *Faragher* v. *City of Boca Raton* (1998) and *Burlington Industries, Inc.*, v. *Ellerth* (1998), the Court broadened laws against sexual harassment, holding employers responsible for the misconduct of their supervisors even if the employers did not know of the misconduct. At the same time, the ruling made it easier for employers to limit their liability by clarifying what was a proper sexual harassment policy.

Suggested Readings: Linda Greenhouse, "The Justices Decide Who's in Charge," *New York Times*, June 27, 1999, sec. 4, p. 1; "High Court Stays Its Conservative Course, *Congressional Quarterly Almanac*, 1993, p. 325; "1996 Supreme Court Decisions," *Congressional Quarterly Almanac*, 1996, p. 5-47; "1997 Supreme Court Decisions," *Congressional Quarterly Almanac*, 1997, p. 5-21; "Supreme Court Cautious, Pragmatic," *Congressional Quarterly Almanac*, 1994, p. 310; "Supreme Court on Internet Free Speech, June 26, 1997," *Historical Documents*, 1997, p. 290; "Supreme Court on Sexual Harassment, June 26, 1998," *Historic Documents*, 1998, p. 438.

Related Entry: Election of 2000.

SURPLUS, BUDGET. *See* **Budget, Federal.**

T

TALBOTT, NELSON STROBRIDGE (STROBE), III. (April 25, 1946, Dayton, Ohio– .) Ambassador-at-Large to the former Soviet republics, 1993–1994; Deputy Secretary of State, 1994–2001.

A close friend of Bill Clinton since their days together as Rhodes scholars in Oxford, England, Strobe Talbott played a key role in shaping the administration's **foreign policy**. Prior to Clinton's election, Talbott worked as a journalist for *Time* magazine. An expert on **Russia**, he served as ambassador-at-large to the former Soviet republics and special adviser to the secretary of state in 1993 and was promoted to deputy secretary of state, the second-highest post in the State Department, on February 23, 1994. Talbott's views of the world were sharply shaped by the **Vietnam** War, which he opposed. Many experts considered him a neo-Wilsonian who, along with National Security Adviser **Anthony Lake**, felt that the United States should pursue humanitarian ideals abroad.

Born in Dayton, Ohio, the son of an investment banker, Talbott attended Hotchkiss prep school in Connecticut and earned his B.A. from Yale University in 1968. Exhibiting a keen interest in Russia early on, he wrote his senior thesis on Russian poet Fyodor I. Tyuchev. After graduating from Yale, he spent three years at Oxford University on a Rhodes scholarship, where he roomed with Bill Clinton. Talbott spent part of his time in Russia furthering his study of the country. Upon completing his studies, Talbott went to work for *Time* magazine. His first appointment was as an intern at *Time*'s Moscow bureau. He rose to the posts of diplomatic correspondent, Washington bureau chief, and editor at large. He simultaneously wrote numerous books, including *Endgame: The Inside Story of SALT II* (1979), *Deadly Gambits: The Reagan Administration and the Stalemate in Nuclear Arms Control* (1984), *The Russians and*

Reagan (1984), and, with Michael R. Beschloss, *At the Highest Levels: The Inside Story of the End of the Cold War* (1993).

While Talbott was often critical of Ronald Reagan's hawkish stance toward the former Soviet Union, he had little trouble winning confirmation as ambassador. Talbott continued to write while working for the State Department; many of his articles appeared in leading magazines and newspapers, such as *Foreign Affairs, Foreign Policy*, and the *New York Review of Books*. Throughout Clinton's presidency, Talbott remained the administration's expert on Russia, often advising the president not to inflame the former Soviet Union. He opposed expanding **NATO** too rapidly and favored fostering an alliance with Russia. After **Madeleine Albright** became secretary of state and the United States adopted a more interventionist posture in the Balkans, tensions grew between the United States and Russia, which was suspicions about U.S. and European actions against Yugoslavia. Indeed, during the **Kosovo** war, Talbott worked with Russia's envoy and former Prime Minister Viktor Chernomyrdin to achieve an accord before the war drove the United States and Russia further apart.

Suggested Readings: Michael Clough, "The White Man Who Brings Diversity to Clinton's Foreign-Policy Team," *Los Angeles Times*, January 9, 1994, p. M2; William Hyland, *Clinton's World* (Westport, CT: Praeger, 1999); David Rosenbaum, "Crisis in the Balkans," *New York Times*, June 7, 1999, p. A11.

TAXES. *See* **Budget, Federal**; **Budget-Reconciliation Bills of 1997**; **Domestic Policy**.

TECHNOLOGY. *See* **High Technology**.

TENET, GEORGE JOHN. (January 5, 1953, New York, New York– .) Director of the Central Intelligence Agency (CIA), 1997– .

After serving as acting director of the Central Intelligence Agency (CIA) for over six months, George Tenet was formally sworn in as the director of the CIA in July 1997. He assumed leadership of a troubled agency that was struggling to overcome a series of espionage scandals and morale problems, the latter stemming in part from its search for a clear mission in the post–Cold War world. Tenet was nominated after **Anthony Lake**,

Clinton's national security adviser, withdrew his name from consideration in the face of opposition from key conservative senators.

Born in New York, Tenet earned his B.S. from the School of Foreign Service at Georgetown University in 1976 and his M.I.A. from the School of International Affairs at Columbia University in 1978. Shortly after graduating, he joined the staff of Pennsylvania senator John Heinz. In the mid- and later 1980s, he worked for the **Senate** Select Committee on Intelligence, serving as the staff director of this key committee under Senator David Boren of Oklahoma. As staff director, he coordinated all of the committee's oversight and legislative activities. This included overseeing historic arms-control negotiations between the Soviet Union and the United States. After Bill Clinton was elected president in 1992, Tenet served on Clinton's national security transition team and then on his National Security Council. He became the deputy director of the CIA in July 1996. Upon John Deutch's resignation as director of the CIA, Tenet became the acting director. Unlike his predecessors, Tenet enjoyed a relatively uncontroversial tenure as director of the CIA.

The most interesting development during Tenet's tenure as director of the CIA was the agency's increasing involvement in the **Middle East**. Traditionally seen as an agent of U.S. interests in the cold war, the CIA cast itself as a natural arbiter of disputes between Israel and Palestine. More precisely, the Clinton administration pushed Israel and Palestine to agree on peace plans that depended on outside and/or impartial verification. While the CIA did not have a history of playing this role, Tenet contended that the CIA was well suited to verify whether the agreements were being upheld. Journalist Douglas Waller even nicknamed Tenet the "diplo-spy," suggesting that Tenet was forging a new role for the CIA as an agent of espionage and diplomacy. Whether the CIA would prove able to play this role remained to be seen.

Suggested Readings: Neil King, Jr., "Top Man at CIA Becomes Visible as Peace Broker in Israeli Crisis," *Wall Street Journal*, Eastern edition, October 6, 2000, p. A19; Douglas Waller, "The Diplo-Spy," *Time*, October 23, 2000, p. 37.

Related Entry: Foreign Policy.

TERM LIMITS. During the 1990s, public discontent with the federal government produced a growing demand for term limits on members of Congress. Tapping into this discontent, the Republican Party's **"Contract with America"** called for a constitutional amendment to limit the terms of members of Congress to twelve consecutive years. In 1995, the **U.S. House of Representatives** voted 227–204 for such an amendment, 61 votes short of the two-thirds majority necessary to pass a constitutional amendment. Two years later, the vote was 217–211, even further short of the number needed to pass the amendment. In the interim, U.S. Term Limits, a group dedicated to the cause of passing such an amendment, sponsored nine separate statewide ballot initiatives in favor of adding term limits to the Constitution. Although the initiatives passed in all nine states, the U.S. **Supreme Court** let stand a lower-court decision that ruled that such statewide restrictions were unconstitutional because they violated Article 5 of the U.S. Constitution, which stated that constitutional amendments had to originate in either Congress or special constitutional conventions. Two years earlier, the U.S. Supreme Court had struck down state laws that sought to limit the terms of their congressional representatives. Ironically, the defeat of over thirty incumbents in the **election of 1994** lent weight to the argument that such an amendment was no longer necessary. In addition, as Republicans from the class of 1994, many of whom campaigned on the promise to limit terms, were reelected, they grew less enthusiastic about limiting their own terms. For example, in 1994, George Nethercutt upset Thomas Foley, the longtime Democratic congressman from the state of Washington and the Speaker of the House. One of Nethercutt's primary promises was that he, unlike Foley, would limit the time he remained in Washington, D.C. Like other advocates of term limits, Nethercutt implied that power had corrupted the nation's political leaders, who were out of touch with the desires of their constituents. In 1999, however, Nethercutt announced that he would run for a fourth consecutive term. Among the reasons he gave for reneging on his promise to resign after six years was that he still had work to finish. Nethercutt also stated that he no longer saw why "we need them [term limits]" (Rauch, "Is There an Excuse," p. 2579). He narrowly won reelection.

Suggested Readings: John Rauch, "Is There an Excuse for George Nethercutt?" *National Journal*, August 12, 2000, p. 2579; "Term Limits Amendment Falls Short," *Congressional Quarterly Almanac*, 1992, p. 1-35.

TERRORISM. The United States experienced numerous terrorist attacks during Bill Clinton's presidency. Some were committed by foreigners against U.S. facilities and citizens abroad; some were committed by foreigners against Americans living within the United States; but the most notorious act of terrorism of the era, the **Oklahoma City** bombing, was committed by a U.S. citizen against his fellow citizens. The U.S. government arrested and obtained convictions of many of the perpetrators of these terrorist attacks, although some of the alleged terrorists remained at large.

On February 26, 1993, a little over a month after President Clinton was inaugurated, a bomb exploded in the basement garage of the World Trade Center in New York City. The bomb killed 6, injured over 1,000, and terrified thousands more who were trapped in the skyscraper. Six Middle Eastern men were later convicted for this act of terrorism, which allegedly was committed to retaliate against U.S. support for Israel.

On April 19, 1995, a car bomb exploded outside a federal office building in Oklahoma City, Oklahoma. The bomb killed 168 people, including 19 children. It was the worst act of domestic terrorism in U.S. history. Shortly after the incident, Timothy McVeigh and Terry Nichols were arrested. While McVeigh did not testify at his trial, most assume that he sought to avenge the federal government's raid against the Branch Davidians in **Waco**, Texas, which took place exactly two years before the Oklahoma City bombing. He was sentenced to death.

On June 25, 1996, 19 American servicemen were killed and several hundred others were injured when the military housing complex in Dhahran, Saudi Arabia, was bombed. Following lengthy questioning by the FBI, the United States arrested Hani al-Sayegh for participating in the bombing, but U.S. District Court Judge Emmet Sullivan subsequently dropped charges against al-Sayegh on the grounds that he did not understand the plea agreement he had signed at the time of his arrest and that not enough evidence existed to prosecute him.

On July 27, 1996, a pipe bomb exploded at Centennial Olympic Park in Atlanta, Georgia, in the midst of the Summer Olympics. One woman, Alice Hawthorne, was killed, and 110 others were injured. The bombing dampened the festive spirits of the games, although the Olympic organizers refused to suspend the remaining events. The FBI originally suspected that Richard Jewell, a security guard who uncovered the bomb shortly before it went off, of committing the act of terrorism, but Jewell was later cleared. Subsequently, in the fall of 1998, the FBI accused Eric Robert Rudolph, one of the most wanted fugitives in the nation, of having committed the act of terrorism during the Olympic Games. Rudolph was already the lead suspect in the bombing of two abortion clinics, one in Atlanta and the other in Birmingham, Alabama, on January 29, 1998. He was also wanted for the bombing of the Otherside Lounge, a bar in Atlanta that attracted a large lesbian clientele. Despite a massive manhunt, Rudolph evaded federal authorities. Many suspected that he lived in the wild in the hills of North Carolina and enjoyed the support of some locals who saw him as an antigovernment and antiabortion renegade.

On August 7, 1998, bombs exploded at the U.S. embassies in Kenya and Tanzania, killing 190 people, including 8 Americans. The U.S. accused Islamic militant Osama bin Laden of orchestrating the attacks and responded by striking bin Laden's base in Afghanistan with cruise missiles. Several individuals of Middle Eastern descent were arrested and charged with conspiracy in relation to these two bombings and were extradited to the United States for trial. In late May 2001, all four suspects were found guilty and await sentencing.

On October 12, 2000, the warship USS *Cole* was attacked in Port Aden, Yemen, by suicide bombers who detonated their explosives-packed boat next to the ship as the *Cole* refueled in the harbor. The attack killed 17 and wounded 39 U.S. sailors. While a naval investigation cleared the commander of the USS *Cole* of any wrongdoing, the bombing prompted the military to reevaluate its security procedures, particularly in nations like Yemen that had a long history of harboring terrorists.

Suggested Readings: Beau Grosscup, *The Newest Explosions of Terrorism: Latest Sites of Terrorism in the 1990s and Beyond* (New York: New Horizon Press, 1998); "Patterns of Global Terrorism, 1999," http://www.state.gov/www/global/terrorism/1999report/1999index.html.

Related Entry: Crime.

THOMASES, SUSAN. Adviser to First Lady Hillary Clinton.

Susan Thomases, a partner at the New York law firm Wilkie Farr and Gallagher, had no official title at the White House, but as a longtime friend and adviser to Bill and **Hillary Clinton**, she gained a good deal of attention in the mid-1990s due to her answers, or lack thereof, to questions posed by a **Senate** banking committee investigation into the **Whitewater** affair. Republicans on New York senator Alfonse D'Amato's committee insinuated that Thomases, along with White House Deputy Chief of Staff **Harold Ickes** and Hillary Clinton's chief of staff **Margaret Williams**, had committed perjury when they testified that they could not recall numerous events in 1993 and 1994, particularly what happened in the wake of **Vincent Foster**'s death. White House spokespersons and Democrats on D'Amato's committee challenged these accusations, terming them election-year propaganda aimed at electing Senator **Robert Dole** president—D'Amato chaired Dole's campaign. Ultimately, independent counsel **Kenneth Starr** chose not to indict Thomases, Ickes, or Williams.

Susan Thomases grew up in Englewood, New Jersey. She first met Hillary Clinton in the fall of 1974 while she was helping Bill Clinton in his unsuccessful run for Congress. Prior to their meeting, Thomases had worked for various liberal causes, including Eugene McCarthy's 1968 campaign for the Democratic presidential nomination and George McGovern's 1972 presidential bid. Thomases had met Bill Clinton in 1970. Thomases and Hillary Clinton found that they shared much in common, including a penchant for liberal politics and similar backgrounds. When Thomases earned her law degree from Columbia University and went to work as a corporate lawyer, she found that she had even more in common with the future first lady, and they remained close. Hillary Clinton recommended Thomases for the board of directors of the Children's Defense Fund. In 1992, Thomases went to work for the Clinton campaign, first as a part-time adviser and then full-time in charge of scheduling. After Clinton's election, she stayed in Little Rock to participate on Clinton's transition team. Even though several of Clinton's aides found her tactless, she could have had a top post in the Clinton administration, but she chose to remain in the private sector as an unofficial adviser.

In the latter part of the 1990s, after the dispute over her testimony passed, her name continued to surface regarding other matters connected to the Clintons. Some credited her with initiating the Million Moms March, a demonstration that took place on Mother's Day 2000, largely to show support for **gun control** and other goals of the Clinton administration. In fact, Thomases's sister-in-law, Donna Dees-Thomases, was the leading organizer of the march. Thomases also helped Hillary Clinton in her successful run for the U.S. Senate in the **election of 2000**.

Suggested Readings: Lloyd Grove, "The Clintons' Bad Cop," *Washington Post*, March 2, 1993, p. E1; Martin Walker, "Net Closes In on First Lady," *Guardian*, June 12, 1996, p. 2.

Related Entry: Election of 1992.

TORT REFORM. For over a decade, conservatives argued that American businesses were hurt by unnecessary civil suits and exorbitant penalties. Such litigation, conservatives contended, added to the cost of insurance, stifled innovation, and ultimately hurt consumers. To rectify this situation, the Republican Party pledged in its **"Contract with America"** to reform the nation's tort laws. Democrats, by and large, opposed such efforts, arguing that suits and the threat of litigation acted as one of the few protections afforded consumers in their relations with corporations. In March 1995, the Republican-controlled **House of Representatives** passed sweeping tort reform that significantly limited punitive-damage awards. This included limits on penalties in medical-malpractice and product-liability cases. In the **U.S. Senate**, however, conservatives proved less successful in passing such sweeping legislation. Unable to break a filibuster over the House proposal, the Senate settled for a bill that limited damages in product-liability suits alone.

Senate and House members did not work out a bill acceptable to both houses until the following year, at which time they settled for a bill much like the one passed by the Senate the year before. Even though President Bill Clinton threatened to veto the bill, it was passed by both houses of Congress, largely along party lines. Senator **Robert Dole** pushed hard for passing the bill even though he believed that Clinton would veto it, calculating that he and the Republicans could use it effectively as a political issue in the upcoming presidential campaign. Clinton vetoed the bill, nonetheless. The House of Representatives voted 258–163 to override President Clinton's veto, short of the necessary two-thirds majority. During the presidential campaign, Republican nominee Bob Dole pursued the issue, but largely without great effect.

During his second term as president, Clinton continued to oppose broad federal tort reform. However, he did sign a bill that set a limit on the liability that companies faced stemming from the so-called Y2K problem. Many predicted that computers would have great difficulty recognizing the year 2000 in their data bases, producing mass problems. Since few computers crashed at the beginning of the new millennium, the impact of the bill that Clinton signed was minimal.

Suggested Readings: Mark Hofman, "Clinton Cool to Tort Reform," *Business Insurance*, July 26, 1999, p. 3; "House Sustains Product Liability Veto," *Congressional Quarterly Almanac*, 1996, p. 3-9; Bob Van Voris, "Clinton's a Surprising Tort Reformer," *National Law Journal*, August 14, 2000, p. A1.

Related Entry: Deregulation.

TRADE DEFICIT. While nearly all economic indicators documented the exceptional performance of the **economy** during Bill Clinton's presi-

Table 17
Merchandise Trade Deficit (in Billions of Dollars)

	1990	1995	1997	1998	1999
Exports	394	585	689	682	695
Imports	495	743	871	912	1,025
Trade balance	−102	−159	−182	−230	−330

Source: Statistical Abstract of the United States, 2000; Economic Report of the President, 2001.

dency, one lingering concern was the trade deficit. Month after month and year after year, the federal government announced new record trade deficits. For instance, in the summer of 1999, the trade deficit reached $24.6 billion, up from $21.2 billion the month before. The annual trade deficit skyrocketed to over $330 billion (Table 17). This represented a 40 percent rise from the year before. Critics warned that these record trade deficits would ultimately end the economic expansion and reduce Americans' standard of living. Yet other economists observed that these absolute numbers overstated the problem. The trade deficit as a percentage of the gross domestic product actually declined in the 1990s. Increasing trade deficits, many economists added, displayed the relative strength of the American economy and the confidence of American consumers. As the Clinton presidency drew to a close, however, worries about growing trade deficits increased, in part due to the swelling dependence of America on foreign oil, whose price escalated in the later years of the decade. During the 1970s, increasing energy costs had contributed to the nation's economic difficulties. During much of the 1980s and 1990s, the United States had benefited from cheap oil prices (in real terms). The prospect of a renewed episode of energy price hikes thus concerned economists and consumers alike. In the first nine months of 2000, the United States imported nearly $80 billion worth of petroleum, compared to about $40 billion worth of petroleum products a year earlier. Republican presidential candidate **George W. Bush** tapped into these fears by arguing that the Clinton-Gore administration had no energy policy and had allowed the United States to become increasingly dependent on foreign oil. Gore responded weakly to these charges, shifting the debate to Bush's ties to "big oil" and away from the efforts, or lack thereof, of the Clinton administration to reduce energy consumption. Whether energy price hikes combined with ballooning trade deficits would end the economic expansion, however, remained to be seen.

Suggested Readings: http://www.census.gov/foreign-trade/www/press.html; John B. Judis, "Out of Commission: Clinton Ducks the Trade Deficit," *New Republic*, April 14, 1997, p. 14; *Statistical Abstract of the United States, 2000* (Washington, DC: GPO, 2000).

TRAVELGATE. One of the first scandals to plague the Clinton administration was "travelgate." This scandal involved the firing of employees of the White House travel office. Like many of the other scandals of the Clinton years, this one produced no criminal convictions of any top White House officials, nor did it lead to any charges against the president or First Lady **Hillary Clinton**. Nonetheless, travelgate helped set the tone of the Clinton presidency, displaying the drive of Clinton's adversaries to damage his presidency and the administration's tendency to obfuscate rather than admit any possible wrongdoing.

On May 19, 1993, White House Press Secretary **Dee Dee Myers** announced that seven longtime employees of the White House travel office had been fired because of "financial mismanagement" and "shoddy accounting procedures." One of those fired was Billy Dale, a thirty-year veteran of the office who was responsible for arranging the travel details of the president and his entourage. Dale was replaced by Catherine Cornelius, Clinton's twenty-five-year-old cousin. Noting that Cornelius had coordinated the travel plans of the Clinton campaign, Myers stated that her hiring did not signify nepotism by the president. Myers did not note, however, that all seven employees of the travel office had been fired without a hearing nor that those who would take over the duties of the travel office were close friends of the Clintons and contributors to Bill Clinton's presidential campaign.

Although the administration had the legal right to replace the travel-office employees, the incident gained notoriety for several reasons. Not long after the firing, reporters revealed that Harry Thomason, a friend of the Clintons and a leading supporter of Bill Clinton's campaign, had initiated the move to fire the seven travel-office employees and had instigated the rumor that the office was corrupt. Later reports revealed that Hillary Clinton and her top aide, David Watkins, had played a key role in replacing the seven employees. Rather than admit that they might have acted improperly, Hillary Clinton and other White House officials countered that the travel-office employees, not the White House, were in the wrong. After reporters began to investigate the firing, **Vincent Foster** was put in charge of damage control. His suicide death further left a cloud over the firings.

In time, the independent counsel's office and several congressional committees investigated travelgate. None of these investigations uncovered any criminal action on Hillary Clinton's part. The House Government Oversight and Reform Committee, led by its chairman, Congressman William Clinger, a Republican from Pennsylvania, which spent nearly two years investigating the matter, concluded that the Clintons, on the urging of Hollywood producer Harry Thomason, ordered the travel workers fired in 1993 so that the president could reward his cronies. The committee report, which only its Republican members endorsed, further charged the White House with "a colossal damage-control effort." Still, Clinger's committee did not uncover evidence that could lead to criminal charges. Similarly, in the summer of 2000, independent counsel **Robert Ray** concluded that there was not enough evidence to file charges against either Bill or Hillary Clinton for obstruction of justice. Ray argued that Hillary Clinton had played "a role" in the affair by influencing David Watkins to fire the employees and not fully cooperating with efforts to uncover the history of the matter. However, like investigators before him, Ray did not determine that the first lady had broken the law.

Suggested Readings: Angie Cannon, "Travelgate: No Charges," *U.S. News & World Report*, July 3, 2000; Elizabeth Drew, *On the Edge: The Clinton Presidency* (New York: Simon & Schuster, 1994), pp. 174–181; Jeffrey Toobin, *A Vast Conspiracy* (New York: Random House, 1999).

TRIANGULATION. *See* **Morris, Dick**.

TRIPP, LINDA R. (1950, Whippany, New Jersey– .) Key Player in the Monica Lewinsky scandal.

Until January 1998, Linda Tripp was an obscure public affairs specialist at the Pentagon. Overnight she gained fame and notoriety, or infamy, depending on one's perspective, by providing independent counsel **Kenneth Starr** with tapes she had made of telephone conversations she had had with **Monica Lewinsky**. These tapes seemed to reveal that Lewinsky had engaged in a sexual relationship with President Bill Clinton and suggested that the two had sought to cover up their relationship. To confirm the information on the tapes, Starr arranged for Tripp to meet Lewinsky at a hotel bar and wired Tripp with a secret microphone to record further evidence of Lewinsky's and Clinton's dalliance and cover-up. On January 16, 1998, four days after first meeting with Starr, Tripp met with **Paula**

Linda Tripp.
January 22, 1998.
AP/Wide World Photos.

Jones's lawyers, who were on the eve of deposing President Clinton in regard to Jones's sexual harassment suit against the president. Information Tripp provided to Jones's lawyers allowed them to ask detailed questions about his relationship with Lewinsky. In turn, Clinton's responses to these questions provided the basis for the perjury counts against him and to a large extent the charges of obstruction of justice that led to his **impeachment**.

On January 21, 1998, reports of Clinton's alleged affair with Lewinsky broke in the press. Henceforth, as the story unfolded, Tripp became the target of extreme scrutiny and curiosity. Born Linda Carotenuto in Whippany, New Jersey, in 1950, Tripp suffered through her parents' painful divorce as a teen. After attending secretarial school at a Katherine Gibbs school in Montclair, she married Bruce Tripp, a career army man. For twenty years, she traveled from post to post with her husband, bearing two children and working at a variety of jobs. In 1991, she gained temporary employment in the secretarial pool at the White House, at the time occupied by **George Bush**. In 1992, she divorced her husband and kept working at the White House. When Clinton became president, she landed a position in the office of the White House counsel. Tripp found the atmosphere of the Clinton White House to her disliking. Before she met Lewinsky, Tripp contacted **Lucianne Goldberg**, a literary agent, in the summer of 1996 to discuss the possibility of writing a kiss-and-tell exposé on the Clinton White House. While Tripp chose not to go forward with this project, she provided *Newsweek* reporter Michael Isikoff with information that seemed to confirm a rumor that Clinton had "groped" **Kathleen Willey**, a White House volunteer, in 1993. At about the same time, Tripp suggested that Isikoff should investigate the president's relationship with an unnamed intern.

Tripp took detailed notes of her conversations with Lewinsky and, in October 1997, began secretly recording their telephone conversations. Tripp later testified that she taped the conversations to protect herself, even suggesting that she feared for her own safety and that Clinton and/or his aides had a reputation for dealing roughly with their adversaries, but many suggested that Tripp had other motives, noting her desire to publish a book on sex in the White House. Indeed, in August 1994, over a year before Lewinsky's and Clinton's first encounter, Tripp was transferred, against her desire, to the Pentagon. Even though she received a hefty pay raise as a "public affairs specialist," she remained unhappy. Tripp even complained that she had been forced out of the White House because she knew too much about the **Whitewater** scandal and because she had questioned the official story about what had happened to **Vincent Foster**. Ironically, because she was a political appointee, Lloyd Cutler had no responsibility to find her a new job when he arrived as the new White House counsel in 1994 with his own personal secretary, but sympathetic with Tripp's plight as a divorced mother of two, he helped her gain employment at the Pentagon. At the Pentagon, Tripp met Lewinsky, who, like Tripp, had been moved there from the White House. Tripp befriended Lewinsky, who soon began to tell Tripp about a relationship she was having with a "married man" in the White House.

In the midst of the scandal, Maryland State Prosecutor Stephen Montanarelli launched a grand-jury probe into whether Tripp had violated Maryland state wiretapping laws that prohibited taping a phone conversation without the knowledge of all parties. Conservatives rallied behind Tripp, citing Montanarelli's probe as proof of the heavy-handedness of

Clinton and his supporters. Liberals, in contrast, criticized the hypocrisy of conservatives, who insisted on impeaching the president because of his alleged perjury in Jones's sexual harassment suit but simultaneously dismissed Montanarelli's probe as overkill. After the **U.S. Senate** acquitted Clinton on impeachment charges, Montanarelli indicted Tripp. Even though investigators showed that Tripp had been informed that it was illegal to tape a phone conversation without the other party's knowledge, in the wake of several unfavorable pretrial rulings, all charges were dropped against her. On January 19, 2001, Tripp was fired from her job at the Pentagon. While conservatives cried foul, as a political appointee, she was supposed to tender her resignation, as did all political appointees in the final days of Clinton's presidency. When she did not, her boss at the Pentagon terminated her employment.

Suggested Readings: "Key Player: Linda Tripp," http://www.washingtonpost.com/wp-srv/politics/special/clinton/players/tripp.htm; Richard A. Posner, *An Affair of State* (Cambridge, MA: Harvard University Press, 1999); Elaine Sciolino and Don Van Nutta, Jr., "Testing of a President: The Confidant," *New York Times*, March 15, 1998, p. 1; Jeffrey Toobin, *A Vast Conspiracy* (New York: Random House, 1999).

TSONGAS, PAUL. (February 14, 1941, Lowell, Massachusetts–January 18, 1997, Boston, Massachusetts.) U.S. Senator, 1979–1985; Candidate for Democratic presidential nomination, 1992.

During the 1992 presidential campaign, Paul Tsongas, a former senator and congressman from Massachusetts, posed the most serious threat to Bill Clinton's quest for the Democratic nomination. Running somewhat as an antipolitician, Tsongas advocated relatively un-Democratic or anti-liberal solutions to the nation's economic woes. In particular, he opposed a middle-class tax cut, one of Clinton's promises, favored cutting the capital-gains tax rate, a Republican goal, and emphasized the need to cut the federal **budget** deficit. Unlike most Republican candidates, however, Tsongas was a liberal on most social issues. After winning the New Hampshire primary, Tsongas found it difficult to compete with Clinton in the South and lost in several big-state primaries to the former Arkansas governor. Having recently recovered from lymphatic cancer, he had difficulty matching Clinton's energy. Moreover, his relatively dry style was no match for Clinton's charm. Tsongas ultimately endorsed Clinton for president over **George Bush** or **H. Ross Perot**.

After the general election, Tsongas joined with former Republican New

Hampshire senator Warren Rudman to form the Concord Coalition, which developed proposals for cutting the federal budget deficit. In many ways, Clinton adopted Tsongas's priorities. Rather than implementing a tax cut, he focussed on cutting the deficit and agreed to cut the capital-gains tax. In addition to campaigning for deficit reduction, Tsongas fought to bring minor-league baseball and hockey back to his hometown of Lowell, Massachusetts. He died of pneumonia, stemming from his ongoing battle with cancer, in 1997.

Suggested Readings: "Obituary: Paul Tsongas," *Boston Globe*, January 20, 1997, p. B4; Paul Tsongas, *Journey of Purpose* (New Haven, CT: Yale University Press, 1995).

Related Entries: Domestic Policy; Election of 1992.

TUCKER, JIM GUY. (June 13, 1943, Oklahoma City, Oklahoma– .) Governor of Arkansas, 1992–1996; Whitewater defendant.

On July 15, 1996, Arkansas governor Jim Guy Tucker resigned in the face of his conviction on fraud and conspiracy charges. He was convicted of fraud and conspiracy along with **Susan McDougal**, one of the Clintons' partners in the original **Whitewater** development investment. Tucker served eighteen months of home detention. Subsequently, in the face of a separate charge, in exchange for a promise of immunity against further prosecution, he agreed to cooperate with independent counsel **Kenneth Starr**'s Whitewater investigation. Twice he testified before the Whitewater grand jury in Little Rock, Arkansas. The value of his testimony, however, was problematic, and it did not lead to the indictment of either President Bill Clinton or **Hillary Clinton**.

Ironically, Tucker and Clinton had vied for the Democratic nomination for governor of Arkansas in 1982. Tucker, a congressman, attacked Governor Clinton's record on **crime** in 1979–1981. Clinton countered that Tucker was a tool of labor and an opponent of food stamps. On primary day, Clinton won the plurality of votes, with Tucker finishing third behind the lesser-known Joe Purcell. After Clinton defeated Purcell in the Democratic runoff, he went on to beat Frank White in the general election. Tucker successfully ran for governor in 1992, replacing Governor Clinton, who was focussing on winning the presidency.

Suggested Readings: Steve Barnes, "Arkansas Governor Resigns after Furor," *New York Times*, July 16, 1996, p. A10; "Jim Guy Tucker Makes Second Appearance before Whitewater Grand Jury," http://www.nando.net/newsroom/nt/421tucker.

html; Susan Schmidt, "Ex-Governor to Cooperate with Starr," *Washington Post*, February 21, 1998, p. A1.

TYSON, LAURA D'ANDREA. (June 28, 1947, Bayonne, New Jersey– .) Chair, Council of Economic Advisers, 1993–1995; Director, National Economic Council, 1995–1996.

Laura D'Andrea Tyson, who first came to Bill Clinton's attention during his 1992 campaign for the presidency, played a key role in shaping the administration's economic policy. After the election, Clinton appointed her chair of the Council of Economic Advisers, and in 1995 she was promoted to the post of director of the **National Economic Council**. She resigned from the government and returned to her teaching job at the University of California at Berkeley after Clinton was reelected in 1996. At that time, she could take pride in the steady expansion of the **economy**, which she, along with several of Clinton's other key advisers, helped bring about.

Born in Bayonne, New Jersey, Tyson earned her B.A. from Smith College in 1969 and her Ph.D. in economics from Massachusetts Institute of Technology in 1974. After a brief period as an economist at the World Bank, she accepted a teaching position at Princeton University. In 1978, she moved to the University of California at Berkeley, rising to the position of full professor in 1988. Upon an invitation by Bill Clinton's longtime friend **Robert Reich**, she attended an economic summit in Little Rock, Arkansas, in the summer of 1992, where she met Bill Clinton. Tyson caught his ear by arguing in favor of something akin to **Robert Reich**'s national industrial policy. Clinton was also impressed by her ability to express complicated economic ideas simply and forcefully.

As chair of the Council of Economic Advisers and director of the National Economic Council, Tyson called upon Clinton to retreat from his promise of cutting the deficit in half by 1997, arguing that such a drastic cut would jeopardize the economy's recovery. She also promoted the president's economic stimulus package, which Congress did not enact. At the same time, Tyson proved more fiscally conservative than many in the administration when it came to the proposed **health care reform** package, which Tyson estimated would prove more costly than First Lady **Hillary Clinton** admitted. Nonetheless, Tyson and Clinton remained close. Perhaps most important, Tyson battled with the Republican-controlled Congress in 1995 over how best to balance the federal **budget**, stridently opposing tax cuts at the expense of Medicare and Medicaid. As she observed, the administration had achieved deficit reduction without drastically cutting entitlement programs. When Republicans countered that they favored a freeze, not a cut, she explained how a freeze actually reduced benefits to recipients.

Suggested Readings: Keith Bradsher, "In the Line of Fire," *New York Times*, July 7, 1995, p. D1; *Current Biography Yearbook*, 1996, p. 595; Susan Dentzer, "Laura D'Andrea Tyson," *Working Woman*, August 1993, p. 30.

Related Entry: Domestic Policy.

U

UNFUNDED MANDATES. Part of the Republican Party's **"Contract with America"** was a pledge to curb the power of the federal government by limiting its ability to enact regulations without providing the funds to pay for these regulations. Republicans lived up to this pledge by passing the Unfunded Mandate Act of 1995. Indeed, the act was one of the first to be passed by the Republican-controlled **U.S. House of Representatives** and **U.S. Senate**. The measure made all unfunded costs over $50 million to state and local governments subject to specific procedural rules that could only be overridden by a majority of voting members in the House and Senate. While President Bill Clinton opposed many of the goals of the "Contract with America," he signaled that he would support the unfunded-mandate measure in his 1995 State of the Union Address. Clinton understood that broad support for such a measure existed. For instance, in 1994, the National Conference of Mayors and the National Association of Counties had endorsed the concept of an unfunded-mandate bill. Hence, on March 22, 1995, at a ceremony attended by numerous governors and mayors, Republicans and Democrats, many of whom had long complained about the ability of the federal government to compel state and local governments to pay for programs without funding them, President Clinton signed the act. At the time, Senator Robert Byrd of West Virginia remarked that it would be very difficult to determine the ultimate impact of the measure. Five years later, it was still quite difficult to decide what it had been, since many existing mandates were exempted by the new law. In addition, complex court decisions narrowed the reach of the law that Congress passed in 1995.

Suggested Readings: Theresa A. Gullo and Janet M. Kelly, "Federally Unfunded Mandate Reforms: A First-Year Retrospective," *Public Administration Review* 58:

5 (September/October 1998), p. 379; "Clinton on Unfunded Mandates Legislation, March 22, 1995," *Historic Documents*, 1995, p. 141; "Law Restricts Unfunded Mandates," *Congressional Quarterly Almanac*, 1995, p. 3-15.

Related Entry: Deregulation.

V

VIETNAM. Following the **election of 2000**, President Bill Clinton made a historic three-day trip to Vietnam, becoming the first U.S. president to visit the country since the end of the Vietnam War. Clinton's visit, which was highlighted by stops in Hanoi and Ho Chi Minh City (formerly Saigon), marked the culmination of his administration's policy of normalizing relations with the United States' onetime foe. In 1995, the Clinton administration reestablished diplomatic relations with Vietnam. The administration also negotiated bilateral trade agreements with Vietnam and rescinded travel restrictions to the region. Even though Congress did not endorse the trade agreements, few doubted that barriers between the two nations were disappearing. The two most important remaining obstacles to fully normalizing relations were U.S. allegations of human rights violations in Vietnam and demands for more cooperation in finding the remains of U.S. servicemen and soldiers still missing in action (MIAs). Steady progress toward overcoming both of these concerns allowed Clinton to travel to Vietnam with little protest by veterans' groups or conservatives in the United States. Ironically, Clinton's historic visit to Vietnam received little attention in the United States because the public was consumed with the ongoing dispute over who had won the presidential election. Clinton's stop in Hanoi had to share headlines with the battle over whether or not to recount the votes in Florida and, as a result, tended to get crowded out of the headline news.

Vietnam figured in the Clinton presidency in one other way. During the 1992 and 1996 presidential campaigns, opponents of Clinton sought to discredit his credentials as a leader by arguing that he had dodged the draft during the Vietnam War. Investigative reporting suggested that Clinton had manipulated the system to avoid service. The fact that both President **George Bush** and Senator **Robert Dole** were World War II veterans made Clinton's lack of military service and his criticism of the Vietnam War a liability, particularly among conservatives. Clinton's defenders argued that the comparison was unfair, noting that many of his opponents who were similar in age likewise had not served in Vietnam. For instance, **Dan Quayle** had served in the National Guard. During the 2000 presidential campaign, Vice President **Al Gore** sought to contrast his military service in Vietnam to **George W. Bush**'s record. The Texas governor and son of President George Bush had served in the Air National Guard. Yet Gore gained little political capital from Bush's record on Vietnam, showing that Vietnam was a much less controversial issue in 2000 than it had been in 1992.

Suggested Readings: "Bringing Closure to Vietnam," *Chicago Tribune*, November 16, 2000; "Old Foes, New Fans: In Vietnam, Clinton Finds That the Postwar Generation Has a Crush on America," *Newsweek*, November 27, 2000, p. 50; "Success in Indochina," *Washington Post*, November 21, 2000, p. 41.

W

WACO. In the early months of Bill Clinton's presidency, the nation was gripped by a showdown between federal forces and members of the Branch Davidians, a religious cult in Waco, Texas. A splinter group of Seventh-Day Adventists, the Davidians, under the lead of David Koresh, readied themselves for the apocalypse at their compound, which they called Ranch Apocalypse. Based upon reports that the Davidians were accumulating illegal weapons, the U.S. Bureau of Alcohol, Tobacco, and Firearms (ATF) sought to execute a search of the premises on February 28, 1993. Viewing the ATF's search as a sign of an impending apocalyptic assault, the Davidians repelled the ATF agents by force. Four ATF agents were killed and sixteen were wounded in the skirmish, as well as an unknown number of Branch Davidians.

For the next fifty-one days, federal authorities laid siege to the Branch Davidians' complex in Waco. Special FBI agents sought to convince the heavily armed cult members to turn themselves in peacefully. The media encircled the camp, allowing the nation to follow the showdown. On April 19, 1993, the siege came to a tragic end when FBI agents in armored vehicles rushed the compound and fired tear gas into it. A fire erupted that quickly spread through the edifice, burning Koresh and 79 others, including women and children. Many Americans, particularly conservatives, viewed the attack with alarm. Some cast it as proof of the ineptitude of the Clinton administration, the callousness of liberals toward the religious right, and the dangers of a powerful federal government. Attorney General **Janet Reno** defended the actions of federal agents, adding that she would not have "approved the plan" had she known that it would end in a mass suicide.

Over the course of the rest of Clinton's presidency, the Waco incident remained a bone of contention between Clinton and conservatives. In

The Branch Davidian compound near Waco, Texas, April 9, 1993. AP/Wide World Photos.

1995, two subcommittees of the House Judiciary Committee convened hearings into the raid. Conservative Florida congressman Bill McCollum, who would later play a leading role in the **impeachment** of President Clinton, declared, "Until we learn the truth and restore accountability to government, we cannot begin to rebuild faith in federal law enforcement." (*CQ Almanac*, 1995, p. 6-33). McCollum conceded that the FBI had not broken the law, but he suggested that the administration had been in the wrong. Subsequently, the Justice Department conducted a special investigation into the affair. Its investigation suggested that the FBI had not been forthcoming with its own representation of what had taken place the day of the raid. Yet, in a strange twist, in the waning days of the Clinton presidency, a conservative federal prosecutor, who had claimed that the FBI had covered up its actions, was himself accused of covering up his own negligence in the case. In other words, he had allegedly cast aspersions on the FBI to evade closer inspection of his own actions.

Suggested Readings: "Hearings Probe 1993 Waco Siege," *Congressional Quarterly Almanac*, 1995, p. 6-33; "Clinton on Deadly Attack on Armed Cult Compound, April 20, 1993," *Historic Documents*, 1993, p. 293; http://www.pbs.org/wgbh/ pages/frontline/waco/; Dick J. Reavis, *The Ashes of Waco* (Syracuse, NY: Syracuse University Press, 1998); Stuart A. Wright, ed., *Armageddon in Waco* (Chicago: University of Chicago Press, 1995).

WELFARE REFORM. In 1992, Bill Clinton pledged to "end welfare as we know it" if he were elected president. This promise was central to his characterization of himself as a "New Democrat." During the first two years of his presidency, he did not push Congress to fulfill this pledge, focussing instead on **health care reform** and other issues. After the Republicans took control of both houses of Congress in the **election of 1994**, welfare reform once again became a prominent issue. The Republicans' **"Contract with America"** contained a promise to radically change welfare. The 1995 Republican **budget**-cutting package included welfare-reform provisions. In December 1995, Clinton vetoed the Republican proposal, arguing that it was too harsh. However, in his January 1996 State of the Union Address, President Clinton reaffirmed his desire to reform welfare as long as Congress proved willing to accommodate his specific criticisms of the Republicans' earlier proposal.

Through much of the spring of 1996, it appeared that Congress and the president would not reach an agreement on welfare reform. Republicans remained committed to simultaneously reforming welfare and Medicaid, while President Clinton insisted that he would sign only a more narrowly tailored welfare-reform bill. Believing that the public desired welfare reform, **Robert Dole**, who was the **Senate** majority leader and the odds-on favorite to win the Republican nomination for president, seemed to relish another Clinton veto.

Much to the surprise of many, the deadlock over welfare changed rapidly in the summer of 1996. Republican leaders in the **U.S. House of Representatives**, chastened by the **government shutdown** and public reaction to it, suggested that they would pass a bill that the president could sign. After Dole resigned his Senate leadership post to commit his full attention to the presidential campaign, his replacement, **Trent Lott**, helped work a welfare-reform bill through the upper house. Although he objected to some of the bill's provisions, President Clinton pledged to sign the bill, a pledge he kept on August 22, 1996.

The welfare-reform bill ended the sixty-one-year guarantee of federal aid to all families with dependent children. In its place, the federal gov-

WELFARE REFORM 363

ernment agreed to provide block grants to the states that they could use with broad discretion. Already the federal government had allowed several states to experiment with welfare reform. Such block grants, however, came with two key restrictions aimed at cutting, not insuring, benefits. Specifically, adult recipients of welfare funded by the federal government would have to obtain employment within two years, and recipients were limited to a total of five years of welfare. Proponents of these provisions contended that they were necessary to end the cycle of dependency that existing programs allegedly created. President Clinton objected to a third specific restriction, one that prohibited providing welfare to immigrants who were legally in the United States, but he signed the bill nonetheless, pledging to undo this provision in the future.

Even before the 1996 welfare-reform bill was enacted, welfare caseloads had begun to decline, particularly in states that had been granted waivers by the federal government and had been allowed to experiment with the delivery of aid. In the years after the welfare-reform bill was passed, the number of Americans who received aid dropped significantly, allowing both Republicans and President Clinton to take credit for the reduction in the welfare rolls. In August 2000, the administration announced that welfare caseloads had fallen to a thirty-five-year low. In January 1993, 14.1 million Americans received welfare; as of December 1999, 6.3 million did. During the same time period, the administration proclaimed that initiatives to move people from welfare to work had been very effective. The administration added that its support for health and child care and an expansion of the earned-income tax credit contributed to the success of welfare reform.

Critics of welfare reform argued that the Republican-sponsored measure would punish millions of children who through no fault of their own were born into **poverty**. Conservative proponents of the measures countered that welfare reform would encourage behavior that in the long run would reduce the risk of becoming poor. While the decline of the welfare rolls suggested that the conservatives judged the situation more accurately, a number of experts argued that only time will tell exactly who was right. Much of the reduction of the welfare rolls, they observed, was due to the expansion of the **economy**, which created a much tighter job market than had existed in the 1970s and 1980s. This tight job market produced millions of new jobs and an upward pressure on wages. However, they warned, a downturn in the economy could quickly undo the gains made in the latter half of the 1990s. Many also acknowledged that it would become much more difficult to move the approximately 6 million individuals who remained on welfare than it had been to move others off the welfare rolls because those who continued to draw welfare were the least educated and skilled and thus the most difficult to place in the job market.

Suggested Readings: "After 60 years, Most Control Sent to States," *Congressional Quarterly Almanac*, 1996, p. 6-3; "Clinton Says Welfare Bill Is a 'Real Step Forward,'" *Congressional Quarterly Weekly Report*, August 3, 1996, p. 2216; Jason De Parle and Steven A. Holmes, "A War on Poverty Subtly Linked to Race," *New York Times*, December 26, 2000, p. A1; "Fact Sheet on Welfare Reform," August 22, 2000, http://*Historic Documents*, 1996, p. 450; Mary Ellen Hombs, *Welfare Reform* (Santa Barbara, CA: ABC-Clio, 1996); Jack A. Meyer, "Assessing Welfare Reform: Work Pays," *Public Interest* 136 (Summer 1999), p. 8; Robert Reich, "Working Principles," *American Prospect*, June 19, 2000, p. 21.

WHITE HOUSE DEFENSE TEAM (DALE BUMPERS, GREGORY CRAIG, DAVID KENDALL, CHERYL MILLS, CHARLES RUFF, AND NICOLE SELIGMAN).

During the **House** Judiciary Committee hearings on impeaching the president and even more prominently during the trial phase of the **impeachment** process in the **U.S. Senate**, President Bill Clinton was represented by a team of lawyers, most prominently Dale Bumpers, Gregory Craig, **David Kendall**, Cheryl Mills, and Charles Ruff. Several other attorneys, including his private attorney, Nicole Seligman, and Deputy White House Counsel **Bruce Lindsey**, also helped present his defense against the House impeachment charges. A brief description of each as well as the role they played follows.

Dale Bumpers, a longtime friend and mentor of Bill Clinton, was a senator from the state of Arkansas from 1975 to 1998. Prior to becoming senator, he had been governor of Arkansas. In a populist style, Bumpers delivered an emotional closing address that summarized the case for not convicting the president.

Gregory Craig had about twenty-five years of experience as an attorney in Washington, D.C. He had served as a Senate staff member and had been a partner at the prominent firm of Williams and Connelly. Prior to joining Clinton's defense team, he held a post with the State Department as director of policy planning.

David Kendall represented Clinton as his private attorney for over four years, during the bulk of independent counsel **Kenneth Starr**'s **Whitewater** investigation. Like Craig, Kendall was a partner at Williams and Connelly. Until 1998, Kendall largely avoided the public limelight. He first met Clinton and his wife while he was a law student at Yale Law School.

Cheryl D. Mills, who served as deputy White House counsel during most of the Whitewater investigation, was, like Kendall, not widely known until the Senate trial. As a relatively young, **African American**, female attorney, she made a strong impression on the public with her staunch defense of the president. (The thirteen House prosecutors were all white men.) A graduate of the University of Virginia and Stanford Law School, Mills worked briefly for the Washington, D.C. firm of Hogan and Hartson before joining Clinton's transition team. After the impeachment process was completed, Mills turned down a chance to become Clinton's chief legal counsel to work in the private sector.

Charles Ruff defended President Clinton from a wheelchair, to which he had been confined by a poliolike affliction. Ruff was the most experienced of Clinton's attorneys, having served as the chief Watergate prosecutor and having defended numerous politicians in other high-profile cases. Ruff took over the White House counsel position from Jack Quinn in January 1997. He presented the opening statement during the Senate trial in the impeachment process.

Nicole Seligman, the least known of Clinton's defense team, clerked for **Supreme Court** Justice Thurgood Marshall and was also a partner at Williams and Connolly. Seligman had a great deal of experience as a criminal defense lawyer in Washington, D.C., having defended Oliver L. North from charges stemming from the Iran-Contra case.

Suggested Readings: http://washingtonpost.com/wp-srv/politics/special/clinton/ defense.htm; Robin Toner, "For a Tough Clinton Lawyer, a Tough Decision to Leave," *New York Times*, August 16, 1999, p. A10; Richard Stevenson, "President Tripple-Teams His Lewinsky Problem," *New York Times*, August 5, 1998, p. A20.

WHITEWATER. The Whitewater investigation dogged Bill Clinton's presidency and indirectly led to his **impeachment** by the **U.S. House of Representatives**. Yet as Clinton prepared to leave office, it remained unclear whether Whitewater should have received as much attention as it did. In mid-September 2000, independent counsel **Robert Ray**, who succeeded **Kenneth Starr**, wrapped up a six-year investigation of the president's involvement in an Arkansas land deal that had gone sour long before the **election of 1992**. After spending approximately $52 million to determine whether the president or First Lady **Hillary Clinton** had committed any crimes, including covering up their involvement in the

Whitewater affair, the independent counsel concluded that there was "insufficient" evidence to prove that either Bill or Hillary Clinton had "knowingly participated in any criminal conduct." Neither the president nor the first lady commented on the independent counsel's report, which seemed to vindicate their long-standing position that the Whitewater investigation had been politically motivated all along. Instead, in the words of White House spokesman Joe Lockhart, they would "leave it to the American people to make up their own minds on whether this was a useful exercise" (*Baltimore Sun*, September 21, 2000, p. 1A).

As one reporter aptly wrote in the midst of the impeachment process, "It all started with a little real estate deal 20 years ago" (David Froomkin, "Untangling Whitewater"). In 1978, Bill Clinton, who was then the attorney general of the state of Arkansas, and Hillary Clinton, formed a partnership with **James and Susan McDougal** to purchase over two hundred acres of property along the Whitewater River in Arkansas. Their partnership was known as the Whitewater Development Corporation. Fourteen years later, in 1992, the partnership was dissolved due to years of poor performance. At the time, the Clintons reported having lost more than $40,000. Yet in March 1992, after the *New York Times* revealed the Clintons' ties to the Whitewater land deal, the Resolution Trust Corporation (RTC), the federal agency responsible for resuscitating the savings and loan industry, began to investigate the remnants of Madison Guaranty Savings and Loan, a thrift once owned by the McDougals. In 1986, federal regulators had forced James McDougal to step down as president of Madison Guaranty due to his mismanagement of the corporation. Among the federal government's concerns was that McDougal had made risky loans to "shell" corporations that either he or his associates owned. In the fall of 1992, RTC investigators referred their investigation of Madison Guaranty to the FBI and the U.S. attorney's office in Little Rock, Arkansas.

Initially, this probe had nothing to do with Whitewater, but the government soon expanded its investigation to determine if Madison Guaranty had illegally contributed to Bill Clinton's 1984 gubernatorial campaign and investigated allegations made by David Hale, an Arkansas politician, that Governor Clinton had pressured him into donating funds to Capital Management Services, Inc., another investment firm owned by Susan McDougal. While the Whitewater investigation received relatively little attention in the waning days of the 1992 presidential campaign, it gained increasing attention following President Clinton's inauguration. Conservatives suggested that **Vincent Foster**'s suicide grew out of his involvement in the Whitewater affair or the ongoing effort to cover up the president's involvement in the scandal. The cry for an independent counsel grew when stories broke that friends of the president had allegedly paid **Webster L. Hubbell**, a former law partner of Hillary Clinton and associate attorney general to buy Hubbell's silence regarding the Whitewater deal.

In January 1994, Attorney General **Janet Reno** named **Robert B. Fiske, Jr.**, a Republican and onetime U.S. attorney, as independent counsel to investigate the Whitewater affair. After Fiske reported that investigators had found no evidence of wrongdoing in Vincent Foster's death, both houses of Congress initiated their own hearings into Whitewater. While these hearings raised questions about the honesty and forthrightness of several members of Clinton's administration, including Deputy Treasury Secretary **Roger C. Altman**, a longtime friend of the Clintons and the acting chief of the RTC, the Senate Banking Committee reported that "no law or ethical standards had been breached." A minority of members of the committee, however, all Republicans, accused Altman of lying to them and left the door open for further hearings. Indeed, in the summer of 1995, with Republicans now in the majority, the Senate Special Committee on Whitewater released a 769-page report that, in the words of *Congressional Quarterly*, "portrayed Mrs. Clinton as the chief culprit in White House attempts to impede investigations into the failed Arkansas land deal" (*CQ Almanac*, 1996, p. 1-46). At about the same time, James and Susan McDougal and **Jim Guy Tucker**, the Democratic governor of Arkansas, were indicted for bank fraud in cases that did not stem from the Whitewater investment. All three were eventually found guilty. In spite of much fanfare, the Republican-led Senate hearings failed to produce any major new revelations about the president and may have hurt some Republicans politically. Not only was Clinton reelected in November 1996, but New York senator Alfonse D'Amato of New York, who chaired the committee, lost his reelection bid to Charles Schumer in 1998.

Meanwhile, Kenneth Starr had taken over for Robert Fiske as the independent counsel on August 9, 1994. Starr, who had ties to conservative activists, drew the fire of Democrats from the start. They claimed that he lacked prosecutorial experience and would not act in an impartial manner. In February 1997, Starr announced that he would resign to accept an offer to be dean of Pepperdine Law School. Starr subsequently withdrew his resignation and expanded his investigation, focusing particularly on Hillary Clinton's relationship to Madison Guaranty while she was a partner at the Rose Law Firm. For nearly two years, the White House maintained that it could not locate documents relating to Hillary Clinton's work for Madison Guaranty. After two years, Carolyn Huber, a member of Hillary Clinton's staff, announced that the subpoenaed documents had remarkably appeared among numerous storage boxes in her office. Ironically, the documents that were produced tended to support the administration's oft-repeated statements that Hillary Clinton had done minimal work for Madison Guaranty.

As 1997 came to a close, Starr had not uncovered enough evidence to pursue an indictment of the first lady or the president, but then his investigation took a totally unexpected turn that would lead to President Clinton's impeachment. **Linda Tripp**, a former White House worker and confidante of **Monica Lewinsky**, contacted Starr's office and turned over tape recordings of her telephone conversations with Lewinsky that suggested that Lewinsky and Clinton had had a sexual affair. Even though Clinton's affair was not illegal and even though it had no bearing on the Whitewater land deal, Starr received permission from the U.S. Court of Appeals for the District of Columbia to expand his investigation to include examining the Lewinsky matter. Starr contended that the president's affair with Lewinsky and, more specifically, his efforts to conceal it revealed a pattern of behavior consistent with obstructing justice. The following day, Clinton was deposed in the **Paula Jones** sexual harassment case. The president denied to the public and to Jones's lawyers that he had had sex with Lewinsky. From this statement, the independent counsel's office built a case that Clinton had committed perjury and obstructed justice. Building on Starr's charges, the House Judiciary Committee held hearings on the Lewinsky matter and recommended that Clinton be impeached. On December 19, 1998, largely voting along partisan lines, the full house impeached the president on two charges. On February 12, 1999, the **U.S. Senate** acquitted President Clinton of all charges.

In the wake of the impeachment trial, Starr resigned, leaving to Robert Ray the task of wrapping up the Whitewater investigation. Even before Ray issued his final report, the independent counsel's office had revealed that it would not indict either of the Clintons for their involvement in the Whitewater matter. Yet Ray left open until Clinton's final day in office the possibility that he might indict the president for matters stemming from the Lewinsky scandal. On his second-to-last day in office, President Clinton conceded that he had testified falsely in the Jones case. In exchange for this written admission, Ray promised not to pursue the case any further.

While Ray concluded that not enough evidence existed to indict the

president in the Whitewater matter, many conservatives remained convinced that the Clintons were thoroughly corrupt and deserved the
scrutiny they received. Regardless of the merits of these claims, the
Whitewater affair left the public with a distaste for the law that created
the independent counsel's office and, perhaps most important, tended
to reinforce public cynicism about politicians. This helped account for
the difficulty **Al Gore** had in capitalizing on the remarkably good economic record of the Clinton years and for the low voter turnout in the
election of 2000. The complexity of the Whitewater affair also baffled
the public, which tended to conflate all of the scandals into one when it
came to evaluating the president's character. In other words, much of
the public, as displayed by polls regarding Bill Clinton's character, apparently agreed with Starr that Clinton exhibited a pattern of unethical
behavior, in spite of the fact that the lengthy investigation into Whitewater revealed no specific illegal acts on either his or the first lady's part.

Suggested Readings: "No Clinton Charges in Whitewater," *Baltimore Sun*, September 21, 2000, p. 1A; "Panel Issues Whitewater Report," *Congressional Quarterly
Almanac*, 1996, p. 1-46; Robert N. Roberts and Marion T. Doss, *From Watergate
to Whitewater* (Westport, CT: Greenwood Press, 1997); "Rough Whitewater Ride
for Clinton," *Congressional Quarterly Almanac*, 1994, p. 108; Harry Shearer, *It's
the Stupidity, Stupid* (New York: Ballantine, 1999); "Untangling Whitewater,"
http://www.washingtonpost.com/wp-srv/politics/special/whitewater/whitewater.htm.

WILLEY, KATHLEEN. Witness in impeachment of President Clinton.
    On March 15, 1998, in the midst of the **Monica Lewinsky** scandal,
Kathleen Willey, a former volunteer in the White House Social Office,
dropped another bombshell on the public when, in an interview aired
by the popular *60 Minutes* television show, she claimed that President
Bill Clinton had "groped" her in the Oval Office on November 29, 1993.
The public had first been made aware of this incident by *Newsweek* reporter Michael Isikoff in August 1997. In his story, Isikoff relied heavily
on an interview with **Linda Tripp**, who told him that Willey had told her
(Tripp) that "the president had taken her (Willey) from the Oval Office
to his private office, a small adjoining hideaway, and kissed and fondled
her" (Isikoff, "A Twist in *Jones v. Clinton*," p. 30). Yet partly because
Tripp was unknown at the time and because the president's legal team
strongly denied the story and partly because Willey herself did not speak
with Isikoff about the alleged incident, it did not create much of a stir at
the time. But after the Lewinsky affair was raised by the press, the public

began to pay more attention to Willey's story and to possible efforts by the Clinton administration to silence her.

Willey informed *60 Minutes* that she had gone to the president to ask for a paying job to help her ease her family's financial troubles. She was shocked, she explained, when the president groped her and placed her hands on his genitals. In the *60 Minutes* interview, Willey added that the president had perjured himself by denying in his grand-jury testimony that he had made sexual advances to her. Clinton's lawyers challenged Willey's allegations, releasing information that cast doubt on her story. For instance, Clinton's advisers noted that Willey remained a strong supporter of Clinton through the 1996 campaign, suggesting that the incident had never taken place. Willey, they added, was distraught at the time of their 1993 meeting. In fact, her husband committed suicide later that same day. One key player in determining the veracity of the story was **Julia Hiatt Steele**. Willey contended that she had informed Steele about the president's behavior the day of the incident. While Steele initially confirmed this claim, she subsequently recanted her support of Willey's allegations. In response, independent counsel **Kenneth Starr** indicted Steele on obstruction-of-justice charges.

While many opponents of the president sought to use the alleged Willey affair to muster support for his **impeachment**, the specific charges against him did not contend that he had perjured himself in regard to the Willey matter. The fact that Steele's trial for perjury ended in a hung jury and that Starr chose not to retry her cast some doubt on Willey's story. Nonetheless, many remained convinced that the president had in fact made advances to Willey or, at the least, that her charges were credible.

Suggested Readings: Jennifer G. Hickey, "The Longest Hug on Record," *Insight on the News*, April 6, 1998, p. 7; Michael Isikoff, "A Twist in *Jones v. Clinton*: Her Lawyers Subpoena Another Woman," *Newsweek*, August 11, 1997, p. 30; "Key Player: Kathleen Willey," http://www.washingtonpost.com/wp-srv/politics/special/clinton/players/willey.htm; Leef Smith and Patricia Davis, "Clinton's Hands Were 'All over Me,'" *Washington Post*, May 5, 1999, p. A5.

WILLIAMS, MARGARET ANN. Chief of Staff to First Lady Hillary Clinton, 1993–1997.

Insofar as **Hillary Clinton** played a more prominent and active role than most first ladies, so too did her chief of staff, Margaret Ann Williams. Insofar as Hillary had a tumultuous tenure as first lady, so too did Margaret Williams as her adviser. One source (Ruth Marcus) described Williams's job as "huge." Early in Bill Clinton's presidency, she had to help Hillary orchestrate the drive to gain **health care reform** while simultaneously managing the first lady's staff and the White House's social functions. When the investigation into **Whitewater**, including Hillary's involvement, thickened, Williams was dragged into the fray. Indeed, a **U.S. Senate** committee led by Senator Alfonse D'Amato recommended indicting Williams on perjury charges because of her inability to recall much when she was asked about **Vincent Foster**'s death and numerous other matters. Her name arose again following Clinton's reelection in regard to her role in **Chinagate**, the alleged exchange of favors to Asian businessmen (and perhaps Chinese officials) for campaign funds. In particular, Williams received a $50,000 check from **Johnny Chung** in 1995 in a reception room inside the White House. Aides responded that Williams did not solicit the funds but rather simply delivered the check to the Democratic National Committee. In spite of these legal entanglements, Williams remained loyal to the first lady and the president.

Williams came to her job from the Children's Defense Fund (CDF). Williams worked as communications director for the CDF when Hillary Clinton worked for the organization. Unlike most other chiefs of staff to the first lady, Williams also held the title of aide to the president, a sign of Hillary's unusual prominence within the administration. In May 1997, Williams married William Barrett at Trinity College, her alma mater. Both Bill and Hillary Clinton attended the wedding. In 1997, Williams departed the Clinton administration and went to work as a consultant. She supported Hillary Clinton's run for the U.S. Senate in 2000.

Suggested Readings: David Maraniss, "First Lady's Aide Again in Spotlight," *Washington Post*, March 7, 1997, p. A4; Ruth Marcus, "Williams Is Assistant to Both the Clintons," *Washington Post*, August 5, 1994, p. A8.

WOMEN. Bill Clinton owed his election as president in large part to women who voted for him by substantial margins in the **elections of 1992** and **1996**. Conservatives tended to express their befuddlement over this "gender gap," arguing that Clinton gained the support of so-called soccer moms, (the term used to describe middle-class suburban housewives) through acts of symbolism, such as expressing his concern for children and education rather than deeds or his own personal behavior. Clinton and his supporters, in contrast, argued that women favored the Democratic candidate for president because they correctly judged his policies as profamily and prowomen and because they trusted him more than conservative candidates who, in Clinton's views, threatened gains women had made in recent times.

During the 1992 campaign and throughout his presidency, Clinton staked out a clear position on several issues that had special significance for women. He ardently defended abortion rights. One of the first pieces of legislation that he signed was the **Family and Medical Leave Act**. When Congress refused to enact his **health care reform** proposals, he won lesser protections for children in the **Children's Health Insurance Program (CHIP)**. The administration touted its support for increased funding for breast cancer research, domestic violence shelters, and the Small Business Administration's Women's Business Centers. In addition, the administration heralded its support of the Violence against Women Act, which provided federal funds to police departments, and the Paycheck Equity Act, which aimed at strengthening laws that prohibited wage discrimination against women to encourage them to pursue domestic violence cases.

Perhaps just as important, **Hillary Clinton** was one of the most active and visible first ladies in history. As a friend and associate of many prominent women's rights activists, Hillary Clinton helped her husband win and maintain support from much of the women's movement even during the **impeachment** process. She advised the president on key appointments in the days leading up to and after his inauguration and headed the president's health care reform effort in 1993 and 1994. In the mid-1990s, Hillary played a less visible role, although she regularly made appearances before women's audiences, touting the accomplishments and vision of the Clinton administration. During the impeachment process, Hillary fervently defended her husband and saw her approval ratings rise. Both Hillary Clinton and the State Department, under the direction of **Madeleine Albright**, sought to make women's rights a global issue. To this end, they prodded the United Nations to sponsor its first International Women's Conference, in which Hillary played an active part. The administration also pressured congress to approve the UN convention on women's rights, which conservative Republican senator Jesse Helms of North Carolina opposed.

Women served in the administration in key positions and in record numbers. Forty percent of all administration appointees were women. They included Madeleine Albright and **Janet Reno**, the first women to serve as secretary of state and attorney general, respectively. Other prom-inent women **cabinet** members and advisers were **Donna Shalala**, the secretary of health and human services, **Carol Browner**, the head of the Environmental Protection Agency, and **Laura D'Andrea Tyson**, the chair of the Council of Economic Advisers and director of the **National Eco-nomic Council**. Nearly one-third of all of Clinton's judicial appointees were women, including **Ruth Bader Ginsburg**, a longtime defender of women's rights, his first nominee to the U.S. **Supreme Court**.

During the Clinton presidency, the number of women in the work force continued to grow, and the wage gap continued to narrow. Hillary Clinton's election to the **U.S. Senate** in 2000 stood as one more example of the progress that women, including open advocates of women's rights, made during her husband's presidency.

Suggested Readings: "America's Commitment—Federal Programs Benefiting Women and New Initiatives as Follow-up to the UN Fourth World Conference on Women," *WIN News* 24:2 (Spring 1998), p. 79; "Hillary Power," *Newsweek*, April 7, 1998, p. 58; http://clinton3.nara.gov/WH/New Womens—History/accomps. html; Kathleen Hall Jamieson, Erika Falk, and Susan Sherr, "The Enthymeme Gap in the 1997 Presidential Campaign," *PS: Political Science and Politics*, March 1999, p. 12.

WOOD, KIMBA M. Unconfirmed nominee for Attorney General, 1993.

After President Bill Clinton's first nominee for the post of U.S. attorney general, **Zoë Baird**, withdrew her name for consideration following re-ports that she had hired illegal immigrants to work in her house, the president announced that he would nominate Kimba Wood for the post. Less than a week after making the announcement, however, Clinton changed his mind when a background check suggested that she too had improperly hired an illegal immigrant as her baby-sitter. Pundits quickly called this the nannygate problem. Even when it was learned that Wood had not violated any law—she had hired the sitter before the Simpson-Mazzoli or Immigration Reform and Control Act of 1986 made it illegal to hire illegal immigrants as baby-sitters—Clinton refused to reinstate Wood as his nominee. Prior to announcing her nomination, Clinton had asked Wood if she had a "Zoë Baird" problem. Wood answered that she did not. Perhaps President Clinton felt for public relations purposes that she should have been more forthcoming. Yet the two aborted nomina-tions were a public relations fiasco for the administration, making it look inept and confirming fears that Clinton's young aides and Arkansas friends lacked the experience and savvy to run the government. More-over, the Baird and Wood incidents raised a whole set of other questions about the reason why Clinton needed or wanted to appoint a woman to the post of U.S. attorney general in the first place and about the presi-dent's real commitment to gender equity in the workplace. The Baird and Wood fiascoes angered many feminists who had supported Clinton for president. They observed that male nominees had never been asked about who worked in their household. Some also complained that Baird's violation of the law was technical at worst and that Wood had committed no wrong.

Two possible positive byproducts of the aborted nominations were that they raised public awareness of the difficulties that professional **women** faced, which their male counterparts did not, and generated discussion of the need to improve day care for all citizens. The entire process was complicated further by the fact that Wood, a federal district-court judge in New York, had been appointed to the court by Ronald Reagan and that she enjoyed the support of Senator Alfonse D'Amato, a New York Republican. In place of Wood, Clinton displayed his resolve to appoint a woman by nominating **Janet Reno** as U.S. attorney general. While Wood did not become the first female attorney general, she remained a federal district-court judge. In early 2001, **George W. Bush** nominated Linda Chavez to serve as his secretary of labor. Chavez's nomination, like Wood's, was derailed when it was revealed that she had harbored an illegal immigrant and had not informed the FBI or Bush's aides about this potentially damaging news. Chavez asserted that she was the victim of the politics of personal destruction. Ironically, in 1993, she had criti-cized both Baird and Wood for hiring illegal immigrants to work as day-care providers.

Suggested Readings: Richard L. Berke, "Clinton Chooses New York Judge for Jus-tice Post," *New York Times*, February 5, 1993, p. A1; "A Teach-in on Nannies," *New York Times*, February 9, 1993, p. A20.

WOOLSEY, JAMES, JR. Director of the Central Intelligence Agency (CIA), 1993–1994.

James Woolsey served as director of the Central Intelligence Agency (CIA) for the first two years of Bill Clinton's presidency. His brief tenure as head of an agency that was in search of a mission at the end of the cold war was a troubled one. Woolsey experienced limited access to the president and poor relations with Congress, particularly with Senator

Dennis DeConcini, the Arizona Democrat who chaired the Senate Select Committee on Intelligence. In addition, many covert-operations officers within the CIA disliked Woolsey because of his distrust of covert operations. Yet it was Woolsey's search for a suspected traitor within the agency that hurt Woolsey the most. While this investigation revealed that Aldrich Ames, a career CIA officer, had sold secrets to the Soviet Union for nearly a decade prior to Woolsey's taking over as director, Woolsey caught much of the political flak for the episode. The fact that Woolsey did not dismiss other CIA officers or agents in the case in spite of evidence that they should have suspected Ames hurt him with the press. Ironically, while Woolsey dealt leniently with agents because he wanted to maintain high morale, his call for a radical reshaping of the agency, to better meet the post–cold war mission of the CIA, upset many career officers.

Woolsey was a graduate of Stanford University and Yale Law School. An army veteran, in 1968 he worked for Eugene McCarthy, the anti-**Vietnam** War candidate for the Democratic nomination. Like Bill Clinton and several other members of his administration, Woolsey was a Rhodes scholar. Although he was an opponent of the Vietnam War, he went to work for Paul Nitze, who represented the Richard Nixon administration at the Strategic Arms Limitations Talks (SALT). Subsequently, Woolsey worked as the general counsel for the **Senate** Armed Services Committee, chaired by the neoconservative Democrat Henry M. Jackson of Washington. Woolsey also served as the under secretary of the navy during Jimmy Carter's presidency and practiced law in the 1980s, representing numerous defense contractors. Although he was a Democrat, he advised the Republicans on national security matters during the 1980s. He worked with National Security Adviser Brent Scowcroft on conventional-arms-reduction talks during **George Bush**'s presidency. While Clinton did not dismiss him, Woolsey found his years in the Clinton administration frustrating. He resigned in the face of news critical of his handling of the Aldrich Ames spy case and lack of support from the White House. In 1996, he endorsed Senator **Robert Dole** for president on the grounds that Clinton was undermining national security via what he claimed was haphazard conduct of American **foreign policy**.

Suggested Readings: Michael Gordon, "The New Presidency: The C.I.A." *New York Times*, January 11, 1993, p. A1; Tim Weiner, "Director C.I.A. to Leave," *New York Times*, December 29, 1994, p. A1.

WORKFORCE INVESTMENT ACT OF 1998. The Workforce Investment Act (WIA), passed in 1998, required states to form locally based one-stop

service-delivery systems to deliver many employment and training services funded by the federal government. A number of factors led to passage
of the act. Government investigators determined that existing employment and training systems were fragmented and inefficient. These reports
dovetailed with general criticism of government waste to prod the Clinton administration to develop an alternative to existing mechanisms for
providing adult education and job training. Even before the act was
passed, a number of states had experimented successfully with the "one-
stop" concept. The absence of a federal mandate, however, according to
many experts, inhibited other states from doing the same. The Workforce
Investment Act of 1998 mandated that all states established such centers.
Early reports indicated that the unified delivery systems were more effective than their predecessors in achieving their goals of providing job training and adult and vocational education. The initiative built on the
School-to-Work Opportunities Act, which President Clinton had signed
into law in 1994. This bill, jointly administered by the Departments of
Education and Labor, provided federal support to states and communities
to develop adult learning programs. The Workforce Investment Act
merged these educational programs with other federally funded job-
training efforts under a single system of delivery, based upon the notion
that both programs were aimed at the same goal and served similar constituents.

Suggested Readings: R. D'Amico and R. Fedrau, *An Evaluation of the Self-Service
Approach in One-Stop Career Centers: Final Report* (Menlo Park, CA: Social Policy
Research Associates, July 1999); D. Kogan, Katherine P. Dickinson, Ruth Fedrov,
et. al., *Creating Workforce Development Systems That Work: An Evaluation of
the Initial One-Stop Implementation Experience: Final Report* (Menlo Park, CA:
Social Policy Research Associates, August 1997).

WORLD TRADE CENTER BOMBING. *See* **Terrorism**.

WRIGHT, SUSAN WEBBER. Presiding judge in Paula Jones lawsuit.

In July 1994, U.S. District Court Judge Susan Webber Wright was appointed to oversee **Paula Jones**'s sexual harassment lawsuit against President Bill Clinton. Over the course of the next five years, she issued
numerous rulings, including some that angered Clinton and his supporters and others that infuriated Clinton's detractors. Most notably, in
April 1998, she dismissed Paula Jones's sexual harassment suit, ruling that
even if he had made sexual advances to her, Clinton had not sexually

harassed Jones as defined by the law. Yet in July 1999, after the **U.S. Senate**'s **impeachment** trial, Judge Wright fined Clinton $90,000 and held him in civil contempt of court for giving false testimony about his relationship with **Monica Lewinsky**. "I take no pleasure in imposing contempt sanctions against the Nation's President," Wright declared, "and no doubt like many others grow weary of this matter." Yet, she continued, "The Court has determined that the President deliberately violated the Court's discovery orders, thereby undermining the integrity of the judicial system" (quoted in Suro, "Clinton Is Sanctioned," p. A1).

Wright had known Clinton through most of her adult life. After graduating from Randolph-Macon Women's College, she enrolled in law school at the University of Arkansas at Fayetteville. Clinton was one of her law-school teachers. Nonetheless, she worked for his opponent, Republican congressman John Paul Hammerschmidt, in Clinton's first race for public office, his unsuccessful run for Congress in 1974. After graduating, Wright clerked for Judge J. Smith Henley, who had recommended Clinton as a teacher. For more than a decade, she taught at the University of Arkansas at Little Rock. In 1990, **George Bush** nominated her to the U.S. District Court in Little Rock.

Wright also was involved in several **Whitewater**-related rulings. She held **Susan McDougal** in contempt for refusing to cooperate with the grand jury investigating the Whitewater matter. She also ruled that White House lawyers did not have to provide independent counsel **Kenneth Starr** with notes of conversations that had had with **Hillary Clinton**. A U.S. court of appeals overturned this decision.

Suggested Readings: "Case against Clinton Brings Former Professor before His Former Student," *New York Times*, July 11, 1994, p. B7; "Key Player: Susan Webber Wright," http://www.washingtonpost.com/wp-srv/politics/special/clinton/players/wright.htm; Susan Schmidt, "Trial Judge in Jones Case," *Washington Post*, May 29, 1997, p. A11; Robert Suro, "Clinton Is Sanctioned in Jones Lawsuit," *Washington Post*, July 30, 1999, p. A1.

Y

YELLEN, JANET A. (August 13, 1946, Brooklyn, New York–   .) Chair, Council of Economic Advisers, 1997–1999.

Janet Yellen chaired the Council of Economic Advisers (CEA) from 1997 to 1999, two of the best years for the nation's **economy**. Born in Brooklyn, New York, Yellen earned her B.A. from Brown University in 1967 and her Ph.D in economics from Yale University in 1971. After teaching at Harvard University and serving as an economist for the Federal Reserve Board, she joined the faculty of the Haas School of Business at the University of California at Berkeley. In 1994, President Bill Clinton nominated her to serve on the Federal Reserve Board. After being reelected, he nominated her to assume the chairmanship of his Council of Economic Advisers. Along with **Laura D'Andrea Tyson** and **Alice Rivlin**, Yellen's appointment reflected Clinton's commitment to nominating **women** to positions traditionally held by men. Yellen returned to the University of California at Berkeley after resigning as head of the CEA.

Suggested Reading: Ron Fournier, "Clinton Names CEA Chief," *Associated Press*, December 19, 1996, on Lexis-Nexis.

YELTSIN, BORIS. *See* **Russia**.

YUGOSLAVIA. *See* **Bosnia and Herzegovina**; **Kosovo**.

TIMELINE

1991

May 8   Arkansas governor Bill Clinton and Paula Jones meet in hotel room in Little Rock, Arkansas.

Oct. 3   Bill Clinton announces that he will run for president.

1992

Jan. 26 Bill and Hillary Clinton appear on *60 Minutes* television show to respond to scandal regarding his alleged affair with Gennifer Flowers.

Feb. 6   New concerns regarding Clinton's evasion of the draft appear in the press.

Feb. 18 In spite of scandals, Clinton comes in second in New Hampshire presidential primary and is dubbed the "comeback kid."

July 16 Bill Clinton accepts Democratic Party's presidential nomination.

Nov. 3   Bill Clinton is elected president with 43 percent of popular vote.

1993

Jan. 20 William Jefferson Clinton is inaugurated as forty-second president of the United States.

Jan. 21 Zoë Baird's nomination as U.S. attorney general is withdrawn in wake of reports that she had hired an illegal immigrant as a nanny.

Jan. 25 President Clinton appoints his wife, Hillary, to head Task Force on National Health Care.

Jan. 27 President Clinton announces six-month "don't ask, don't tell" policy regarding gays and lesbians in the military. Policy later becomes permanent.

Feb. 26 Terrorists bomb World Trade Center in New York City, killing 6 and wounding 1,000.

April 19	Fifty-one-day-seige in Waco, Texas, culminates with death of 80 Branch Davidians following FBI and ATF raid of and fire at Davidians' compound.
May 20	President Clinton signs Motor Voter Bills.
June 26	United States bombs Baghdad, Iraq, in retaliation for alleged attempt to assassinate former President George Bush.
July 20	Vincent Foster, Clinton friend and White House counsel, is found dead in apparent suicide.
Aug. 10	Clinton signs budget deficit-reduction plan, which had been narrowly passed by Congress without any Republican support.
Sept. 13	Israeli prime minister Yitzhak Rabin and PLO leader Yasir Arafat sign peace accord and shake hands at White House.
Sept. 22	President Clinton officially unveils plan for national health care insurance.
Oct. 3	Eighteen American soldiers are killed in firefight in Somalia.
Nov. 13	President Clinton delivers moving address at black church in Memphis, Tennessee, where Dr. Martin Luther King, Jr., had delivered his last sermon.
Nov. 30	President Clinton signs "Brady bill" requiring five-day waiting period for buying a handgun and criminal background check.
Dec. 8	President Clinton signs bill implementing North American Free Trade Agreement (NAFTA).

1994

Jan. 20	Robert Fiske is appointed independent counsel to investigate Whitewater affair.
May 6	Paula Jones files sexual harassment lawsuit against President Clinton for his alleged misconduct in 1991.
July 26	U.S. Congress begins Whitewater investigations.
Aug. 9	Kenneth Starr is appointed new Whitewater independent counsel.
Sept. 13	President Clinton signs Anti-Crime Bill.
Sept. 18	Haitian military dictators relinquish power in face of armed invasion by U.S. forces; Jean-Bertrand Aristide is restored as leader.
Sept. 26	Health care reform package dies in Congress.
Oct. 21	North Korea agrees to discontinue its nuclear development program in exchange for U.S. and Japanese economic aid.
Nov. 8	Republicans win control of both houses of Congress in midterm elections. Newt Gingrich is elected new Speaker of the House.
Dec. 1	U.S. Senate ratifies global tariff agreement (GATT).

1995

Jan. 31   President Clinton authorizes emergency $20-billion financial bail-
               out of Mexico.

March 22   President Clinton signs Unfunded Mandates law.

April 19   Bomb explodes outside Alfred P. Murrah Federal Building in
               Oklahoma City, Oklahoma, killing 168; Timothy McVeigh and
               Terry Nichols are charged with murder and later convicted.

June 28   Webster Hubbell, former U.S. associate attorney general and law
               partner of Hillary Clinton, is sentenced to twenty-one months in
               mail-fraud and tax-evasion case.

Aug. 30   NATO initiates two-week bombing campaign against Bosnian Serbs
               in retaliation for their attacks on Sarajevo.

Sept. 19   President Clinton defends affirmative action, stating that the coun-
               try needs to "mend it" rather than "end it."

Nov. 4   Israel's prime minister Yitzhak Rabin is assassinated by an Israeli
               extremist.

Nov. 14   U.S. government is shut down as a result of impasse between
               Republican-controlled Congress and President Clinton.

Nov. 15   Bill Clinton and Monica Lewinsky's sexual relationship begins.

Nov. 21   Balkan leaders sign "Dayton Peace Accord" ending conflict in Bos-
               nia and Herzegovina; U.S. troops are to be sent to region to main-
               tain peace.

Nov. 30   President Clinton visits Northern Ireland and is welcomed warmly
               by thousands in Belfast and Londonderry.

Dec. 16   Government shuts down for second time over budget dispute.
               This shutdown lasts until January 5, 1996; public tends to blame
               conservative Republican leaders for shutdown.

1996

Jan. 23   In State of the Union Address, President Clinton declares that the
               "era of big government is over." The president also pays tribute to
               his wife, whose appearance before a grand jury is pending.

Jan. 25   Hillary Clinton testifies before federal grand jury that is examining
               the Whitewater matter.

April 3   Secretary of Commerce Ron Brown and 31 other Americans and
               two Croatians are killed in airplane crash in Dubrovnik, Croatia.

April 4   President Clinton signs landmark farm bill remaking federal gov-
               ernment role in agriculture.

April 29   Vice President Al Gore attends fund-raising event at Buddhist tem-
               ple in Los Angeles. Conservatives will later accuse the Clinton ad-
               ministration of violating campaign finance laws and covering up
               their violations.

May 9	President Clinton testifies by videotape in trial of Whitewater defendants Susan and James McDougal.
May 28	James and Susan McDougal and former Arkansas governor Jim Guy Tucker are convicted of fraud.
June 25	Terrorists attack U.S. military complex in Saudi Arabia, killing nineteen Americans.
July 27	Olympic Games in Atlanta, Georgia, are disrupted by bombing in public park that kills 1 and wounds 110.
Aug. 3	President Clinton signs Food Quality Protection Act.
Aug. 6	President Clinton signs Safe Drinking Water Act.
Aug. 20	President Clinton signs law that increases minimum wage.
Aug. 21	President Clinton signs Health Insurance Portability and Accountability Act (HIPAA) of 1996.
Aug. 22	President Clinton signs welfare-reform law.
Aug. 28	Clinton is renominated by the Democratic Party, declaring that "hope is back" and promising to build a "bridge to the 21st century."
Sept. 24	President Clinton signs Comprehensive Nuclear Test-Ban Treaty; Senate, however, does not ratify.
Nov. 5	Clinton defeats Senator Robert Dole to become the first Democrat elected to two consecutive presidential terms since Franklin D. Roosevelt.

1997

Jan. 20	Clinton is inaugurated for second term as president.
March 11	U.S. Senate approves investigation into campaign fund-raising irregularities by Clinton administration and members of Congress.
March 29	Clinton and Monica Lewinsky have last sexual encounter.
April 24	U.S. Senate approves chemical weapons-ban treaty.
May 27	U.S. Supreme Court rules that Paula Jones's sexual harassment suit against President Clinton may proceed.
Aug. 5	President Clinton signs legislation promising to balance federal budget by 2002. Budget allows for $125 billion in tax cuts, a hike in the minimum wage, restoration of welfare benefits to legal immigrants, and health care coverage for uninsured children.
Oct. 3	Justice Department concludes that President Clinton did not violate any laws during 1996 campaign fund-raising efforts in so-called Chinagate scandal.
Dec. 5	Paula Jones's lawyers name Monica Lewinsky as potential witness.
Dec. 28	White House secretary Betty Currie retrieves gifts that President Clinton had given Monica Lewinsky.

1998

Jan. 7   Monica Lewinsky signs affidavit denying relationship with President Clinton.

Jan. 12–21   Linda Tripp meets with independent counsel Kenneth Starr; Starr requests and is granted authority to expand his investigation; news stories of relationship between President Clinton and Monica Lewinsky break. Clinton is deposed in Paula Jones's suit. In interview with PBS moderator Jim Lehrer and in televised address, President Clinton denies having had a "sexual relationship" with Lewinsky.

Jan. 27   In State of the Union Address, President Clinton calls for using budget surplus to "save Social Security first."

April 1   Paula Jones's sexual harassment suit against President Clinton is dismissed by federal district-court judge Susan Webber Wright.

April 10   Catholics and Protestants agree to Good Friday Peace Accords in Northern Ireland.

July 22   President Clinton signs Internal Revenue Service Overhaul bill.

July 28   Monica Lewinsky agrees to cooperate with Starr investigation.

Aug. 17   President Clinton testifies before grand jury regarding his relationship with Monica Lewinsky; in televised address, Clinton admits improper relationship with former intern.

Aug. 20   Following terrorist attacks on U.S. embassies in Nairobi, Kenya, and Dar es Salaam, Tanzania, United States retaliates by bombing alleged bomb factory in Sudan and separate site in Afghanistan.

Sept. 9   Independent counsel Kenneth Starr issues 453-page report to Congress that finds numerous grounds for impeachment. Report is rapidly released to the public on the Internet. At prayer breakfast, President Clinton apologizes for having "sinned."

Oct. 8   House of Representatives authorizes impeachment hearings.

Oct. 23   Israeli prime minister Benjamin Netanyahu and Palestinian leader Yasir Arafat sign Wye River Memorandum.

Nov. 3   Democrats make gains in midterm election, although Republicans maintain control of both houses of Congress.

Nov. 6   In the wake of the election and in the face of brewing scandal regarding his own fidelity to his wife, Speaker of the House Newt Gingrich announces that he will not seek reelection as Speaker and will leave Congress at the end of his term.

Nov. 9   House Judiciary Committee begins impeachment hearings.

Nov. 19   Paula Jones settles suit with President Clinton for $850,000.

Dec. 19   House of Representatives impeaches President Clinton on two of four articles drawn up by House Judiciary Committee.

1999

Jan. 7   Impeachment trial of President Clinton begins in the U.S. Senate.

Feb. 12   President Clinton is acquitted by U.S. Senate of all impeachment charges.

March 24   NATO begins air war on Serbia. Seventy-nine days later, bombing is halted after Yugoslavia's president Slobodan Milosevic agrees to withdraw his forces from Kosovo.

March 29   Dow Jones industrial average closes above 10,000 for first time.

Oct. 13   President Clinton fails to gain two-thirds majority vote in the U.S. Senate in favor of nuclear test-ban treaty.

Nov. 30   Demonstrators protest outside World Trade Organization meeting in Seattle, Washington.

2000

Feb. 1   Commerce Department reports that economic expansion is longest in American history.

Feb. 6   Hillary Clinton formally announces candidacy for U.S. Senate seat in New York.

May 24   House of Representatives passes bill granting China most-favored-nation status.

Aug. 14   President Clinton speaks at opening day of Democratic National Convention.

Aug. 25   Clinton announces that two weeks of negotiations at Camp David have failed to produce agreement between Israel and Palestinians.

Sept. 20   Independent counsel Robert Ray reports that government lacks enough evidence to charge the president or Hillary Clinton with any crime stemming from the Whitewater affair.

Oct. 6   Following protests in Belgrade, Slobodan Milosevic is compelled to give way to Vojislav Kostunica, who had won Yugoslavia's presidential election.

Oct. 12   USS *Cole* is attacked by terrorists while in port in Yemen.

Nov. 7   Election ends without a clear victor in presidential race, although Bill Clinton's wife, Hillary Clinton, easily wins seat in U.S. Senate. Subsequently, Democratic Party candidate Al Gore pushes for a manual recount of votes in key counties in Florida; Republican Party candidate George W. Bush files suit in opposition to recount; Florida Supreme Court orders recount in three countries and resets deadline for certification; U.S. Supreme Court hears appeal of Bush's suit, vacates Florida Supreme Court decision, and remands it to state court.

Nov. 19   President Clinton ends historic trip to Vietnam.

Dec. 13   Al Gore concedes election after U.S. Supreme Court ruled 5–4 in George Bush's favor by overturning Florida Supreme Court decision to go ahead with recount.

2001

Jan. 19   President Clinton and independent counsel Robert Ray make a deal whereby Clinton admits that he testified falsely in deposition in Paula Jones lawsuit and Ray pledges not to pursue case against Clinton any further.

Jan. 20   President Clinton issues 140 pardons. Among those pardoned are Susan McDougal and former Secretary of Housing and Urban Development Henry Cisneros.

INDEX

Page numbers that appear in **bold** indicate main entries.

About the Author

PETER B. LEVY is an Associate Professor in the Department of History and Political Science at York College of Pennsylvania. He is the author of numerous books and articles, including *The Encyclopedia of the Reagan-Bush Years* (Greenwood Press, 1996), *America in the Sixties—Right, Left, and Center: A Documentary History* (1998), *The Civil Rights Movement* (1998), *100 Key Documents in American Democracy* (1999), and *Let Freedom Ring: A Documentary History of the Civil Rights Movement* (Greenwood Press, 1992). He also serves as the editor of the Greenwood series Shapers of the Great Debates. He is currently completing a case study of the civil rights movement in Cambridge, Maryland, and is investigating the question, What can one do with a history degree?